D0991327

Justice Joseph Story by Gilbert Stuart
HARVARD UNIVERSITY LAW SCHOOL COLLECTION

GERALD T. DUNNE

Justice Joseph Story
and the Rise of the Supreme Court

SIMON AND SCHUSTER
NEW YORK

First printing

SBN 671-20665-6
Library of Congress Catalog Card Number: 70-139620
Designed by Edith Fowler
Manufactured in the United States of America

Acknowledgments

Some of the chapters in this book originally appeared as articles in various journals. Permission to reprint the following pieces is gratefully acknowledged.

"The American Blackstone," 1963 *Washington University Law Quarterly* 321 (1963). Reprinted with permission.

"Joseph Story: The Age of Jackson," 34 *Missouri Law Review* 307 (1969). Copyright © 1969 by The Curators of the University of Missouri. Reprinted with permission.

"Joseph Story: The Germinal Years," 75 *Harvard Law Review* 707 (1962). Copyright © 1962 by the Harvard Law Review Association. Reprinted with permission.

"Joseph Story: The Great Term," 79 *Harvard Law Review* 877 (1966). Copyright © 1966 by the Harvard Law Review Association. Reprinted with permission.

"Joseph Story: The Great Term—1837," 14 *Saint Louis University Law Journal* 1 (1969). Reprinted with permission.

"Joseph Story: The Lowering Storm," 13 *American Journal of Legal History* 1 (1969). Reprinted with permission.

"Joseph Story: The Middle Years," 80 *Harvard Law Review* 1679 (1967). Copyright © 1967 by the Harvard Law Review Association. Reprinted with permission.

"Joseph Story: The Salem Years," *Historical Collections*, Vol. 101, 1965. Copyright © 1965 by the Essex Institute. Reprinted courtesy of the Essex Institute.

"Justice Story: 1812 Overture," 77 *Harvard Law Review* 240 (1963).

Copyright © 1963 by the Harvard Law Review Association. Reprinted with permission.

"Mr. Justice Story and the American Law of Banking," 5 *American Journal of Legal History* 205 (1961). Reprinted with permission.

"The Story-Livingston Correspondence (1812–1822)," 10 *American Journal of Legal History* 224 (1966). Reprinted with permission.

Letter from Henry Clay, February 9, 1845, in Manuscript Collections. Reprinted courtesy of the Historical Society of Pennsylvania.

Letter to Richard Peters, February 2, 1835, in Richard Peters Papers. Reprinted courtesy of the Historical Society of Pennsylvania.

Letter to Robert J. Walker, May 22, 1841, in Manuscript Collections. Reprinted courtesy of the New York Historical Society.

To Nancy

Contents

Foreword

Why did I write this book? It all goes back to a Story opinion on negotiable instruments which I encountered years ago in the course of my work as a junior member of the legal staff of the Federal Reserve Bank of St. Louis. At that time I was struck by what seemed to me the extraordinary combination of Story's legal scholarship and his practical knowledgeability, and this circumstance led me to two other discoveries. One was that Justice Story had been president of one bank and vice-president of another while serving on the Supreme Court. The other was that, notwithstanding his enormously critical influence on American law and life, no modern, full-length biography of this great man existed.

Initially, I had no intention of filling the lacuna. Rather, my original aim had been only to examine Story's dual role as judge and banker as a means of exploring the origins and consequences of his ideas on the law of money, banking, and commerce. Undertaken with a grant from the Ford Foundation (herewith gratefully acknowledged) and published in the *Journal of American Legal History*, this effort led, inevitably but imperceptibly, to the larger project. Basically, I suspect the motivation rested upon the fact that at the range of a century I had been captivated by Story's fundamental decency and goodness, and was accordingly moved to pay a tribute to his memory by placing his accomplishments (and recording his shortcomings) in a modern perspective.

There was, however, far more to it than an effort to add another wreath to Story's laurels. Indeed, transcending any purely personal delineation was that aspect of Story's career which struck me almost from the first—namely, the perspective it afforded for an examination of the role of the Supreme Court in the emergence of the American nation-state (an influence which, in my view of the evidence, seems far more the result of pressure at the periphery than any *coup de main* at the center) and, distinct but related, an appraisal of the rise of an authentic American law and its interplay in the American ethos and American culture.

I have tried to weave these strands into this book, which is an amateur effort in every sense of the term. It was a labor of love written not in the milieu of the academic world but as an evening and holiday avocation in the course of an absorbing succession of jobs at the Federal Reserve Bank of St. Louis. While its errors and deficiencies are mine alone, it is much the better for the help and kindness of others. Here I would like to thank particularly my dear friend Ross Robertson of Indiana University, whose own work in economic history has abundantly proved that sweep and style make the best framework for specialized and technical exposition. My heartfelt appreciation also goes to Joseph Losos for his constant encouragement and perceptive criticism. Next I must mention those young lions of the law, the article editors of law reviews at Harvard, Washington, Missouri and St. Louis Universities, who checked my citations, corrected my errors, and polished my prose. To them and to their publications (and also to the *American Journal of Legal History* and the Essex Institute) my thanks both for editorial assistance and for permission to reprint herein material originally published in periodical form. Also, I am indebted to a great number of law librarians and especially to Professor Jean Ashman of Washington University. And, finally and greatest of all, I must record my debt to my wife, Nancy, and our six children. Justice Story took a great deal of time which belonged to them. For their love and forbearance, my grateful appreciation.

Gerald T. Dunne

St. Louis, Missouri
May 30, 1960 – December 24, 1969

PART ONE

The Germinal Years

CHAPTER I

Our Man in Salem

Like a wolf's head thrust out to the sea, Essex County on the upper Massachusetts coast reaches due east into the Atlantic. Newburyport rests high on the forehead; Cape Ann is the muzzle; Salem, seemingly about to be gulped down, lies deep in the open mouth; the Marblehead promontory forms the lower jaw. It is a sea-born country, hard and beautiful, where blazing summer and frigid winter alike are periodically shaken by fierce inbound storms which seek to take back what the sea has given.

Its men have matched geography and weather, and the snarling wolf's head appropriately symbolizes the long series of confrontations there—white man and red, patriot and Tory, Unitarian and Congregationalist, immigrant and Yankee. It would be difficult to select the most hate-filled and divisive of the conflicts, yet as bitter as any was that which pitted Jeffersonian against Federalist at the beginning of the nineteenth century. The very nomenclature of its political discourse suggested the depth of suspicion. The Federalists, certain that President Jefferson was about to bring a guillotine to every New England common, labeled their opponents as the "Democratic" or "French" Party and so suggested an ideological nexus with Jacobin Terror. Not to be outdone in insinuations of subversion, the Jeffersonians called themselves "Republicans" to imply that the Federalist opposition was but a step away from a royalist coup. They also labeled that opposition's inner establishment "the Essex Junto," thereby neatly combining the latter group's geographical location and its supposed instinct for extraconstitutional intrigue.

The Federalist–Jeffersonian hatred found its customary outlet in rhetorical abuse copiously inserted in periodical, pamphlet, and flyer, and, frequently enough, rhetoric turned to violence. Cutting across the lines of family and class—although wealth and station were a good working index of Federalism—the hatred permeated every aspect of daily life. It dictated the paper a man read, the church where he prayed, the bank where he borrowed, the tavern where he drank, and the assembly where he danced.

Unquestionably, it was Essex County's climate of intrigue and maneuver which made Secretary of the Treasury Albert Gallatin seek a discreet and nonroutine procedure when, in the summer of 1806, word reached Washington that the collector of customs at Newburyport was dispensing with the oath on the drawbacks. The drawbacks, a subsidy to American shipping, were a refund of duties on reexported goods and, like all subsidies, carried a hedge of congressional restrictions—the goods had to be actually landed on American soil, held in the original package, and shipped out within a year. Compliance with these conditions was ensured through an inspection by the collector, a counterinspection by the naval (port) officer, and the oath of the shipper.

Oaths were taken seriously, and any dispensation, if true, would be a serious breach of duty. Even more serious, however, would be the indiscretion of sending a federal official to formally investigate the accusation. Hence the Secretary besought Congressman Jacob Crowninshield, a member of one of the few Essex merchant-prince families with a Jeffersonian allegiance, to recruit a local Republican for the task. Crowninshield, with a bluff seaman's distaste for intrigue, was most unenthusiastic, and it took almost a year of Gallatin's coaxing to bring him round. He finally capitulated with the announcement that he "had selected Joseph Story, Esq. . . . to manage the business."[1]

[1] Jacob Crowninshield to James Gallatin, May 2, 1807, Crowninshield Papers, Peabody Museum, Salem, Mass. (hereinafter cited as Crowninshield Papers).

Crowninshield gave no details on the proposed investigator. Perhaps Gallatin remembered the name from an appointment imbroglio some four years past when a young lawyer called Joseph Story had jockeyed his way into being nominated for the office of Salem's port officer over more senior claims and then declined the post when it was formally tendered. Had Gallatin requested particulars, Crowninshield would have responded much in the way he would have described a fo'c'sle hand—that Story was twenty-seven, five feet eight, left-handed, by marital status widower, by occupation lawyer, and capable equally of talking and of fighting his way out should anything untoward develop in Newburyport.

Pressed for detail, the Congressman probably would have added that Story attended Salem's East Church—Unitarian and Republican—and had graduated from Harvard with second honors in 1798. Doubtless the Congressman would have emphasized that his candidate had been born of unimpeachable Republican antecedents in little Marblehead just across Salem harbor, with a father, Dr. Elisha Story, an ex-Bostonian, who had been both physician and party stalwart, and with an uncle, the Reverend Isaac Story, who had attended Princeton with Secretary of State James Madison. In a final effort, Crowninshield might have suggested that Story should know the way around bureaucracies, particularly maritime bureaucracies, thanks to a grandfather who had served as clerk of the Colonial Court of Vice-Admiralty and subsequently with the old Navy Board which sat in Boston during the Revolution.

And that would have been that. Crowninshield would not have written, nor probably did he know, that his candidate was the descendant of Elisha Story, a cordwainer who had come over from England at the beginning of the eighteenth century.[2] Still less would he have detailed the more significant characteristics of the proposed investigator—the slight dumpiness of jawline, the

[2] See, generally, Derby and Gardner, "Elisha Story of Boston and Some of His Descendants," *Essex Institute Historical Collections*, L (1914), 297.

incipient baldness, the debonair dress and bearing, the buoyant personality, the phenomenal memory, the flash-point temper, the quick step, or the nervous, sinewy gestures.

Had Gallatin bothered to check with his friend the Reverend William Bentley, an influential Salem Republican and pastor of East Church, the report on Story's pugilistic capabilities would have been verified. Dr. Bentley had an eagle eye and he kept a diary. "Mr. Martin & Story had a fight, & since that time affairs are more quiet," ran one entry.[3] "Mr. Joseph Story & Hearsey Derby had an open engagement at fisty cuffs," ran another.[4] Yet when the Bentley diary passed from fact to judgment, the results showed that Story had spent twenty years under the critical gaze of a man who despised him, who meticulously noted all his faults, who resolved every doubt against him, and who persistently prophesied his downfall and attempted to bring it about. What would Dr. Bentley have said of Story's suitability for the New-buryport assignment? "His ambition is boundless," ran a more temperate diary passage, "his principles those of youth and inexperience, his mind active, but not strong. His flights are quick, but not high. He skims, but does not rise."[5]

Crowninshield undoubtedly was aware of Dr. Bentley's opinion of Story. Yet what the clergyman saw as Story's moral deficiency seemed to the Congressman, if anything, harmless idiosyncrasy. Crowninshield himself once had brought an elephant all the way back from Calcutta, and he was inclined to allow any man an eccentricity or two. He was, moreover, genuinely fond of Story and hence transmitted the nomination with the endorsement "This gentleman is in every way well qualified to . . . carry on the investigation."[6] Yet the Congressman's distaste for the whole business invested his recommendation with some decidedly ambiguous undertones. And before a fortnight had passed, these im-

---

[3] Bentley, *The Diary of William Bentley* (4v., 1905-14; hereinafter cited as Bentley), III, 142. See also Dow, "William Bentley, D. D., Salem Diarist," *Proceedings of the American Antiquarian Society*, XXXII (1922), 52.
[4] Bentley, III, 18.
[5] *Ibid.*, 16.
[6] Letter to Gallatin, May 2, 1807, Crowninshield Papers.

plications were borne out. Story reneged on the assignment. "[H]e informed me," Crowninshield wrote Gallatin, "that he found himself obliged to set off immediately on a journey to the southward. . . . He had not done anything in the affair."[7]

Jacob Crowninshield learned early enough that where Joseph Story was concerned, a considerable gap might separate promise and performance. "Mr. Storey [sic] . . . promised to write me while I remained in Washington," he complained during his first tour in Congress. "I have not yet been favored by a single word from him."[8] Both the unwritten letters and the untended investigation typified an anomalous mixture of industry and indiscretion on the part of a man who had an extraordinary capacity to become involved because of his wish to say the pleasing word and his unwillingness to refuse a friend's request. The more important commitments often ran on to the point where some abrupt and painful action was required to set things to rights. Almost inevitably when he made his move to get free of a tangle of his own creation, Story demonstrated an uncanny instinct for the course best suited for his long-run advantage.

Rejecting the investigation in favor of the trip southward hazarded antagonizing two powerful members of the Administration. The action almost took—to use a New England phrase—the impudence of a dancing master, for part of his mission contemplated an interview with Gallatin himself to press the claims of more favored clients. Yet when the issue was forced upon him, Story made his choice, and things turned out none the worse for him. There was perhaps another element in his decision which lay below the level of consciousness. For many years he had been bemused with an idealized Southland. In declining the job of naval officer he closed his letter by mentioning "a desire to migrate southward" and requesting information on "any situation favorable to my views."[9] In early 1805 he was writing Crownin-

---

[7] Letter to Gallatin, May 13, 1807, Crowninshield Papers.
[8] Letter to Nathaniel Silsbee, Dec. 5, 1803, Crowninshield Papers.
[9] Letter to Gabriel Duvall, March 30, 1803, in W. W. Story, *Life and Letters of Joseph Story* (2 v., 1851: hereinafter cited as W. W. Story), I, 103-4.

shield "that Virginia is & always hath been the most patriotic, disinterested and magnanimous state in the Union."[10] Later that year he was telling a Baltimore classmate of his desire for "any respectable situation"[11] in that city, and in early 1806 he was still signing himself "really at bottom a Virginian."[12]

A quarter century later Story asserted that his youth had been "little infected with Virginia notions,"[13] and in a certain qualified sense this was quite true. Equally typical of the exasperating complexity of Story's character was that when he stopped talking of going south, he actually began preparations for such a journey. His preparations were well under way when, with a characteristic manifestation of industry and indiscretion, he attempted to take on the Newburyport investigation which his engagements at home and elsewhere precluded his fulfilling. His Southern commitments seem to have involved two assignments. One concerned some Treasury claims which Story, the last man to minimize the importance of his work, belittled as being "of no great consequence."[14] The other was as immense as the first was small. It was the big case, the traditional turning point of a legal career; beside it, all conflicting commitments shriveled into insignificance.

[10] Letter to Crowninshield, Jan. 24, 1805, Crowninshield Papers.
[11] Letter to Nathaniel Williams, June 6, 1805, in W. W. Story, I, 105.
[12] Letter to Crowninshield, Jan. 4, 1806, Crowninshield Papers.
[13] W. W. Story, I, 129.
[14] Letter to Samuel P. P. Fay, May 30, 1807, in W. W. Story, I, 152.

CHAPTER II

A Young Man of Talents

Story first went south toward the end of 1794, and it was not much of a trip—only as far as Cambridge.

He had burned his bridges at Marblehead Academy; impelled "to chastise" a schoolmate there, he had been chastised in turn by a teacher, disproportionately, and on this note the academy and the scholar parted company forever. His uncle, Reverend Isaac Story, took him to Harvard College to arrange for his late enrollment. The school's decision was that matriculation depended not on merely passing the usual entrance examination but on equaling the current attainment of the incumbent freshman class. This meant that the applicant had six weeks to cover the fall semester's work, largely by himself. In Homeric Greek he was completely on his own, and he went through the *Iliad* as reader, grammarian, and lexicographer. He appeared at Harvard in January of 1795 and passed the entrance examinations with flying colors.

As young Joseph Story was demonstrating his proficiency in the classics, talents of a more mundane type were being displayed in Augusta, Georgia, where four land companies purchased an immense quadrilateral that ran from the Chattahoochee to the Mississippi and from Tennessee to western Spanish Florida. It was beautiful country, fertile, and irrigated by a network of rivers with strange Indian names like Yazoo. Some thirty-five million acres were involved. The price was half a million dollars. The tract lay allegedly within Georgia's shadowy western frontier. It also fell within the shadow of the historic claims of the Spanish Crown. More to the point was its occupancy by a powerful Indian confederacy as to whom only the federal government held the constitutional power to negotiate in peace or the military power to break by war. The tangled legal title would have depressed the price in any event. The purchasing land companies lowered it yet further by corrupting the legislature almost to the last man.

Coincidently with the sale, however, came the disclosure of its circumstances. Georgia erupted in fury, and the end of 1795 saw a new legislature swept into office. The grant was repealed; the records were destroyed; a denunciation of the transaction was written into the state constitution. In a spectacular bit of ceremony the state dignitaries assembled in the capital and summoned fire from heaven with a sunglass to burn the original act as an official intoned, in accordance with directions (which included capitalization and punctuation marks), "GOD SAVE THE STATE!! AND LONG PRESERVE HER RIGHTS!! AND MAY EVERY ATTEMPT TO INJURE THEM PERISH AS THESE CORRUPT ACTS NOW DO!!!!"[1]

Simultaneously, a group of enterprising Yankees were buying the entire holdings of one of the original land companies. The sale comprised eleven million acres, one third of the Yazoo tract, and the price was ten cents an acre. The deal was fairly complex, involving installment payments, certain cedings and recedings of the land, and the formation of a New England Mississippi Land Company to serve as both vehicle and shield for subsequent sales. Whether by accident or design, the formal deed of purchase and the Georgia repealing act bore the same date, February 13, 1796 The sequence that followed suggested design rather than accident.

[1] Beveridge, *Life of John Marshall* (4v., 1916-19; hereinafter cited as Beveridge), III, 565.

The New England Company sought a legal opinion of its rights from Alexander Hamilton, who was practicing law in New York. The company had it in hand by the middle of March, 1796. Hamilton concluded that Georgia's attempted repeal was barred by the provision of the United States Constitution forbidding a state to impair the obligation of contracts. In short, the rescission was a nullity, and "the courts of the United States . . . will be likely to pronounce it so."[2] A few months later the company's legal fortifications were completed when Robert Goodloe Harper, prominent Federalist, Baltimore lawyer, and charter member of one of the purchasing land companies, published a pamphlet which began with the premise that the validity of the original sale concerned the courts, not the legislature, and concluded with the proposition that not even the courts were empowered to set the transaction aside.

The national government was also interested in the Yazoo transactions, and not from the standpoint of abstract theories of law or ethics. Of acute concern to George Washington's Administration was the problem of the Indians within the Yazoo lands and that of the Spaniards to the south of them. Of equal importance was the desirability of Georgia's following the lead of its sister states and surrendering its western domains to the nation for the formation of future states. After seemingly interminable backing and filling, the turn of the century saw a compromise worked out whereby the United States took over the lands as a territory, with five million acres being reserved to settle the mare's nest of private claim and counterclaim. To this end the heads of the Departments of State and Treasury, together with the Attorney General, were constituted a commission to hear the investor's case and report to Congress.

The end of the eighteenth century witnessed other changes, some great, some small. Joseph Story was back in Marblehead studying law. He had graduated from Harvard in the summer

2 *Ibid.*, 569.

of 1798 "with regret" and with "many bitter tears."[3] Neither his tears nor his regrets could match those with which New England Federalists greeted the election of Thomas Jefferson in 1801. There was, however, one place in New England where Federalist and Jeffersonian might meet in fine bipartisan concord, and that was in the service of the New England Company. For one minor consequence of the Jeffersonian ascendancy was that a Republican commission would propose whatever settlement was offered the New England claimants, and a Republican Congress would validate it. No longer did the company cite Hamilton and Harper in support of its claims. Instead it sought advocates of sterling Jeffersonian antecedents to support its cause in a long-term lobbying effort.

Perez Morton, who in a few years would be Story's predecessor as the Republican Speaker of the Massachusetts House of Representatives, went into virtual exile as the Washington agent of the New England Company. Gideon Granger of Connecticut, Jefferson's Postmaster General, went him one better and actually took to the floors of Congress to press the company's case in a lobbying effort which one day would cost him the very seat on the Supreme Court that Joseph Story filled. Together these stalwarts authored a petition to Congress, "Memorial of the Agents of the New England Mississippi Company to Congress with a Vindication of their Title at Law Annexed." The company had its representatives inside as well as outside. Congressman Ezekiel Bacon, a western Massachusetts Republican, watched over its interests in the House of Representatives. Senator John Quincy Adams, Bostonian Federalist, performed a like duty in the Senate. Not that Senator Adams could do too much, for overt Federalist support for the claimants might be fatal. "[T]he most effectual aid I can give . . ." Adams noted, "is by remaining silent."[4]

[3] Letter to William W. Story, Jan. 23, 1831, in *Miscellaneous Writings of Joseph Story*, ed. W. W. Story (1852; hereinafter cited as *Miscellaneous Writings*), 17.
[4] John Quincy Adams, *Memoirs*, ed. C. F. Adams (12v., 1874–77; hereinafter cited as J. Q. Adams, *Memoirs*), I, 423.

The commission's report was forthcoming on February 16, 1803, and recommended that the New England Company investors be paid off at approximately their out-of-pocket cost. An enabling bill was introduced in Congress. The claimants, the Administration, and practically everyone else devoutly hoped that such legislation would slide through as a matter of routine. They could not have been more disappointed, for they had failed to take into account Congressman John Randolph of Roanoke, who had seen at first hand the events surrounding Georgia's repealing act and doubtless was powerfully impressed by the elaborate ceremonial. Time and again he rose in the House to defeat the New England claims by his scathing, flamboyant oratory and parliamentary skill. "I observe," Jacob Crowninshield's wife, Sally, wrote him in early 1805, "there have been warm debate on the Georgia Lands."[5] Dr. Bentley otherwise forwarded his views to his Congressman: "As to the Georgia affair, I execrate it. . . . It was base speculation, which had the vilest principles and the worst measures as its basis."[6]

But Sally Crowninshield's prim understatement and Dr. Bentley's ire were untypical New England reactions. Far more characteristic was the union of Federalist and Republican under the standard of the New England Company. The adhesion of his nominal copartisans from the North only intensified Randolph's fury. "Of what consequence is it," he shrilled, "that a man smiles in your face, holds out his hand, and declares himself the advocate of those political principles to which you are also attached, when you see him acting with your adversaries upon other principles. . . ?"[7]

On other issues President Jefferson might run Virginia with the efficiency of a machine; on this he could not. As New England coalesced around the Yazoo claims, the unity of Virginia shat-

[Feb. 20, 1805, Crowninshield Papers.
Letter to Crowninshield, Feb. 18, 1805, Crowninshield Papers.
Henry Adams, *History of the United States under the Administration of Thomas Jefferson* (2v., 1930; hereinafter cited as H. Adams, *Jefferson*), Vol. Bk. II, 214.

tered. A few of its Congressmen stood with the President; the overwhelming majority, including both of Jefferson's sons-in-law, joined Randolph. Washington observers began to note that "so there is no being in nature which a Virginian hates as much as a New England Democrat."[8]

Not only Southerners were taking a critical second look at some Yankee Republicans; so were New England Federalists. They had given Story a particularly hard time of it when he first moved from Marblehead to Salem to engage in the practice of law. "[This] is to lay the foundation that Story will not be received in the Supreme Court when he comes to apply," wrote Jacob Crowninshield. "What will not Federalism attempt to carry out."[9] The preemptive disbarment failed, but the Federalists were not finished with young Story. "Mr. Story is marked out for destruction, he has aided the cause of the Gover't. & the people," Jacob Crowninshield wrote in 1802. The Federalists, he added, "had a 'Court Ball' last week and no republican was asked," and afterward they "voted to exclude certain persons among whom we find our names, Silsbee, Story . . . and all [their] ladies . . ."[10] And there were other incidents. The works of a New England divine contain the description of how Story was "on account of his political opinions, knocked down in the street, beaten, and forced to take shelter in the house of a friend, whither he fled, bleeding, and covered with the mud of the streets."[11]

Story's vanity ensured that he would never surrender to snub or violence. Patronage, however, succeeded where persecution failed. By 1807 ruling spirits of the New England Company were assured by Story's public and private career that here was their man. His maverick tendencies and insistence on his own way had even broken, albeit cryptically, into the press. "It is well known,"

[8] Manasseh Cutler to Dr. Joseph Torrey, Feb. 2, 1805, in *Life, Journals and Correspondence of Rev. Manasseh Cutler,* ed. W. P. and J. P. Cutler (2v. Cincinnati, 1888), II 189.
[9] Letter to Richard Crowninshield, Nov. 15, 1800, Crowninshield Papers.
[10] Letter to Richard Crowninshield, Nov. 24, 1802, *ibid.*
[11] Theodore Parker, *Additional Speeches, Addresses, and Occasional Sermons* (1855–1867), I, 178.

chuckled the Federalist *Salem Gazette*, "that there has been for some time considerable disagreement and disorder in the democratic ranks in this town and that sharp contensions have taken place . . ."[12]

How Story was brought into the ranks of the New England Company is not a matter found in newspapers. The lackluster Republican lobbyists may have sought out his assistance. Perhaps the invitation came from one of the Federalists who had felt his steel in the courtroom. But in any event the bid came and was accepted. Hence, even before Story accepted Crowinshield's commission, Robert Goodloe Harper received a letter from a hard-bitten New England Federalist, Harrison Gray Otis, which suggested in which direction the wind was blowing.

> I shall in a few days give to a Mr. Story from this place a line of introduction to you, at his particular request, and will thank you to pay him such attentions as may be consistent with your convenience and leisure. He is a young man of talents who commenced Democrat a few years since and was much fondled by his party. He discovered however too much sentiment and honour to go *all lengths*, & acted on several occasions with a very salutary spirit of independence & in fact did so much *good*, that his party have denounced him, and a little attention from the right sort of people will be very useful to him and to us.[13]

[12] *Salem Gazette*, Nov. 4, 1806.
[13] Letter to Harper, May 1, 1807, in Samuel E. Morison, *Life and Letters of Harrison Gray Otis* (2v., 1913; hereinafter cited as Morison, *Otis*), I, 283.

CHAPTER III

Transformation

TRAGEDY

The *Gazette* was the voice of the Federalist Party in Salem. Its stock in trade was a torrent of vituperation which was met, measure for measure, by the screeds of the Salem *Register*, to which Dr. Bentley and Joseph Story both contributed. Story had written the *Register's* motto and for him it was singularly appropriate; it began with a Jeffersonian flourish, struck a middle note of nationalism, and then ended with a canon of Federalism:

> *Here shall the Press the People's right maintain,*
> *Unawed by influence and unbribed by gain;*
> *Here Patriot Truth her glorious precepts draw,*
> *Pledged to Religion, Liberty, and Law.*[1]

This ambivalence was reflected in the treatment the *Gazette* meted out to Story. Sometimes the Federalist sheet praised him sometimes it upbraided him. Occasionally it referred to him in a manner which might be that of hearty commendation or cutting sarcasm. However, its enmity was not apparent in the early summer of 1805 when its obituary notices included:

[1] W. W. Story, I, 127.

. . . very suddenly, on Saturday evening last, Mrs. Mary
Lynde Fitch Story, aged 23 . . . Her superior and cultivated
understanding afforded rich treasures for her own enjoyment,
and the pleasure of her friends. . . .[2]

The retiring and sensitive disposition suggested in the brief elegy
had been noted in an even more fleeting reference toward the end
of the previous autumn, with the publication of *The Power of
Solitude*, "in Plain handsome binding, . . . 1.25 cents—in calf,
gilt 1.50."[3] Joseph Story was the author of this collection of
poems, but he concluded the preface with the acknowledgment
"that a few of them are not my own composition."[4] The book

> Lovely lock of auburn hair
> Let me catch thy varied curls . . .

was the second edition of the work; the first, a slim volume of
one hundred pages, had been published in 1802, and it was to a
supplementation of other pieces that the comment referred.

Doubtless the cryptic mention was as much as the Reverend
Thomas Oliver's daughter would permit on the part of a man not
her husband. Not that such a condition persisted for long. She
and Story were married on December 9, 1804, thus happily con-
cluding a year whose midpoint found the young lawyer noting
that despite all inclinations to move elsewhere "my situation here
grows daily better, and I have less power to contend against the
pleasure of being near Mary."[5] All this ended on June 22, 1805.
Reminiscent of the ceremony in Georgia, Story collected and
burned all the copies of *Solitude* he could find.

Doubtless grief underlay his action, although the sharp criticism
that the poetry received (when it attracted attention at all) was

[2] *Salem Gazette*, June 25, 1805. It is of course possible that the notice was
submitted by a bereaved relative or friend.
[3] Salem *Register*, May 30, 1805.
[4] Story, *The Power of Solitude*, 2nd ed. (1804), 4. One such poem, which
may reflect both Mary's poetry and Story's red curly hair, may be "Lover's
Whims" (p. 230):
[5] Letter to Samuel P. P. Fay, June 11, 1804, in W. W. Story, I, 101.

also involved. The critical reception was justified, for by any aesthetic index the book was appallingly poor. Yet as a relic of a brief and tragic love ("Maid of my heart . . . accept this humble gift . . ."[6]) it has flashes of extraordinarily touching appeal here and there in the mediocre text.

Hard on the heels of this tragedy came a second. In late August of 1805 Elisha Story, age sixty-three, died at Marblehead. "Never," wrote Dr. Bentley, "was a man more sincerely lamented in a Town . . . He was a man of good person & of most amiable character."[7] Indeed, this twice-married fishing-village physician was an extraordinary figure. Member of the Boston Tea Party and veteran of the Sons of Liberty and the Continental Army, Dr. Story made the easy transition from pre-Revolutionary Whig to post-Revolutionary Jeffersonian. Characteristic was his last will and testament. After making his wife executrix, he requested her "not to distress the poor, who may owe me at my decease, but to receive their debts as they may be able to pay in ever so small a sum." There followed a reference, worth ten of Dr. Bentley's barbs, to my "son Joseph, to whom I recommend her and her concerns; and though this perhaps is needless, I do it to mark my special confidence in his affections, skill, and abilities."[8]

We have Story's word for it that this succession of losses brought him to the brink of moral disintegration. He sought escape by throwing himself with redoubled energy into his professional work. "I have just crawled into my office, and am now endeavoring to drown all recollection in the hurry of business. My spirits have been so depressed, and my anguish so keen, that for three months I have been solitary and closeted, unknowing and unknown in the world," he wrote a classmate.[9]

It is tempting to see the events of the summer of 1805 as the crucial pivot of Joseph Story's life. One can find the dilettante

[6] Story, *The Power of Solitude* (1804), 7.
[7] Bentley, III, 187.
[8] W. W. Story, I, 13.
[9] Letter to Samuel P. P. Fay, Oct. 8, 1805, in W. W. Story, I, 114.

transformed—the visionary poet writing *The Power of Solitude* and the pragmatic lawyer burning it. To be sure, there are signs of change. Solitude was the last thing Joseph Story appeared to want thereafter. We hear no more of his yearning to start off again in faraway places, and reports of engagements at "fisty cuffs" disappear. An extraordinary self-possession thereafter marks his conduct in an age when invective was the standard coin of debate. "Keep a constant guard upon temper and tongue," he would later warn his Harvard classes. "Always have in readiness some of those unmeaning but respectful formularies [as for example] 'the learned gentleman . . .' "[10] A frontal attack could still smoke him out, but in the absence of direct provocation Story's mode of conduct became *nisi bonum* both of the living and of the dead. There appear, moreover, the signs of one scarred with an extraordinary psychological trauma. "[W]ith the world, I dare say, I pass for a cheerful man," he subsequently wrote, "and so I am; but my cheerfulness is the effect of labor and exertion to fly from melancholy recollections, and to catch at momentary joy."[11] In particular, his conversational bent took on the overtones of a man who cannot bear a moment of silence and seeks to destroy it with his own voice. One acute observer recognized the compulsive nature of Story's famous garrulity: "when he was in the room few others could get in a word; but it was impossible to resent this, for he talked evidently not to bear down others, but because he could not help it."[12]

We must be wary, however, of turning a chronological chain of events into a causal one. Story had early manifested the com-

[10] Rutherford B. Hayes, *Diary and Letters*, ed. Williams (Columbus, O., 1922), I, 113.
[11] W. W. Story, I, 333.
[12] G. W. F. Howard (Lord Howard of Morpeth), *Travels in America* (New York, 1851; in Library of Congress), 23. See also Robert H. Gardiner, *Early Recollections* (Hallowell, Maine, 1936), 105: "I dined once with Story when Webster, Otis and other gentlemen of that standing were at the table. Story engrossed the whole conversation for several hours. William H. Prescott, the historian, who sat next to me whispered: 'It's too bad. I have been trying to get in a word edgeways and can't succeed.' "

plex strains of his personality. His exhibitionist instinct had cropped up when he was a disputatious youngster who loved to confound his elders in the Marblehead barbershop. Likewise do we catch glimpses of his underlying melancholia in the small boy who sat brooding on the striated cliffs which gave his native town its name. Equally significant perhaps was his sense of estrangement from Marblehead, which, despite his praise of its Spartan virtues, always seemed to him a place of "general poverty" with "little room for the pride of scholarship, or the triumph of superior knowledge."[13] Harvard opened an entirely new world, and he left it with deep regret to return home in 1798. He took up the law largely for the lack of anything better to do, and—although he cried over the gnarled prose of Lord Coke—he seems to have taken to it from the very first.

Yet transformation of poet to lawyer was not a simple, lineal process. While studying with his characteristic dedication, Story persistently complained of the lack of intellectual companionship and nostalgically recalled

> . . . *sweet Friendship, who in* HARVARD's *bowers,*
> *With calm enjoyment winged my youthful hours,*[14]

as he read good law and scribbled bad verse in the first draft of *Solitude*. Significantly, his reservations on his choice of a career did not seem to focus on any temperamental incapacity for legal studies, but, rather, on an apprehension of material failure in their practical application. "Law," he wrote a friend, "I admire as a science; it becomes tedious and embarrassing only when it degenerates into a trade."[15] And there were other complications duly noted by Pastor Bentley with all the scorn of a true Salemite for the little village across the harbor: "Captain Nichols . . . wishes to dissolve an intimacy formed between his Daughter & Story the Poet of Marblehead."[16]

[13] Letter to William W. Story, Jan. 23, 1831, in *Miscellaneous Writings*, 7.
[14] Story, *The Power of Solitude* (1804), 64.
[15] Letter to Thomas Welch, Oct. 19, 1799, in W. W. Story, I, 83.
[16] Bentley, II, 358.

THE LAW

One day perhaps someone will investigate the seeming aptitude of second-rate poets to become first-rate jurists. Story exemplifies the phenomenon on one side of the Atlantic; Lord Mansfield and Sir William Blackstone—both of whose careers contain parallels to Story's—show it on the other. We have it on the authority of Alexander Pope (which, to be sure, must be qualified by Pope's penchant for flattery to friends in high places) that Mansfield might well have been another Ovid. And Sir William Blackstone even dipped into verse to say goodbye to poetic composition in "The Lawyer's Farewell to His Muse":

> *Me, wrangling courts and stubborn law*
> *To smoke, and courts, and cities draw*
> *No room for peace, no room for you—*
> *Adieu, celestial nymph, adieu.*

Perhaps Blackstone's eminently readable *Commentaries* so sparked Story's interest in the law as to preclude a repetition of formal adieu, even though he used almost identical words in forsaking poetry. For Blackstone is a symbol of a tradition which contended for, and seems to have won, the allegiance of a man who left Harvard unsettled in spirit and with a pronounced taste for Rousseau and the French *philosophes*. Certainly Story's attitude to the Alien and Sedition Acts of 1798 seems to have been so much in the best libertarian traditions that many years later he felt called upon explicitly to apologize for it. "He who lives a long life & never changes his opinions," Story wrote at thirty-nine, "may value himself upon his consistency; but rarely can be complimented for his wisdom. Experience cures us of many of our theories . . ."[17]

Indeed, hostile reaction to Federalist law-and-order legislation

---

[7] Letter to Harrison Gray Otis, Dec. 27, 1818, in Morison, *Otis*, I, 122-23.

may well have been the last chapter in Story's Jeffersonianism, for it would seem that by the time the legal apprenticeship was over the English Enlightenment had triumphed over its French counterpart. Perhaps "triumph" is too strong a word, for Rousseau and Blackstone have their similarities as well as their differences. Both are prophets of nationalism, and both predicate a natural law finding its best exemplification in the safeguarding of life, liberty, and property. In emphasis, the differences are profound. One is speculative and critical, the other analytic and conservative. Of the triad of life, liberty, and property, one gave priority to man freed of all restraints, while the other saw liberty as inseparable connected with property and, indeed, receiving there its exemplification.

Not all lawyers are conservatives, but, as de Tocqueville perceptively observed, most of them are, and this in the very necessities of the case. For if law becomes something more than a way of making a living or an appendage to a political career, it imparts —or attracts men with a predisposition to—"habits of order, a taste for formalities . . . , [an] instinctive regard for the regular connection of ideas, which naturally renders them hostile to the revolutionary spirit and the unreflecting passions of the multitude."[18] De Tocqueville noted other consequences of this condition—that in America lawyers come from the people but form a counterpoise to the democratic order, and that if an aristocracy existed anywhere in the United States it was found in the American bench and bar. Story disliked de Tocqueville, whose work, he wrote, "has had great reputation abroad, partly founded on their ignorance that he has borrowed the greater part of his reflections from American works, and little from his own observations. The main body of his materials will be found in the Federalist, and in Story's Commentaries on the Constitution; *sic vos non vobis.*"[19]

[18] A. de Tocqueville, *Democracy in America* (Vintage edition, 1960; hereinafter cited as de Tocqueville), I, 283.
[19] Letter to Francis Lieber, May 9, 1804, in W. W. Story, II, 330. Actually, de Tocqueville's recently discovered work sheets contain a gracious acknowledgment of his dependence on Story; see de Tocqueville, II, 395 n.

Story's own extensive use of paste and shears did not inhibit his having an acute proprietary interest in his own work. Lack of acknowledgment was certain to spark a resentful hostility. But there may have been other reasons converging to the same end. Certainly de Tocqueville set down on paper some general propositions which, Story felt, went without saying but were best left unsaid. And de Tocqueville's clinical analysis of the role of law and lawyers in America may have been a shaft that struck home as far as Story's personal career was concerned. Jefferson's reflections in the last year of his life were much to the same end. "[W]hen . . . the honeyed Mansfieldism of Blackstone," wrote the aged ex-President, "became the student's hornbook, from that moment, that profession (the nursery of our Congress) began to slide into toryism, and nearly all the young brood of lawyers now are of that hue. They suppose themselves . . . to be whigs, because they no longer know what whigism or republicanism means."[20]

MEN AND WOMEN

"I brood in secret over my former love," wrote Story a year and a half after his Mary's death, "and darkness sweeps across my mind."[21] It is barely possible that had Mary lived, Story could well have taken his poetry more and more seriously to the extent that his share in the American heritage would have been a collection of third-rate poetry. There was a strain of unconventionality in the family, which cropped out in his clerical uncle's stormy ecclesiastical career and again, after the Justice's death, in Story's only son, who, close to forty and well on his way to success as a public servant and legal scholar, emigrated to Italy to become a sculptor and spent his father's hard-won competence in living like an English milord. But Mary Story's long-range influence was never felt. For some of the qualities that did emerge in Story

[20] Letter to Madison, Feb. 17, 1826, in Jefferson, *Works*, ed. Ford (12v., 1904–5; hereinafter cited as Jefferson, *Works*), XII, 456.
[21] Letter to Samuel P. P. Fay, Dec. 19, 1806, in W. W. Story, I, 141.

—drive, energy, and competence—we might look to another and most extraordinary woman, Mehitable Pedrick Story. She had married his widower father at nineteen. "[M]y beloved, faithful, and affectionate wife," Dr. Story described her, ". . . did during the whole time in which I have lived most happily with her, take on her the charge and management of my children, whom I had by a former wife, and did conduct that trust reposed in her with great patience and prudence, which probably have few examples."[22] And indeed she had raised the seven children of her husband's first marriage and her own eleven with such impartiality that her firstborn, Joseph, grew up thinking he was one of the orphan brood.

Very probably the doctor's generous amiability caused his wife's talents to be exerted to the utmost. To the extent that parental influence can be taxed with children's characteristics, Story drew on both mother and father. His kindness, his generosity, his genuine liking for people, his dislike of hurting or of disappointing, can all find reflection in his father's image; his energy, ambition, and sense of his destiny were maternal legacies. And while the strains were happily mixed, his mother's influence seems dominant. We can only guess to what extent it furthered his love of reading and indulged his attitude of wanting to be captain or nothing in his childhood games. Unquestionably, the memory of his crowded, happy childhood home made his widowerhood doubly depressing. ("Kiss the children for me" was a customary close of his letters to married friends.) A second marriage had been deterred, he recalled, by "my difficulty in meeting with an individual to whom I could offer the free homage of my heart . . ."[23] Perhaps he had not been so much pursuing as pursued. Many years later he read *The Pickwick Papers* and commiserated with Mr. Weller on the moving sympathy of "widders" for those "who have lost their wives."[24]

[22] W. W. Story, I, 14-15.
[23] Letter to Joseph White, Jr., May 28, 1808, in W. W. Story, I, 169-70.
[24] Letter to Sarah Wetmore Story, Jan. 28, 1838, in W. W. Story, II, 284.

The political warfare of turn-of-the-century New England min-
imized his chances of finding a second wife among the ladies of
the maritime aristocracy. In Salem the merchants' wives held their
levees in the beautiful McIntyre houses and outdid each other in
featuring excellent food, vintage wines, and sparkling conversation. Yet as far as Joseph Story was concerned, on his arrival in
Salem much of this fine society might have been in far Cathay. "I
should as soon have expected to see a cow in a drawing-room as a
Jacobin,"[25] recalled an old lady of the days when Jeffersonians
were considered beyond the pale.

There was, however, one Federalist who did not treat Story to
the customary ostracism. This was William Prescott, whose fortune it was to go down in American history as the son of the
American commander at Bunker Hill and the father of the distinguished historian. Yet his influence in that history may be as
profound as it was unspectacular, for if we seek a gray eminence
in Joseph Story's life we may find it here. "From the moment I
came to the bar," recollected Story, "he treated me with un-
hesitating kindness and respect; and when such occurrences were
rare from other quarters, I constantly received from him invita-
tions to the parties at his house, as if I belonged to the circle of
his own friends."[26] How much this "kindness and respect" must
have meant to a young man in whom an instinctive affability was
conjoined to social and intellectual ambition. The consequences
show up over a period of time in scattered but extremely significant manifestations. It was to Prescott that Story gave an advance copy of his *Dartmouth College* opinion.[27] It was to Prescott that Story turned when weighing the possibility of resigning
from the Supreme Court.[28] It was to Prescott that he dedicated
his great *Equity Jurisprudence*. Indeed, the formative influence

[25] H. Adams, *Jefferson*, Vol. I, Bk. I, 92.
[26] Letter to William W. Story, Jan. 23, 1831, in *Miscellaneous Writings*, 22.
[27] Shirley, *The Dartmouth College Causes and the Supreme Court of the United States* (1879; hereinafter cited as Shirley), 305.
[28] Fairman, "The Retirement of Federal Judges," *Harvard Law Review*, LI (1938), 397, 413.

in Joseph Story's life was not John Marshall (whom Story did not even mention in the memoir he addressed to his son) but, rather, William Prescott, "whose regard," Story acknowledged thirty years after their first meeting, "would flatter my pride, and whose censure would infuse the most serious doubts into the estimate of my own conduct."[29]

THE JUDGES

"[T]ho' the people have this Judiciary check against the usurpations of the Legislature, what check have they against the usurpation of the Judiciary?" inquired a Yankee Republican in an Independence Day speech in 1805. "A judicial monarch," he went on, "is a character as abhorrent as an executive or legislative monarch in my view." The speaker also thrust at the bar as well as the bench—"the host of lawyers who infest our land like the swarms of locusts in Egypt."[30] The number of lawyers in the Republican Party was small enough. Utterances such as this— virtual canons of Jeffersonianism—must have made these few, or at least the ones who took their profession seriously, acutely uncomfortable. Story not only was a Republican lawyer but had been chosen to represent his party in the state legislature at the spring elections of that year of 1805. He was, moreover, a lawyer who took his profession most seriously, for February of that year had seen the publication of his *Pleadings in Civil Actions*, "a valuable New Work for Gentlemen of the Law . . . (five dollars)."[31] Though priced four times as high as *Solitude*, the lawbook was as much a success as the poetry was a failure. It was also an index to the future and the past. It foretold Story's pedagogic gift (the immediate consequence of the book was so to illuminate the procedural mysteries as to bring lay pleaders into court, and this in turn led to a formal apprenticeship and licensing for the Massa-

---

[29] Letter to William W. Story, Jan. 23, 1831, in *Miscellaneous Writings*, 22.
[30] John Leland, quoted in Robinson, *Jeffersonian Democracy in New England* (1916), 120 and n.81.
[31] Salem *Register*, Feb. 7, 1805.

chusetts bar); it showed that the young man in Salem with more time than clients was enough enamored of the law to explore its ways at his own expense; and it betokened an increasing self-assurance, for it was Story's second. The first, *American Precedents of Declarations*, appeared in 1802 with the anonymous indication that it was the work of two members of the Essex bar.[32]

The leisure gradually filled with professional employment, and with this came increasing public recognition. Story was appointed to a committee to revise Salem's ordinances in 1802, was placed on its school committee in 1804, and was elected to the state legislature shortly before the tragic summer of 1805 came upon him. He was reelected in 1806, and for the first time a majority of Republicans was returned to the lower house with him. The Jeffersonians were at long last in a position to fit some state policies to their ideas, and one of these was to put a bridle on the Federalist bench of Massachusetts. The battle between court and legislature was inevitable in the Jeffersonian ascendancy. One reason was philosophical. "Without controlling the Judiciary," Henry Adams stated the Jeffersonian principle, applicable alike on the state and national levels, "the people could never govern themselves in their own way; and although they might, over and over again, in every form of law and resolution, both state and national, enact and proclaim . . . , it was none the less certain that Chief Justice Marshall and his associates would disregard their will and would impose upon them his own."[33]

The other cause was practical and arose from the simple chronological fact that the Federalist Party was organized first and the Republican Party second. As the Jeffersonians took legislatures and governorships, Congress and the Presidency, they found al-

[32] Letter of W. W. Story to R. H. Dana, May 3, 1851, in W. W. Story, II, 21; *Legal Papers of John Adams*, ed. Wroth and Zobel (3v., Cambridge, Mass., 1965), I, 30 n. Story's co-worker was apparently Benoni Perham, and the Library of Congress so catalogues the book. However, a letter from Story bound with the Harvard copy claims the authorship. My thanks to Mr. George A. Strait of the Harvard Law School Library for this information.
[33] H. Adams, *John Randolph* (1898), 130-31.

most everywhere that a long-term judiciary had been organized
and left behind by the party they displaced. The inevitable ouster
attempt took various forms in various places. In Massachusetts the
Republicans adopted the tack of an "inflexible opposition to an
increase of the judges' salaries (at a time when they were con-
fessedly inadequate to their support) with a view to keep them
in a state of humiliating dependence, or to force them to resign
their places . . . "[34] The first round in this campaign of starvation
came on May 29, 1806, when Theophilus Parsons was appointed
Chief Justice of Massachusetts. Parsons' hidebound Federalism
framed an extraordinarily analytic and creative mind. He was
said to have more information on any given subject than most
men, and he knew more law than anything else. Parsons had indicated, however, that he would not ascend the bench unless the
salary were improved and made permanent. His attitude grew
out of the legislative practice of paying the judges in hit-or-miss
fashion and then only on judicial petition. This condition of
Parsons', Story recalled, "was known to his friends only, and was
communicated to me." (Was William Prescott the conduit?)
Story accordingly suggested a bill not only to regularize but also
to increase the judicial salaries. His motion to set up a committee
to report the bill was promptly voted down, but after a strong
speech by Story it passed easily. The favorable committee report,
drawn up by Story as chairman, contained a flowing eulogy to
the "inflexible integrity, the profound knowledge, and strict impartiality" of the Massachusetts Supreme Court. His performance
during the floor debate split his own party and rallied enough
Federalists to pass the measure.[35]

Flushed with this success, Story took the field again at the
January, 1807, meeting of the legislature with proposals to sys-
tematize and extend the jurisdiction of the state judiciary. He had
some able collaborators in the work. "I have employed myself in

[34] *Salem Gazette*, Aug. 23, 1811, quoting the *Worcester Gazette*.
[35] W. W. Story, I, 130-36. See also C. Warren, *History of the Harvard Law
School* (1908; hereinafter cited as Warren, *Harvard*), I, 263 n.1.

a careful revisal of the bills rec'd. from you,"[36] wrote Judge Sewell, whose Marblehead law apprentice Story had been. And a subject that would be particularly close to Story's heart was suggested by Judge Sedgwick: "I addressed a letter to you . . . enclosing a bill on the subject of equity."[37]

The second effort was a dismal failure. "Story," gloated Pastor Bentley, ". . . discovered that his ambition outstepped his Judgment. His first act was to aid the bill for raising the salaries of the Judges, a matter which could not obtain in Federal times. He succeeded. He has since attempted the new judiciary bill & failed. He called for it again & failed by a greater majority. Not a single Republican was found to adhere to him."[38] The defeat seemed to provoke a flash of the old fire. "Mr. Story . . . moved, that the committee on the Judiciary be discharged from all further duty. Which was immediately voted; and when he, as the Chairman of that committee, delivered the papers to the Chair, they were committed to new committees. Mr. Story was excused from the committee on the penal laws, and Mr. Bacon substituted."[39] Yet Story was far from finished with either his subject or his party. Massachusetts' rising tide of Jeffersonianism continued as the May elections of 1807 gave the Republicans both the legislative and executive branches of the state government. Dr. Bentley preached a powerful sermon, as the Salem Gazette fumed in impotent wrath: "Democrats hate lawyers: they have . . . therefore chosen a lawyer for governor, a lawyer for lieut. governor . . . [and in] this town they have chosen the only democratic lawyer that could be found in it for representative . . ."[40] With typical Federalist petulance, the Gazette did not know when its principles were in good hands. In compliance with a suggestion in the new governor's inaugural, a study of the general arrangements and powers of the state judiciary was submitted to a committee headed

[36] Letter to Story, Jan. 2, 1807, Story Papers, Library of Congress.
[37] Letter to Story, Jan. 27, 1807, ibid.
[38] Bentley, III, 273.
[39] Salem Gazette, Jan. 27, 1807.
[40] Ibid., May 29, 1807.

by Story. The committee was also directed to consider the introduction of equity jurisdiction. But Story was not home for the
election or the inaugural. He was riding south on the Yazoo
claims.

PART TWO

Lawyer and Lobbyist

CHAPTER IV

_____

Two Trips to Washington

_____

THOMAS JEFFERSON

In late May of 1807 Story came clattering into the national capital "reduced to a mere jelly" by the bouncing of the Baltimore–Washington stagecoach.[1] Had he made the trip in summer or winter, the discomforts would have been far worse. He was fated to do a great deal of traveling on behalf of the Yazoo claimants, and the sheer torture that these undertakings involved was a good index of his dedication to their cause. A lawyer, it is often insisted, is not to be identified with his clients or his case. Like all general propositions, this is a question of degree, and the answer requires some additional questions. What is the depth of his commitment to the legal theory he asserts? Is it one culled from many with professional detachment? What is the value of the cause? What activity does he expend on it? On these counts the assimilation of Story and the Yazoo claimants was complete. His emerging attitudes on the supremacy of the courts over the legislature we have already seen. The possible value of claims on the fertile Southern lands grew to fantastic proportions as the cotton exports of the United States jumped from 73,000 to 178,000 bales between 1800 and 1810. The energy he gave it in his years of advocacy was

[1] Letter to Samuel P. P. Fay, May 29, 1807, in W. W. Story, I, 148.

immense. "I wish the Georgia claimants," once complained a relative, "were in the black hole of Calcutta or some other place for keeping you from us."[2]

Although the Yazoo claims were the catalyst of Story's philosophical Federalism, the behavior of the dominant core of the Federalist Party was sufficient to inhibit any thought of formal transfer of allegiance. As the tension from the Napoleonic Wars mounted, the rule-or-ruin attitude of the Federalist ultras increasingly polarized around a sectional Anglophilism which not only reinforced the traditional barrier between conservative Republicans and the Federalist Party but estranged the Federalist moderates within it.

Story had lost his inherited religious conviction at Harvard, but his college years had reinforced a strong nationalist bent, which probably began with his father's tales of soldiering in the American Revolution. Story's college days had begun inauspiciously enough, for his latecomer status meant that he took his place in the class friendless and alone. Yet his compelling personal charm and appetite for scholarship so paved his way that when the undeclared war with France broke out in Story's senior year, he helped draft the Harvard memorial endorsing President Adams' policy. Prophetically perhaps, the Franco–American tension resulted in the French oration being dropped at the Harvard commencement of 1798 and also produced a rash of cockades throughout New England. The Federalists adopted the black cockade of the old Continental Army; a few Republicans wore the red-white-blue of Revolutionary France. Significantly, his first confrontation between nationalism and ideology, between revolution and conservatism, saw Story wearing the black cockade and wearing it proudly.

But all this was almost ancient history when Story arrived in Washington in May of 1807, hard on the heels of Crowninshield's letter announcing the uncontemplated turn of events in the Newburyport investigation. If Gallatin, hard pressed for revenues in

[2] Joseph White to Story, Feb. 19, 1810, Story Papers, Library of Congress.

a deteriorating foreign situation, was irked by the Newburyport development, he showed little sign of it; on the contrary, Story found him "plain and modest in his demeanor" and was impressed with the Secretary's "promptitude, accuracy, and distinctness."[3] A far more important visit was paid to James Madison, incumbent Secretary of State and his Uncle Isaac's Princeton schoolmate, whom Story found "a most agreeable, modest, and unaffected man."[4] Madison would become President in two years and place Joseph Story on the Supreme Court in four. They were two of a kind—pedantic, fussy, middle-sized men. They were alike in their nervous indecision in the face of crisis, alike in a flintlike tenacity once the crucial decision was made, and alike in the complexity of their crypto-Federalism. Story's admiration of any man was essentially a function of reciprocity, and we may glean Madison's view of Story by reading backward from the latter's profuse praise of the fourth President's "private virtues, his extraordinary talents, his comprehensive and statesman-like views." When Story wrote this tribute, thirty-five years after his first meeting with Madison, he could not forbear coupling it with a belittling reference to Madison's predecessor in office: "[I]n wisdom I have long been accustomed to place him [Madison] before Jefferson . . . I know something more of each of them in trying times, than the common politicians of our day . . . "[5]

On May 29, 1807, Story was little more or less than a common politician of the day, and he was delighted, as such, to be received by the President of the United States. In a sense the meeting was the midpoint of his career. Less than twenty years before, when Joseph Story was a boy at Marblehead, President George Washington had come to town on a state visit; Story's silence on this incident suggests that he and his family participated only as onlookers. Less than twenty years later another Virginia President would enter Salem in a coach-and-four for a visit whose highlight

[3] Letter to Samuel P. P. Fay, May 30, 1807, in W. W. Story, I, 152.
[4] *Ibid.*
[5] Letter to Ezekiel Bacon, April 30, 1842, in W. W. Story, II, 420.

would be a glittering reception for James Monroe at the residence of Mr. Justice Story.

Now with his fortunes at midpassage, he wrote home enthusiastically of his reception at the Executive Mansion and noted Jefferson's kindness and courtesy. His praise was tinctured with a guarded and uncharacteristic note of prim disapprobation: "The negligence of his dress a little surprised me. He received us in his slippers, and wore old-fashioned clothes, which were not in the nicest order, or of the most elegant kind . . ."[6] It was perhaps a most significant touch, for the British minister had been received under like circumstances and had treated Jefferson's slippers as a studied insult to the Crown. Jefferson had more on his mind than clothes: troubles beset him from all points of the compass. In the Atlantic the republic was pressed between two millstones as the British behaved with their customary phlegmatic, unselfconscious arrogance, while Napoleon treated American interests with sweetness and light one day and maniacal fury the next. To the south there were the Spanish in Florida. The West was still rumbling from the aftermath of the Burr conspiracy and the possibility of more separatist plots to come. To the north the Essex Junto bided its time for the chance to put its rule-or-ruin ideas into action. To this assortment of troubles was added the Yazoo claims, a minor but persistent festering complication. As leader of the opposition Jefferson might preach the doctrine of strict construction, states' rights, and the most austere morality in government. On every count he should have stood with Randolph. But Jefferson in power dismissed as metaphysical subtleties the doctrines he formerly preached, and on the Yazoo case he threw his weight on the side of practical compromise. No doubt his basic reaction to the Yazoo controversy was to join Story's brother-in-law in the wish that the Yazoo claimants with their interminable bleats of injured innocence were in the Black Hole of Calcutta.

But what was for Jefferson a minor complication swollen out of all proportion to its importance was for Story almost the fixed

[6] Letter to Samuel P. P. Fay, May 30, 1807, *ibid.*, I, 151.

center of his universe. Perhaps the most important part of his work was done on the return swing. The first stop, at Baltimore, showed Story's rise in professional prominence as the patronage of an equal replaced the supplication of an applicant. ("[A] man of talents, well versed in his profession in Massachusetts, need not shrink from an honorable competition."[7]) Ironically, he was the unknowing recipient of the same type of patronage he was dispensing. Robert Goodloe Harper, both a firsthand participant in the Yazoo affair and the leading advocate for the claimants, paid him the heed which the hardbitten Otis had suggested. ("Mr. Harper was very polite in his attentions."[8]) And perhaps the intelligence as to the young lawyer's Achilles' heel was sent to New York, where the Federalist Rufus King received him in a two-hour interview. ("As a young man and a stranger, I preserved silence . . ."[9])

SUMMER INTERLUDE

Story got back to Salem about the same time that the news of the *Chesapeake* outrage reached New England. Even moderate Federalists were shocked on hearing that an American man-of-war had fallen under a surprise cannonade from a supposedly friendly English frigate, had struck her colors, and had lost four of her crew to the press gang. Anglo–American relations had been going from bad to worse since May of 1805, when Sir William Scott, sitting in the High Court of Admiralty, delivered his judgment in the prize case of the *Essex.* Sir William was a remarkable man, whose sensitive personal honor was not above baiting the American minister at a dinner party and whose instinct for shaping the law into new and creative forms included an ability to bend it to the wishes of George III. Whether he merited Mr.

[7] Letter to Samuel P. P. Fay, June 10, 1807, *ibid.,* 154.
[8] *Ibid.,* 153.
[9] Letter to Samuel P. P. Fay, June 18, 1807, *ibid.,* 154.

Justice Story's subsequent encomium as a jurist "whose eminent qualifications . . . entitled him to great reverence"[10] is another question.

But there was no such gracious appraisal in 1805 when Scott's *Essex* decision came like a thunderclap across the Atlantic. In a sense the judgment hinged on the narrowest of technicalities. Previously Sir William had held in the *Polly* case that the American customhouse entries were virtually conclusive evidence that foreign goods had been incorporated in American stocks and so lost any belligerent taint. The American carrying trade accordingly boomed under the forced-draft pressure of the Napoleonic Wars. Needless to say, so did the drawbacks.

With all of his other virtues, Scott was also a realist who comprehended the role of lawyers in the fate of empires. He decided *The Polly* when the Anglo–French conflict was yet in its fluid, formative stages and neutrals were potential allies and placated as such. He decided the *Essex* when the lines of the rivalry were hardening into the last climactic decades and the few neutrals of the world were no longer blandished but coerced, as each protagonist tried to outdo the other in preempting by force the economic resources of the world. For the United States this meant a seemingly endless rain of blows as decrees poured forth from Napoleon and countervailing orders issued out of the British Privy Council.

Sir William's decision in the *Essex* could be read at two levels. At the lowest, it was no more than a simple demand for proof—that whether the *Essex's* cargo was bona-fide American goods required more evidence than the fact that it had been landed in the United States and the American duty paid. Behind this façade was another message—that American ships and seamen henceforward sailed under the terms the British prize courts and press gangs would allow. Napoleon responded that any submission to British

[10] *Charles River Bridge v. Warren Bridge,* 11 PETERS at 596 (1837). See also the tribute as *"jurisperitorum eloquentissimus"* in *Miscellaneous Writings,* 282-85.

rules would make any American ship liable to French confiscation. Caught in this battle, "the United States could only be likened to an unfortunate rat worried by two terrier bulldogs; whether it fought or whether it fled, its destiny was to be eaten up."[11] From a standpoint of abstract logic, the only choices were to fight or to submit. And to fight was to fight both, for to take but one was to submit to the other. The American dilemma initially manifested itself in sharp words and little else. "The noted Judge Scott," wrote Jacob Crowninshield, "is a member of the King's Privy Council . . . [who] receives his orders & then goes upon the pot of judgment & gives a decision against neutrals under what he pretends is the law of nations . . . "[12] Story was even harsher, comparing the learned judge to a pirate: "one depredates . . . on the ocean, the other plunders clothed in the hypocritical ermine of Justice."[13]

Salem was hit disastrously by the new British policy. A town meeting was held and solemn protest was entered against the belligerent infringements of the neutral trade. Story authored the tedious and prolix memorial solemnly proving that the High Court of Admiralty was not adhering to its own precedents,[14] and sent it down to Crowninshield enclosing an extra copy for "some Republican Senator to be presented to the Senate."[15] Crowninshield reported back "that the Memorial is spoken of in the highest terms of commendation. It does honor to its authors & I have no doubt it will be read with lively interest wherever it is seen."[16] Story perhaps needed some words of comfort after the *Gazette*'s sharp bite: "We this day publish the *Memorial* voted by about an *hundred* persons, on Monday last, to be presented to [the] Gov-

[11] H. Adams, *The Life of Albert Gallatin* (1879; hereinafter cited as H. Adams, *Gallatin*), 380.
[12] Letter to Nathaniel Silsbee, Dec. 29, 1805, Crowninshield Papers.
[13] Letter to Jacob Crowninshield, Dec. 17, 1805, Crowninshield Papers.
[14] *Miscellaneous Writings*, 43 (1835).
[15] Letter to Jacob Crowninshield, Jan. 21, 1806, Crowninshield Papers.
[16] Letter to the Committee of the Town of Salem, Jan. 31, 1806, Crowninshield Papers.

ernment, as the doings of the Town of Salem, which contains between one and two *thousand voters*."[17]

Jefferson's response to the *Essex* decision took the form of economic sanctions. Crowninshield was strongly behind the President. "Our ships are plundered in every sea," roared the shipowning Congressman, "our seamen are impressed . . . I am ready to act."[18] Crowninshield, proposing a total bar on British and French imports, was more extreme than the Administration, which settled for import prohibitions on a specified list of products. Up in Salem Joseph Story gave an inkling of his future break with Jefferson as he confessed his skepticism of passive refusals to buy. "It would cripple our commerce without giving us material advantages," he wrote Crowninshield. "We must depend for ultimate effect on measures more decisive . . ."[19]

Reciprocal miscalculation occurred on both sides of the Atlantic. Jefferson shared the Napoleonic delusion as to the degree of pressure required to bring a nation of shopkeepers to heel. And the British regarded the philosophical idealism of Jefferson's reaction to the *Essex* decision as the response of a poltroon. Hence, the *Chesapeake* incident came as almost the inevitable upshot of an inherently unstable relationship between the two countries, complicated further by misunderstanding.

Jefferson could have had a declaration of war that summer for the asking and could have taken a virtually united nation into armed hostilities. Yet he stayed his hand, refused to call Congress into immediate session, and contented himself with certain halfway measures. Thus far his philosophic hatred of war coincided with widespread intuition of the practical futility of formal belligerence. Salem reflected the mood of New England and, to a lesser degree, of the whole nation. A town meeting was held.

[17] *Salem Gazette*, Jan. 24, 1806.
[18] *Annals of Congress*, XV (1806), 411. (In citing Congressional material, I have followed the unofficial volume designations used for the *Annals of Congress* and the *Register of Debates* respectively and cited the *Congressional Globe* by Congress and session.)
[19] Letter to Jacob Crowninshield, Dec. 17, 1805, Crowninshield Papers.

Story was included in a committee to draw up a remonstrance. The document as written vigorously protested the outrage but stopped short of an outright appeal to arms. Instead, the protestors resorted to the ambiguity of "honorable measures which may be adopted to obtain redress for our recent injuries."[20] Yet, almost as the committee wrote, a Salem divine was preaching a sermon defending the British action, and Chief Justice Parsons was giving his extrajudicial opinion that British impressment of American merchant seamen was wholly legal. To Republicans such attitudes verged on treason; to Federalists it was a recognition of the simple fact that the Royal Navy was the shield of American independence. Napoleon, they insisted, had been diverted from his designs on the North American continent only temporarily and would promptly reassert them when his major obstacle was crushed. Massachusetts' Senator Timothy Pickering, most irreconcilable of the Federalist ultras, decried what seemed to him the Jeffersonian attempt to "hasten the glorious period when to the lofty titles of Emperor of France and King of Italy and Protector of the Confederation of the Rhine shall be added that of Emperor of Two Americas."[21]

JOHN MARSHALL

Congress reconvened October 26, 1807. For the Yazoo claimants, developments were all to the good. The fortunes of domestic politics had placed a Massachusetts Republican in the speakership of the House of Representatives and had resulted in a weakening of John Randolph's legislative power. The increasingly critical state of foreign affairs, moreover, put a premium on settling the sectional rivalry of the Yazoo controversy in the interest of national unity. Deterioration of foreign relations had been the only fruit of Jefferson's extraordinary forbearance in the *Chesapeake* episode. The British disavowed the incident in a manner which

---

[20] Salem *Town Records, 1800–1818*, 264-66 (July 10, 1807).
[21] Sears, *Jefferson and the Embargo* (1927), 188.

added insult to the original injury, and the contest of oppression of American interests between their Orders in Council and the Napoleonic decrees proceeded with new vigor.

In December of 1807 Jefferson played his trump card, requesting and obtaining from Congress a total embargo of American overseas trade. Only by the accident of the Speaker's eye falling elsewhere did the measure fail to bear Crowninshield's name; the Salem Congressman had been the first on his feet to urge its adoption when Jefferson's message was read to the House of Representatives. Jefferson had seen the practical advantages of boycotts in the critical days preceding the American Revolution. A passive refusal to buy was one thing for a colony but quite another for a sovereign country. Simple passivity could be damaging, but it still gave belligerents access to American resources through third-party intermediaries and, most important of all, left American cargoes and seamen free to wander the high seas with full vulnerability to foreign searches and seizures. Contrariwise, the extreme economic sanction of embargo had two inherent disadvantages. Lacking the spectacular flavor of an appeal to arms, it depended on dull routine and the long pull. Closely related was the fact that this lever to move the British to good behavior had its fulcrum in New England, the headquarters of the American carrying trade. Only if New England stood firm could the embargo succeed.

The first consequence of the Embargo Act became apparent with the beginning of 1808. Ship after ship came into Salem harbor to tie up and ride empty-hulled at the wharves. Behind the ships, Salem's entire economic complex—the foundries, the sail lofts, the banks, the insurance companies—began to lapse into inactivity. Yet the Jeffersonian Yankees seemed to be holding the line. "[N]o man likes the embargo," wrote a hard-shell New England Federalist, "and nineteen in twenty detest it; yet party hatred is stronger, and will dictate the declaration . . ."[22] Na-

[22] George Cabot to Timothy Pickering, Jan. 28, 1808, in Lodge, *Life and Letters of George Cabot* (1877), 376.

tional adversity was, however, the New England Mississippi Land Company's opportunity. With the first of the new year Joseph Story was off southward again. Dr. Bentley watched him go "to manage the mad Yazoo business."[23] Offsetting the clergyman's disapproval was the word which was increasingly noised about in Federalist circles. "Though he is a man whom the Democrats support," wrote one charter member of the Essex Junto to another, "I have seldom if ever met with one of sounder mind on the principal points of national policy. He is well worthy [of] the civil attention of the most respectable Federalists . . . "[24]

Both Congress and the Supreme Court were in session when Story reached Washington. His business was strictly with the legislative branch, but, like a busman on a holiday, he spent his spare time in the courtroom. Of even more value to him was a boardinghouse companionship with the familyless Justices. For it was doubtless in the boardinghouse that he first met John Marshall and fell captive to the Chief Justice's compelling personal charm. "I love his laugh," Story wrote home, "—it is too hearty for an intriguer . . ."[25] With this one sentence Story abjured the virtual pivot of the Jeffersonian creed, for in that creed John Marshall was the "crafty chief judge, who sophisticates the law to his mind, by the turn of his reasoning," and so headed a "subtle corps of sappers and miners constantly working under ground to undermine the foundations of our confederated fabric."[26] How sharply the meeting of Story and Marshall must have contrasted with the strained interview at the White House the preceding summer. The young lawyer and the middle-aged Chief Justice both loved to talk, and they had a host of matters to talk about. Doubtless the Georgia claims headed the list, as Marshall's own family estate lay in the shadow of expropriatory state legislation.

[23] Bentley, III, 341, 346.
[24] George Cabot to Timothy Pickering, Jan. 28, 1808, in Lodge, op. cit. supra (note 22), 377.
[25] Letter to Samuel P. P. Fay, Feb. 25, 1808, in W. W. Story, I, 167.
[26] Jefferson to Thomas Ritchie, Dec. 25, 1820, in Jefferson, Works, XII, 177-78.

This accidental point of consensus was, however, the superficial index of a far more pervasive affinity of experience and attitude. Marshall loved poetry, and Story had written a volume. Story revered Washington, and Marshall had just completed a Washington biography. Both authors had been involved in dismaying experiences with publishers. In terms of shared experience, immediate or vicarious, there were the New Jersey campaigns of 1777, in which Captain John Marshall and Surgeon Elisha Story both served. There were common bonds in their Unitarianism, in an apprehension of the extremes of the Jeffersonian faith, and, above all, in a reverence for the judicial process.

The long conversations—each waiting for the other to stop talking—alone must have been to Story worth the trip to Washington. Whether they compensated for the failure of his mission and the humiliation which accompanied it only he could tell. The Yazoo claimants had sent Story to Washington to address not John Marshall but the House of Representatives. He must have worked extremely hard on his speech and anticipated the triumph he thought his vigorous, if florid, oratorical powers would provoke in the halls of Congress. He had good reason to pride himself on his speaking ability. As a stripling of twenty he had delivered the eulogy on Washington's death before the Marblehead town meeting, and the gathering had responded by appointing "a Committee to present the thanks of the Town to Mr. Joseph Story for his Oration delivered this day and request a Copy for the press."[27] Even Dr. Bentley could appraise one of Story's perennial Fourth of July speeches as "highly poetical & with unnumbered Classical allusions & with some very just remarks."[28] Alas, the speech which was intended to galvanize Congress turned out to be love's labor lost. To be deprived of rendering it was bad enough, but the circumstances were particularly galling. On February 12, 1808, Story waited in silence all day (for him the cruelest of punishments) as debate raged in the House of Repre-

[27] Marblehead *Town Records, 1789–1801*, 402 (Jan. 2, 1800).
[28] Bentley, III, 97.

sentatives on whether he might address it. A fiery Georgian capped the issue with the inquiry as to whether the House "could be so lost to a sense of its own dignity as to enter into a controversy on its own floor with speculators or their agents."[29] The response was an overwhelming rejection of Story's request to be heard.

Story stayed on a few days longer. One of his last actions was to visit the Senate galleries, where he heard Virginia's Senator William Branch Giles level a blistering condemnation at John Marshall. "Never," Story wrote to a friend, "did I hear such all-unhinging and terrible doctrines . . . [Giles] attacked Chief Justice Marshall with insidious warmth . . . You shall hear from me *intimately* respecting the judges and bar, hereafter."[30]

[29] *Annals of Congress* XVIII (1808), p. 1602.
[30] Letter to Samuel P. P. Fay, Feb. 13, 1808, W. W. Story, I, 159.

CHAPTER V

Congressman Story

NOMINATION AND ELECTION

On January 18, 1808, Jacob Crowninshield collapsed in the House of Representatives. Down with him as he fell came the real political power of the Crowninshield family, down went the last truly personal tie which held Story to an authentic Republican allegiance, and down went any chance the embargo had for success. Crowninshield made a great fight for his life, but his seaman's constitution was not proof against this last illness. He died April 15, 1808. Story and Dr. Bentley united in eulogy. "[M]y honored and lamented friend . . . ," said Story, "a man of excellent understanding, of manly feeling, and incorruptible integrity."[1] "I have known him from a lad & have nothing to blame in him," mourned Dr. Bentley. "Had he not been confined in his early education & early been engaged in the business of the Seas he would have left none before him."[2] At some point during Crowninshield's last illness, Story cast his eye on the Salem seat in the House of Representatives. So did the dying Congressman's brother, Benjamin. "I heard the other day," gibed Story's brother-

[1] Letter to William W. Story, Jan. 23, 1831, in *Miscellaneous Writings*, 29.
[2] Bentley, III, 355.

in-law to apparently receptive ears, "the Republicans were talking strongly of putting B[enjamin] C[rowninshield] Jr up as Representative to Congress—do not you think some of our good folks mad?"[3] Shortly after Congressman Crowninshield's death on April 15, the brother and Story locked horns at the Republican caucus which had been convened in Salem to nominate a successor. Procedure was fairly free and easy, with the result that a host of Storys who had come over to the meeting from Marblehead provided the slim margin making Story the party choice.[4]

Dr. Bentley simmered over what he felt were sharp tactics in the party councils, and he felt his worst fears confirmed when the Federalists failed to nominate a candidate of their own: "J[oseph] S[tory] will answer as well for them as any man they could chuse."[5] To much the same effect ran an ambiguous accolade in the local Federalist paper when the formality of election transformed Story from candidate to Congressman-elect: "May his usefulness, in this new station, be equal to his talents."[6] Up from Washington came another significant note of congratulation. "I shall with pleasure . . ." wrote Congressman Ezekiel Bacon, "resign into your hands the next winter the sole management of *Yazooism* in the national councils."[7] Other Republicans in Washington, whose political horizons were broader than the Yazoo controversy, likewise found Story's election a circumstance of congratulation, and the *National Intelligencer* duly reported his victory.

Certainly the consequences of the spring elections in Massachusetts made the Jeffersonians seek all the consolation they could find. The Republicans carried the commonwealth, reelecting Governor James Sullivan. They had saved the Salem seat in the by election. Otherwise the Federalists scored a smashing comeback,

[3] Joseph White, Jr., to Story, Feb. 28, 1808, Story Papers, Library of Congress.
[4] Bentley, III, 360.
[5] *Ibid.*, 361
[6] *Salem Gazette*, May 24, 1808.
[7] Letter to Story, June 1, 1808, Story Papers, Library of Congress.

carrying both houses of the legislature. To be sure, their margin was small, but its very narrowness reinforced party cohesion. Ten years earlier Thomas Jefferson had fathered the doctrine of state interposition to any federal laws which attempted to press central authority beyond the letter of constitutional authority. From the Federalist point of view, Jefferson had thus sown the wind in his opposition to the Alien and Sedition Acts; it would be fitting retribution that he reap the whirlwind over the embargo.

One of the principal targets of vengeance was Federalist Senator John Quincy Adams, who had cast his vote for the embargo. Although Adams' term had a year to run, the Massachusetts legislature elected his successor. The Essex Junto had marked their man well. Responding in icy and intellectual contempt, Adams promptly submitted his resignation. Another item was a legislative memorial excoriating the embargo itself, and here they were on safer ground. Massachusetts' Democratic governor himself had referred to the embargo as a great calamity justified only by alternative evils, and Story's position was far from enthusiastic. That May of 1808 did more than return the Federalists to power; it also witnessed the Spanish revolt against Napoleon and thus provided the Federalist argument that the pro-Napoleonic cast of the embargo was doubly perverted by its operation against a nation struggling for its own freedom.

Certainly the Federalists had a point. England's control of the seas did make the ostensibly impartial embargo the American complement of Napoleon's Continental System. England's control of the seas, however, made her oppressions immediate and Napoleon's remote. The two parties united in decrying foreign violations of American rights. Party division occurred on the issue of which oppressor was the worse. The Jeffersonians reacted against the enemy at hand, not the enemy over the horizon. The Federalists outdid each other in denouncing the Corsican tyrant. On this index Story tended toward the Federalist camp. In the legislative session of 1807 he had drawn up a memorial against belligerent infringements and vigorously resisted attempts to substitute the phrase "royal proclamations and imperial decrees" for his own words condemning "imperial mandates."[8]

When the 1808 session of the legislature debated the resolution condemning the embargo, Story outdid any Federalist in his denunciation of Napoleon. Nominally defending the Administration, Story's efforts must have made many Jeffersonians wish to be saved from such friends. He undercut the core of the policy of passive resistance by urging a large Navy. As to the embargo itself, Story said he would have voted against it, but now that it was in force it should be given a chance. "[C]onfessedly brilliant," applauded a Federalist paper.[9] Dr. Bentley thought otherwise: "Mr. S[tory], our member, had his long speech, this & that & finally voting with after he had weakened his friends. Leading men to a precipice from which they know not how to escape. Give me a firm man who reflects, but decides."[10]

THE BRIGANTINE *WILLIAM*

Dr. Bentley's assessment of Story was appropriate. Story seemed to have as many positions on the embargo as a weathervane on a gusty day: the embargo never should have been tried; it should have been given a chance; it was the only way to avoid war, "measures more decisive" (whatever those might be) were necessary.[11] "The picture which you give me of public sentiments on the embargo," Congressman Bacon acknowledged in April, "is just as I had expected. Party considerations here as elsewhere . . . prevent a candid disclosure of opinions, but they must eventually leak out."[12] Perhaps the indecisive spring elections, in which the Federalists fell short of scoring a mortal blow, changed Story's covert disapproval to halfhearted endorsement. Perhaps the catalyst came in his new Washington status and the consequent op-

Amory, *Life of James Sullivan* (1850), II, 263.
W. W. Story, I, 137, quoting the *Columbian Centinel*, May 28, 1808.
[0] Bentley, II, 363.
[1] Letter to Jacob Crowninshield, Dec. 17, 1805, Crowninshield Papers.
[2] Letter to Story, April 24, 1808, Story Papers, Library of Congress.

portunity to trade off a supported embargo for a successful Yazoo settlement. In any event, by midsummer his views seemed to be swinging behind the Administration, with Congressman Bacon inquiring as to the status of Story's "projected pamphlet in vindication of the embargo."[13] By fall, the Congressman-elect was in the thick of the fight.

The occasion was the trial of the brigantine *William*[14] at Salem. The ship had been caught in a violation of the embargo law. In itself this was no problem, because New England juries were wont to acquit embargo violators whatever evidence the United States Attorney produced. This time the Federalists struck for the jugular and based the defense on the unconstitutionality of the law. Massachusetts' Chief Justice Parsons had been giving his extrajudicial opinion to this effect, and now the Essex Junto was prepared to put his words to the test. Specifically the issue was over the failure of the law to carry a terminal date, and this omission had been sharply debated in both Cabinet and Congress. As a practical matter, the omission was a necessity if the British were to be convinced that American passive resistance would continue as long as their active depredations. Logically, however, it permitted the Federalists to throw Jefferson's strict construction back in his face. The Constitution said not one word about an embargo. To be sure, it might be used in time of war, but how could the war power be summoned to stay out of war? As the case came on for trial, the *Salem Gazette* summed up the issue as "whether the Congress and President have a right BY THE CONSTITUTION *forever* to prohibit commerce to the people of the United States . . ."[15]

The Jeffersonians had good cause to be apprehensive. As the embargo began to take hold, evasions mounted. The biggest loophole was the coastal trade, and the Administration attempted to supply the deficiencies of the statute by elaborate regulations granting virtually plenary power to United States collectors. The

---

[13] Letter to Story, April 22, 1808, Story Papers, Library of Congress.
[14] *United States v. The William*, 28 FED. CASES 614 (1808).
[15] *Salem Gazette*, Sept. 20, 1808.

regulations had been voided by a Jeffersonian appointee, Justice William Johnson, sitting on circuit in South Carolina. Now the law itself was to be tested in New England, and the district judge of the United States who would test it was an old-line Federalist, John Davis.

Governor Sullivan had been apprehensive enough over his own state judges. "There is no way to carry on a war," he wrote Jefferson, ". . . without the decisive aid of a Judiciary . . . We shall, if a war takes place, be instantly plunged in a civil war in this State if the Judiciary continues as it is at present . . . " But even worse, apparently, was John Davis. "[T]he Judiciary of the United States in this district," Sullivan continued, "is still more unpropitious . . ."[16]

Such, supposedly, was the judge. The defense was in the hands of William Prescott and Samuel Dexter. The United States Attorney was one George Blake, Yazoo claimant, who summoned his brother, Francis, as co-counsel. The brother's presence was presumably found inadequate, as Dexter delivered what was considered "his *greatest* argument [and] one of the ablest he ever made"[17] on the constitutional issue. At the eleventh hour ("Until . . . last evening, I had not expected to take a part, in this elaborate and protracted discussion . . ."[18]) Joseph Story joined the prosecution. He made a powerful plea to the court. Many years later Story would assert that he had "ever considered the embargo a measure which went to the utmost limit of constructive power under the Constitution."[19] However, he permitted no such doubt in the Salem courtroom:

> Since it was first contemplated to submit this inquiry to the test of judicial decision, I have read many ingenious newspaper essays . . . Such, however, has been either my inflex-

[6] Letter to Jefferson, Dec. 7, 1807, in Sears, *Jefferson and the Embargo* (1927), 58.
[7] William Sullivan, *Familiar Letters on Public Characters* (Boston, 1834), 27.
[8] Blake, *An Examination of the Constitutionality of the Embargo Laws* 1808); in Pamphlet Collection, Essex Institute, Salem, 7.
[9] Letter to William W. Story, Jan. 23, 1831, in *Miscellaneous Writings*, 34.

ible pertinacity, or insuperable dullness of apprehension, that they have rather had a tendency to strengthen my former impressions; and my first and last opinion on this subject, yet remains firm and unshaken.[20]

Indeed, "inflexible pertinacity" aptly described the Yazoo claimants. Even here their claim was pressed: one of the Blake brothers argued that the absence of a terminal date did not make a law perpetual; on the contrary, he argued, with an obvious eye on the Georgia repealer, almost any law might be repealed, the sole exception being one involving a grant, and *"though the record of such a grant be committed to the flames, the infamy of the outrage will remain an imperishable record; the grant itself is adamantine, and can never be consumed!"*[21]

On October 4, 1808, Judge Davis handed down a powerful opinion which astonished Federalists and delighted Republicans by holding the embargo valid and constitutional. Republican delight was not, however, enough to forgive or forget Story's earlier vacillation. Scarcely two weeks after Judge Davis' decision, the Republican caucus met to select a candidate for the next full congressional term. Story was passed over in favor of a little-known physician. "He is a firm man," rejoiced Dr. Bentley. "Mr. Story has been too vacillating."[22] Story took this defeat, if defeat it was, in his stride, and was enough of a partisan to deliver a strong speech backing the Administration when the Salem town meeting on October 26 voted down a proposal to condemn the embargo. Yet the town meeting was a false precursor of the November elections. Due in part perhaps to some Federalist tinkering with the electoral laws, Massachusetts returned to the Federalist column and Salem elected as its Congressman the very Federalist whom Jacob Crowninshield had turned out of office years before. "The principal cause of our suffering," mused Dr. Bentley, "is from the young Lawyer Story whose duplicity ha

[20] Blake, *op. cit. supra* (note 18), 8.
[21] *Ibid.*, 12.
[22] Bentley, III, 390.

been very injurious to us. We could not agree to put him up & many were attached to him because we rejected him."[23]

THIRD TRIP TO WASHINGTON

The second session of the Tenth Congress convened on November 7, 1808. Story, a "lame duck," arrived and was sworn into office December 20. He made up for lost time with a furious burst of activity, proposing an increase in the Navy, a bounty on fish, and the employment of unemployed seamen on coastal gunboats. All of these measures fell within the traditional service that a Congressman was supposed to render his constituency.

Henry Adams has asserted that Story came to Washington determined to end the embargo and, what is more, that he collaborated with the Essex Junto, the British minister, and John Randolph to force Jefferson to sign a humiliating repeal as the last act of his administration.[24] Yet Story's correspondence suggests that an indecisive effort to be all things to all men persisted up to the moment of final decision. What finally forced his hand? It must have been the climax of the war of nerves which the Essex Junto carried on throughout 1808. "I attended a private meeting of several of the principal characters in Boston . . . ," wrote a British traveler early in the year. "[A]ll agreed that memorials from all the towns . . . should be immediately transmitted to the Administration, and a firm determination expressed that they will not cooperate in a war against England.[25] In keeping with the blueprint, memorials did pour in upon the White House, and the Federalist papers clamored incessantly with threats of resistance and hints of secession.

Machiavelli observes that the successful prince must combine the characteristics of the lion and those of the fox. John Quincy Adams had neither. His analogy in the animal kingdom must be the stag—heroic, aloof, and perpetually at bay. And while the

23 *Ibid.*, 395.
24 H. Adams, *Jefferson*, III, 432-34.
25 *Ibid.*, 246.

stag may excite our admiration, his inevitable end is to go down before the pack. Thus did Adams, who had seemingly sacrificed his political career for the embargo, succumb to the Federalist war of nerves and conclude that the measure must be abandoned. "The democratic representatives from Massachusetts," crowed a Federalist paper, "have received a letter from Mr. John Quincy Adams, announcing to them that the embargo must be given up, or, democracy dies forever in the east."[26] The Administration made one last effort to save the day. On January 9, 1809, Congress passed the Enforcement Act giving Secretary Gallatin all-encompassing powers of search, seizure, and detention. "It was a terrible measure," concludes Henry Adams, "and in comparison with its sweeping grants of arbitrary power, all previous enactments of the United States Congress sank into comparative insignificance."[27] Carrying water on both shoulders up to the last, Story voted for the act. Yet the measure was the last burst of refulgence from a plan that had burned itself out. The embargo was lost the following day, when Congress turned its back on passive resistance and, over Administration objections, voted (Representative Story was not recorded) to place the Navy on immediate war footing.

From this point on, the Jeffersonian leaders were concerned only with preventing a retreat from becoming a rout. On February 2, 1809, the House defeated a proposal to end the embargo the following June. This was no victory, for the terminal date had been selected to spare Jefferson the indignity of repealing the embargo within the closing days of his second term. The configurations became clear two days later when, by a voice vote, the House fixed the last day of Jefferson's Presidency as the last day of the embargo. Jefferson was thunderstruck. "[A] sudden and unaccountable revolution of opinion," he wrote a few days later, "took place last week chiefly among the New England and New York members, and in a kind of panic they voted the

[26] See John Quincy Adams, *Writings*, ed. Ford (7v., 1913–17; hereinafter cited as J. Q. Adams, *Writings*), III, 280 n.1.
[27] H. Adams, *Gallatin*, 378–79.

4th of March for removing the embargo . . . "[28] He later satisfied himself as to the source of the turnabout: "I ascribe all this to one pseudo-Republican, Story. He came on (in place of Crowninshield, I believe,) and staid only a few days; long enough, however, to get complete hold of Bacon, who, giving in to his representations, became panic-struck and communicated his panic to his colleagues, and they to a majority of the sound members of Congress."[29]

Story conceded that he had been "unwearied" in his efforts to impress other members of Congress with the dangers of continuing the embargo, and, his mind resolved in the end, he stood firm as the Administration's legislative lieutenants vainly "scolded, privately consulted, and argued with" him.[30] How different things might have been had the resolute and uncomplicated Crowninshield continued to hold the Salem seat in Congress. To be sure, there was a host of other reasons why the embargo failed. There were the bountiful harvests of 1808, which fortified British domestic resources, and the Spanish revolt, which opened a new foreign source of supply. There was the persistent stream of Federalist oppositionist sentiment, duly transmitted to Westminster in the British diplomatic pouch, which persistently undercut Administration announcements. And, finally, the embargo probably asked too much of human nature.

Story sowed the seed of repeal; he was missing when the harvest was fathered. "Mr. Story . . . ," noted Dr. Bentley toward the end of January, "has returned to Salem. The political character of this man is very doubtful among us."[31] The *Salem Gazette* was also moved to comment on his return. "By the way," it asked, "what has become of the bounty on . . . fish? Has Mr. Story deserted his post, and left the fish to swim as chance directs?"[32]

[28] Letter to T. M. Randolph, Feb. 7, 1809, in Jefferson, *Works*, XI, 97.
[29] Letter to Gen. Dearborn, July 16, 1810, in Jefferson, *Works*, XI, 143.
[30] W. W. Story, I, 187.
[31] Bentley, III, 412.
[32] Feb. 14, 1809.

CHAPTER VI

Fletcher v. Peck

SALLY WETMORE

Story's late arrival and early departure from his legislative duties were perhaps excusable. He had cases at the November setting of the Supreme Judicial Court of Massachusetts. He also had them early in the year at the Rockingham court in New Hampshire. Yet his departure might also be due—to use his own phrase—to the law of love rather than a love of the law, for the preceding August he had remarried. His bride was Sarah Waldo Wetmore, a distant relative of his first wife and, appropriately, the daughter of a judge of the Boston Court of Common Pleas. The second romance did not have the lyrical note of the first ("Esteem . . . ripened into affection," Story put it[1]), and perhaps Story took care that it did not. Nonetheless the marriage was to last for thirty-seven years, during which Story would be the model of husband and father.

It might be truly said that Judge Wetmore had not lost a daughter but had gained a son. The judge had a habit of leaning on his in-laws. He seems to have gotten in over his head in the original Boston speculations in the Yazoo lands, whence he had been rescued by one of his wife's relatives who had been unfor-

---

[1] Letter to Joseph White, May 28, 1808, in W. W. Story, I, 170.

tunate enough to have gone surety on his note. Story fell into the pattern as the judge eventually moved to Salem and assumed, thanks to Story's influence, the office of high sheriff of Essex County. Down through the years the pattern continued in varying configuration.[2]

One of the judge's coadventurers in the Yazoo lands and other enterprises was a man named John Peck. Unlike the judge, Mr. Peck managed to effect his payments on schedule and secure his claim to the Southern lands. He was extremely active in the subsequent pattern of sales, and his name was prominent on the memorials that went down to Washington.[3] His name also appeared as the defendant in a suit which was filed in the federal circuit court at Boston in May of 1803 by Robert Fletcher of New Hampshire. This proceeding, to say the least, had its unusual features. Federal jurisdiction was obtained not on substantive constitutional grounds but on the diverse state citizenship of the litigants. Moreover, the suit arose out of Mr. Peck's sale of some Yazoo lands to Fletcher; the transfer had scarcely been completed when the buyer turned around and attempted to set the transactions aside. The specific ground for the attempted rescission was the claim that the Georgia repealing act had divested Peck of his rights and left him nothing to sell. The claim was somewhat bizarre, since the alleged infirmity in title was almost seven years old and had been well known to the buyer before he bought. More relevant, perhaps, to the sequence of events was the virtually contemporaneous report of the Yazoo commissioners, which seems to have gone out of its way to emphasize the shaky legal position of Mr. Peck and his associates in the New England Com-

[2] Judge Wetmore seems to have spent a lifetime in overextended activities— and overdue notes—which crossed his son-in-law's career in both the Supreme Court (see *Brown v. Gilman*, 4 WHEATON 255 (1819) and the bank of which Story was president: "My note at the Merchants' bank . . . due this week" (Judge Wetmore to Story, Nov. 23, 1813, Story Papers, Essex Institute); "The request of William Wetmore [for discharge of endorser's liability] cannot be complied with" (directors' minutes, Merchants' Bank, now Merchants-Warren National Bank, Salem, Jan. 24, 1817).
[3] *American State Papers*, XXVIII, 145 (Report No. 75, Feb. 22, 1803).

pany. "[W]ithout pretending to affirm that the Legislature of the State of Georgia was competent to make the decision," the commissioners asserted, "[we] feel no hesitation in declaring . . . the title of claimants cannot be supported."[4] The claimants, of course, might be forgiven for disputing this denial of the very heart of their cause. In any event, the pendency of the Boston litigation fitted hand in glove with the revised plea of the New England Company that the question of title should have a judicial determination. The determination was slow in coming. Then, in October of 1807, Mr. Justice Cushing, sitting as circuit justice, handed down the decision of the court resolving all issues in favor of Peck: the original transfer was good, the Georgia repeal was void, and Peck had passed a valid title when the sale was made.

While the tangle of events prevent any conclusions from rising above the dignity of intuition, it is not an impermissible assumption to note that the judgment of the circuit court did powerfully reinforce the oral argument which Story was to have delivered to Congress at the beginning of 1808. Whether or not the attempts to obtain legislative and judicial determination of right were related, the fact remains that efforts were apparently pressed on both fronts. The lobbying efforts went forward unabated. Fletcher took an appeal to the Supreme Court, whose decree would be a final resolution of all legal aspects of the matter.

The appeal itself held an extraordinarily significant character reflecting a recovery of judicial and Federalist nerve. Back when the Yazoo investors were importuning Congress, their pleas included a petition to make specific provision for the Supreme Court to pass on the merits of their case. Their request went unanswered, but thanks to adroit procedural tactics, they had achieved their long-sought objective.

Oral argument opened on March 1, 1809. Fletcher was represented by a Maryland lawyer, Luther Martin. Peck's counsel was also a Marylander, none other than Robert Goodloe Harper. The

[4] *Ibid.*, 122 (Report No. 74, Feb. 16, 1803).

sole Yankee flavor to this New England controversy was provided by Harper's associate, John Quincy Adams. In Adams' view the case hinged on the single question whether legislative corruption should be rewarded by expropriating New England creditors. With characteristic pessimism he deprecated his five-hour argument before the Supreme Court as "dull and tedious almost beyond endurance."[5] His depression must have been compounded by an experience at Madison's inaugural ball two days later. "The crowd was excessive—the heat oppressive, and the entertainment bad,"[6] Adams noted. Worse yet was the news whispered by Mr. Justice Livingston—that the Court was reluctant to decide the Yazoo case at all, "as it appeared manifestly made up for the purpose of getting the Court's judgment."[7] And finally, to complete his misfortunes, the Senate unexpectedly tabled his appointment as minister to Russia.

From this low point, things brightened. The Supreme Court entered a technical judgment on the Yazoo case, setting it down for reargument in 1810. President Madison persuaded the Senate to reverse itself and approve Adams' ministerial appointment. Adams accordingly wound up his affairs preparatory to departing for St. Petersburg. Joseph Story succeeded him as counsel in the *Fletcher v. Peck* proceeding. The succession clearly marked Story's arrival as a man of affairs. His behavior on the embargo issue seems not to have affected his political fortunes in the slightest. Typical of his complex character was his prompt return to the state legislature in the face of his previous declaration that he "would not continue in the public councils for a salary of $10,000 per annum."[8] Also typical was a growing display of an instinct for knowing (as a Federalist paper would later put it) "how far he *must* go with his party and when he may spurn at them."[9]

[5] J. Q. Adams, *Memoirs*, I, 543.
[6] *Ibid.*, 544.
[7] *Ibid.*, 546.
[8] Letter to Samuel P. P. Fay, Jan. 9, 1809, in W. W. Story, I, 182.
[9] *Salem Gazette*, March 16, 1810.

At approximately this time, Story was putting another pay raise for the state's Chief Justice through the legislature. There was no need of intermediaries now; Parsons simply sent for Story and made known his needs. Story complied, to the applause of the Federalist press. Likewise illustrative of Story's devotion to the law were his American editions of Chitty's *Bills and Notes*, Abbott's *Ships and Shipping*, and Lawe's *Assumpsit*, and continuing of his *Digest of the Law*, intended as a compendium of Anglo-American jurisprudence. Story never managed to complete his grand design, at least in the form originally contemplated. Nevertheless, the mere fact that the project was begun despite the pressure of professional and public duties may be taken as the index of institutional commitments.

VICTORY

February of 1810 found Story back in Washington. Almost two years to the day after his humiliating rebuff before the House of Representatives, Story spoke at length before the bar of the high court. Not that John Marshall, or anyone else, needed argument on the controversy which had been discussed up hill and down dale for over a decade. If anyone wanted an indication of where the Chief Justice's attitude lay, an insight could be had for the asking in the fifth volume of his biography of Washington. There Marshall had condemned in the strongest terms the repudiation of public and private contracts during the period of preconstitutional confederation. Marshall stated sympathetically the Federalist insistence on "the exact observance of public and private engagements" and "rigid compliance with contracts," to which the "faith of a nation, or of a private man was deemed a sacred pledge." Further, the "imprudent . . . could not be protected by the legislature from the consequences of their indiscretion . . ." Finally, "the new course of thinking which had been inspired by the adoption of a constitution that was understood to prohibit all laws impairing the obligations of contracts, had in great measure restored that confidence which is essential to the internal prosperity of nations."[10]

Marshall announced the Court's opinion on March 16, 1810. It was written in his characteristic soldier's prose—terse, lucid, persuasive, and free of a single legal citation. In it he conjoined Hamilton's argument on the contract clause and Harper's plea of natural law to express "the unanimous opinion of the court, that, in this case, the estate having passed into the hands of a purchaser for a valuable consideration, without notice, the state of Georgia was restrained, either by general principles, which are common to our free institutions, or by the particular provisions of the constitution of the United States, from passing a law whereby the estate of plaintiff . . . could be . . . rendered null and void."[11] Equally characteristic was Marshall's skill in welding essentially divergent views into "the unanimous opinion of the court." Justice Johnson of South Carolina was agreeable to the conclusion as a matter of natural law, but objected to pushing the contracts clause to this extreme. He also objected to giving a judgment in "a mere feigned case." He did so, however, on the basis of his confidence that "the respectable gentlemen who have been engaged for the parties . . . would never consent to impose a mere feigned case upon this court."[12]

Various commentators have analyzed the Johnson views. Some have seen a tribute to Story's integrity; at least one other has read it as none too subtle sarcasm. Doubtless such differences prolonged the doubt as to whether the proceeding was a mere sham battle to get a legal decision fortifying the Georgia claims.[13] Certainly Mr. Peck treated his legal bills with a nonchalance more worthy of a justice-of-the-peace proceeding than a great constitutional case,

[10] Marshall, *Life of George Washington*, V (1807), 85, 178.
[11] 6 CRANCH at 139.
[12] *Ibid.*, 147-48.
[13] See, generally, Magrath, *Yazoo: Law and Politics in the Young Republic* (1966), which both generously noted my first publication on Story's pre-Court career and abundantly proved—contrary to my suggestion that the matter would ever remain an open question—the Yazoo case to be a collusive proceeding.

and his attitude scarcely suggests the existence of an agreement in which every detail had been prearranged. In mid-1810 Harper forwarded his bill to Peck in care of Story, who acknowledged: "In truth, the expense is a concern of the whole Company, and they are taking measures to collect from all parties . . ."[14] Yet, for all of these fine words, time dragged on and the bill continued outstanding. "[R]emind Mr. Peck once more . . . ,"[15] pleaded the unpaid Harper to Story. "Eighteen months have now elapsed . . . and surely it is time that the money should be paid." The lawyer finally got his fee in late 1812, with Story wringing the money from the reluctant Peck "at the heels of an execution."[16]

[14] Letter to R. G. Harper, June 9, 1810, in Heaney, "The Letters of Joseph Story," *American Journal of Legal History*, II (1958), 69.
[15] Letter to Story, Aug. 31, 1811, in Story Papers, Essex Institute, Salem.
[16] Letter to Harper, Nov. 3, 1812, in Heaney, *op. cit. supra* (note 14), 70.

CHAPTER VII

Wanted: One Judge

MANY ARE CALLED

Story passed the summer of 1810 busy in the practice of law and politics at Salem. Not many miles away in Scituate, Associate Justice William Cushing, full of years and honors, lay dying. His passing on September 10, 1810, reduced the Supreme Court to six —three Federalists, three Republicans. Time and mortality seemed slowly accomplishing what frontal attack could not. Jefferson's first term had begun with a solidly Federalist Court; his second had closed with three of his appointees there. Hence the embittered ex-President found Cushing's death a "circumstance of congratulation." "[O]ld Cushing is dead," he gloated. "At length then, we have a chance of getting a Republican majority in the Supreme Judiciary."[1] Jefferson noted, however, that the opportunity was combined with danger. "[I]t will be difficult," he had written Madison, "to find a character of firmness enough to preserve his independence on the same Bench with Marshall." Jefferson doubtless also was concerned with the ultimate disposition of a suit which had been brought against him in Virginia on the basis of action taken while he was President. In any event, he had his man to supply the requisite counterpoise: Levi Lincoln, his

[1] Letter to Gallatin, Sept. 27, 1810, in Jefferson, *Works*, XI, 153.

old Attorney General and more recently Governor of Massachusetts.[2]

The appointment had to come from New England. There was
the political necessity of maintaining a sectional balance on the
Court. There was also the need for a judge versed in local law
in days when the Justices spent far less time in Washington than
they did in riding circuit to hear both original actions and intermediate appeals. Madison noted how the stony soil of New England seemed to be growing a bumper crop of candidates. "Lincoln obviously is the first presented to our choice . . . ," he wrote
his predecessor. "Granger is working hard for it . . . Neither
Morton, nor Bacon, nor Story have yet been brought forward."[3]
Inasmuch as Story's name was fifth on Madison's list at the outset
and seventh before the matter was settled, his chances of appointment seemed most remote. "The office," he wrote years
later, "was conferred on me without any solicitation on my part,
and came upon me quite unexpectedly."[4] Every word was literally true, but the implication of innocent surprise was not. Story
had a champion in his friend Ezekiel Bacon, now the powerful
chairman of the Ways and Means Committee. To be sure, Bacon
occasionally lost heart when the combination of Story's youth
and the more powerful claims of others seemed insuperable. On
one occasion he even suggested that his candidate might make
the best of a bad situation by endorsing Granger except "I . . .
should not expect that you would assist in *kicking over your own
dish.*"[5]

The possibility of the thirty-four-year-old Bacon or the thirty-
two-year-old Story being sent to the high court filled Jefferson
with horror. "Story and Bacon," he warned Madison, "are ex-
actly the men who deserted us [on the Embargo Act]. The for-

2 Letter to Madison, May 25, 1810, *ibid.*, 140.
3 Letter to Jefferson, Oct. 19, 1810, in C. Warren, *The Supreme Court in
United States History* (2v., 1937; hereinafter cited as Warren, *Supreme
Court*), I, 407.
4 Letter to William W. Story, Jan. 23, 1831, in *Miscellaneous Writings*, 35.
5 Letter to Story, Oct. 22, 1810, in Brant, *James Madison* (6v., 1941–56; hereinafter cited as Brant), V, 168.

mer unquestionably a tory, and both are too young."[6] Jefferson strongly endorsed Gideon Granger of Connecticut, former Postmaster General and Yazoo lobbyist par excellence. "His abilities are great," recommended the ex-President. "I have entire confidence in his integrity."[7] Granger pressed his own candidacy with the diligence formerly shown for the New England Company. He cast his net from the Maine border to the New York line, condemning rivals with faint praise and causing a flood of testimonials to descend on the Executive Mansion. Yet Madison had a Virginian's dislike of being pushed too hard, whether the pressure came from his venerated mentor at Monticello or the ebullient politician from Connecticut. "[T]he only legal evidence of [Granger's talents] . . . known to the public," Madison demurred to Jefferson's suggestion, "displays his Yazooism." And the President even turned the flood of testimonials to Granger's discredit. "The means by which this has been done are easily conjectured, and outweigh the recommendations themselves."[8]

Over Levi Lincoln's objections, Madison submitted his name to the Senate. (Lincoln himself once had a candidate, Massachusetts Attorney General Barnabas Bidwell. Bidwell, however, was now a fugitive in Canada following discovery of a shortage in his accounts.) The Senate confirmed Lincoln's appointment on January 3, 1811, and seemingly concluded the matter. Lincoln's failing eyesight forced him to persist in a refusal to serve. The nonplussed President waited a month and then nominated the darkest of dark horses, Alexander Wolcott, the federal revenue collector of Connecticut. If loyalty on the embargo was the test, Wolcott qualified admirably. Not only had he harried embargo-breakers with the zeal of a grand inquisitor, but he repeatedly defended the measure in the press. Just as Granger's flagrant Yazoo activities provoked the threat of a Southern veto, so did Wolcott's enforcement activity produce an actual Northern one. The Federalists, of course, were delighted to throw their weight

[6] Letter to Madison, Oct. 15, 1810, *ibid.*
[7] *Ibid.*
[8] Letter to Jefferson, Oct. 19, 1810, Brant, V, 168-69.

against the Administration, and passing over Connecticut's favorite son in favor of a lesser light was asking for trouble. All of these causes converged in a mortifying Administration defeat when the Senate rejected the nominee by the crushing vote of twenty-four to nine.

Madison's reaction was to give the Senate a nominee it could not reject. On February 22, 1811, he nominated John Quincy Adams, and the Senate immediately responded with a unanimous confirmation. Unhappily, Madison had repeated his *gaffe* of making a selection without the prior assent of the nominee, and the slow-traveling return post from St. Petersburg brought him a refusal and a suggestion. Adams declined the position outright. "[Legal] studies were never among those most congenial to my temper . . . ," he wrote the President.[9] The minister to Russia, however, did have a candidate—Judge Davis of the Brigantine *William* case, who "on one signal and not untrying occasion, manifested . . . his determination to support at the post allotted to him the administration of government in all constitutional measures."[10]

Selecting any Federalist was simply out of the question, even though Madison seemed to be getting close to the end of the limited list of Yankee lawyers of his own party. The problem of the judiciary was, moreover, compounded by the death in June of another member of the Court—Samuel Chase of Maryland. The new vacancy precipitated a tug of war between Maryland and Virginia for the succession. The sectional controversy coincided with a bitter Cabinet crisis. Under the circumstances, the President understandably took his time with respect to further action. Then, on November 15, he sent the names of Joseph Story and Treasury Register Gabriel Duvall to the Senate as the respective successors of Justices Cushing and Chase. His action seemed a matter of administrative routine. So did the Senate confirmation which followed three days later.[11]

[9] Letter to Madison, June 3, 1811, in J. Q. Adams, *Writings*, IV, 95.
[10] *Ibid.*, 96.
[11] And, on Story's nomination and confirmation generally, see Dowd, "Justice Joseph Story and the Politics of Appointment," *American Journal of Legal History*, IX (1965), 265.

MR. JUSTICE

"I entertain some very heretical opinions upon the merits of . . . *common law*, so idolized by all English common lawyers and by all who . . . [parrot] their words in America."[12] So John Quincy Adams wrote his aged father on declining Madison's offer of a seat on the Supreme Court. Joseph Story took a diametrically opposite tack and for diametrically opposite reasons when the shopworn offer finally came his way. To be sure, he hesitated. The salary involved was $3,500, and Story, who knew the perils of low judicial salaries, commanded a professional income of almost twice that amount. And this affluence was but the promise of even better things for a man on his way up in the world. In January, 1811, Story had been chosen Speaker of the Massachusetts House of Representatives. He was active in breaking the Federalist banking monopoly in Massachusetts. He had been nominated for the state Senate. There was so much to consider when Congressman Bacon's letter came up from Washington with the news on Madison's intention to place him on the Supreme Court. What were the factors that prompted acceptance? The "high honor," the "permanence of tenure," and the opportunity "to pursue, what of all things I admire, juridical studies . . ."[13] To John Quincy Adams these considerations were beneath contempt. But Adams was a President's son and could indulge his aristocratic detachment precisely because he was a social and intellectual aristocrat. Story was neither; he was only an ambitious young man who wished desperately to become both if he could do so consistently with his own sense of integrity. His acceptance was preconditioned accordingly.

"That country pettifogger!" roared the Federalists when his appointment was announced.[14] Dr. Bentley's reaction was not much different. "Mr. Story," he noted, "has at length reached the bench of Judges of the U. S. A. This promotion is a seasonable

---

[12] Letter to John Adams, July 21, 1811, in J. Q. Adams, *Writings*, IV, 145.
[13] Letter to Nathaniel Williams, Nov. 30, 1811, in W. W. Story, I, 201.
[14] Quincy, *Figures of the Past* (1883), 158.

relief when his political reputation has deserted him."[15] "[He] boasted to an opposition man that . . . he had now finished his political career & abandoned politics & politicians."[16] And Story's farewell speech to the legislature said as much and more. "Mr. Story," reported the *Salem Gazette*,[17] "in quitting the Legislature, pursues a safe course, and comes off with decency—venturing his praise only on the 'mighty dead'; and of those he names, there were five Federalists to three Democrats . . ."

In late January of 1812, Story left Salem on his fifth trip to Washington. He took his seat on February 3 as the new term of the Court opened. A new order of things seemed presaged by the Justices present. Story and Duvall, the juniors, were Madison's appointments. Justices Brockholst Livingston and Thomas Todd had been placed there by Jefferson. Only Justice Bushrod Washington sat by Federalist commission. Temporarily absent were William Johnson, Jefferson's first appointee, and—most appropriately, it seemed—John Marshall. Two weeks later Story got around to answering his mail. "You ask me," he wrote a Baltimore classmate, "how the ermine rests upon my shoulders. I answer with more ease than I expected."[18]

[15] Bentley, IV, 69.
[16] *Ibid.*, 77.
[17] Jan. 21, 1812.
[18] Letter to Nathaniel Williams, Feb. 16, 1812, in W. W. Story, I, 213.

PART THREE

1812 Overture

CHAPTER VIII

The Twilight's Last Gleaming

MR. MADISON'S COURT

On May 7, 1806, Hartford's *Connecticut Courant* carried a story to the effect that the Jefferson Administration had secretly appropriated two million dollars as a gift to Napoleon for permission to make a treaty with Spain. While false, the story was mild alongside some of the things published about the Jeffersonians, and, moreover, the Jeffersonian papers were fully capable of both attack and defense in any battle of the prints. It was therefore something of a surprise when, despite a general Administration policy favoring freedom of the press, a federal grand jury indicted the paper's editors, not for violating any statute, but for the common-law crime of libel.

The case finally ended with dismissal of the indictment at the 1812 term of the Supreme Court in a rule of decision well fitted to a case so intimately associated with Thomas Jefferson. In dismissing the case, the Court repeated almost verbatim the thesis asserted in the opening lines of Jefferson's Kentucky Resolutions of 1798—that the powers of the federal government consisted of concessions by the states, and that the states expressly retained whatever they did not explicitly concede. From this Jeffersonian premise the Court went to its own judicial conclusion and held that whatever the common law might say on the point, the judicial power of the United States was "a constituent part of those [state] concessions"[1] and hence was without authority to take upon itself the definition and punishment of offenses against the government.

The decision came on the last day of the 1812 term, and its assertion of states' rights and strict construction struck a most appropriate closing note for the first term in which the Court sat with a Republican majority. The Republicans had waited a long time for the day. Over ten years earlier they had captured both Presidency and Congress under a pledge to destroy the works and pomps of Federalist centralism and with a particular proscription framed for its judicial apparatus. "[A]n attempt to describe, in a volume of two or three hundred pages, the crimes of the Supreme Court of the United States," cried an early Republican polemicist, "would be just like proposing to compress the Atlantic into a thimble."[2] For even the Federalists had difficulty with a Court which as early as 1793 construed its constitutional powers with an expansive literality and made itself a forum for a suit against Georgia by a citizen of another state.[3] Variously articulated—the Court spoke in *seriatim* opinions—the basic theory of jurisdiction had shaken all but the most extreme nationalists, for it asserted that fundamental sovereignty rested in the American people rather than the states and that ultimate decisional power, short of constitutional amendment, was held by the Supreme Court. However, this attempted subordination of state power to the federal judicial process was reversed by a constitutional amendment which proposed withdrawing federal jurisdiction from suits of the type in question and which was ratified by the requisite number of states almost within a year of the decision.

Curiously, where the Federalists had bridled the Court with dispatch, the Republicans seemed laggard. Almost a decade of Republican rule came and went with judicial reform unaccom-

[1] *United States v. Hudson and Goodwin*, 7 CRANCH at 33 (1812).
[2] Callender, *The Crisis Before Us* (Philadelphia, 1800), Part II, 5.
[3] *Chisholm v. Georgia*, 2 DALLAS 419 (1793).

plished and the Court surviving as both symbol and instrument of broad construction, implied powers, national sovereignty, and judicial supremacy. Jefferson's years in office opened and closed with the Federalist opposition in control of the tribunal and Chief Justice Marshall holding both President and Congress to a stalemate. Justice Cushing's death, midway in Madison's first term, gave the Republicans their first chance to convert their representation on the Court from minority to majority, and Jefferson emphasized the critical nature of the forthcoming appointment:

> The nation ten years ago declared it's [sic] will for a change in the principles of the administration of their affairs. They then changed the two branches depending on their will, and have steadfastly maintained the reformation in those branches. The third, not depending on them, has so long bid defiance to their will, erecting themselves into a political body, to correct what they deem errors of the nation. The death of Cushing gives an opportunity of closing the reformation by a successor of unquestionable republican principles.[4]

He was less jubilant with his successor's final choice of a candidate to transform the Republicans on the Court from minority to majority. Nonetheless his reservations must have been quieted when he read the opinion of the Court in the *Courant* case, for it made—with Mr. Justice Story's apparent acquiescence—a judicial bow to the popular will in the best Republican tradition. ("[T]his case has been . . . settled in public opinion"[5]); and it did so on the very issue which underlay the Alien and Sedition Acts of 1798[6] and the countering declarations which Madison and he had respectively written for the Virginia and Kentucky legislatures.

Were the Sedition Act still effective at the time of the *Courant*

---

[4] Letter to James Madison, Oct. 15, 1810, in Jefferson, *Works*, XI, 152.
[5] 7 CRANCH at 32.
[6] *United States Statutes at Large*, I, 577 and 596 (1798).

story, the Hartford editors could have been fined two thousand dollars and jailed five years. Yet, perversely, if the common-law tradition prevailed and the lapse of the Sedition Act revived judicial discretion in the area, the editors were in even worse trouble. For if the judicial power of the United States followed British precedent, the absence of statute left federal judges with intrinsic and virtually untrammeled authority to punish any utterance which they deemed subversive to public authority. Moreover, they were free to do so irrespective of the falsity or malice of the utterance, two conditions which the Sedition Act made requisites of guilt.

Given the slanderous tone of the Federalist press, the Republican grand jury which indicted the editors might be forgiven for borrowing the opposition's insistence on the applicability of British precedents in the American courts. So many of the old Republican principles had been compromised over the years of Republican power that one more or less seemed to make little difference. Certainly doctrine after doctrine was vanishing. Condemnation of acquisitions of people and territories had been followed by the Louisiana Purchase. Proclamations of Draconian governmental morality ended with a thoroughly practical settlement of the Yazoo land controversy. Assertions that the best government was the least government disappeared in a web of controls, inspections, and licenses of the neutrality legislation desiged as a *détente* from European strife. Condemnation of newly emerging banking and monetary devices as a source of swindles and fluctuations turned into a counsel to make banks Republican by appropriate use of federal deposits.

Yet, while the press of events showed the difficulty of philosophers' becoming kings and remaining philosophers, two dogmas resisted disintegration under the solvent of power. The first was antipathy toward force in international affairs, and this notwithstanding the most intense British and French provocations, on the one hand, and, on the other, the Federalist taunt that a Republican Administration could not be kicked into a war. The second concerned freedom of speech and of the press, an area where strict construction and libertarian instinct reinforced each other. Jefferson instructed his United States attorneys to let the most incendiary screeds pass without notice, and Madison, on succeeding to the Presidency, was especially faithful to his own Virginia Resolution that any power of suppression was "not delegated by the Constitution, but, on the contrary, expressly and positively forbidden by one of the amendments thereto."[7] Still, lapses from libertarian rigor did occur, partly by way of retaliation for state libel prosecution of Republican journalists; one was the indictment of the Hartford editors, even though the action, after the bitter Republican opposition to the Sedition Act, was inconsistency exemplified.

Dismissal of the charge by the new Republican Supreme Court was virtually preordained. Attorney General William Pinkney set the stage by refusing even to argue the case on behalf of the government's nominal interest. Justice William Johnson, scarcely forty years old but still the senior Republican appointee, followed through with a ringing declaration that the federal courts had no common-law criminal powers as to seditious libel or any other matter. The opinion itself was categorical in tone, and no dissents were entered. A close reading of the text, however, shows that it was not unanimous. A reader might well infer a partisan fission and impute a tacit disagreement to the Federalist holdovers on the Court, Chief Justice Marshall and Associate Justice Bushrod Washington, now relegated to an unfamiliar and insecure minority status. Similarly, it would seem reasonable to assume that Johnson's four Republican colleagues shared his views. Yet presumption here must take account of the Republican Party's two wings, or, more precisely, two generations, both of which were represented on the Court. The elder, which included Justices Johnson, Todd, Livingston, and Duvall, had been born before the American Revolution and had memories of opposition as

[7] Virginia Resolutions, Dec. 24, 1798, in Commager (ed.), *Documents of American History* (1949; hereinafter cited as Commager, *Documents*), 182.

well as power. The younger wing had neither characteristic, but did have all the faults and virtues of youth. Its members were bored by the old doctrines, excited by new ones, and impatient to impose their will. In the Twelfth Congress, sitting one floor above the new Supreme Court in the unfinished Capitol building, they had already shown their temper. Led by Henry Clay, thirty-four, and John C. Calhoun, twenty-nine, they had seized the legislative leadership in an avowed drive for a war which would take Canada and Florida, partly as retributive justice and partly as the natural order of things.

The "War Hawks" had their counterpart in the fifth Republican Justice, Joseph Story. Neither he nor Clay nor Calhoun "could remember the colonial epoch, or had taken a share in public life except under the Constitution of 1789, or had been old enough to feel and understand the lessons taught by opposition to the Federalist rule."[8] On the floor of Congress Clay and Calhoun rejected the old Republican doctrine on peace and war. On the bench of the Supreme Court, Joseph Story did likewise as to judicial power. Externally dissimilar, both convictions sprang from the same armed vision which saw the United States not as composite but as organic, not as derivative but as primary, not as confederation but as sovereignty. Hence, despite the ruffles and flourishes of strict construction, one of the most significant aspects of the libel case was Joseph Story's mute refusal—disclosed in a later case at another time[9]—to construe the constitutional grants of power with strict and critical severity. And the most ironic aspect of this refusal to construe the national authority *strictissimi juris* was not so much that it represented a turnabout view of the second generation of a party originally dedicated to the destruction of Federalist centralism, but that its adherents would be the congressional and judicial coadjutors of the author of the Virginia Resolutions himself in "rebuilding a sovereignty

[8] H. Adams, *History of the United States under the Administration of James Madison* (2v., 1930; hereinafter cited as H. Adams, *Madison*), Vol. II, Bk. VI, 122.
[9] *United States v. Coolidge*, 25 Fed. cas. 619 (1813). See p. 109.

as terrible in peace as in war."[10] Indeed, in partial consequence of Justice Story's mute dissent reversal of the major premise of the *Courant* case was a process which began with the decision itself.

MR. MADISON'S JUDGE

Although he was the youngest man who has ever been appointed to the Supreme Court, Justice Story came to it with an impressive record—as Congressman, Speaker of the Massachusetts House, leader at the state bar, and author of a book of poetry, two volumes on pleading, and three American editions of standard English legal works. Despite these credentials, he had taken his seat on the Court with considerable nervousness. It may have been the low side of the cycle of alternating cheerfulness and depression which persistently beset him. Or it may have been more circumstance than mood, for he came to the Court less than fourteen years out of Harvard and scarcely ten past his admission to the bar. Yet one look at the docket was all he needed for reassurance. A good segment of the cases came out of New England. Another and somewhat overlapping group involved the neutrality legislation of Jefferson's second term which as a Congressman he had been instrumental in framing or repealing. Indeed, if the height of his new position had numbed his vanity, the first round of argument and conference forcibly brought him back to the fact that, for all his youth, he was as learned in the law as any colleague on his bench or lawyer at its bar.

"[B]rother Story, here . . . can give us the cases from the Twelve Tables down to the latest reports,"[11] is reputed to be the mode in which John Marshall closed conferences of the judges, and the Chief Justice could have begun at no more appropriate time than the conference on *United States v. Crosby*[12]

[10] H. Adams, *Madison*, Vol. II, Bk. VI, 114.
[11] W. Plumer, Jr., *Life of William Plumer* (1857; hereinafter cited as *Plumer*), 205-6. See also Goebel, "The Common Law and the Constitution," in William Jones (ed.), *Chief Justice John Marshall* (Ithaca, N.Y., 1956), 101.
[12] 7 Cranch 115 (1812).

held shortly after Story joined the Court. Not that Brother Story had taken the law of the case back quite as far as the twelve tables, but he had linked it to the Codes of the Emperor Justinian. Years before, he had abstracted the very point at issue in a manuscript *Digest of the Law*,[13] and in doing so he covered the common-law British and American cases as well as the Roman tradition manifested in the French, Dutch, and Scots authorities. It was this characteristic knowledgeability which doubtless won him the assignment to write the opinion in the case, and his response came on February 12, 1812, only nine days after he took his seat.

In its way the opinion was a masterpiece, albeit an unusual one. Appropriately, it concerned conflicts of law,[14] but otherwise was taciturn and almost abrupt ("title to land can be acquired and lost only in the manner prescribed by the law of the place where such land is situate"[15]). Not only did the citationless brevity conceal the vast erudition which underlay it, but it marked one of the comparatively infrequent occasions when, as opinion-writing Justice, the versifying Story took the counsel he proposed in "Advice to a Young Lawyer":

> Be brief, be pointed; let your matter stand
> Lucid in order, solid and at hand.[16]

Concealed or exhibited, this formidable learning must have come as an immense asset to the libraryless Justices even though Congress, perhaps prompted by the new political complexion of the tribunal, had just granted them the use of the Congressional Library. Yet, despite the availability of Story's encyclopedic knowledge and the presence of five Republican judges, one circumstance of the 1812 term suggested that the new Court might

[13] See Nadelmann, "Joseph Story's Contribution to American Conflicts Law: A Comment," *American Journal of Legal History*, V (1961), 230, 238.
[14] "In particular the influence of Story has been predominant both in England and America in regard to particular doctrines as well as the whole foundation of this branch of the law." (Allen, *Law in the Making* [1939], 239.)
[15] *United States v. Crosby*, 7 CRANCH at 116.
[16] W. W. Story, II, 88.

very much resemble the old one, for Marshall continued to use the decisional opinion as the voice of a single jural personality and went on writing most of them himself. Indeed, the opinions of all the Republican Justices put together did not match one half of Marshall's output at the term, and Story did not write his second (and last) until adjournment was virtually at hand. This time his effort concerned the statute of limitations ("once the statute runs against one of two parties entitled to a joint action, it operates as a bar to such joint action"[17]). Only a trifle longer than the first, it was again an exercise in self-effacing modesty. Once more Story knew as much on the point as colleague and counsel, having covered the issue—although his opinion gave no hint whatever—in his weighty tome *Pleadings in Civil Actions*.[18]

Little wonder, then, that the transition from lawyer to judge came with facility and Story was able to report early in the term that "as far as my judicial duties go, I find myself considerably more at ease than I expected."[19] Yet he could never rest for long, and as the six-week term approached its close he chafed to be on his way. "As the time approaches," he wrote his wife, "at which I . . . direct my steps to my own interesting home, my heart feels an unusual restlessness and anxiety."[20]

The sentiments were doubtless reciprocated by Sarah Wetmore Story, to whom marriage must have seemed a series of arrivals and departures. Certainly the characteristic note of hers was set scarcely three months after the wedding, when her Congressman husband left for Washington. She did not like being alone then ("I regret," Story wrote in that first separation, "that your time is so solitary as you represent it"[21]), and there is no evidence that her feelings changed as time went on, for her health broke and most of her children died in childhood. Any disposition to resent her lot, however, was sternly inhibited by the standards of the

[17] *Marsteller v. McClean*, 7 CRANCH at 159 (1812).
[18] Story, *A Selection of Pleadings in Civil Actions* (1805), 89.
[19] Letter to Samuel P. P. Fay, Feb. 24, 1812, in W. W. Story, I, 215.
[20] Letter to Mrs. Story, March 12, 1812, *ibid.*, 218.
[21] Letter to Mrs. Story, Jan. 15, 1809, Story Papers, Essex Institute.

day. Perhaps it was checked also by the consciousness of the shadow of her cousin, her husband's first wife.

Nonetheless, Story's second marriage was eminently successful, for, like everything else he undertook, he brought it forethought, persistence, and dedication. If he was often away from home, his letters back were frequent and tender. And they were far more than love letters, for they wove together the political gossip of the day, poetic and philosophical reflections, and perceptive descriptions of social events. In fact, nowhere else in his extensive writings did Story show quite the artistry he reached in his letters home, where he managed to bring the spirit of distant festivities to his wife in her lonely Salem parlor ("The assembly was uncommonly brilliant. . . . The dresses of the ladies . . . costly and superb"[22]) and at the same time make it clear that the writer was not having too good a time) "I quitted the assembly at ten o'clock, being exceedingly fatigued, and willing to resign a scene, which however alluring, was not worth . . . the smiles of a wife"[23]).

However Story might charm his wife, others were impervious to his personable ways. The antipathy which he was capable of provoking could be found in the parallel reactions of two oddly contrasting, brilliant, brittle New England contemporaries. One, Harrison Gray Otis, owed allegiance to the lost world of New England Federalism. The other, the Reverend William Bentley, was committed to the equally lost world of Thomas Jefferson. The first had mercilessly assessed Story's weakness ("a little attention from the right sort of people"[24]) and then berated him for the change of attitude so induced ("Joseph, indeed . . . his coat of many colors"[25]). The second had detested the Justice for years and did not propose to stop because with the appointment to the Supreme Court "this cringing man . . . has risen as he wished."[26]

[22] Letter to Mrs. Story, Feb. 5, 1814, in W. W. Story, I, 251.
[23] *Ibid.*
[24] Letter to Robert Goodloe Harper, May 1, 1807, in Morison, *Otis*, I, 283.
[25] Quincy, *Figures of the Past* (1926), 319.
[26] Bentley, IV, 81.

Story's comings and goings seldom escaped the clergyman's eye or acidulous notation in a compendious diary. The turbulent spring of 1812, however, involved events which overshadowed Story's return to Salem. There were the troubles of the local Republican printer with the threat of seditious libel (still very much the law of the commonwealth), there was the "Gerrymander" by which the Republicans sought to reinforce their tenuous hold on Massachusetts in the forthcoming state elections, there was the embargo laid as a preliminary to war, and, finally, there was the seemingly inexorable approach of war itself.

MR. MADISON'S WAR

Federalist success in making the spring elections a referendum of opposition to the forthcoming war against Great Britain swept their ticket to victory. The state Senate, previously Republican by one seat, went back to its Federalist coloration. So did the state House of Representatives which one year earlier had elected Story its Speaker with thirty votes to spare. Elbridge Gerry, previously the Republican's best vote-getter, and, next to Story, Marblehead's most distinguished son, was turned out of the governor's chair by Caleb Strong. Thus, the stage was set for what Story would label as "the most mortifying and self-humiliating recollections [of] my native state."[27] When the news came to Massachusetts that Clay, Calhoun, and the other young Republicans had finally gotten their war against England at the same time that Napoleon launched his armies in a final effort to conquer Europe, Yankee Federalists felt that their suspicions of Republican subservience to France were completely vindicated. Governor Strong proclaimed a public fast in reparation for hostilities "against the nation from which we are descended,"[28] and all New England seemed to start reading "the Valuable Pamphlet entitled 'MR. MADISON'S WAR'; or a *Dispassionate Inquiry into the*

27 Joseph Story to William Pinckney, 1816, in W. W. Story, I, 296.
28 H. Adams, *Madison*, Vol. II, Bk. VI, 399.

reasons alleged by MADISON for declaring an Offensive and Ruinous War against Great Britain."[29]

Theological and literary polemics next entered a more political phase. Acting under statute and pursuant to the constitutional provision authorizing the nationalization of the state militia on the contingency of invasion, Madison requested a quota of Massachusetts troops. Governor Strong declined and suggested that in his own opinion no invasion threatened. He could have cited the Virginia Resolutions as authority for the determinative character of this judgment. Instead he proffered the advisory opinion of Massachusetts' Supreme Judicial Court that the right to determine the operative fact of imminent invasion "is vested in the Commanders-in-chief of the militia of the several States."[30]

According to Story, the Justices of the Supreme Court of the United States also considered the question at the time and were "unanimously of the opinion that the Governors were bound to obey the requisition; and regretted that neither the President nor Congress had required their opinion on the subject."[31] However, that canon of strict construction which held their tribunal to cases and controversies and debarred it from advisory judgments delayed pronouncement on the militia controversy many years. Appropriately, Story wrote the opinion (". . . the authority to decide whether the exigency has arisen, belongs exclusively to the President, and . . . his decision is conclusive upon all other persons"[32]).

The process of reversal could be said to have begun with the two weeks of bruising travel which it took Story to reach Salem. Yet his arrival home was a pause rather than the end of his travels for the year. Under existing law[33] he was required to preside twice a year in the states assigned to him—he had to be in Portsmouth by May 1, in Boston by May 15 and in Newport by June

[29] Boston *Columbian Centinel*, July 15, 1812.
[30] *American State Papers: Military Affairs*, I, 324.
[31] Quoted in Plumer, 430-31.
[32] *Martin v. Mott*, 12 WHEATON at 30 (1827).
[33] *United States Statutes at Large*, II, 696 (1812).

15. Summer was free, but following it came a swing through the New England fall and winter—to Exeter on October 1, to Boston on October 15 and to Providence on November 15. Sitting in these circuit courts alongside the local federal district judge, Story heard both original actions as well as appeals (largely maritime cases) from the federal district Courts.

It was a wretched system. The physical burden of travel was immense. Story, who had a fairly compact circuit, later estimated he traveled close to two thousand miles a year. It required long sittings to keep to the statutory schedule ("[The case] detained me in court until 8 o'clock in the evening," Story's reporter once complained to his diary[34]). It gave the judges a vested interest in error ("My chief apprehension," wrote Harrison Gray Otis of a Story decree taken from circuit to the Supreme Court, "is that he will now feel pledged to support his opinion"[35]). Still, it was not all loss. It did keep the high court in touch with local law and local problems; perhaps its members were better appellate judges for having presided at the trial level ("Judge STORY summed up the evidence with his usual perspicuity and impartiality, and charged the jury with great independence"[36]).

Nonetheless the circuit system did leave the Justices open to local pressures, and New England antiwar sentiment appeared to have ruled one of Story's first decisions on Madison's proclamations of June 25 and August 9, 1809. The first proclamation withdrew, the second reinstated, nonimportation sanctions against Great Britain, a mortifying sequence which had resulted when the British repudiated the agreement by which their minister had obtained the initial concession. The charge in the case was a violation of the ban on imports, and the defense, which Story sustained, asserted that the second proclamation was a nullity.[37]

[34] John Gallison, Manuscript Diary (Nov. 2, 1814), Massachusetts Historical Society.
[35] Letter to Robert G. Harper, Dec. 2, 1815 (copy), Otis MSS., Massachusetts Historical Society.
[36] Boston Columbian Centinel, Dec. 30, 1818.
[37] The Orono, 18 FED. CASES 830 (1812).

It was a surprising decision, for it traversed a clear legislative intent that the British might have American concessions only *quid pro quo*. Nevertheless, Story, sounding a reprise from the Virginia Resolutions, took as his text a point not at issue ("the president has no common-law prerogative to interdict commercial intercourse"[38]) and struck down Madison's second proclamation. He did so with great civility, but also did so with a decisiveness that left no doubt of his view of the judiciary as the ultimate arbiter of governmental action. To be sure, the opinion was not quite the assertive document it seemed, for Federalists and Republicans alike were heartily sick of the old Republican doctrines of passive resistance. Nevertheless, the opinion is a surprising one, not only being at odds with Story's nationalistic bent, but stultifying Madison on a marginal question with the Presidential signature barely dry on Story's judicial commission.

But he was not countenancing local resistance to the war. Rather, in part his judgment reflected an antipathy toward embargoes, an attitude he had manifested during, and even before, his brief tour in Congress. In part doubtless he was moved to assert a counterpart denial of inherent power to the President if this were the case for the judiciary under the libel decision. In part he may have been influenced by Marshall's position on the point.[39] And, in part, there may have been a compulsion to seize the first chance to show the world he was his own man, independent of, and indeed superior to, the political branches of government.

JUSTICE STORY'S JURISDICTION

The proclamation decision was a highly misleading index of Story's views, for the over-all result of his first swing around the New England circuit showed a juridical nationalism in temper as well as philosophy and luminously prefigured the long and distiguished career in structuring an authentically American law.

[38] *Ibid.*
[39] *President's Proclamation Declared Illegal*, 19 FED. CASES 1289 (1812).

With a stroke of his pen he not only cleared his docket of verdict appeals, but disclaimed any authority in Massachusetts practice to prescribe the procedure of a national court.[40] In another opinion he began his work in structuring the American law of bankruptcy by outlining an expansive outline of preemptive federal authority and correspondingly constrained field of concurrent state power.[41] In still another, he asserted his view of a high judicial prerogative by insinuating a strong doubt whether he could be given other than Supreme Court duties.[42] But most of all his soaring view of the national judicial power was shown on the admiralty side of his court, for if the proclamation case recalled the days of passive resistance, the prize cases showed that the American eagle could carry arrows as well as an olive branch. "The Commissions came for the Privateers," Dr. Bentley noted. ". . . Several . . . have sailed from Salem & four from Marblehead. The spirit increases & a little success would cover the American seas with them."[43] As the privateering cases started to come up on appeal to his circuit court in the fall of 1812 (the legitimacy of seizures was initially adjudicated in the federal district courts), Story was doubtless often reminded of his grandfather William Story, who among other legal clerkships had handled prize proceedings in the Boston Navy Board of the American Revolution, where "six million dollars passed through his hands."[44]

Prize law was now the exclusive province of the federal courts as a consequence of the Supreme Court's partial definition of the constitutional grant of national judicial power to all cases of admiralty and maritime jurisdiction.[45] The partial definition, however, settled only the wartime sweep of admiralty and left open the ques-

[40] *United States v. Wonson*, 28 FED. CASES 745 (1812).
[41] *Babcock v. Weston*, 2 FED. CASES 306 (1812).
[42] *Ex Parte United States*, 24 FED. CASES 737 (1812).
[43] Bentley, IV, 104.
[44] Letter from Isaac Story to James Madison, Oct. 27, 1794, Madison Papers, Library of Congress. See also Wroth, "The Massachusetts Vice Admiralty Court and the Federal Jurisdiction," *American Journal of Legal History*, VI, 251 n.4; and John Adams, *Diaries*, ed. Butterfield (4v., Cambridge, 1961), I, 73, 236, 238, and II, 45-46.
[45] *Glass v. The Sloop Betsey*, 3 DALLAS 6 (1794).

tion of its workaday peacetime scope. This—whatever it might be—the Judiciary Act of 1789 had vested exclusively in the federal courts with a grant which retained the generality of the constitutional language.[46] Precedent offered two answers. On the European Continent, admiralty courts heard all cases connected with the sea or with seafaring men or sea-trading men. Curiously, the opposite situation prevailed in maritime England, where a series of historical accidents had shriveled admiralty to what English law still calls its "inherent"[47] jurisdiction—collisions, salvage, seamen's wages and bottomry bonds.

The abridgement began when Plantagenet politics produced a statute declaring "that the admirals and their deputies shall not meddle henceforth of anything done within the realm but only of a thing done on the sea."[48] It reached its peak centuries later with Sir Edward Coke's vindication of the common law over the courts of the royal prerogative, of which admiralty was one. While praising the admiral as "our English Neptune" (and here, as in the statute, the reference was to the judicial, not the military, officer), Coke nonetheless used his writ of prohibition and his tremendously influential *Institutes* to shear admiralty courts of powers over insurance policies, transport agreements, shipping documents, and other matters technically negotiated "within the realm" and transfer virtually all jurisdiction over maritime contracts to the courts of the common law.[49] His successful efforts were hotly protested by a series of polemics. Most prominent of the books were Godolphin's *View of the Admiralty Jurisdiction* (1661) and Zouche's *Jurisdiction of the Admiralty of England* (1663), while Sir Leoline Jenkins' House of Lords oration on the point was accounted a *"locus classicus."*[50] All united in contradicting Coke's historical arguments and in asserting the superiority of admiralty's substance and procedure for the complexities of a maritime and often international trade.

[46] *United States Statutes at Large*, I, 77 (1789).
[47] See Halisbury, *Laws of England*, ed. Simonds, I (London, 1952), 50.
[48] 13 RICHARD II, Stat. 1, 2, c.5 (1389).
[49] Coke, *Institutes on the Laws of England* (1797), IV, 123-24.
[50] *Dictionary of National Biography* (1937-38), X, 742.

In his manuscript *Digest of the Law*, Story had abstracted points and authorities on the controversy, impartially setting down the common-law orthodoxy of Coke and Blackstone and the unavailing counterprotests of Godolphin and Zouche.[51] Whatever might have been the views of Story the scrivener, there was no doubt that Story the judge opted for the broad, Continental view of admiralty jurisdiction. There was far more here than a taste to hear and decide cases, for the broad theory of jurisdiction would have delivered perhaps half the commercial litigation of the country to the exclusive jurisdiction of the federal courts. A set of parallel conditions doubtless whetted Story's appetite. One was the incongruous fit of the jury-polarized proceedings of the common law to maritime affairs,[52] the other was the extraordinary range which statute-free admiralty offered the judicial process. Even stronger was the naturalist tradition under which "the law" could not be one thing at Athens and another at Rome, and this was fortified by Story's nationalism, which applied the principle *a fortiori* to Salem and Savannah. And even granting that a variegated localism might obtain in essentially parochial matters, no such condition attached to the law of the sea.

Story was the product of a maritime civilization in which the speech of the sea was almost a vulgar tongue.[53] Maritime cases had formed a large part of his law practice.[54] As a judge, he could write an opinion which sounded like an excerpt from a quarter-

[51] Story, *Digest of the Law* (MS., Story Papers Treasure Room, Harvard Law School), I, 503.
[52] "[I]f it be left to a jury not only to find the facts . . . but also to pronounce what is the law resulting from them, it will be next to impossible, to form a system of rules by which a merchant may safely regulate his conduct." (Mr. Justice Livingston, concurring in *Oliver v. Maryland Ins. Co.*, 7 CRANCH at 494-95 [1813].)
[53] "It has been a northeast storm ever since morning." (Letter to Mrs. Story, Jan. 15, 1809, Story Papers, Essex Institute, Salem.)
[54] See *Cleveland v. Fettyplace*, 3 MASS. 344 (1807); *Stocker v. Harris*, 3 MASS. 360 (1807); *Wellman v. Nutting*, 3 MASS. 381 (1807); *Appleton v. Crowninshield*, 3 MASS. 389 (1807); *Cotel v. Hilliard*, 4 MASS. 582 (1808); *Pearce v. Phillips*, 4 MASS. 589 (1808); *Cook v. Essex Fire & Marine Ins. Co.*, 5 MASS. 106 (1809); *Whitteridge v. Norris*, 6 MASS. 109 (1809); *Baxter v. New Eng. Marine Ins. Co.*, 7 Mass. 231 (1811); *Appleton v. Crowninshield*, 8 MASS. 286 (1811).

master's log.[55] Accordingly, maritime law, in Story's view, was of concern "to the lawyer and the merchant; to the statesman and the private gentleman," and indeed to anyone who "wishes well to the commerce of our country [or] wishes to comprehend the advantages resulting from the timely patronage of the government in maritime concerns."[56]

Finally, there was his response to the separatism with which New England greeted the initial military reverses of an unwanted war. "I am thoroughly convinced," he wrote in summer of 1812, "that the leading Federalists meditate a severance of the Union . . . Gracious God!"[57] It was no accident that in the same letter this judge with scarcely six months' experience, without having heard a word of argument on the point, and unconcerned with his previous stand for a common-law interpretation of constitutional powers, categorically asserted the broad, Continental view of admiralty: "I have no doubt that jurisdiction rightfully extends to every maritime contract and tort, and the more its jurisdiction is known, the more it will be courted."[58] Unmentioned was the beneficiary of the courtship—the national judicial power.

[55] "[T]he sloop dropped down the harbor . . . there anchored with two anchors . . . [Later] she had her mainsail up, one anchor upon her bows, the other down, and a crew of five [aboard]." (*The Julia*, 14 FED. CASES at 25 [1812].)
[56] Charles Abbott, *The Law Relative to Merchant Ships and Seamen*, ed. Story (1810), *ix*.
[57] Letter to Nathaniel Williams, Aug. 24, 1812, in W. W. Story, I, 229.
[58] *Ibid.*

CHAPTER IX

The Perilous Night

THE TEMPER OF NEW ENGLAND

"[N]or were my duties during the War," Story once reminisced expansively, "with its preceding accumulation of Causes arising from the Embargo and Non-Intercourse laws, and the War itself, without the most momentous and arduous responsibility."[1] And it was most true that when the national power was at its nadir, Story audaciously proclaimed its prerogatives time and again. Would he have asserted the broad theory of admiralty jurisdiction had the question come before him during those years? The question is open, not because his nerve would have failed the challenge had there been the slightest chance of success, but rather that public opinion in wartime New England simply would not have tolerated it.

The Story family had firsthand knowledge of the consequences of provoking that opinion past the breaking point. Fifty years earlier the administration of the Stamp Act had been committed to the brisk, expeditious and juryless courts of vice-admiralty, and Massachusetts erupted in protest. Both the form of the tax and the method of the levy were regarded as outrages. "But the most grievous innovation of all," asserted one town meeting, "is

[1] Letter to John Brazer Davis, Jan. 3, 1824, in *Proceedings of the Mass. Historical Society*, XLIX (1916), 186.

the alarming extension of the power of courts of admiralty. In these . . . one judge presides alone! No juries have any concern there! The law and the fact are . . . decided by the same single judge . . ."[2] Remonstrances poured across the Atlantic from other colonies. Citizens of Connecticut protested the loss of "one of their most darling rights, that of Tryal by Juries"; Pennsylvania asserted that the new admiralty jurisdiction was "contrary to Magna Charta"; and South Carolina denounced its extension "beyond its ancient limits."[3] Indeed, it was hard to believe that the common law, whose theory of crimes was so repellent to the old-line Republicans, could be the same jurisprudence to which the venerable John Adams referred when, in the sunset of his life, he denounced the Stamp Act for giving jurisdiction "to . . . judges of admiralty, poor dependent creatures, to . . . of the civil law without juries or without any of the open, noble examination of witnesses or publicity of proceedings of the common law . . ."[4]

Massachusetts did more than protest. On August 26, 1765, the mob took to the streets of Boston and attacked the houses of officials charged with administration of the new levy. Despite the denial of William Story that he was "a Promoter and Encourager of the Stamp Act,"[5] his house was the first attacked, his files were destroyed, his personal belongings scattered, and he escaped injury only by fleeing to Ipswich. Happily, the commonwealth accepted his subsequent statement that just prior to the riot he had determined "to resign his said office that he might have nothing to do with that accursed act" and awarded him " £67, 8s., 10d. for losses and suffering in the late times of confusion."[6]

[2] Braintree Resolution, Oct. 14, 1765, in Commager, *Documents*, 57.
[3] Edmund C. Morgan (ed.), *Prologue to Revolution: Sources and Documents on the Stamp Act Crisis* (Williamsburg, Va., 1959), 52-58.
[4] Letter to William Tudor, Aug. 16, 1818, in John Adams, *Works* (10v., Boston, 1850-56), X, 348-49.
[5] Boston *Gazette*, Aug. 26, 1765. I am indebted to Prof. Edmund S. Morgan for this specific reference, which supplements the published account in his *Stamp Act Crisis* (Williamsburg, 1953), 126-27.
[6] Derby and Gardner, "Elisha Story of Boston and Some of His Descendants," *Essex Institute Historical Collections*, L (1914), 297, 300-01.

Against this background it would have taken not only a brave judge but a rash one to lay hands on the institution of jury trial in a commonwealth which had actually written the old English rule on admiralty into its organic law.[7] The spirit of the Stamp Act riots was close enough to the surface as things stood. Congressmen who had voted for the war were hissed on the streets of Boston; and the Representative from Plymouth was actually seized by a mob and kicked through his town. The old political ties buckled under new developments. The Federalists vainly supported an antiwar Republican for the Presidency in the 1812 election. "[T]he price we must pay is great," wrote Story's mentor, William Prescott, "—a temporary association with democracy."[8] The Massachusetts Republicans responded, with equal lack of success, by nominating one of the few war Federalists as their candidate for governor.

It was the stalwart and hitherto nationalistic Federalists, however, who best typified the inversion of the old party attitudes. Even in the act of protesting loyalty to the constitutional forms they treated the Madison Administration as if it were an alien despotism, and some, passing from words to deeds, maintained economic and even social relationships with the British forces. A few (the "Blue Lights") went so far as to signal tactical and navigational information to the Royal Navy. The British responded by keeping a consul in Boston to grant licenses for the Spanish trade in the interest of indirectly supplying their peninsular armies.

Such circumstances that first wartime summer in New England impelled Story to undertake a flanking overturn of the liberal decision with an appeal to Attorney Pinckney to seek a statute

[7] "In all controversies concerning property, and in all suits between two or more persons, except in cases in which it has heretofore been otherwise used and practiced, the parties have a right to a trial by jury; and this method of procedure shall be held sacred, unless, in cases arising on the high seas, and such as relate to mariner's wages, the legislature shall find it necessary to alter it." (Massachusetts Constitution, Art. I, Sec. 15.)
[8] Letter to Theodore Sedgwick, Sept. 28, 1812, in Sedgwick Papers, Massachusetts Historical Society.

granting the federal courts a common-law jurisdiction in criminal matters. Pinckney in turn laid the proposal before Madison. Beset by military reverses as well as domestic sedition and pressed by advice on all sides to forsake his libertarian principles—even Jefferson urged hemp, tar, and feathers for the domestic crisis—Madison held fast to his principles and repeated his long-time detestation of a judge-made system of crimes. The rebuff was discouraging, but more than this was required to stop Story's effort to vindicate his views. Rather, it probably caused him to redouble his efforts to change the position of just one Republican colleague—for this would have overturned the *Connecticut Courant* decision—when he rejoined the Court in February of 1813 for his second term.

In most respects it was a productive period for him. He raised his opinion output to eight. In one he fired the opening gun of his campaign to eliminate the elaborate formalities of corporate procedure and did so by a tour de force which combined precedent and pragmatism ("Public policy, therefore, as well as law . . . fully justifies the doctrine we have endeavored to establish"[9]). Another propounded a liberality of construction for the "full faith and credit" clause of the Constitution by enforcing a New York judgment in the District of Columbia ("Were . . . judgments of the state courts . . . considered *prima-facie* evidence only, this clause in the constitution would be utterly unimportant and illusory"[10]). In a third he showed his dissatisfaction with a Marshall opinion by submitting a concurring one of his own.[11] Yet on the *Courant* case his luck was poor, for apparently all the Republicans stood fast. Undaunted, Story doubled back to the executive in an effort to gain his point through a list of specific statutory enactments. Again his efforts were unavailing, and he came close to despair at what he saw as doctrinaire folly on one hand and unabashed sedition on the other. "The Courts are crippled," he fumed; "offenders, conspirators and traitors are enabled to carry on their purposes almost without check."[12]

[9] *Bank of Columbia v. Patterson's Administrator*, 7 CRANCH at 307 (1813).
[10] *Mills v. Duryee*, 7 CRANCH at 485 (1813).
[11] *Livingston and Gilchrist v. The Maryland Ins. Co.*, 7 CRANCH 506 (1813).
[12] Letter to Nathaniel Williams, May 27, 1813, in W. W. Story, I, 244.

"A MORAL AND RELIGIOUS PEOPLE"

Story's expostulation epitomized the continued political deterioration in New England as both the old and the new nationalists blamed the 1798 resolutions for the existing state of affairs. Ex-President Adams found the behavior he saw on all sides that of "servile mimics . . . copied from examples set them by Virginia and Kentucky."[13] Story, on the other hand, looked to the fruit rather than the root and attributed the local turbulence to the *Courant* decision: "In my opinion, the Government will be completely prostrated unless [Congress] give jurisdiction to their Courts and a common-law authority to punish crimes against the United States."[14]

His specific concern was the case of the recaptured prize, a *cause célèbre* which rocked Boston in the summer of 1813. The root of the matter was the continued and offensive presence of the British consul in Boston, busy granting safe-conducts through the Royal Navy patrols to American shippers. To Story this was the epitome of imperial insolence. To others it was a melancholy fact of life to which the powerless must accommodate themselves and particularly so as to the Iberian trade, which remained perfectly legal under American law. Moreover, some shippers bound for other destinations held a license to sail for Spain in the hope of deceiving any British men-of-war they might encounter. Indeed, Congress itself did not act to penalize the mere possession of such a license until the late summer of 1813.

Even before Congress acted, however, and in the face of a reportedly adverse view of the Attorney General, Story while on circuit announced some new law to make his point ("It has been said, that no case of condemnation can be found on account of the use of an enemy license. Admitting the fact, I am not disposed to yield to the inference"[15]). Pronouncing licensees fair

[13] Quoted in Page Smith, *John Adams*, (2v., Garden City, N.Y., 1962), II, 1111.
[14] Letter to Nathaniel Williams, Aug. 3, 1813, in W. W. Story, I, 247.
[15] *The Julia*, 14 FED. CASES at 31 (1813).

game was cheered in the privateering section of Salem ("The most interesting domestic news to our section of Salem is the condemnation as Prizes of British Licenses, which gives the E. part of Salem above half a million of dollars"[16]). A contrary view prevailed in other quarters, particularly as to "certain picaroons fitted out from some of our own ports obviously, and even avowedly, for the purpose of cruising against the vessels of American citizens."[17]

Hence, when one American vessel sailing with a British license was taken by two privateers, the American owner simply put out in another craft and took it back. To most of Massachusetts this seemed like a fine show of Yankee initiative, and those who thought otherwise learned to hold their tongues. ("Some of our citizens," noted Dr. Bentley, ". . . roughly handled for calling it piracy."[18]) Story was furious. "A disgraceful affair . . . ," he fumed. "I should not be at all surprised that the actors should escape . . . owing to defects in our criminal laws."[19] And if the *Courant* case was decisive he was right, for no act of Congress prohibited the recapture of the prize by the original owner.

Yet there would be no escape if he could help it. Disclaiming to decide whether the United States, as a sovereignty, had entirely adopted the common law, he nonetheless found that by the very design and wording of the Constitution "the existence . . . of the common law is not only supposed . . . but is appealed to for the construction and interpretation of its powers."[20] A minor premise came in a provision of the 1789 Judiciary Act giving the circuit court exclusive original jurisdiction over all crimes and offenses cognizable under the authority of the United States. The conclusion followed easily: that all common-law offenses, including the case before him, were already within his jurisdiction as a result of congressional action some twenty years before.

[16] Bentley, IV, 242-43.
[17] Boston *Columbian Centinel*, Oct. 2, 1813.
[18] Bentley, IV, 185.
[19] Letter to Nathaniel Williams, Aug. 3, 1813, in W. W. Story, I, 247.
[20] *United States v. Coolidge*, 25 Fed. Cases at 619 (1813).

But what about the *Courant* case? That decision, Story said, was "entitled to the most respectful consideration; but having been made without argument, and by a majority only of the court, I hope that it is not an improper course to bring the subject again in review."[21] The language suggested that at least one of the Republicans had been favorably impressed by Story's arguments at the 1813 term of the Court. Yet the prospects of outright reversal of the *Courant* decision were uncertain enough to prompt Story to formulate an alternate theory of criminality drawn from the "admiralty and maritime jurisdiction" clause of the Constitution.

He had a much stronger argument here. Yet his desire to secure an expanded common-law jurisdiction evidently prompted him to "abandon an impregnable fortress to seek battle in an open field."[22] Moreover, trying to prove the point via two theories of jurisdiction involved the hazard of proving it under neither. On the other hand, the alternate theory did distinguish the present proceeding from the *Courant* case and gave the Republican Court a chance, without reversing itself outright, to claim a large and inherent criminal jurisdiction. Moreover, it did so by enhancing the admiralty, a subject very much on Story's mind and one on which he was collecting all the ammunition he could store. One authority had been conspiciously missing from his *Digest of the Law,* and he was diligently seeking to repair the omission. "I would give fifty dollars," he wrote, "for a copy of Sir Leoline's works."[23]

The sea-born quality of Story's quest to enhance the national power was both mirrored and stimulated by the funeral proceedings for Captain James Lawrence, whose dying cry of "Don't give up the ship!" moved the hard-core New England Federalists as little as his living exploits had done. (Lawrence's dashing exploits came as close to winning the heart of New England for

21 *Ibid.* at 621.
22 Du Ponceau, *Jurisdiction of the Courts of the United States* (1824), 10.
23 Letter to Nathaniel Williams, July 27, 1813, in W. W. Story, I, 228.

the war as any feats could, a possibility mirrored in the prim remonstrance of the Massachusetts Senate "that in a war like the
present, waged without justifiable cause . . . , it is not becoming a moral and religious people to express any approbation of
military or naval exploits which are not immediately connected
with the defense of our sea-coast and soil."[24]) Lawrence's funeral,
following his heroic death in the *Chesapeake–Shannon* engagement, had been planned for Salem's North Church, mildly Unitarian, stoutly Federalist, and particularly desirable because of its
organ and its commodious size. Shortly before the ceremony,
however, an apprehension swept the congregation that the funeral
might become a partisan rally. Hero or no hero, use of North
Church was accordingly denied, and proceedings took place in a
smaller edifice. It was still an impressive affair. Elbridge Gerry,
now Vice-President, led the mourners. Dr. Bentley gave the
prayer. The lack of space, however, took something off the ceremonies. "[T]he multitude was so great, that a small part only
could hear the eulogy of the Honorable Judge STORY."[25]

Story might have made a fire-eating speech, for he had a sentimental association with the luckless *Chesapeake*. He would
shortly pass on Commodore Decatur's claim for one twentieth of
the ship's captures,[26] and, in fact, he had been invited by Lawrence to dine aboard shortly before the fatal *Shannon* engagement. But in a larger sense more than sentiment was involved, for
the sea battle and its aftermath epitomized the general state of
affairs in Massachusetts in which denial of the church was the ecclesiastical counterpart of denial of the militia. Even worse, in the
military picture, was the state's interference with the regular
forces by making arrest under collusive process serve as a means
of legalized desertion. ("This very day," Story protested his
limited judicial powers, "I [could not grant] an application to
discharge a soldier. . . . The service has suffered . . . from

[24] Quoted in H. Adams, *Madison*, Vol. II, Bk. VII, 65-66.
[25] *Salem Gazette*, quoted in *Columbian Centinel* of Aug. 25, 1813.
[26] *Decatur v. Chew*, 7 FED. CASES 322 (1813).

fraudulent arrests."[27]) On top of this came widespread commerce with the enemy. Yet, despite these provocations, Story's address avoided recriminations. And if its tone failed to reciprocate the grand hatred so characteristic of Massachusetts politics, its substance praising "the . . . Navy of my country" and "the stars and the stripes which distinguish our flag" was a world away from the philosophy of Virginia.[28]

Yet the detestation which Story seemed to excite in fundamentalist Republican and unreconstructed Federalist alike were the twin anathemas visited upon his head after his speech. "What honor can be paid," sneered the Boston *Advertiser*, "where . . . a Story is chief priest?"[29] And even more intemperate was Dr. Bentley's malediction on the Justice who had left his East Church and would one day join the North Church congregation—"a Deserter to my own, perfidious to our Association & double-minded in his fellowship."[30]

AN INDEPENDENT PARTNER

Part of New England's Federalist fury grew out of losses involved in the shriveling of the American overseas trade, and Story saw such economic reverses at close hand in his encounters with the local insolvency statutes. Yet New England ingenuity, stalemated in one form of enterprise, rapidly turned to another. Manufacturers grew as international commerce declined, and mechanized weaving, the circular saw, and the iron plow suddenly and simultaneously appeared on the American scene. Indeed, the sole opposition to lifting the abortive embargo which the Madison Administration had briefly enforced during the mid-war years came from the nation's infant industrial effort. A disproportionate part of this development came in Story's New England circuit,

[27] Letter to Nathaniel Williams, Aug. 3, 1813, in W. W. Story, I, 244-45.
[28] Quoted in *An Account of the Funeral Honours Bestowed on the Remains of Capt. Lawrence and Lieut. Ludlow* (1813), 48.
[29] Quoted in Charles J. Ingersoll, *The Second War Between the United States and Great Britain* (Philadelphia, 1840), II, 23.
[30] Bentley, IV, 186.

and the constitutional allocation of patent jurisdiction to the federal government made the sudden proliferation of inventions grist for his judicial mill. His response was a creative balancing of incentive for enterprise on one hand and protection of public interest on the other ("[M]onopoly is granted upon the express condition, that the party shall make a full and explicit disclosure, so as to enable the public, at the expiration of his patent, to make and use the invention . . ."[31]). His efforts here were perhaps the most luminous vindication of his many-sided talents, for he started with a taste for books rather than things, and at times he complained of his lack of mechanical aptitude. Nonetheless, he laid the cornerstone of American patent law, and his work was soon commemorated in the dedication of one of its earliest treatises to "the Hon. Joseph Story . . . , to whose learned and luminous decisions the author is indebted . . ."[32]

The stirrings of economic ferment had their counterpart in political changes. February of 1814 saw William Pinckney abruptly resign as Attorney General, to be succeeded by Pennsylvania's Richard Rush. Later that year, George Blake, the United States Attorney for Massachusetts, acting perhaps at Story's explicit suggestion and at least on his indirect prompting, wrote to see if the Justice Department had changed its position concerning the common-law criminal jurisdiction of the federal courts. The answer was in the negative and the rationale was the political theory of "limited political concessions of distinct and independent sovereign States."[33]

Yet, even as the new Attorney General restated the rationale of the Kentucky and Virginia Resolutions and the *Connecticut Courant* case, the Administration's latest judicial appointee was steadily chipping away at the major premise of those doctrines.

[31] *Whittemore v. Cutter,* 29 FED. CASES at 1122 (1813).
[32] Fessenden, *An Essay on the Law of Patents for New Inventions* (1822), xxxiii; See also Prager, "The Influence of Mr. Justice Story on American Patent Law," *American Journal of Legal History,* V (1961), 254.
[33] Letter from Attorney General Rush to George Blake, July 28, 1814, in Warren, *Supreme Court,* I, 439.

Story had early indicated his conviction that whatever the *Courant* case might say on the necessity of congressional action to breathe life into the federal judicial powers, there were wide areas where "whether there be any statute existing . . . is not in my judgment material."[34] Particularly was this true as to the wartime confiscation cases, whose consequences, he insisted, were derived not so much from legislative enactment of a confederation as from the implicit power of a member of the family of nations. For it was here that Story—sometimes in dissent, sometimes in ascendancy—persistently asserted the extreme prerogatives of the sovereignty in arms. His polestar was the Continental internationalist Cornelis van Bynkershoek, "whose rules of law are written in blood," according to a shocked lawyer.[35] Story agreed, but from a contrary point of view. "If Bynkershoek yet remains on the bookseller's hands," he wrote a Baltimore classmate, "take it on my account; the war has whetted my appetite for it."[36] He obviously liked what he found, pronouncing the Dutch jurist of the highest authority, and this notwithstanding John Marshall's more humane views of war.

Again and again the old soldier and the youthful scholar split on the issue of confiscation. Thus, Marshall disavowed "supposed analogies to certain principles . . . avowed by the great maritime and belligerent powers of Europe,"[37] in protesting seizures of neutrals moving between enemy-occupied areas. Contrariwise, Story took his stand on "sound policy and national honor"[38] in unsuccessfully asserting the liability to seizure of enemy property

[34] *The Alligator*, 1 FED. CASES at 529 (1813).
[35] Samuel Dexter noted in *The Aurora*, 8 CRANCH at 216 (1814). "Van Bynkershoek is not moved by the scruples of sentiment," says J. de Leuter. "In war all violence and ruses are permitted, perfidy alone excepted. There is no difference between belligerents and private citizens, still less between combatants and noncombatants; all may be equally killed or enslaved. As to enemy property, whether public or private, . . . all may be forfeited . . . Either war or peace; there is not room for intermediate conditions." (De Leuter in Bynkershoek, *De Domino Maris Dissertatio*, trans. Van Deman [New York, 1923]. II, x.)
[36] Letter to Nathaniel Williams, Aug. 24, 1812, in W. W. Story, I, 229.
[37] Marshall dissenting in *The Commercen*, 1 WHEATON at 396 (1816).
[38] Story dissenting in *Brown v. United States*, 8 CRANCH at 141 (1814).

in America. And so their disagreement on confiscability ran like a line of cleavage through the reports—confiscability of neutral property on an enemy ship (*The Nereide*),[39] of American property in enemy territory (*The Venus*),[40] of enemy goods destined for American buyers (*The Merrimack*),[41] as a consequence of the mere acceptance of a British license (*The Julia*),[42] and as a consequence of a suspectedly collusive capture (*The Bothnea and The Jahnstoff*).[43]

Neither the hostility of his native New England[44] nor Marshall's contrary attitude in these matters caused Story to budge one inch. "I hold it an indispensable duty," Story wrote as he entered his first formal disagreement in *The Nereide* by contradicting Marshall with a six-thousand-word dissent, "not to surrender my own judgment, because a great weight of opinion is against me, a weight no one can feel more sensibly than myself."[45] And in a reference in private correspondence to Marshall's *Nereide* opinion, Story went even further in obdurancy: "[N]ever in my whole life was I more entirely satisfied that the Court were wrong in their judgment."[46]

[39] 9 CRANCH 388 (1815).
[40] 8 CRANCH 253 (1814).
[41] 8 CRANCH 317 (1814).
[42] 8 CRANCH 181 (1814); cf. *United States v. The Matilda*, 26 FED. CASES 1200 (1813).
[43] 2 WHEATON 169 (1817).
[44] See Newmeyer, "Joseph Story and the War of 1812: A Judicial Nationalist," *The Historian*, XXVI (1964), 486.
[45] 9 CRANCH at 455.
[46] Letter to Nathaniel Williams, May 8, 1815, in W. W. Story I, 256. And so much for the legend as variously phrased. E.g., "[H]e was a Federalist in principles from the time he first came under Marshall's influence" (Benjamin Wright, *The Growth of American Law* [Boston and New York, 1942], 55); "When it is remembered that after Story was made Associate Justice his views became identical with those of Marshall on almost every subject . . ." (Beveridge, IV, 118 n.1); ". . . as when Joseph Story comes on, pink-cheeked and thirty-two, as the disciple of Jefferson and lives to utter dire prophecies on those who would not follow where Marshall had led" (Charles Fairman, *Mr. Justice Miller and the Supreme Court* [New York, 1939], 57). Justice Frankfurter summed it all up: Story "had the deepest devotion to Marshall, but he also had views and vanity" (Frankfurter, "John Marshall and the Judicial Process," in Arthur Sutherland [ed.], *Government under Law* [Cambridge, 1956], 10).

A VIRGINIA CONTROVERSY

Yet the issue of war and confiscation did not always find the Chief Justice and the junior associate in separate camps. Rather, they were in complete rapport on what was to be the most important case of all. Originally styled in the Supreme Court *Fairfax's Devisee v. Hunter's Lessee*,[47] the controversy involved conflicting claims to the same Virginia land. One title was asserted on behalf of the hereditary owners, the Fairfax family. The other rested on the expropriatory Virginia legislation of the Revolution. As a young lawyer, Chief Justice Marshall had argued the Fairfax title in the state courts, and later his brother had bought part of the Fairfax lands for the family estate. Hence the Chief Justice was doubly disqualified on this labyrinthine maze of Virginia law and politics whose specific constitutional question (there were fourteen issues in the case) turned on a fine point of timing: Had the confiscation been consummated prior to the Treaty of Paris of 1783, which interdicted any future expropriation? The Virginia trial court held it had not and validated the Fairfax claim. After a long delay, the Virginia Court of Appeals reversed the judgment and asserted that the state-granted Hunter title was the good one. But litigation was not yet at an end. Inasmuch as the Fairfax title had rested its overridden claim on a federal treaty, it fell, nominally at least, under a provision of the 1789 Judiciary Act which authorized further proceedings before the Supreme Court in such cases. The appeal was taken, and the presiding judge of the Virginia court certified the record to Washington ("improvidently,"[48] it developed).

The case was argued shortly after Story first took his seat on the Supreme Court in February of 1812. Decision was deferred until the following year, and it was not until March 15, 1813, that Story handed down the tedious and prolix opinion, reversing

---

[47] 7 CRANCH 603 (1813).
[48] *Hunter v. Martin*, 18 VA. at 1 (1815).

the Court of Appeals and upholding the Fairfax title on the grounds that the confiscation had not been consummated before the treaty became effective. It was a somewhat audacious under- taking, for it bypassed the alternate grounds on which the Vir- ginia Court of Appeals had made its finding. Moreover, Story's opinion gave a strained construction to state legislation and tres- passed on his first judicial declaration that title to land depended on the *lex loci*. Finally, it was tinged with a sectional and minority basis, for the Kentuckian Justice Todd joined the Court's two Virginians in not sitting and South Carolina's Johnson dissented. Only New Jersey's Livingston and Maryland's Duvall joined Story in the three-judge mandate which went back to Richmond.

Yet these very irritants illuminated an infirmity in the consti- tutional design whose previous manifestation—the Supreme Court's assumption of jurisdiction over a private citizen's suit against Georgia—had been aborted in a termination which concealed rather than composed the basic difficulty. This was a widespread assumption that the Constitution reflected the automaticity which ruled Adam Smith's earth and Isaac Newton's heavens. The spirit of the age which saw mechanism and order everywhere was nat- urally disposed to impute a self-equilibrating balance to state and national powers having their being in a common territory and population.

There were a few dissenters. Tough-minded old John Adams insisted that there could no more be two sovereigns in one ter- ritory than two Supreme Beings in one universe. More widespread and far more frequently cited was the analogy that state and na- tional governments should no more clash than parallel lines should meet. Yet the bitter test of history would hold another norm—that these matters were ruled not by the law of Euclid but by that of Parmenides, or, as a later American President, Woodrow Wilson, would phrase it, by an accountability to Darwin, not to Newton.

The confrontations of power were inevitable in the very nature of things, and it was the judicial process which became, so to speak, the cutting edge of the blade. For it was here, to invert de

Tocqueville's thought, that every judicial proceeding carried the germ of a political question, and the irenic generality that national courts should have the last word on federal—including constitutional—matters, and the state courts on all others, solved nothing. Constitutional issues were inevitably bound up with the workaday world of ordinary law, and every jurisdictional question returned to the root of the problem of the finality of power.

The answer of the Virginia school was that neither government —including its courts—should be the final judge of its own powers. Yet, at the absolute extreme, this meant constituting each government the final judge of the other, a proposition as unworkable as the first and, moreover, simply irrelevant to the entangled problems of the real world. Conceding, for example, the right of the commonwealth of Massachusetts to keep holy its Sabbath and the right of the federal government to carry its mails, what should be done with a federal postman not only traveling on Sunday, but "blowing his horn to the disturbance of serious people"?[49] Or, again, did the war powers permit the enlistment of a minor into the regular forces irrespective of what the law of a state might say as to legal competency of infants?[50] Further complicating the judicial cross-set had been the failure of Congress to grant the national courts the full range of their permissible constitutional powers.

The grant that Congress had made in the Judiciary Act of 1789 did provide for equilibrium of a sort. Section 25 of that act provided for an appeal to the Supreme Court whenever a federal, constitutional, or treaty right had been unavailingly claimed before a state court of last resort. To be sure, this process of harmonization presupposed that such appellate jurisdiction might be constitutionally instituted. There was one major consideration supporting, and one opposing, the presupposition. A major difficulty was that the Constitution nowhere permitted it in so many words. On the other hand, a major argument was that Section 25

[49] *Commonwealth v. Knox*, 6 MASS. at 78 (1809).
[50] *Commonwealth v. Cushing*, 11 MASS. 66 (1814).

simply had to be what it was if the national power was to be a fact as well as a name.

Doubtless the latter consideration was persuasive in compelling the acquiescence of a number of state courts to this appellate jurisdiction, but the Virginia Court of Appeals was not numbered among them. That it should join by enforcing a judgment not its own on a question which involved Virginia land law fully as much as the Treaty of 1783, was asking a good deal. And perhaps it was asking too much to expect submission to a mandate plagiarized from the old English forms ("The President of the United States . . . Greeting") and carrying both their hauteur ("there is error in the judgment of the Court of Appeals") and their insolence ("you therefore are hereby commanded"[51]) If ever the substance and circumstance of litigation were calculated to shake loyalty and spread New England unrest to other areas, *Fairfax* seemed to be the case par excellence.

"THIS ONCE HIGHLY FAVORED AND HAPPY LAND"

As 1814 unfolded, disintegration seemed to develop proportionately to an exterior pressure which Britain, victorious in the Napoleonic Wars, was increasingly bringing to bear. Yet even these dark times had their compensation. The important wartime cases began appearing on the docket of the Supreme Court, with the result that it became difficult to keep congressional quorums, "owing to the number of members who crowd to hear the pleadings in the Court."[52] Even more flattering than such attention to ex-Representative Story was his increasing status with his fellow judges. He turned out seven opinions at the term, most of which dealt with the mysteries of prize law, and as to which, he noted with ostentatious modesty, "my brethren were so kind as to

[51] *Hunter v. Martin*, 18 VA. at 1 (1815).
[52] *National Intelligencer*, Feb. 24, 1814, quoted in John Powell, *Richard Rush* (Philadelphia, 1942), 50.

place confidence in my researches."[53] He might have been less assured had he learned of Harrison Gray Otis' reaction to the matter. "[Some of] his colleagues," wrote the scandalized Otis of Story's expertise, "to the astonishment and mortification of their friends in this quarter are considered as giving him the pavé in causes of this description."[54]

A more accurate index of the year than any display of judicial knowledge was provided shortly following the adjournment of the Court. A few days after Story arrived home from the current term the *U. S. S. Constitution* came fleeing into the Salem coastline with pursuing British men-of-war close astern. The almost Melvillian symbolism was a prophetic precursor of the spring which saw the *Fairfax* mandate, and the underlying validity of Section 25 of the Judiciary Act, fiercely argued before the Virginia Court of Appeals, whose reporter noted that "the question whether this mandate should be obeyed excited all that attention from Bench and Bar which its great importance truly merited."[55]

The nationalist slough of despond continued into summer. In Hartford, an American naval officer undertaking to attract a few recruits was arrested "for causing drums to be beat through the public streets of this populous city,"[56] and elsewhere in New England business as usual went on with the nearby British forces ("Yesterday was examined before Judge Story, a young man from Gloucester apprehended in carrying supplies by contract to the enemy"[57]). The climax came with the sack of Washington in August, and as summer passed into fall Story's home-town paper was suggesting that the Union was "virtually dissolved."[58]

[53] Letter to Samuel P. P. Fay, April 24, 1814, in W. W. Story, I, 261.
[54] Letter from Harrison Gray Otis to Robert Goodloe Harper, Dec. 2, 1815 (copy), in Otis MSS., Massachusetts Historical Society.
[55] Quoted in Warren, *Supreme Court*, I, 446-47.
[56] Hartford *Mercury*, Dec. 16, 1816, quoted in *Niles' Weekly Register*, Jan. 4, 1817.
[57] Bentley, IV, 262.
[58] *Salem Gazette*, Sept. 23, 1814, quoted in Ward, *Andrew Jackson: Symbol for an Age* (1962; hereinafter cited as Ward), 215 n.3.

Unquestionably the most devastating blow was the sack of Washington by the British in mid-1814 and the quasi-paralysis which overtook the American financial system as a consequence. An apparent epiphany of regional superiority alongside national incompetence was doubtless seen throughout much of New England as a practical and even ethical validation of the forces of separatism. For while the creedal formalities of the ultra-Calvinism of the old order were in decline, there persisted its habits of thought which viewed prosperity and adversity as the polar counterparts of election and rejection. Even the Merchants' Bank of Salem, cofounded by Story and the *de facto* Republican exchequer of Essex County, could still reflect this self-imputed amalgam of ethical and economic superiority by telling the hard-pressed national Treasury that while federal obligations were virtually irredeemable and circulating at a discount, "this Bank continues to pay its notes in gold and silver."[59]

Hence, the suspension of specie payments throughout much of the country lent an especial persuasiveness to the call which went out through New England "for the Wise and the Good of those States which deemed themselves oppressed" to meet in Hartford in mid-December of 1814.[60] Certainly the appeal fell on many willing ears. If the war were to be continued, wrote a Yankee in far-off India,

> God only knows what may be the consequences, . . . all the commercial men largely in trade I suppose will be ruin'd, the only good effect which can result will be a separation of the States & that is quite uncertain. I hope with all my heart it may happen, the evils attending such an event cannot be greater than to be subjected to the controul [sic] of the Southern and Western States.[61]

[59] Directors' minutes, Merchants' Bank, July 7, 1815.
[60] Massachusetts Protest against War and Embargo, quoted in Dangerfield, *The Era of Good Feelings* (1952), 88.
[61] Henry Lee to P. T. Jackson, Jan. 30, 1813, in Porter, *The Jacksons and the Lees*, II (1937), 1076.

There was more to the restiveness than obdurate regionalism. Rather, a core element in the dissatisfaction was the feeling that the national government had failed in its elementary duty of defense and that its sins of omission would be visited upon New England in the form of invasion and subjection. Hard-shell Federalists made the most of the situation, but even Administration supporters were apprehensive over a possible hostile landing, and Story's bank made provision that "teams be provided to remove stock and books at a moment's notice in case of fire or invasion."[62]

As Story prepared to leave for the 1815 term of the Supreme Court, the only turn of good fortune for him lay in his election to the presidency of the Merchants' Bank. Otherwise the scene was overcast with gloom. On December 15, 1814, the Hartford Convention came to order, and, appropriately, the following day the Virginia Court of Appeals issued its opinion in the Fairfax case, refusing to heed the Supreme Court's mandate and insisting upon its own independence in constitutional matters.

And the fortunes of war formed an appropriate counterpart. The American navy had been swept from the seas, and the American armies seemed immobilized. Maine lay under partial occupation, one British force was poised atop the Hudson Valley's historic invasion route, and a second approached Louisiana from the sea. The coastline was blockaded, the Capitol was a fire-blackened hulk, the currency was in chaos, and the interest on the national debt went unpaid. Pessimistic reactions ranged from Congressman Daniel Webster's prediction of the collapse of the government in sixty days to Justice Livingston's effort to secure a statutory removal of the Supreme Court's 1815 term from Washington to Philadelphia. All in all, it was the appropriate winter of discontent for the messages of alienation which went to Washington from men in Richmond who abhorred centralized power and from men in Hartford who abhorred it when it was not in their hands.

The Hartford message was carried down to Washington by a

<hr>

[62] Directors' minutes, June 7, 1813.

trio of commissioners headed by Harrison Gray Otis, who traveled south at about the same time as Story and did it much in the manner of envoys of one sovereign power to another. The explicit substance of the message seemed innocuous enough: an end to state dynasties in the Presidency; repeal of the slave compromise in taxation and representation; and a concurrent majority for declarations of war, imposition of embargoes, and admission of new states. But the real thrust of the message, outlined like a sword beneath a cloak, was the hint to force even more radical changes by extraconstitutional means if the points sought could not be gained within constitutional procedures. It was the same undercurrent which characterized the Virginia and Kentucky Resolutions almost two decades earlier, and which tinctured in a more complex and subtle form the latest *Fairfax* opinion of the Virginia Court of Appeals. The cycle seemed to have come full turn since the War Hawks got their war in June of 1812. Now Justice Livingston wrote Story assuring him of friendship "[w]hatever may be the fate of this once highly favored and happy land," and the implication of an approaching end of the present order was underscored.[63] Congress appealed to Providence and enjoined prayer and fasting for delivery from a time of "public calamity and war."[64]

[63] Letter to Joseph Story, Sept. 1, 1814, in Dunne, "The Story-Livingston Correspondence, 1812–1822," *American Journal of Legal History*, X, 1966. This letter with six others from the University of Texas Story collection were included in the foregoing article through the kind permission of the Manuscripts Committee of Miriam Lutcher Stark Library and were the first published from this collection.

[64] *United States Statutes at Large*, III, 248 (1814).

CHAPTER X

The Dawn's Early Light

VISITS TO TWO PRESIDENTS

The opening of the Supreme Court's February, 1815, term symbolized the atmosphere of national frustration, humiliation and despondency. Proceedings began February 1 in an "uncomfortable and unfit"[1] parlor in a private home because the regular courtroom, although itself untouched by the British torch, was unusable in the smoke-blackened Capitol. Then, just as the gloom seemed overpowering, news of two astonishing events came like lightning flashes from east and west. "ALMOST INCREDIBLE VICTORY—GLORIOUS NEWS!" headlined the *National Intelligencer*'s extra on the battle of New Orleans.[2] Hard on the heels of the military triumph in Louisiana came word of the equally spectacular diplomatic one at Ghent, where American negotiators had managed to end the war on the basis of a return to the *status quo ante*.

The convergence of these events produced an astonishing turnabout of popular attitude. From one end of the country to the other there were fireworks, oratory and parades. "No one stopped to ask," observed Henry Adams on the change, "why a govern-

---

[1] George Ticknor to Elisha Ticknor, February, 1815, in Hillard, *Life, Letters and Journal of George Ticknor* (1876), I, 38.
[2] Washington *National Intelligencer*, Feb. 4, 1815, quoted in Ward, 5.

ment which was discredited and falling to pieces at one moment, should appear as a successful and even a glorious national representative a moment afterward."³ Yet there was no mystery whatsoever to Adams' great-grandfather. "Mr. Madison's administration," wrote the venerable ex-President, "must be accorded by historians, notwithstanding all the errors, blunders, confusions, distractions, disasters, and factions, . . . the most glorious period of the history of the United States."⁴ On the very same day, Story was echoing the same exhilarating sentiment: "Never did a country occupy more lofty ground; we have stood the contest, single-handed, against the conquerors of Europe."⁵

If the makeshift courtroom exemplified the gloomy way February began, Dolly Madison's glittering reception at the Octagon before the month was out symbolized the glorious change which had come to pass. Story was there, wearing his judicial robe. He doubtless cut a somewhat somber figure alongside the epauleted glitter of the generals or the court dress of the diplomatic envoys, for the affair was indistinguishable in its elegant splendor, and differed only in scale, from those of any court in Europe. Dolly Madison presided regally, and the only persons in the capital who seemed untouched by the joy were the three Hartford commissioners. Overnight the wave of nationalism made them men without a mission and the butt of every jokester in the country. ("Missing," mock-advertised the New York *National Advance*, "Three well looking, responsible men . . . supposed to be traveling towards Washington . . ."⁶) Harrison Gray Otis left Washington in a fury of frustration, unleashing twin barbs against Mrs. Madison's party ("all was tinsel and vulgarity") and the President himself ("what a mean and contemptible little blackguard"⁷).

³ H. Adams, *Madison*, Vol. II, Bk. IX, 80.
⁴ Letter to William Stephens Smith, Feb. 22, 1815, in Page Smith, *John Adams*, II, 1110.
⁵ Letter to Nathaniel Williams, Feb. 22, 1815, in W. W. Story, I, 254.
⁶ Quoted in Morison, *Otis*, II, 167.
⁷ Letters to Mrs. Otis, Feb. 20 and 22, 1815, in Brant, VI, 370.

Notwithstanding these strictures, Mrs. Madison's reception did have a certain significance. It was a pole apart from the simplicity with which Jefferson had attempted to make the White House a symbol of Republican egalitarianism. There was no question as to which of the two worlds Story preferred. Himself debonair and well-groomed, he had been taken aback by Jefferson's negligent dress in the White House; the regal note which the Madisons brought to the Executive Mansion was far more to his taste. ("Mrs. Madison holds a levee every Wednesday evening, and I have just returned from my attendance at her court."[8]) Not that the Federalists, learning nothing but forgetting nothing, were wont to let the Republicans overlook their previous to-do in simplifying the social life of the Presidency. "We recall," noted Boston's *Columbian Centinel*, "with how much boorish malignity the levees of Mrs. Adams were ridiculed."[9]

The reception was, however, an appropriate prelude for the message Madison shortly thereafter sent to Congress. In content it was as far apart from his own Virginia Resolutions as his wife's levee was from Jefferson's social austerity. Yet it might be said that the message was not so much change as growth. The Virginia school of political philosophy had staked everything upon the ability of the United States to develop their (not "its") destinies in institutional and geographic isolation from the influence of European statecraft. Madison's genius, which had managed to transform the unacceptable by withstanding pressure to abandon his libertarian principles during the war, was also equal to accepting that which he could not transform. "Experience has taught us," he wrote, "that neither the pacific dispositions of the American people, nor the pacific character of their political institutions, can altogether exempt them from that strife which appears . . . to be incident to the actual period of the world . . ."[10] Thereafter followed successive Presidential recommendations

Letter to Mrs. Story, Feb. 7, 1810, W. W. Story, I, 195.
Columbian Centinel, Jan. 4, 1812.
[10] Quoted in H. Adams, *Madison*, Vol. II, Bk. IX, 82-83.

which had very little of states' rights and strict construction, but very much of implied powers and national sovereignty: a standing army, a world-ranging navy, a protective tariff, an ample exchequer, a federal university, permanent internal taxation, and that institution which Congressman Madison in 1791 had denounced as an unconstitutional excrescence—a national bank. Indeed, only one item remained for Madison to take every weapon from the Federalist political armory, and that was to find in the federal judicial power the ultimate arbiter of all constitutional issues.

Madison would eventually come round to even this position, but meanwhile other Republicans saw the last traces of the old dispensation pass without remorse, regret or even nostalgia. Typical of the second generation of Clay, Calhoun and himself, Story hailed the turn of events as a glorious opportunity for the Republicans to put themselves "permanently in power."[11] What were his specifics? "Let us extend the national authority . . . Let us have great military and naval schools; an adequate regular army . . . [and] a permanent navy; a national bank, a national system of bankruptcy . . . [and] Judicial Courts which shall embrace the whole constitutional powers . . ."[12]

The reference to the courts was the opening gun in a counter battery fire to the Richmond polemics. Story followed it with a declaration that in safeguarding the Union it was the judicial power which must always remain "a strong and stringent link."[13] He wrote as a man who would soon make good on his words.

SEA CHANGE

The great national triumph of 1815 made that year's term of the Supreme Court almost anticlimactic. Story wrote nine opinions, one in dissent. Exceptionally important in continuing his rigorous exposition of the contract clause, and curiously coinci-

[11] Letter to Nathaniel Williams, Feb. 22, 1815, in W. W. Story, I, 254.
[12] *Ibid.*
[13] Memorandum to William Pinckney, February 1816, *Ibid.*, 293.

dent in dealing with the post-Revolutionary troubles of the Episcopal Church, were his opinions in *Terrett v. Taylor*[14] and *Town of Pawlett v. Clark*.[15]

Another touch of coincidence in the cases was suggested by his own forthcoming informal attendance at St. Peter's, Salem's Episcopal church, to which he would repair when his differences with Dr. Bentley probably became too much to bear. He was home shortly past mid-March, a homecoming signaled by kindness to the children of another family in the face of a loss about to beset his own. "Yesterday afternoon," a Salem matron wrote her husband, "I had the pleasure of seeing Judge Story. He brought books, knives, and pencils for the children."[16] A week later his small daughter, Mary, died ("This is the second time that I have buried a lovely daughter"[17]), and before the year was out the experience was to be repeated with the loss of his namesake, six years old ("My dear little boy . . ."[18]).

Childhood mortality was a common enough occurrence in nineteenth-century America, but in Story's case it applied with a particularly cruel and ongoing pertinacity. His first child had died in early 1811, and he marked the event with a verse which was to have a hauntingly recurring relevance:

> *Sweet, patient sufferer, gone at last*
> *To a far happier shore,*
> *All thy sick hours of pain are past,*
> *Thy earthly anguish o'er.*

> *Ah! never, never, from my heart*
> *Thy image, child, shall flee—*
> *'Tis soothing from the world to part,*
> *'Tis bliss to think on thee.*[19]

[14] 9 CRANCH 43 (1815).
[15] 9 CRANCH 292 (1815).
[16] Mrs. Benjamin Crowninshield to Benjamin W. Crowninshield, March 21, 1815, Crowninshield Papers.
[17] Letter to Nathaniel Williams, May 15, 1815, in W. W. Story, I, 255.
[18] Letter to Williams, Dec. 3, 1815, *ibid.*, 257.
[19] W. W. Story, I, 209-10.

For the verse was not only to be an elegy for the child who died in 1811 and the two who died in 1815, it was to be a prophecy of lament for the child who was to die four years later ("On Thursday, the 1st day of April, 1819, . . . died my dear little daughter, Caroline Wetmore Story, aged six years"[20]) and for still another who was to be taken from him in his middle years ("one of the most beautiful and attractive of human beings, and at ten . . . every thing her parents could wish"[21]).

Bitter enough in the ordinary course of things, the fate was doubly cruel in being laid upon a man for whom the angel of death held an extraordinary mixture of fear and fascination.[22] Perhaps the latter attitude was rooted in childhood exposure to the ultra-Calvinist preaching of his clerical uncle, who, by Story's recollection, seemed obsessed with the doctrines of depravity, death, and damnation. In any event, his reaction to adversity was to lose himself in extraordinary activity. "[H]aving been a like sufferer," he wrote Webster on the death of the latter's wife, "I can say, that the great secret of comfort must be sought, so far as human aid can go, in employment. It requires effort and sacrifices, but it is the only specific remedy against unavailing and wasting sorrow; that canker which eats into the heart and destroys its vitality."[23]

Fortifying the impulse which sought in legal writing an anodyne for grief was the economic spur provided by his inflation-riddled salary. Doubtless his banking connection helped some, but other supplementation was badly needed. By 1813 he was seeking

[20] Ibid., 332.
[21] Letter to Chancellor Kent, June 24, 1831, in W. W. Story, II, 56.
[22] "Perhaps when I am in my grave you will take comfort in these little details" (letter to William Wetmore Story, Jan. 23, 1831, in W. W. Story, I, 2); ". . . the tomb closes in on greatness . . ." (letter to Samuel P. P. Fay, May 18, 1807, ibid., 144; "Within my own short political life, the tomb has closed over the generous Knox, the intrepid Lincoln, the learned Dana, and the accomplished Sullivan" (speech of Jan. 17, 1812, in Miscellaneous Writings, 65); "We too must pass away to the tomb" (speech of Sept. 4, 1821 ibid., 241; ". . . death has been annually busy in thinning our numbers' (speech of Aug. 31, 1836, ibid., 377).
[23] Letter to Daniel Webster, Jan. 27, 1828, in Webster, Private Correspondence, ed. Fletcher Webster (2v., 1857; hereinafter cited as Webster), I, 446

the publication of law reports of his circuit court. ("A volume of my Reports is prepared by the reporter, but he finds no person willing to print them and pay any value for the copyright."[24]) The following year he was corresponding with Attorney General Rush on the possibility of their preparing a compilation of United States laws. By the start of 1815, and perhaps earlier, he had turned entrepreneur in a joint publishing venture. "About the middle of February," wrote his reporter, "I commenced the publication of the first volume of Circuit Court Reports. I was on the safe side for the whole expense was to be borne by Judges Story & Davis & W. S. Shaw, Esq. I was to contribute only the labor, & to have the copy right & an equal share of all profits for my reward."[25] The undertaking, particularly when conjoined with his effort to escape grief, seems to have prompted an almost assembly-line production of elaborate legal essays designed as an inventory, so to speak, in the event a question litigated before the circuit court came seeking an opinion. And one essay which Story urgently wished to link to an opinion was the one on admiralty jurisdiction, a subject now doubly important as the new sense of nationalism coincided with an upsurge in the blockade-freed maritime traffic carrying three American harvests to Europe. Not that Story necessarily required a case in point to get his convictions on the record; *obiter dictum* could do as well, and by May of 1815 he had made his views crystal clear. "In my judgment, and I speak after having given the subject a very grave consideration, the admiralty has always rightfully possessed jurisdiction over all maritime contracts . . ."[26]

Then, "with a manuscript dissertation on this subject nearly finished,"[27] the square issue was transferred from his study to his court. A suit, *De Lovio v. Boit*,[28] involving a contract of marine

[24] Letter to Nathaniel Williams, Aug. 3, 1813, in W. W. Story, I, 248.
[25] John Gallison, Manuscript Diary, July 4, 1815, Massachusetts Historical Society.
[26] *The Jerusalem*, 13 FED. CASES at 565 (1815).
[27] Letter to Henry Wheaton, Sept. 5, 1815, in W. W. Story, I, 267.
[28] 7 FED. CASES 418 (1815).

insurance, was appealed from the district court to the circuit court on the question of admiralty jurisdiction. Under the Continental rule, admiralty would decide the case. Under the English rule, it could not. Which would prevail? Story suggested that whatever the question was, it would be long: "The opinion will not be short of seventy pages, as the materials are great, and the learning spread over a wide surface."[29]

With this forewarning came a four-stage, 26,000-word exegesis of the terse constitutional phrase "admiralty and maritime jurisdiction." "The vast importance and novelty of the questions," Story half apologized at the outset, ". . . render it impossible to come to a correct decision without a thorough examination of the whole jurisdiction . . ."[30] First came a three-thousand-word history tracing admiralty to its half-fabled beginnings and undertaken more as a tender of credentials than as an exposition of law. The need for credentials became apparent with the second stage— a sustained attack on common-law position as set out in Lord Coke's *Institutes,* a work which had reduced him to tears of frustration during his law apprenticeship. Now with poetic justice the thirty-five-year-old judge let it be known that he was not one of the many who were dismayed by "encountering any opinion supported by the authority of Lord Coke."[31] The avenging thrust delivered, Story then swept through a systematic contradiction of Coke's doctrines, cases and citations ("unless I am very much mistaken, they entirely fail of their intended purpose . . . "[32]) to a conclusion that the common law had no authority to rule affairs of the sea ("indefensible . . . inconsistent and contradictory"[33]). All this was still prelude to the third stage—"whatever may in England be the binding authority . . . in the United States we are at liberty to re-examine the doctrines . . ."[34] Here Story

[29] Letter to Nathaniel Williams, Sept. 8, 1815, in W. W. Story, I, 263.
[30] 7 FED. CASES at 418.
[31] *Ibid.,* 421.
[32] *Ibid.,* 425.
[33] *Ibid.,* 441.
[34] *Ibid.*

used the resurgent nationalism to underline his point. ("Indeed the doctrine that would extend the statutes of Richard to the present judicial power of the United States seems little short of an absurdity."[35]) Having maneuvered for position with this exhaustive series of marches and countermarches, he was now in position to drive home his thrust with matched appeals to deductive and empirical logic. The first went to textual analysis, and here he found that by adding three words, "and maritime jurisdiction," the constitutional draftsmen had widened the admiralty powers of the federal courts to the widest limits. The other was a candid citation of "the advantages resulting to the commerce and navigation of the United States, from a uniformity of rules and decisions in all maritime questions."[36] Combined, these two propositions reduced the many thousands of words of the opinion to a terse imperative: "national policy, as well as juridical logic, require the clause of the constitution to be so construed, as to embrace all maritime contracts, torts, and injuries . . ."[37]

A particularly masterful touch was the disposition of the thorny history of admiralty in the colonies. Here he made a virtue out of adversity by dismissing the historical sticking point with an obscure, seemingly offhand footnote reference that the Vice-Admiralty Court of Massachusetts, before the Revolution, exercised a jurisdiction far more extensive than that of the admiralty in England.[38] Unhappily, he was still a step away from full mastery of his powers, and he marred the magnificence of his creation with the nervous and uncertain note on which he ended: "[N]or can I pretend to conjecture, how far a superior tribunal may deem

---

[35] *Ibid.*, 443. *Cf. Niles' Weekly Register*, X (1816), index, vi: "British insolent decision about salvage."

[36] 7 FED. CASES at 443. See Deutsch, "Development of the Theory of Admiralty Jurisdiction in the United States," *Tulane Law Review*, XXXV (1960), 117.

[37] 7 FED. CASES at 443.

[38] *Ibid.*, 442 n.46. *Cf.* Mr. Justice Campbell (dissenting): "The opinion is . . . celebrated for its research, and remarkable, in my opinion, for its boldness in asserting novel conclusions, and the facility with which authentic historical evidence that contradicted them is disposed of." (*Jackson v. Steamboat Magnolia*, 20 HOWARD at 336 [1857].)

fit to entertain the principles, which I have felt it my solemn duty to avow . . ."[39] In fact, he almost seemed to seek reversal by quoting an English judge: "I have made several decrees since I have had the honor to sit in this place, which have been reversed in another place; and I was not ashamed to make them, nor sorry when they were reversed by others."[40]

He need not have been so apprehensive. The year was 1815, not 1812, must less 1765. His opinion accorded with the new spirit of the times. "To my surprise," Story conceded, ". . . the decision is rather popular among merchants. They declare that in mercantile cases, they are not fond of juries."[41]

THE STRONG AND STRINGENT LINK

For all the heartbreak 1815 brought Story, it brought some triumphs too. There was the unexpectedly welcome reception of his *De Lovio* opinion on admiralty jurisdiction. There was the LL.D. award by Brown University, and as the year drew to a close Harvard included his name in the enumeration of the "distinguished sons . . . of the University" selected to serve on the Society to Promote Theological Education at Harvard,[42] a special establishment for theological education. Specialized training for the ministry, whose preparation previously had been considered part and parcel of a general Harvard education, and indeed its principal object, was merely one straw in the winds of change which doubtless sent Story to the 1816 term of the Court with high hopes of overturning the *Connecticut Courant* decision. An extraordinary opportunity to do so was presented by the case of the recaptured prize, in which his condemnatory decree had gone up to the Supreme Court on a *pro forma* certificate of division between Story and District Judge John Davis. Yet, on this point,

39 7 FED. CASES at 444.
40 *Ibid.*
41 Letter to Nathaniel Williams, Dec. 8, 1815, in W. W. Story, I, 270.
42 *Columbian Centinel*, Dec. 16, 1815; I am advised by Dr. Conrad Wright of the Harvard Divinity School, author of *The Beginnings of Unitarianism in America* (Boston, 1955), that notwithstanding the impressive title, the Society was in the nature of a "friends" group.

the changing times had not produced a reversion to the old Federalism, but, rather, an unprecedented environment both drawing on and differing from Federalist centralism and Republican philanthropy.

Some Federalist dogma was assimilated. Some was not. One item cast irretrievably into outer darkness was a system of crime and punishment drawn from the judgment rolls of pre-nineteenth-century England. Thus, Attorney General Rush observed the precedent of his predecessor and refused even to argue the case of the recaptured prize when it came up on the docket. Justice William Johnson followed the Attorney General's lead and summarily dismissed the case—over Story's sulky objection—on the authority of the *Courant* decision.[43]

Story need not have been so petulant. He had promised to "submit with utmost cheerfulness to the judgment of my brethren."[44] Moreover, the case of the recaptured prize was affirmed not so much on the rule of *stare decisis* as it was on that of "the letter killeth and the spirit giveth life." For, almost at the same time, another case on the 1816 docket gave Story his chance to pulverize the formal major premise of the *Courant* case. The occasion was the old *Fairfax* proceeding, back once more under the style of *Martin v. Hunter's Lessee*[45] and back with four separate opinions of the Virginia Court of Appeals.[46] These asserted and reasserted, with appropriate citations to the Resolutions of 1798, that the Constitution was a compact of confederated sovereignties in which the derivative center and the integral states were divided by object and function; that neither central nor state government touched the other, coerced the other, or, most emphatically, could be the final judge of its own power; that any law of Congress which presumed to make a federal court the censor of state judiciaries traversed the organic basis of its very legitimacy and was, therefore, unconstitutional and void.

One decade earlier this probably would have been a deadly

---

[43] 1 WHEATON 415 (1816).
[44] 25 FED. CASES at 621 (1813).
[45] 1 WHEATON 304 (1816).
[46] *Hunter v. Martin*, 18 VA., 1 (1815).

riposte to Story's original *Fairfax* opinion and all the more persuasive for adopting much of the formula by which Chief Justice
Marshall asserted his veto over national legislation. And in fact
one of the Virginia judges suavely cited Marshall's *Marbury v.
Madison* opinion to attest that the ill-considered nature of the
1789 Judiciary Act "has been detected and admitted"[47] by the Supreme Court itself. The issue, however, had passed the point-
counterpoint of scholastic disputation, for, as Henry Adams observes, the Virginia court had the misfortune to speak in accents
of state sovereignty and strict construction at a time when "the
national authority sprang into vigor unknown before."[48] Had it
used the tongues of angels, the state tribunal could not have overcome Story's countering opinion.

With it Story came into his own. He used his new-forged instrument of power delicately enough. The title question was
scrupulously reexamined, although there was no obligation to do
so and when indeed the sole issue of jurisdiction turned on the
right to decide it wrongly. And when the mandate went down
for a second time, it went directly to the trial court, perhaps to
spare Richmond sensibilities and perhaps to avoid the possibility
of a second defiance. But on the basic issue of power and of the
federal judiciary as the final judge of that power, Story delivered
his judgment with the incisiveness of a diamond-cutter's stroke.
There was not a trace of the nervousness with which he closed
his admiralty opinion, nor of the duplicative logic which had dis-
figured his circuit decree in the case of the recaptured prize.

Rather, now he manifested, par excellence, an assured certitude.
Characteristic was the beginning, in which he seemed to go out
of his way to demolish the cornerstone of the *Courant* opinion
with the assertive declaration that "the constitution was not . . .
necessarily carved out of existing state sovereignties, nor a surrender of powers already existing in state institutions . . ."[49]
What, then, was its source? In an echo of his youthful preoccupa-

[47] *Ibid.*, at 28.
[48] H. Adams, *Madison*, Vol. II, Bk. IX, 191.
[49] 1 WHEATON at 325.

tion with general will and the social contract, Story submitted that it was "emphatically, as the preamble of the Constitution declares, by 'the people of the United States.' "[50] Then, reminiscent of his footnote disposition of the Massachusetts admiralty controversy, he sought to prove his point by citing one of the very amendments designed to hold the central government to the strict letter of its authority: "the powers not delegated to the United States by the constitution, nor prohibited by it to the states, are reserved to the *states* respectively, or *to the people*."[51] Given this source and this character for federal powers, it was a fairly easy matter to make the opinion a didactic treatise on the nature and function of the federal judiciary. Did the Judiciary Act of 1789 grant too much power to the national government's judicial arm? Nonsense, Story asserted, any constitutional infirmity in the act arose because it granted too little. ("If, then, it is the duty of Congress to vest the judicial power of the United States, it is a duty to vest the *whole judicial power*. The [constitutional] language, if imperative as one part, is imperative as to all."[52]) Then followed an elaboration of the portions of the Federalist Papers dealing with judicial jurisdiction, which wound up with a luminous and precise aphorism of a final federal superintendence over the state judiciaries in all constitutional proceedings: "It is the *case*, then, and not *the court*, that gives the jurisdiction."[53]

To be sure, there was far more to the opinion, but the terse sentence tells the story. Its brilliantly epigrammatic quality raises the question whether Chief Justice Marshall was as remote from the case as his self-disqualification suggests. Story's son has remarked on the stylistic anomaly of the opinion,[54] and Story himself wrote a cryptic sentence that Marshall "concurred in every word of it."[55] Yet it is also certain that Marshall did not dictate

[50] *Ibid.*, 324.
[51] *Ibid.*, 325.
[52] *Ibid.*, 330.
[53] *Ibid.*, 338.
[54] W. W. Story, I, 257.
[55] Letter to George Ticknor, Jan. 22, 1831, in W. W. Story, II, 49.

the opinion and Story merely sign it. The categorical assertion that Congress *had* to give the full range of judicial powers to a national judiciary has far more in it of Story than of Marshall, and the work is otherwise characterized, conceptually and verbally, with a multitude of Story hallmarks.

Rather, the authorship seems a joint one. "Much of the opinion," says Henry Adams, "bore the stamp of Marshall's mind; much showed the turn of Story's intelligence . . . the same principle lay beneath the whole."[56] Manifestly, Marshall and Story must have discussed, if not the case, at least its principles time and time again. Against this background the epigram, as well as the other swathes of Marshallian prose, merely attests that Story had an extraordinary recall for what he heard as well as what he read and therefore reproduced verbatim, consciously or otherwise, Marshall's remarks on the subject.[57]

However, the test of the opinion does not lie in what Story (or Marshall) had to say. The Supreme Court had spoken before on its asserted role in the constitutional design when it heard the suit of the private citizen against sovereign Georgia back in 1793.[58] In that case the power and brilliance of the *seriatim* opinions of James Wilson and John Jay were every inch the equal of the Story–Marshall product in the final *Fairfax* proceeding. Yet, in establishing the basic relationship of state sovereignty and federal judicial power, it was the latter opinion which passed the test of survival in a triply ironic tour de force. It was the Republican Court which succeeded where the Federalist Court had failed. It did so on a far more marginal salient of constitutional law. It did so through the medium of old Cushing's successor, who cast into systematic, comprehensive and extreme form Cushing's concept of the Court as the "common umpire."[59]

---

[56] H. Adams, *Madison*, Vol. II, Bk. IX, 191.
[57] I am indebted to Prof. Mortimer Schwartz, co-editor with John C. Hogan of *Joseph Story* (1959) for this theory, which he suggested in private correspondence; see also Beveridge, IV, 164, and Commager, "Joseph Story," in *Gaspar Bacon Lectures* (1953), 48.
[58] *Chisholm v. Georgia*, 2 DALLAS 419 (1793).
[59] *Ibid.*, 469.

Yet, in the transformation of a union of sovereignties to a sovereign union, any error of the Federalist Court lay not so much in failure of vision as in prematurity of response. For the message of that Court was an idea which had to await its season. The season came in 1816 when Justice Joseph Story gave his answer to the question put by Justice James Wilson a quarter century earlier:

The question to be determined is, whether this State, so respectable, and whose claim soars so high, is amenable to the jurisdiction of the Supreme Court of the *United States*. The question, important in itself, will depend on others, more important still; and, may, perhaps, be ultimately resolved into one no less *radical* than this—"do the people of the *United States* form a NATION?"[60]

[60] *Ibid.*, 453. And, generally, see Harris, *The Judicial Power of the United States* (1940).

PART FOUR

The Great Term

CHAPTER XI

1816: The Year of Assertion

ARRIVALS AND DEPARTURES

"I am glad to hear of the safe arrival and health of our worthy President," an ambitious bank clerk wrote Secretary of the Navy Benjamin W. Crowninshield in early 1816. "Please make my respects to him and inform him that we are all well at home."[1] Title and tone suggested James Madison as the object of the remarks. In point of fact, the clerk's message concerned Joseph Story, recently arrived in Washington for the new term of the Supreme Court. Mr. Justice Story as we know, was also president of the Merchants' Bank of Salem, and it was under the latter title that the clerk of the bank, out of mixed servility and presumption, chose to refer to him.

No one seemed particularly concerned that Story held both judicial and corporate office. On the contrary, the Blackstonian division of corporations into *"civil and eleemosynary,"*[2] that is, into organs of government and instruments of philanthropy, made it quite proper that a man prominent in the world of affairs should undertake supplementary public service as a bank president. Certainly this was the case at Merchants' Bank, where

[1] John Treadwell to Secretary Benjamin W. Crowninshield, Feb. 13, 1816, in Crowninshield Papers.
[2] Blackstone, *Commentaries*, I, 458.

Secretary Crowninshield had been the first president and Justice Story the second of an institution that was bound by so many charter obligations to the state and the public as to make it, theoretically at least, as much an instrument of communal welfare as a vehicle of private enterprise.[3] And nowhere was the conception of corporate organization as being of a quasi-public nature better shown than in the vocabulary of the day. "[W]hen I was a boy, and for many years afterwards," went one recollection of early-nineteenth-century New England, " 'the Corporation,' in common conversation, always meant the [Harvard] College Corporation . . ."[4]

Yet each day separated the facts a little further from the theory, and the growing discrepancy was evidenced in the first changeover in the presidency of the Salem bank. "Our Merchant's Bank," mourned Dr. Bentley, "by passing from the Crowninshield interest to the Story . . . has not the same friends."[5] Not that Dr. Bentley was an unprejudiced witness as to Story ("the Ambitious wretch"[6]), but his comment did bear witness to the increasingly proprietary nature of the corporate organization. Changing corporate character was in turn but one facet of a revolution in credit, enterprise, and industralization—a revolution whose roots went far back in history but which was flowering spectacularly in the boom times that followed the War of 1812. The resultant change in economic attitudes both reflected and reinforced a new nationalism, which was working a parallel political mutation of its own.

In this era of change, it was highly appropriate that Joseph Story should hold the office of corporation president, for his career and philosophy particularly exemplified the passing of one order and the arrival of another. It was also appropriate that the corporation should be a bank, for the rise of banking cut the fabric of tradition with an especial sharpness. Though the sig-

[3] See *Mass. Special Laws, 1806–1814,* IV, ch. 82.
[4] Theophilus Parsons, II, *Memoir of Theophilus Parsons* (1861), 285.
[5] Bentley, IV, 347.
[6] *Ibid.,* 297.

nificance of the change was barely grasped and rarely articulated, the growing importance of banking amounted to a revolution in the traditional system of credit, which forced profound changes in outlook and values. Sharply challenged were the old agrarian views under which gold and silver, like fields and flocks, were the true essence of wealth. Rather, wealth was changing in form to the intangible—to paper bank notes, deposit entries on bank ledgers, shares in banks, in turnpikes, in canals, and in insurance companies. More important, perhaps, debt was no longer necessarily the badge of improvidence or misfortune. And from the creditor's point of view debt, in the form of bank notes or bank deposits, became an instrument of power.

The consequences of this revolution could be seen in the behavior of the party of Jefferson, Madison, and Story, which was now changing its name from Republican to Democrat, and changing its principles even faster. In the beginning, it had denounced banking with the same agrarian fervor with which it praised states' rights and strict construction of the Constitution. Back in 1803, young Joseph Story had been one of the principal guests at an Independence Day dinner at which a characteristically Jeffersonian toast had made a heavy-handed comparison of banking with the Newfoundland fisheries: "To Banking: May our only Banks be the Grand Banks and my our *Bankers* be rich indeed."[7] Yet in that very month, President Jefferson signaled the passing of the old order with a counsel to make all banks Republican. Two years later, in the Massachusetts legislature, Representative Joseph Story responded by discreetly lending his influence to secure bank charters for his copartisans.

Even more significant was the change in the party's attitude toward a federal,[8] or "national" (to use the then current vocabulary), bank. In 1791, Congressman James Madison, speaking in the accents of strict construction and assailing the heresy of implied

---

[7] Manuscript Program, Crowninshield Papers.
[8] Hammond's deliberately anachronistic "federal bank" is followed here. See Hammond, *Banks and Politics in America* (1957), 205.

powers, had vainly attacked the organization of such an institution as unconstitutional; in 1811, Joseph Story, as Speaker of the Massachusetts House, apparently helped bring the institution to an end when the assembly over which he presided petitioned the commonwealth's congressional delegation not to renew the federal bank's charter. Yet by 1815 the deleterious wartime and peacetime consequences of state-chartered banking corporations upon commerce, currency, and prices prompted President Madison to forsake states' rights for Hamiltonian centralism and to call for a second Bank of the United States. In this appeal he had legal and constitutional fortification, for Mr. Justice Story, his most distinguished judicial appointee, delivered the extrajudicial opinion that a federal bank was one of the "enlarged and liberal institutions [by which] the Government of the United States will be endeared to the people."[9] A proposal to charter such an institution had been introduced in the session of Congress that had met shortly before Story's 1816 trip to Washington, and its pendency prompted a postscript to the clerk's letter to Secretary Crowninshield: "If the Bill to establish a national bank should pass we must beg your good offices in procuring ours to be made a branch, if it will be for our advantage. The Judge and you will consult on this subject."[10]

THE DEUTERO-FEDERALIST

At the time of his arrival in Washington in early 1816, Joseph Story was thirty-six years old, but he had already sat for over four years on the bench of the Supreme Court. Appropriately perhaps, there was a touch of baldness around his temples and a plumpness in his figure that helped offset a certain vivacity and even boyishness of manner. One could easily see the judge and

[9] Joseph Story to Nathaniel Williams, Feb. 22, 1815, in W. W. Story, I, 253, 254.
[10] John Treadwell to Secretary Crowninshield, Feb. 13, 1816, Crowninshield Papers.

bank president in him, and if one looked hard enough, he might still catch a glimpse of the curlyheaded, poetry-writing brawler of 1800 who had relished Rousseau, defended Jefferson, and denounced the Alien and Sedition Acts. His *embonpoint* appropriately exemplified his and his party's transformation to the service of commerce, property, and nationalism. Story was in the forefront of the turnabout and claimed virtually every one of the Federalist Party canons as his own. In fact, it was difficult to see what he omitted in his enthusiastic advocacy, which covered everything from a standing army to a national system of bankruptcy.

The banking and credit revolution made it particularly logical for a federal bankruptcy system—briefly tried under the Federalists and repealed by the Jeffersonians virtually out of hand—to be reinstated. In this case, Story needed no political transformation in the party to press for the revival. Demand for a bankruptcy law could draw on the very philanthropy that was the cornerstone of the Jeffersonian ethic. For the same humanitarian sensibility now burgeoning in proposals for education, for aid to the handicapped, and for mitigation or even abolition of slavery emphatically rejected the hitherto commonplace idea, expressed in Dr. Bentley's diary, that "the terrour of Imprisonment"[11] should be the natural consequence of hard times and business failure.

Fortifying this ethic, the combination of bank presidency and judicial office gave Story a particularly perceptive appreciation of the need for accommodating national commerce with a national law of debtor and creditor. Virtually all state laws operated to the procedural, and often the substantive, disadvantage of out-of-state lenders. Moreover, the provisions of these laws were patchwork personified, ranging from the stern Blackstonian canon making a debtor liable with his "body, lands, and goods"[12] to a variety of emendations, some humanitarian and some otherwise. The proposal that this disarray be replaced with a national bankruptcy act

[11] Bentley, IV. 398.
[12] *Ehrlich's Blackstone*, ed. J. W. Ehrlich (San Carlos, 1959), 706.

provoked what Story would later call a "strange medley of the most opposite views."[13]

There were many lines of cleavage in the controversy. Liberal construction of the Constitution collided with strict. British precedent traversed the American sense of experiment. Debtors and creditors were found on both sides of the status quo, depending on the laws of particular states. Some jurisdictions gave the real estate of planters and farmers almost complete immunity from execution. Others afforded a creditor the most summary methods of jailing his debtor on initial process and keeping him imprisoned virtually for life. Each set of advantages might be lost if a national bankruptcy law were enacted, and this lent a special interest to the question of the relationship between the bankruptcy powers given the federal government by the Constitution and the residual right of states to provide for insolvency, to free the person and property of debtors from oppressive claims, and to regulate process and procedure in their own courts. The constitutional problem was further complicated by the ban on any state legislation that impaired the obligation of contract. On these issues, Associate Justice Washington, an old-line Federalist and senior member of the Supreme Court, had taken one polar position. While sitting on circuit in 1814, Washington had voided the Pennsylvania insolvency statute on the ground that the mere grant of bankruptcy power to the federal government automatically annulled all state legislation that bore on the subject of insolvency.[14] Yet, in setting out such an opinion in a judicial record, Washington was a latecomer. Two years earlier, young Justice Story, sitting on circuit for the first time, tersely had implied the same idea in dictum.[15]

Story's action was predictable, for although a combination of motives underlay his support for a bankruptcy act, such legislation was particularly close to his heart because of its potential

[13] Joseph Story to John Brazer Davis, Dec. 11, 1821, in *Proceedings of the Mass. Historical Society*, XLIX (1916), 183.
[14] *Golden v. Prince*, 10 Fed. Cases 542 (1814).
[15] *Van Reimsdyck v. Kane*, 28 Fed. Cases 1062 (1812).

enhancement of the prestige and power of the federal judiciary. Yet it would have been contrary to the nature of things for the Supreme Court to resist the centralizing trends already transforming the Presidency and Congress, and Story's concept of the judicial function made him uniquely attuned to the spirit of the times. Appointed to destroy (or so some thought), he remained to fulfill.

As we have seen, he began badly enough, sitting in silent dissent when the inherent criminal jurisdiction of the federal courts was denied by the narrowest of margins, and, similarly, his first opinions were the epitome of taciturn self-effacement. This image of the model Jeffersonian judge quickly vanished, and his opinions —categorical, lengthy, citation-studded—exemplified a change which, in terms of private law, asserted an exclusive federal admiralty jurisdiction covering perhaps half the commercial litigation of the country[16] and, with respect to public law, proclaimed the Supreme Court the superior of all state tribunals in constitutional proceedings.[17]

As part of the transformation, he had written a commentary on a bankruptcy proposal pending in the first session of the Fourteenth Congress and had sent it on to the Attorney General. Indeed, he welcomed what a future President feared—that such powers would bring "the jurisdiction of the federal courts into the bosom of every community . . . and make those courts the arbiters in almost every case of contract."[18] And in addition to this, he had drawn a bill, complete with commentary, designed to give the Court common-law criminal powers and to do far more. Indeed, it proposed to eliminate existing restrictions on the national courts and to give them the full range (as seen by Justice Story) of constitutional powers. His proposal was the jurisdictional counterpart of another bill which suggested material support through increased judicial salaries, still at the level

---

[16] *De Lovio v. Boit*, 7 FED. CASE. 418 (1815).
[17] *Martin v. Hunter's Lessee*, 1 WHEATON 304 (1816).
[18] James Buchanan, in *Annals of Congress*, XXXIX (1822), 1284-85.

first established in 1789. Hence, the clerk's letter on the concerns of the Merchants' Bank was but one item on a bursting schedule which guaranteed that if there were any conflict of interest between Story the banker and Story the judge, the character and press of judicial concerns would override those of the bank during Story's stay in Washington in early 1816.

CLAIM AND CONSEQUENCE

The intended sponsor of Story's judiciary bill was Representative William Pinkney of Baltimore, the uncrowned king of the American bar, who at this critical juncture accepted the ministry to Russia and transferred his attention from legislative to diplomatic concerns. Story's judiciary proposals were thereupon placed in the ineffectual hands of some obscure Federalist members of Congress.

The fortunes of the federal courts were far from lost, however. On March 20, 1816, Story delivered the opinion in the case from Virginia, *Martin v. Hunter's Lessee*,[19] asserting the power of federal courts to review the decisions of state judiciaries in all constitutional cases. Possibly with an eye on the fate of his judiciary bill, he further insisted that Congress was constitutionally *required* to give the federal courts their full jurisdiction. Moreover, even though five out of the seven members of the Supreme Court had been drawn from the party of Thomas Jefferson, not one justice dissented. One, however, did enter a concurring opinion that varied considerably in outlook and attitude from that of Story. William Johnson of South Carolina, senior Republican appointee, rejected Story's Federalist logic and attempted to rationalize the old and the new in a theory of concurrent powers that made the Supreme Court the final arbiter of constitutional cases but also insisted that such authority operated only upon litigants and not upon state courts.

The concurrence was half as long as Story's opinion. For this

[19] 1 WHEATON 304 (1816).

reason, probably, it was the first in print, appearing in the quasi-official *National Intelligencer* of April 6. A few days previously, the newspaper had noted the adjournment of the Court "after a session of nearly seven weeks"[20] and, apparently concerned more with speed than with substance, remarked approvingly that "the records of no court of appeals in the Union exhibit such instance of dispatch of business where the questions in dispute are so momentous."[21] Back home in Salem, Story seemed to find the compliment outweighed by the publicity given Johnson's views, for he dispatched an urgent letter to the Court's reporter:

> I observed in the National Intelligencer of Saturday last Judge Johnson's opinion in the case of Martin v. Hunter. I cannot say that I think it drawn up in his best manner. But some of his opinions will, I fear, have an unfavourable effect upon the Judicial Bill now before Congress. I wish very much therefore to have the opinion of the Court published as soon as may be in New York, & republished in the National Intelligencer. Will you procure this to be done without delay? Cannot you also write something in the National Advocate in favour of the bill for increasing the salaries of the judges, & the bill for giving a compensation to the reporter? Both of their objects are so purely national, that it seems to me, that they ought to be put upon grounds of public policy.[22]

The reporter responded with explanations, promised to make amends, and then closed with a comment whose impertinence lost none of its edge because of his unofficial status: "Mr. Justice Johnson places the decision of the Court on a quicksand—yours

[20] *National Intelligencer*, March 23, 1816.
[21] *Ibid.*
[22] Joseph Story to Henry Wheaton, April 11, 1816, in Wheaton Papers, Pierpont Morgan Library, New York, N.Y. (quoted with permission and hereinafter cited as Wheaton Papers). This letter obviously negates the conclusion of "extraordinary action of withholding the Court's opinion from the newspapers and giving them, instead, Justice Johnson's strange and self-contradictory views . . ." (Crosskey, *Politics and the Constitution* [1953; hereinafter cited as Crosskey], II, 1244.)

on a rock. And I am therefore the more anxious to see it before the public."[23] Nonetheless, reporter Wheaton had a point. As far back as the Washington administration, the relationship between state sovereignty and national judicial power had been sensitive and critical, but if the subject were to be touched at all, it was desirable to deal with it firmly. Probably it should have been so dealt with, despite the fact that the last time the Court had asserted its power over a sovereign state, the Eleventh Amendment had subsequently ousted it from the jurisdiction it had claimed. If such an incident had occurred back in Federalist times, there was reason to be apprehensive, even in the Democratic-Republican Thermidor. Indeed, some two weeks before the *Martin* decision, but possibly prompted by the fact that the case was pending, Senator Nathan Sanford of New York had introduced a proposed constitutional amendment authorizing the President, upon appropriate address by Congress, to remove from office any federal judge "when . . . the public good will be promoted."[24]

Of more direct interest to Story at the moment was the spate of bills in which he was interested. The answer came soon enough. Congress adjourned on April 30 without action on any of them save one—the rechartering of the federal bank. Perhaps this neglect of the legislation concerning the judiciary was vengeance for the *Martin* decision. Perhaps it was merely inertia. Or perhaps both these factors combined with the Johnson opinion to shift the scale at a moment of delicate balance. Whatever the reason, the failure of legislation was a cruel blow to Story and carried a particular sting. For Congress, which had already increased its own compensation in response to the postwar price level, had postponed indefinitely a similar adjustment for the judiciary. Story did not explicitly suggest that this was the consequence of his *Martin* opinion, but by directing his criticism at particular states he did hint at the powerful hand of Virginia. ("I am

[23] Letter from Henry Wheaton, April 19, 1816, in Wheaton Papers.
[24] *Annals of Congress*, XXIX (1816), 171.

ashamed of Maryland, for adding her vote to the disgraceful abandonment of the Judges."[25])

In 1811, the inadequacy of the $3,500 salary of an associate justice had made Story hesitate in accepting appointment to the Court. The wartime inflation of 1812–1815 cut the purchasing power of the sum even more, a development that pressed Story particularly hard, for he had come to the Court without inherited or accumulated fortune, but with a wife, two small children, and a widowed mother whom he helped support. Hence, and notwithstanding his dislike of supplication, he felt impelled to mention the "utterly inadequate" judicial salaries in sending his judiciary bill to Pinckney and to insist "how injurious to the public interests a much longer continuance of this false economy will be."[26] But Pinckney's preoccupation with his forthcoming diplomatic service held the same sad consequences for Story's salary that it had for Story's jurisdiction bill. In a purely personal way, however, the Congressman more than made up for any legislative neglect, for he offered Story his Baltimore retainers, which were worth at least ten thousand dollars a year. For Story, the offer must have been an ironic reminder of his repeated efforts in the early days of a meager Salem practice to secure a professional connection in the bustling Maryland city. But there were also memories of the occasions in the Massachusetts legislature when he broke party ranks to prevent the Federalist bench of Massachusetts from being starved into surrender. The latter memories were the more characteristic ones, and they predetermined his response to Pinckney's offer. To be sure, he was tempted. "You know that I am poor," he wrote a relative, "and that an acquisition of property would be highly grateful to me."[27] He even wasted some time before returning his answer. Predictably, it was a declaration, "notwithstanding the meanness of Con-

[25] Letter to Nathaniel Williams, May 22, 1816, in W. W. Story, I, 279.
[26] Commentary on a bill to extend the judicial system of the United States, probably addressed to William Pinckney, in W. W. Story, I, 301. Internal evidence suggests that it was written in January of 1816.
[27] Letter to Stephen White, Feb. 26, 1816, in W. W. Story, I, 278.

gress, to remain on the Bench."[28] He had every reason so to declare. His opinion in *Martin v. Hunter's Lessee* on the Court's constitutional power was intended to be not an end, but a beginning.

[28] Letter to Nathaniel Williams, May 22, 1816, *ibid.*, 279.

CHAPTER XII

1817: The Year of Deployment

The groundwork for the vindication of Story's *Martin* opinion was laid even before the year 1816 was out. It derived from three widely separated events—a statute passed that June in New Hampshire, a lawsuit filed that October in Massachusetts, and a bank opened that December in Maryland. However diverse, these matters were all to occasion the assertion of a strong national judicial power. Story was associated in an extrajudicial way with some facet of each.

A NEW HAMPSHIRE UNIVERSITY— AND AN APPOINTMENT

The first episode began in the spring of 1816, almost as Story was returning home to Salem from the completed term of the Court. Over the border in New Hampshire, William Plumer, an old friend, was elected governor and carried the Democrats into control of the state legislature. Plumer won office in an unusual campaign whose issues involved a college and a court. The first was Dartmouth, where the self-perpetuating trustees had exercised their rights under a royal charter to turn the president out of office, only to see his cause taken up by the Democrats. The second issue concerned the state's highest tribunal. A Federalist law of 1813 had swept the bench clean and instituted, according to the Democratic protests, a "Supreme Judicial Court, which exists by an *act of usurpation* now disgracing our Statute book."[1] The polemic could claim some eminent judicial or, more precisely, extrajudicial authority, for Plumer noted in his diary that Joseph Story had "mentioned, of his own accord," that the law establishing the new judiciary was unconstitutional.[2]

After the election, amends were quickly made in both ousters. On June 27, 1818, Plumer approved two remedial statutes. The first replaced the Federalist judicial system with a reconstituted Democratic one; the second converted Dartmouth College into Dartmouth University, raised the number of trustees from twelve to twenty-one, and, in a modified imitation of Harvard, placed the reformed institution under the superintendence of a board of overseers. The two measures, for all their local associations, also reflected a general attitude of reform. Two other statutes, passed at the same time as the Dartmouth legislation, bear witness to the trend. One was an act revising methods of execution against turnpike and other similar corporations and, like the Dartmouth Act, was framed on the theory that the state could control and change at will the operations and incidents of institutions of its own creation; the other act was for the relief of imprisoned debtors, and was a product of the same rising philanthropic sense that saw in education an important instrument of human betterment.

Indeed, for the reform of Dartmouth Governor Plumer had been in touch with the aging Jefferson, himself busy with plans for the proposed University of Virginia, and Plumer had no doubt whatever as to the legal or moral rectitude of the legislation. Immensely ambitious on behalf of the reformed institution, he sent a formal announcement to his old friend Mr. Justice Story: "You are appointed one of the Board of Overseers of DARTMOUTH UNIVERSITY; the certificate of your appointment,

[1] *New Hampshire Patriot*, Oct. 31, 1815.
[2] Plumer, 431.

and a copy of the Act amending the Charter of that institution is [sic] herewith enclosed."[3] Story seemed an ideal choice. He was well known in New Hampshire, where he had tried cases as a lawyer and where he now held circuit court twice a year. His long-time concern with education ranged from membership on the Salem school committee to current service with the Society to Promote Theological Education at Harvard. His literary credentials included not only works on the law but a book of poetry. Yet a few items might have given Plumer pause. There was the Yazoo land-fraud case, in which Story the lawyer had successfully pleaded that what a government has yielded it cannot reclaim.[4] There was a case involving a British gospel society in which Story the circuit judge had voided a New Hampshire statute allowing tenants to recover the value of improvements and made the point (particularly relevant to Dartmouth's royal charter) that "the division of an empire works no forfeiture of rights previously acquired."[5] There was a Supreme Court case involving Virginia church lands in which Mr. Justice Story had explicitly denied state power to abrogate the rights of any "private" corporation, "upon the principles of natural justice, upon the fundamental laws of every free government, upon the spirit and the letter of the constitution."[6]

Just what letter of the Constitution might have been involved in the Dartmouth reform act was suggested that autumn of 1816 when Boston's *Columbian Centinel* declared: "Any act of the legislature, altering or impairing the contract without the consent of the Trustees, must . . . be considered . . . a violation of the 10th section of the first article of the Constitution . . ."[7] Perhaps a like apprehension of constitutional infirmity prompted

Announcement of appointment, July 3, 1816, in Story Papers, Library of Congress.
Fletcher v. Peck, 6 CRANCH 87 (1810).
Society for the Propagation of the Gospel v. Wheeler, 22 FED. CASES at 63 (1814).
Terrett v. Taylor, 9 CRANCH at 52 (1815).
Columbian Centinel, Sept. 14, 1816.

Story's disengagement from Plumer's nomination. Or perhaps he prudently withdrew from the fight he saw coming when eight of the twelve trustees (thereafter called the "Octagon"[8]) elected to stand their ground, rejecting the Dartmouth Act as invalid and informing Governor Plumer that they "EXPRESSLY REFUSE TO ACT UNDER THE SAME."[9] Whether for these or for other reasons, Story did not attend the first overseers' meeting on August 29 (although he had found time to attend to Harvard's business a little earlier), and, as summer ended, Dartmouth University dropped his name from its list of overseers.[10]

A NEW YORK BANKRUPT
— AND HIS OLD COMPANION

Two overseers who did not resign were Secretary of the Navy Benjamin Crowninshield and Dr. Bentley. That the Secretary should cling to an office that the Justice declined was characteristic of their star-crossed careers. Crowninshield began life as the heir of a salem merchant-prince family; Story was one of eighteen children of a fishing-village physician in Marblehead just over the harbor. Story taught himself Homeric Greek to enter Harvard; Crowninshield, for all of Dr. Bentley's tutoring, failed of admission. However, like all the Crowninshield boys, he qualified early as master mariner and wore his title of "Captain" with dignity. Even in rapport, when Story and Crowninshield were both young Jeffersonian militants, they showed significant differences. as the report of a Federalist editor, published in 1802, indicated:

On Saturday evening, 6th Nov. Capts. Richard and Benjamin Crowninshield and Mr. Joseph Story came to my house, desir-

[8] See Current, "It Is . . . a Small College," *American Heritage*, August 1963, p. 14.

[9] *New Hampshire Patriot*, Sept. 3, 1816.

[10] See Lord, *A History of Dartmouth College, 1815-1909* (1913; hereinafter cited as Lord), 684.

ing to see me by myself. . . . Capt. B. Crowninshield informed me that they had come on unpleasant business, viz. respecting certain recent publications in my paper, of an abusive nature, and personal to him and his friends. After the business was opened by Captain Benjamin Crowninshield, Mr. Story took it up, and enlarged upon it.— He complained that he and some of his friends had, by my paper, been placed before the public in an injurious point of view . . .—that he had no objection to his arguments being fairly combated, but that he would not submit to be dragged before the public in the manner he had been.

Capt. B. Crowninshield immediately followed Mr. Story. He laboured to impress upon me, that many of my publications had been highly improper and injurious . . . that if I continued to publish such things . . . by God he would shoot me in the dark if he could not do it in the day time.[11]

In competition the two men's differences in talent and temperament showed up even more clearly. In 1808, Story bested Crowninshield in a contest for Congress. Later they served together in the state legislature, in which Story put through a pay raise for the Federalist judges over Crowninshield's unavailing objection.[12] And if Dr. Bentley may be believed, Story, moving up through the State House, deprived Crowninshield of the speakership and later virtually compelled Crowninshield to leave Salem and the Merchants' Bank for the Madison Cabinet. ("Mr. B. C. could never remove the competitions which Judge S. had created

[11] *Salem Gazette*, Nov. 12, 1802. Of interest is a communication expressing the other side of the controversy: "Cushing [the editor] . . . has come out with a pretended statement of facts and Story & Ben say only about half of it is true. The great object of it was to prove that Story said he was a writer in the Register [the local Jeffersonian paper] & that Ben dropped *sic*] something about powder or a pistol etc. The first assertion is to lay the foundation that *Story shall not be received in the Supreme Court* when he comes to apply & the other is to bind Ben over to the peace. What will not federalism attempt to carry out." (Jacob Crowninshield to Richard Crowninshield, Nov. 15, 1800, Crowninshield Papers. The letter is obviously misdated; the "1800" should be "1802." See Whitney, "The Crowninshields of Salem," in *Essex Institute Historical Collections*, XCIV [1958], 28, n.97.)
[12] *Salem Gazette*, June 16, 1809.

. . . so that his advancement in this neighborhood . . . was hope-less."[13])

Richard Crowninshield, the third man on the nocturnal visit to the Federalist editor, shortly after the episode and perhaps because of it sought his fortune in New York. He led a spectacular life there, failing in business, marrying an Irish girl (it was hard to tell which shocked Dr. Bentley more), and almost landing in debtors' prison. In November of 1811, as "an insolvent debtor . . . being prosecuted and impleaded,"[14] he sought the protection of a newly enacted New York insolvency statute, listed his creditors, assigned his property, and requested a discharge from his debts. A creditor named Josiah Sturgis, who had lent Crowninshield over $1,400 only weeks before the insolvency statute was passed, opposed the discharge. It was nonetheless granted, and Crowninshield returned to the Salem area, where he recouped his fortunes in a textile enterprise. Yet he seemed to succeed too well; Sturgis, the New York discharge notwithstanding, filed suit on Crowninshield's notes at the October 1816 term of Story's circuit court in Boston.

A BANK IN BALTIMORE
—AND A BANKER IN SALEM

In December of 1816, the federal bank opened a branch in Baltimore. It was unthinkable that the institution should fail to

[13] Bentley, IV, 304. Another indication of the Story–Crowninshield relationship can be seen in a letter from Mrs. Crowninshield to her husband: "Yesterday afternoon I had the pleasure of seeing Judge Story . . . He told me you may be at home in May . . . Does he say true? . . . He likewise says you have fine times with the girls in the house . . . [I also understand there are] so many ladies that almost every evening you send for music and dance. Now you have never told me this and I have many times asked you how you pass your evenings but not a word in reply. I hope in the course of your evenings you sometimes recollect you have a wife at home peering over her knitting work and two daughters studying their lessons by her side." (Letter dated March 21, 1815, Crowninshield Papers.)
[14] *Sturges v. Crowninshield,* Statement of Case, manuscript record on file at the National Archives, Washington, D. C. The official style misspells the plaintiff's name, which was Sturgis.

be represented there, for the rich and enterprising Chesapeake metropolis, which once had called, sirenlike, to young lawyer Story, was vigorously contesting staid Philadelphia's status as the nation's financial capital. In fact, Baltimore had made a spirited bid against the Quaker City to be the headquarters of the federal bank.

Maryland's reaction differed somewhat from that which prevailed elsewhere up and down the seaboard and even far into the interior. Selection as a site of a branch of the Bank of the United States was to Baltimore a disappointing consolation prize. To virtually every other American city, however, possession of one of these semiautonomous banking offices represented both financial advantage and civic prestige.

To be sure, civic pride and local self-interest were but one part of the spectrum of public reaction to the federal bank in general and to branches in particular. The old controversy over liberal versus strict constitutional construction flared again, sometimes in good faith, sometimes as camouflage for a bewildering variety of interests which, like the bankruptcy controversy, cut across sectional, occupational, and social lines. Old-line Jeffersonians candidly reversed themselves and supported the bank. New strict-constructionists expressed doubt over congressional power to authorize branches outside Washington. Hard-money conservatives saw the bank's note-issue function as dangerous radicalism; inflation-biased speculators, inside and outside banking, found the prospect of its regulatory hand intolerable.

Little hostility, however, was apparent on the Salem scene, where, even before the chartering act was passed, the clerk of the Merchants' Bank was writing Story on the possibility of securing a branch in the area, and by October of 1816, the Merchants' board of directors was locked in a spirited contest with Boston for the prize. The issue was never really in doubt. Notwithstanding whatever fortification to Salem's claim might have been lent by Mr. Justice Story's extrajudicial endorsement of the second federal bank, the town was passed over and Boston chosen as the branch city. By December 7, 1816, the office there was in operation. Undismayed, the Merchants' directors marked the turn of the year with a formal resolution on the last day of 1816, asking Story to request the Boston branch of the federal bank for the governmental deposits—mainly customs money—originating in Salem. If Story made the request it went unheeded. In any event, the directors moved to present their case to a higher court through an especially persuasive advocate, declaring

> that it be of great importance to this bank to obtain the deposits of the U. States revenue from the public officers in this vicinity, [and] that the President be requested on his journey to Washington to make application to the President and directors of the National Bank requesting that they would authorize the Branch at Boston to collect the . . . revenues in this vicinity through the agency of this bank.[15]

GOOD FEELINGS AND BAD

The 1817 journey to Washington was one that Story especially wished to make. Replacing Pinckney as his legislative surrogate was young Congressman Daniel Webster from the Sixth (Portsmouth) New Hampshire District. From the second session of the Fourteenth Congress, Webster reported good news on the possibility of passing a bankruptcy law and even showed some optimism in regard to Story's judiciary bill. Webster, Dartmouth '01, was an unusually astute judge of men and events, and his opinion meant a good deal. Indeed, his talent had already been recognized at his alma mater, where both sides had sought his services. He had originally more or less committed himself to the president in the latter's battle with the trustees, but later effected a disengagement and joined the Octagon, his presence ("the Portsmouth Oracle"[16] and theories ("Most horrid! Oh, most foul and horrid!"[17]) badly unsettling the New Hampshire Democrats.

[15] Directors' resolution, Jan. 17, 1817.
[16] *New Hampshire Patriot*, Jan. 28, 1817.
[17] *Ibid.*

The Story–Webster relationship was the acme of reciprocal convenience and cordiality. Moreover, it should be emphasized that the relationship was compatible with then contemporary standards for judicial interests and behavior. No one was particularly scandalized by Webster's legislative activity on Story's behalf, nor by Webster's action in requesting Story's intercession with the reconstituted New Hampshire court to secure a clerkship for an associate. Between the voluble and effervescent Story and the intense, brooding, and comparatively taciturn Webster, prevailed the strong attraction that sometimes unites very different men—and perhaps the antipathy between Story and Dr. Bentley was that which often occurs between men who are very much alike.

Certainly, Webster's prophetic vision seemed justified by the favorable climate for the judiciary that Story found on his arrival in Washington. No more seemed to be heard of the Sanford amendment proposing removal of judges, and, on the positive side, the bill to give the Court its official, paid reporter was gathering new strength. Best of all, in his last annual message to Congress, President Madison had cited both the status of the Supreme Court and "the juridical reputation of their country"[18] in proposing that the Justices be relieved of circuit riding.

There were some countervailing items. Perhaps Story regretted that Mr. Chief Justice Marshall drew heavily on the theory of concurrent powers in endorsing the reporter bill:

> [E]ven in cases where the decisions of the Supreme Court are not to be considered as authority except in the courts of the United States, some advantage may be derived from their being known. It is certainly to be wished that independent tribunals having concurrent jurisdiction over the same subject should concur in the principles on which they determine the causes coming before them.[19]

Certainly also, he must have been irked to learn that his bank's

[18] Eighth Annual Message, Dec. 3, 1816, in Richardson (ed.), *Messages and Papers of the Presidents* (10v., 1896; hereinafter cited as Richardson), I, 577.
[19] Marshall to Senator Dudley Chase, Feb. 7, 1817, in Crosskey, II, 1246.

pleas to the federal bank had gone unrewarded, for he received yet another resolution from the Merchants' directors to "make known the state of our money market to the Treasury Department and to respectfully request the head of that department to cause the customhouse bonds to be collected by this bank."[20]

The frustration attending the Merchants' quest for governmental deposits foreshadowed other failures. Despite Webster's optimistic estimate, Congress adjourned without taking action on the bankruptcy bill. Similarly lost were Story's judiciary bill and the proposal to mitigate the hardships of circuit riding. But Story's trip was not wasted. On the contrary, the Monroe inauguration alone made it worthwhile. Moreover, the 1817 term had its interesting and, indeed, significant aspects. The expanding Western frontier manifested itself in the question whether a buffalo road in Kentucky might be an appropriate item in a land description, with Story and Marshall dividing on the point.[21] The great expansion of commercial enterprise which was transforming the character of corporate organization was reflected in a revisionary Story opinion on negotiable instruments. (The old doctrine on this subject, it declared, "was made at a time when the principles respecting mercantile contracts were not generally understood."[22]) And finally the *Martin* opinion was, in effect, restated in the review of judgments called up on writs of error.[23] More important, the Court itself received a vote of confidence when the bill providing its official, paid reporter was finally signed into law. Once again, the Justices left Washington with the compliments of the Administration's unofficial gazette on their "long session" of "six weeks without interruption," and with the paper repeating the Presidential recommendation that they be relieved of "the extremely fatiguing duties" of circuit riding.[24]

However, the Justices were not the only ones riding that spring

---

[20] Directors' resolution, Feb. 14, 1817.
[21] *Shipp v. Miller's Heirs*, 2 WHEATON 316 (1817). See also Crosskey, II, 831
[22] *Raborg v. Peyton*, 2 WHEATON at 387 (1817).
[23] *Slocum v. Mayberry*, 2 WHEATON 1 (1817); *Otis v. Walter*, 2 WHEATON 18 (1817); *Inglee v. Coolidge*, 2 WHEATON 363 (1817).
[24] *National Intelligencer*, March 17, 1817.

of 1817. Shortly after his inauguration, President James Monroe embarked on a grand tour of the United States. In sharp contrast to the simplicity with which Jefferson had sought to surround the Presidential office, Monroe traveled in a coach-and-four with outriders, and was greeted with booming cannon and military reviews—all reminiscent of the pomp and circumstance of Federalist days and of George Washington's tour of New England almost thirty years before. Yet there were differences. When Washington came to Marblehead, ten-year-old Joseph Story must have been indistinguishable from the village urchins who, by his own account, were his daily companions. When James Monroe came to Salem, however, the high spot of the visit was the July evening when the President "honored with his presence a brilliant assembly at Judge Story's."[25]

The Boston *Columbian Centinel* declared that the Monroe trip exemplified a new era of good feelings. Although the description involved some exaggeration, it received considerable support when the President crossed into New Hampshire. There Monroe accepted honorary degrees from both Dartmouth College and Dartmouth University, as the two contending institutions fashioned a temporary truce in the controversy, which now centered around a replevin suit by the Octagon trustees against the university treasurer for the college records. The Octagon lawyers had rested the bulk of their case on two asserted violations of the New Hampshire Constitution. The first was that the Dartmouth legislation was essentially a forfeiture and, therefore, a matter of judicial rather than legislative competence. The second was that the statute confiscated private property and represented an expropriatory violation of natural law that even the judiciary could not enforce. (Story had relied on both points in voiding the tenant-improvement statute in the British gospel society case.) Finally, almost as an afterthought, came a plea that the royal charter was a federally protected contract, and the reformatory statute an unconstitutional impairment of it.

This sequence of theories represented a prudent strategic estimate, for the current judicial exegesis of the contract clause suggested that, notwithstanding the burgeoning deutero-Federalism, strict construction of this clause would continue. Or at least such seemed to be the import of a decision rendered at the April, 1817, term of the United States Circuit Court for New York.[26] In the decision Mr. Justice Brockholst Livingston had validated the retroactive application of the very law whose protection Richard Crowninshield had sought years before and was now asserting in defending the suit against him before Story's circuit court. Livingston rejected claims that the statute conflicted with both the contract clause and the bankruptcy power of Congress and, in a powerful opinion, ably matched, point for point, the contrary views of Justice Washington in *Golden v. Prince*.[27]

Between them, Livingston and Washington not only exhausted the constitutional issues involved, but also underlined the necessity of the Supreme Court's exercising its power of final decision. Hence, while Story, faced with the Crowninshield litigation, doubtless regretted being unable to add anything new to the analysis, he was in a tactical position to speed the issues to a conclusion. In the spring of 1817, Richard Crowninshield's counsel wrote to the creditor's attorney: "The court has desired me to inform you that the action against Captain Crowninshield will come on to be tried on Tuesday . . . He [Story] proposes that the Court shall divide and carry the case to the Sup. Court without argument or opinion here."[28]

---

[26] *Adams v. Storey,* 1 FED. CASES 141 (1817). "I presume you have heard that Judge Livingston has decided, at the circuit, our insolvent law to be *constitutional*, and that too in a contract made . . . before the passage of the Act under which the debtor was discharged." (Henry Wheaton to Joseph Story, April 17, 1817, Wheaton Papers.)

[27] 10 FED. CASES 542 (1814).

[28] William Prescott to Leverett Saltonstall, May 17, 1817, Saltonstall Papers, Massachusetts Historical Society, Boston.

CHAPTER XIII

1818: The Year of Advance

A JUDGE IN PORTSMOUTH

In a similar burst of speed, the suit of the Dartmouth College trustees was taken by consent on an agreed statement of facts to the highest state tribunal for decision on "the naked question of . . . *constitutionality*."[1] The result was a vigorous disquisition by Chief Justice William Merchant Richardson on the judicial process. ("For if a private right be thus infringed to-day, and that infringement be sanctioned by a judicial decision to-morrow, there will be next day a precedent for the violation of the rights of every man in the community."[2]) The Chief Justice also kept in mind that it was a constitution he was expounding: "[S]itting here as judges, we have nothing to do with the policy or expediency of the acts of the legislature."[3]

His opening premises established, Richardson addressed himself to the nature of corporate organization, emphasizing the associational element and proposing a new and creative analysis on the basis of the property rights involved. This, he suggested, would produce division into essentially private corporations, such as

[1] *New Hampshire Patriot*, Sept. 30, 1817.
[2] *Trustees of Dartmouth College v. Woodward*, 1 N.H. at 114 (1817).
[3] *Ibid.*

banks and manufacturing companies, and public ones, such as counties and towns. Where did Dartmouth fit into this division? "A corporation," asserted Richardson, "all of whose franchises are exercised for public purposes, is a public corporation. . . . A gift to a corporation created for public purposes is . . . a gift to the public."[4] This statement disposed of the major issues of the case. Only the constitutional question of the Dartmouth contracts remained. Here, Richardson seemed to write with an eye on Story's work as counsel and judge, for he went out of his way to distinguish the suit before him from both the Virginia church case and the Yazoo land-fraud controversy. He then noted that the contracts clause was "obviously intended to protect private rights" and must be taken "in its common and ordinary acceptation . . . [and] not . . . to limit the power of the states in relation to . . . public officers . . . or . . . civil institutions."[5] After citing marriage and divorce to prove the latter point, the Chief Justice once more reverted to Story's work, this time in an entirely different vein. He closed the opinion with a powerful affirmation of the *Martin* opinion by pointing out that there was "another tribunal where . . . our judgment [can] be reversed or affirmed, as the law of the case may seem to that tribunal to require."[6]

The losing trustees promptly took the state Chief Justice at his word and appealed to the United States Supreme Court, with the final papers and stipulations being hurriedly completed on Christmas Day of 1817. The respondents gave full cooperation. Governor Plumer declared that the Octagon trustees could have "no rational grounds for success in the National Court,"[7] and Dr. Bentley, who had been the host of the head of Dartmouth University, reported that his guest felt it would be "a service to the University . . . to have the case speedily passed on in the Su-

4 *Ibid.*, 117.
5 *Ibid.*, 132.
6 *Ibid.*, 138.
7 Current, "It Is . . . a Small College," *American Heritage*, August, 1963, p. 82.

preme Court of the United States."[8] The general optimism of the supporters of the university was based on the unlikelihood of a reversal of the New Hampshire judgment on the narrow issue of contract impairment. Webster, particularly pessimistic on the basis of "sundry sayings of a great personage,"[9] proposed that the college faction double back and try all issues *de novo* by filing new suits in Story's Circuit Court for New Hampshire.

To like effect was a contemporary letter from a Salem resident which also cited *"high authority* among us"[10] on the futility of an appeal narrowed to the contracts clause. Story may or may not have been the source of these presentiments, but there is no question that he had become firmly entangled in the controversy. Thus, the *New Hampshire Patriot* might as well have published his name when it boasted that the Dartmouth Act had been reviewed and approved by "a gentleman of the highest legal and literary attainments."[11] From the other side also came a harvest of rumors. One made Story not the reviewer but the "framer of the law";[12] another traduced him as "about to sit as a judge in a cause in which he has been a feed counsellor."[13] Doubtless the welter of suspicion and rumor made Story happy to leave for the 1818 term of the Court, at which the Dartmouth controversy might be reviewed in an atmosphere of greater detachment. And there was another pleasant aspect to his trip to Washington. For once, he seemed to be free of written requests to tend to the business of the Merchants' Bank.

A JUDGE FROM CHARLESTOWN

Notwithstanding an oral argument in which Webster reached new heights, the 1818 term of the Supreme Court adjourned with-

[8] Dr. William Bentley to Secretary Benjamin Crowninshield, Jan. 21, 1818, Crowninshield Papers.
[9] Daniel Webster to Jeremiah Smith, Dec. 8, 1817, in Webster, *Private Correspondence,* I, 267.
[10] David A. White to Francis Brown, Nov. 26, 1817, in Lord, 142.
[11] *New Hampshire Patriot,* April 30, 1816.
[12] T. J. Murdock to Francis Brown, Dec. 27, 1817, in Lord, 142.
[13] Joseph Hopkinson to Charles Marsh, Dec. 31, 1817, *ibid.,* 143.

out a decision in *Dartmouth College v. Woodward.* "The chief and Washington . . ." Webster noted, "are with us, DuVall and Todd perhaps against us. . . . I cannot much doubt but that Story will be with us in the end, and I think we have much more than an even chance for one of the others."[14] At the same time, the judicial impasse was paralleled by a legislative one. Congress ostensibly postponed, but actually killed, a new bankruptcy proposal, and on the subject of judicial stipends it seemed as indisposed as ever to better the lot of the "learned and honorable men, whose salaries have been kept meanly low."[15]

In fact, for Story the most memorable event of the 1818 term was the open break between himself and Mr. Justice William Johnson. Antagonism had been building for a long time, as the *Martin* opinions implied, and, indeed, a reciprocal antipathy seemed to exist from the time they first saw each other. As a young lobbyist, Story confessed an inability to describe Johnson's "mathematical" face.[16] And for his part, Johnson could not resist a highly ambiguous comment in his concurring opinion in *Fletcher v. Peck* on attorney Story's innocence of imposing "a mere feigned case upon this court."[17] On the bench, the two parted company from the first on the issue of common law crimes, and Johnson was the only member of the Court to oppose the provision of Story's judiciary bill that would have authorized such powers. The first open pass at arms came in 1813 when Johnson, dissenting from Story's vigorous validation of the full faith and credit clause, taxed the New Englander as subservient to "technical nicety."[18] However, the real break did not come until the 1818 term. One confrontation arose in *Gelston v. Hoyt,*[19] in which the two agreed that a federal officer is liable for exceed-

[14] Daniel Webster to Jeremiah Smith, March 14, 1818, in Webster, *Private Correspondence*, I, 276.
[15] *Columbian Centinel*, Feb. 2, 1818.
[16] Letter from "Matthew Bramble" (Joseph Story) to Samuel P. P. Fay, Feb. 25, 1808, in W. W. Story, I, 168.
[17] *Fletcher v. Peck*, 6 CRANCH at 148 (1810).
[18] *Mills v. Duryee*, 7 CRANCH at 487 (1813).
[19] 3 WHEATON 246 (1818).

ing statutory authority. Story, however, used the case both as a vehicle to state his views on the judiciary as the ultimate arbiter of the constitutional design and to plead for congressional enactment of his judiciary bill. Johnson's concurrence was worse than dissent: "As the opinion delivered in this case goes into . . . a variety of topics . . . not . . . essential to the case, I will present a brief view of all that I consider . . . decided."[20]

But an even more offensive episode during the term came in Johnson's comment on a case Story had sent up from circuit for final review: "There are eleven questions certified from the circuit court of Massachusetts; but of those . . . two only appear to me to arise out of the case . . . I here enter my protest. . . . We are constituted to decide causes, and not to discuss themes, or digest systems."[21] The venom in this observation was doubly apparent because it revealed knowledge that could have come only from the almost involuntary intimacy of the Marshall Court. Specifically, the reference showed an awareness of Story's plans to undertake a digest of decisions with the Court's reporter, Henry Wheaton, and probably of Story's authorship of several of the anonymous "themes" that had adorned the first two volumes of Mr. Wheaton's reports.[22]

Johnson was a formidable enemy—"a man of considerable talents, and law knowledge, but a restless, turbulent, hot-headed, politician caballing Judge," John Quincy Adams called him.[23] A vigorous writer, he was at work on a biography of General Nathanael Greene, undertaken ostensibly because the availability of the Greene papers permitted a firsthand account of the Revolution, but also as a Jeffersonian reply to the Federalist polemics that Chief Justice Marshall had written into his biography of Washington. In addition, the project was doubtless prompted by a desire to supplement his salary, for Johnson too was feeling the

<hr />

[20] *Ibid.,* 333.
[21] *United States v. Palmer,* 3 WHEATON at 640-41 (1818).
[22] See W. W. Story, I, 283.
[23] Quoted in Donald Morgan, *Justice William Johnson* (1954; hereinafter cited as Morgan), 107.

financial pinch and was angling for an appointment as collector of the port of Charleston, his home town.[24] However, authorship was uppermost in his mind when, after the 1818 term of the Court, he made a summer journey north to examine other source materials. "I was richly rewarded for the journey,"[25] he later commented. In another context, the comment was not without a certain significance.

A JUDGE IN ALBANY

Shortly after the argument of the Dartmouth College case in Washington, another aspect of New England academic life was manifested in New Haven in the assembly of a "College Congress" composed of the clergymen presidents of Harvard, Yale, Bowdoin, Vermont, Middlebury, Williams, Andover Theological Seminary, and Dartmouth College, but *not* Dartmouth University. A Boston paper would later point to "this Congress of Divines" as exemplifying "the Good Feelings and Liberality of the times."[26] To Dartmouth University, however, the Congress seemed a defensive alliance proving what the president of Dartmouth College wrote to the president of Harvard—that the case "has now become substantially the cause of every literary establishment in the country."[27]

Although Dartmouth College's appeal to its sister institutions for funds had been unsuccessful, New England colleges did send observers to the arguments at the 1818 term of the Supreme Court. Indeed, it was not reporter Wheaton but a Yale professor of rhetoric who recorded Webster's closing peroration about the small college and those who loved it. This academic concern with a case under submission to the Supreme Court was certainly un-

[24] *Ibid.*
[25] William Johnson, *Sketches of the Life and Correspondence of Nathanael Greene* (2v., Charleston, 1822), *vii.*
[26] *Columbian Centinel*, Sept. 2, 1818.
[27] Francis Brown to John Kirkland, Nov. 15, 1817, in Warren, *Harvard*, I, 336.

derstandable, but it placed an ambiguous cast on the academic honors that were suddenly showered on some of the Justices. Unhappily, Princeton chose this time to give an LL.D. to her two alumni on the Court, Brockholst Livingston and William Johnson. Harvard followed suit, making a like award to those two at the August commencement, at which Mr. Justice Story was "among the auditors."[28] Story had every right to be there, for he too had shared in the shower with his election to the Harvard board of overseers in April.

However otherwise unseemly, the honors did have a certain symbolism in circumstances in which campus seemed to be displacing court as the cockpit of controversy. In early summer, New York's venerated Chancellor Kent had visited Dartmouth University, where he had allegedly read and pronounced his approval of Chief Justice Richardson's opinion upholding the Dartmouth Act. "The truth is," Webster complained, "the . . . opinion is able, ingenious, and plausible."[29] It had, moreover, been given wide circulation, but this was a game at which two might play. By way of retaliation, Webster had his own Supreme Court argument printed and distributed. The Democratic press denounced the work as a "construction of sophistry,"[30] but Webster had already sent copies to Story for further distribution to the other Justices "in the manner least likely to lead to a feeling that any indecorum has been committed by the plaintiffs."[31] One important fruit of this extrajudicial maneuvering soon bloomed. Chancellor Kent reversed his position, asserting that Webster's argument "gives a new *complexion to the case*."[32] The significance of the turnabout was suggested by a letter that the president of Dartmouth College dispatched from Albany in early autumn of 1818:

[28] *Columbian Centinel,* Aug. 29, 1818.
[29] Daniel Webster to Joseph Story, Sept. 9, 1818, in Webster, *Private Correspondence,* I, 287.
[30] *New Hampshire Patriot,* Oct. 6, 1818.
[31] Daniel Webster to Joseph Story, *supra* (note 29).
[32] Chancellor James Kent to Charles Marsh, Aug. 26, 1818, in Shirley, 263.

Judge Johnson has been here. This the chan[cellor] mentioned, & he also said that the judge conversed on our case, & remarked that the court had a cause of "awful" magnitude to decide &c. From what I learn from other sources the judge has formally requested the chan's opinion. This opinion, if given, will also have great influence on Judge Livingston.[33]

A JUDGE IN SALEM

Story had scarcely arrived back in Salem from the 1818 term when he found, notwithstanding efforts at the highest levels on behalf of the Merchants' Bank, "that the deposits, on account of the customs, by the Collector of this District are not regularly made in this Bank agreeably to the instructions of the Treasury Department."[34] The bumbling of this fairly minor matter exemplified the malaise afflicting the second Bank of the United States. Saddled with almost impossible tasks, administered by incompetents, the bank was under increasing attack from its widely diversified opposition. One thrust came in a statute that Maryland adopted early in 1818, laying a discriminatory and avowedly extirpatory tax on all banking offices in the state not chartered by it. The target was the national bank's Baltimore branch, whose enemies rejoiced that they had found "the scourge to drive away the bank"[35]—a scourge that was speedily applied. On May 8, 1818, a suit to collect the tax and penalties was filed in the Baltimore County Court. A judgment adverse to the bank was quickly handed down and immediately appealed to the state court of appeals on an agreed statement of facts. The judgment was affirmed, and, as in the Dartmouth College case, a further appeal was summarily sought, allowed, and docketed in the Supreme Court.

Scheduled to argue the case for the bank was William Pinckney, who had returned home and resumed his law practice. Pinckney

[33] Francis Brown to Daniel Webster, Sept. 8, 1818, in Shirley, 265.
[34] Director's minutes, April 28, 1818.
[35] Niles' Weekly Register, March 7, 1818.

also had another retainer, for the Dartmouth University authorities, increasingly apprehensive that their lackluster attorneys had given away half their case on stipulation and the other half on argument, belatedly secured his services. His entry into the case served further to unsettle Webster, who was already acutely apprehensive about the outcome of the contracts issue before the Supreme Court and had caused new cases attacking the Dartmouth Act to be filed in the United States Circuit Court for New Hampshire. These would permit, in effect, a trial *de novo* on the complete controversy. The new development seemed to have support in high places. "I saw Judge Story . . ." he wrote in April; "he is evidently expecting a case which shall present all the questions."[36]

As in the original cause, the three new cases were speeded along by use of a special verdict, and Story assisted in offering to hold an adjourned term of his court if necessary in order to dispatch the cases to Washington in time for the 1819 term. It was a session that Story keenly anticipated, and had he accepted Pinckney's offer he might have argued its great cases. "The next term of the Supreme Court," he wrote, "will probably be the most interesting ever known. Several great constitutional questions, the constitutionality of insolvent laws, of taxing the Bank of the United States, and of the Dartmouth College new charter, will probably be splendidly argued."[37] Given Story's interests, advocacy, and principles, it would take an immensely splendid argument to secure his assent to the right of a state to tax the federal bank out of its borders. It would take a similar effort to persuade him of the constitutionality of state insolvency laws, particularly retrospective ones. But much closer questions were whether Dartmouth's royal charter came within the sanction of the contracts clause, and that of defining the nature of corporate organization.

[36] Daniel Webster to Jeremiah Mason, April 28, 1818, in Webster, *op. cit.*, I, 282.
[37] Joseph Story to Henry Wheaton, Dec. 9, 1818, in W. W. Story, I, 313.

As Chief Justice Richardson's opinion showed, the old "civil-charitable" dichotomy was inadequate. But if a property-rights doctrine was substituted, what would be the norms of division, the legal rights and responsibilities, the relationship between governmental power and individual right? All were hard questions, and some years previously a Massachusetts Attorney General had struggled with them indecisively.[38] Chief Justice Richardson's "public-practice" division seemed a marked advance, but its logic made educational corporations "public" par excellence, for, as the preamble to the Dartmouth Rechartering Act itself declared, "knowledge and learning generally diffused through a Community are essential to the preservation of a free Government."[39]

Understandably, Story took a long time to make up his mind. However, he had finally resolved the question before he took the coach to Washington, and he cryptically wrote the Court's reporter:

> I have nearly finished an opinion in the Dartmouth College case. You know I was without one after the argument. But after the closest examination & study I am perfectly satisfied, & never felt more clear in my whole life—When we meet you shall see the opinion; & in the meantime you must guess at the side on which it is.[40]

Another letter, written a few days earlier, had given at least a hint of the substance of the answer: "He who lives a long life & never changes his opinions may value himself upon his consistency; but rarely can be complimented for his wisdom. Experience cures us of many of our theories."[41] Story was then thirty-nine years old.

---

[38] See Oscar and Mary Handlin, *Commonwealth* (1969; hereinafter cited as Handlin), 254-61.

[39] *Laws of New Hampshire, 1811–1820* (Concord, N.H., 1820), VIII, 505.

[40] Joseph Story to Henry Wheaton, Dec. 30, 1818, Wheaton Papers.

[41] Joseph Story to Harrison Gray Otis, Dec. 27, 1818, in Morison, *Otis*, I, 122-23.

CHAPTER XIV

1819: The Year of Decision

THE GREAT TERM

Story traveled part of the way to Washington with Daniel Webster and Harvard's President John Thornton Kirkland, the latter having been invited to review plans for a national university with President Monroe. Doubtless the Dartmouth College case was uppermost in Dr. Kirkland's mind, as it was in Webster's. ("Nor has Harvard College any surer title than Dartmouth College," Webster had argued. "It may, to-day, have more friends; but to-morrow it may have more enemies."[1]) Normally, Story would have been considered a prize traveling companion, for he was accounted an outstanding talker in an age when conversation was a necessary social art. Yet he never talked law, and hence it must have been an extraordinary journey, with the voluble Justice speaking on every subject except the one preoccupying his companions. On that topic Story kept his own counsel well, and the anxious Webster, after a quick canvass of the situation on arrival, wrote home: "Not a word has as yet fallen from any judge on the cause."[2] What he did know was unsettling

---

[1] *Trustees of Dartmouth College v. Woodward*, 4 WHEATON at 568 (1819).
[2] Daniel Webster to Timothy Farrar, a member of the Octagon, Feb. 1, 1819, in Shirley, 243.

enough—that Pinckney, appalled at the overgenerous stipulation of the university counsel, had prepared for reargument on the ground that New Hampshire's immense land grants made it the founder of Dartmouth College and endowed it with all rights of visitation and government.

Pinckney was prepared to take the first opportunity to move for reargument. It never came. Immediately upon convocation (appropriately, in a "splendid new room" in the Capitol[3]), Mr. Chief Justice Marshall announced that during vacation the Justices had reached agreement on the original Dartmouth College case. Plucking a manuscript from the sleeve of his gown, he commenced reading an opinion that gave the day to the college forces on virtually all counts. The furious Pinckney now had to revert to the three auxiliary causes and pressed Webster hard for an enlarged stipulation of fact with respect to them. For his part, Webster would admit nothing, lest these cases, which he had previously seen as his last defense, become his undoing. Accordingly, Webster moved to have them remanded undecided to the circuit court on a "certificate which shall enable Judge Story to know what to do with them in May."[4]

The immediate work of the Court, however, had to go on. On February 8 and 9, the bankruptcy case was heard. Webster (who at times had served as Richard Crowninshield's counsel) listened to the argument and predicted the forthcoming judgment of the Court despite the fact that the absence of the ill Justice Todd portended a possible deadlock: "The general opinion is that the six judges now here will be equally divided. . . . I confess, however, I have a strong suspicion there will be an opinion . . . *against* the State laws."[5] As a forecaster, Webster was right as usual. On February 17, Mr. Chief Justice Marshall delivered an apparently unanimous opinion, striking down Crowninshield's discharge as an unconstitutional impairment of the obligation of

[3] *Niles' Weekly Register*, Feb. 20, 1819, quoted in Warren, *Supreme Court*, I, 483.
[4] Daniel Webster to Timothy Farrar, Feb. 9, 1819, in Shirley, 244.
[5] Webster to Jeremiah Mason, Feb. 15, 1819, *ibid.*, 240.

contract. Not for eight years would it be known how spurious was the unanimity or how brilliantly Marshall steered the Court out of an apparently irreconcilable deadlock in which the pre-emptionist theories of Washington and Story conflicted with the more latitudinarian views of Johnson, Livingston and Duvall. Apparently, Story and Washington gave way to Marshall's compromise holding ("The minority thought it better to yield something than risk the whole"[6]) to the effect that the mere grant of national bankruptcy power did not of itself void state insolvency legislation. Neither did the contracts clause inhibit state abolition of imprisonment for debt, whether past or future. What the latter clause disabled, according to Marshall, was state law insulating a debtor's property from obligations incurred prior to its enactment. This left unresolved the issue. "[The decision] will have a most important bearing upon the fate of the bankrupt act now before Congress. . . . If so, God speed the act!"[7])

Dartmouth College v. Woodward and *Sturgis v. Crowninshield* were, however, essentially prologues for the biggest case of all, involving the Maryland tax on the federal bank. The first two cases involved resort to the letter of the Constitution as set out in the contracts clause. The third, however, went to the very essence of implied powers, for it turned both on a congressional authority to create corporations—an authority nowhere specifically granted in the Constitution's text—and on the authority of Congress to limit the state power to tax, a power that the Constitution seemed explicitly to preserve. For these issues, nine days of argument were set aside; the most distinguished counsel in the country, including Webster, Attorney General Wirt, Luther Martin, and especially Pinckney, outdid themselves. On Saturday March 6, 1819, Marshall read the opinion of a unanimous Court, validating the federal bank as an exercise of the implied powers of Congress and striking down the state tax as an unconstitutional

[6] *Ogden v. Saunders*, 12 WHEATON at 273 (1827); see also Story's comment in *Ex Parte Eames*, 8 FED. CASES at 237 (1842).
[7] Joseph Story to Stephen White, Feb. 17, 1819, in W. W. Story, I, 326.

attempt at frustrating those powers. Much of the opinion was not new, but, rather, reproduced verbatim the state paper on the federal bank that Hamilton had written some twenty-eight years earlier, when the issue of strict construction had been vainly proclaimed by Thomas Jefferson within the Washington Cabinet and by James Madison on the floor of the House of Representatives.

But now the federal bank had been proposed by President Madison, established by a congressional majority of Madison's party, and validated by a court of like composition. Moreover, the judicial validation reasserted the proposition put forward by Story in the Martin case of 1816, for the judgment overrode that of a state court. But most significant of all was the *de facto* congressional validation of this exercise of judicial power. In sharp contrast to the legslative reaction of 1816, the Great Term of the Court saw no retribution. On the contrary, in the interval between the Dartmouth and Crowninshield cases, the long-awaited judicial pay raise was approved. The Chief Justice's annual salary was increased to $5,000 and that of the Associate Justices to $4,500. Story was immensely pleased: "it is most satisfactory to me to know that hereafter my salary will be such as to make me feel easy in respect to the future increase of my family."[8]

THEME AND VARIATION

While Story wrote of the future increase of his family, the event he had in mind had already occurred. This was the birth, on February 12, 1819, of William Wetmore Story, who would reverse his father's course by rejecting the law for the arts and, as a distinguished painter, sculptor, and litterateur, share the world of Lowell, the Brownings, Hawthorne, and Henry James. The son was Story's second. He had already lost his first, and death was again waiting on his return to Salem. "On Thursday, the 1st day of April," he noted in a journal "at ten o'clock in the evening, died my dear little daughter Caroline Wetmore Story,

[8] *Ibid.*

aged six years. This day [the fourth] is her birth-day."[9] His typical response to this, the latest of many personal tragedies, was to lose himself in the mazes of the law, and the newest sorrow doubtless impelled him to check, polish, rephrase, and rearrange the concurring opinion he had written on the Dartmouth controversy. The mere fact that it was written flew in the face of Mr. Chief Justice Marshall's unwritten rule that the Court speak with but a single voice. Yet on the Dartmouth question the unity was rent, when the opinions finally came in, not only by Mr. Justice Duvall's opinionless dissent, but by a complex and bewildering pattern of nominal concurrence. Like Story, Mr. Justice Washington wrote a separate opinion vindicating Dartmouth College. Mr. Justice Livingston, who had written down but did not publish his own views, endorsed all three opinions reaching this result.[10] Mr. Justice Johnson, on the other hand, joined the Chief Justice but pointedly withheld his approval from Story's and Washington's views.

The opinion Marshall published was not quite the one he read. Here Story exerted a delicate hand. ("I . . . am highly gratified,"[11] wrote the Chief Justice of Story's changes.) The modifications were doubtless both subtle and peripheral, for Story's views were different, and in any event Marshall's approach was a characteristic seizure of the high ground at the outset with the assertion that it required no argument to prove that the charter of the college constituted a contract. Mr. Justice Washington, however, felt obliged to explore the point the Chief Justice had not examined. Was the Dartmouth charter a contract? Implying that a negative answer might be reached were the question open, Washington held it was a contract, but only on the ground of the old Yazoo land case. And having decided that there was little difference between grants of land and grants of status, the Virginia judge went on to distinguish between "corporations aggre-

9 W. W. Story, I, 332.
10 Henry Wheaton to Joseph Story, May 13, 1819, Wheaton Papers.
11 John Marshall to Joseph Story, May 27, 1819, in Beveridge, IV, 274-75.

gate, viz., such as are for public government, and such as are for private charity."[12] His purpose was "to prevent any implied decision by this court of any other case than the one immediately before it."[13]

Why was this distinction asserted? Not so much against the Chief Justice, for Marshall's opinion only parallels Washington's governmental–charitable division of corporations. The target could only have been the opinion in which Story had brought business corporations into the division, and which he had displayed with pride to confidants both on and off the bench. That he undertook such exhibition prior to the Court's decision suggests that Story considered his arguments virtually invincible. Nonetheless, the university partisans, who had not seen the opinion and who were determined to make a virtue out of adversity when the auxiliary causes were sent back to Story's circuit, still held high hopes "that the fact of the State's being the *principal donor* can be proved so as to remove the doubts of even an *unwilling* judge."[14] However, the brave words were belied by their efforts to have the case postponed from the May to the October term.

The attempt was unavailing. On May 1, 1819, at Portsmouth, Story rendered provisional judgment for the college, reading an opinion that was "very learned and able and covered all the facts that have been raised in the case."[15] But Story did not quite foreclose the issue. After indicating that the "new facts" had been considered in Washington, he made a gesture of fairness, both ominous and ostentatious, inviting the university counsel to present any additional material at the June term of his Boston court.

It is unlikely that the university could have possibly adduced any further grounds on which to overturn Story's twenty-thou-

---

[12] 4 WHEATON at 659.
[13] *Ibid.*
[14] Governor Plumer to Salma Hale, a New Hampshire Representative, April 8, 1819, in Baxter, "Should the Dartmouth College Case Have Been Reargued?," *New England Quarterly*, XXXIII (1960), 28.
[15] Exeter *Watchman*, quoted in *Columbian Centinel*, May 8, 1819.

sand-word opinion, which was based on several propositions. First, it indicated that Pinckney's belated "principal donor" theory had already been considered and rejected by the Supreme Court. Second, it agreed with Chief Justice Richardson's division of corporations into public and private—but with two profound and significant reservations. The first concerned the word "public," which, Story insisted, had two senses, one "popular," the other "strictly legal."[16] The "popular" concerned any beneficent purpose, the "strictly legal" correlated such purpose with government ownership. From this it followed that the element of private property was critical to any classification. While he did not cite the Merchants' Bank by name, the institution whose presidency he held perfectly fitted his distinguishing example:

> [A] bank, whose stock is owned by private persons, is a private corporation, although . . . its objects and operations partake of a public nature. The same doctrine may be affirmed of insurance, canal, bridge, and turnpike companies. In all these cases, the uses may, in a certain sense, be called public, but the corporations are private. . . .[17]

A misunderstanding about the term "public," Story went on, had led to the proposition "that the government [shall] have the sole right, as trustees of the public interests, to regulate, control, and direct the corporation, and its funds and its franchises, at its own good will and pleasure."[18] This, he asserted, could not be; "such an authority does not exist in the government."[19] From this it was a short step to find in Dartmouth's case the requisite donation of private property, establishing both the institution's character and its immunity from state control.

Two other components were involved in the grand design. One involved elimination of the associational element in corporate

[16] 4 WHEATON at 671.
[17] Ibid., 669.
[18] Ibid., 671.
[19] Ibid., 671-72.

organization, a step that required revision of Story's previous ideas. When he had heard the British gospel society case,[20] Story had virtually equated the corporation with its members. Now he suggested that it was a distinct entity ("a charter . . . brings the corporation into existence without any act of the natural persons who compose it. . . ."[21]), although it would still take him a few more years to work out the consequences of this change. The other step was to envelop his thesis—written largely in a natural-law idiom but with fortifying appeals to history and tradition—with constitutional trappings. Here he had to play his cards with care, for his long suit was limited to the contracts clause, and he accordingly purported to validate legislative changes in corporate charters if made pursuant to a reserved power to do so. Subsequently, he would sharply qualify this position, but at the time it enabled him to meet, head on, Chief Justice Richardson's suggestion of divorce laws as an example of civil institutions whose contractual character did not necessarily transfer them from state control to federal constitutional superintendence. Story's response was oblique in incidence but dispositive in scope:

> [I]f the argument means to assert that . . . a contract [of marriage can be ended] without any breach on either side, against the wishes of the parties, and without any judicial inquiry to ascertain a breach, I certainly am not prepared to admit such a power, or that its exercise would not entrench upon the prohibition of the constitution.[22]

Predictably, nothing was shown in Boston to change Story's views, and he made his judgment final, thus bringing the Great Term to an end with a powerful vindication of his own *Martin* opinion. In purely material terms too, 1819 was a good year for him. The judicial-salary adjustment ended his nagging sense of

[20] *Society for the Propagation of the Gospel v. Wheeler,* 22 FED. CASES 756 (1814).
[21] 4 WHEATON at 691.
[22] *Ibid.,* 696.

insecurity, and the new albeit modest affluence, as well as the judicial vindication, were appropriately reflected by oil paintings of himself and his wife which Gilbert Stuart executed in Boston that summer. But not all consequences were complimentary. Typical was the *New Hampshire Patriot*'s indisposition to receive the judgments of the Supreme Court with either acquiescence or respect. The paper most sarcastically suggested that the state legislature "consult Mr. Chief Justice Marshall, Mr. Justice Story, etc., . . . and then pass such laws as they may approve relative to our local concerns,"[23] and it did so to follow up its printing a letter to the editor:

FACTS

Which should be published with the late "Opinion" of the Supreme Court of the United States in the College cause, as a KEY by which some may, perhaps, better understand the case:

Mr. Justice Todd:	—*Absent*
Mr. Justice Duvall	—*Dissents from the opinion*
Mr. Chief Justice Marshall Mr. Justice Washington	—*In the views of the "Octagon"*
Mr. Justice Livingston Mr. Justice Johnson	—*Between the argument and the decision created LL.D.'s by certain colleges*
and Mr. Justice Story	—*Between the argument and the decision elected a member of the corporation of Harvard College*

Alas! poor human nature!

A Plain Man[24]

23 *New Hampshire Patriot*, June 1, 1819.
24 *Ibid.*, Apr. 20, 1819.

Yet far more significant than irascible outbursts of defeat was the vast, silent, and amorphous referendum of acquiescence. Its extent and character would take time to become apparent. Ultimately, it would show that Marshall expressed, as much as he led, opinion when at the Great Term he took the instrument of federal judicial supremacy, as cast by Story in *Martin v. Hunter's Lessee,* and inscribed upon the *tabula rasa* of the constitutional text a codex of national power and private property.

In this codex, Story's hand appeared not only in the casting of the instrument of inscription, but in filling out a critically important portion of the text itself. For it was judicial theories of the nature and function of corporate enterprise that would profoundly influence national economic development.[25] Perhaps nowhere better was the extraordinarily complex and personalized nature of his contribution better symbolized than in the denouement of the drama that he had entered as commissioned reformer and closed as defender of vested right. It came, not in 1819, the year of the Great Term, but five years later, when the onetime overseer-designate of Dartmouth University was tendered the LL.D. of Dartmouth College—in recognition of "affectionate regard . . . repeatedly manifested for this institution."[26]

[25] See Handlin, 156-58: "Joseph Story perceived that the original character of the corporation stood in the way of a clear line turning on function or organization. In the Dartmouth College case he expounded a broader based conception. . . . The distinction, he maintained, arose from the kinds of right involved. Private corporations were those invested with private property; public, those charged only with government or administration. . . . Story's reasoning was acute enough to focus on the central significance of property rights. . . . Despite . . . weakness, Story's opinion profoundly influenced the American law of corporations. For decades thereafter arguments over what was public and what was private revolved about his definition. . . . The corporation, stripped of its original connotations, stood forth primarily a profit-making institution, a business vehicle serving the interests of investors rather than a public agency utilizing private capital. . . . [I]t had become in practice more like noncorporate businesses than like nonbusiness corporations."

[26] Bennett Taylor to Joseph Story, Aug. 19, 1824, in Story Papers, Library of Congress.

PART FIVE

The Middle Years

CHAPTER XV

A Portrait at Forty

During the summer of 1819, a month or so before his fortieth birthday, Justice Joseph Story had his portrait done in oils. Gilbert Stuart was the artist, and the painting was not one of Stuart's better works, for the colors were somber and the pose was stiff. Perhaps the artistic deficiency lay in overwork, for Stuart was especially busy that summer. Or possibly any shortcoming there was resulted from quantity discount, for Stuart did Mrs. Story at the same time.[1] Nonetheless, Story seems to have been pleased with the picture, and his attachment certainly contradicted his detractors. Doubtless, were the Justice as vain as some suggested, he would have had his reservations about a work in which he showed up balding, bland and thick-featured.

Possibly Story's liking for the portrait was due to the fact that it represented the first fruits of the long-overdue increase in his judicial salary. More likely, however, he valued it because it had been done just after the Great Term of 1819 and thereby served as a memento of the Supreme Court's towering trilogy of decisions.

Certainly the 1819 term had provoked enormous interest, and

The Story picture hangs in Langdell Hall of Harvard Law School, having been left to the university by Story's will. The companion painting of Story's wife was subsequently sold to a private collector. My thanks to Miss Agnes Mongan of the Fogg Museum, Cambridge, for this information.

it was barely over when the Court's reporter proposed printing the reports in two parts, "the first to appear as soon as it can possibly be got out, and to contain the Insolvent & Dartmouth College cases, the former of which is loudly called for & much wanted."[2] Demand, however, was no index of approval. Chief Justice Marshall scarcely had arrived home in Richmond when he wrote that the *McCulloch* opinion "had aroused the sleeping spirit of Virginia, if indeed it ever sleeps,"[3] complained of the sharpness of the printed polemics assailing the decision, and warned that the legislature intended to reformulate and republish the Virginia Resolutions of 1798. In Boston, the conservative *Columbian Centinel,* which had assailed New Hampshire's effort to reform Dartmouth College, apprehensively viewed the *Sturgis v. Crowninshield* decision on state insolvency laws: "Persons, we learn, who have been discharged many years from debts and have since acquired property have had it attached to pay old debts."[4] In New Hampshire, the defeated reformers in the Dartmouth College case showed no sign whatever of behaving like good losers when called on for costs ("LOOK AT THIS!"[5]). To much the same point, ending all talk of a national university, was the protest that "the governors of nearly every college north of the Delaware . . . exerted all their influence to procure a decision which should forever place them beyond the control of the people."[6]

The pattern of events was not all hostile, however. Not only had Congress given the Supreme Court its first salary adjustment in history, but President Madison had made a strong effort to end circuit riding for Supreme Court Justices and thereby free them to give full time to final appellate business in Washington. And, finally, up in New York the courts voided the retroactive aspect of its insolvency law in deference to the *Crowninshield* decision.

[2] Henry Wheaton to Story, March 19, 1819, Wheaton Papers.
[3] John Marshall to Story, March 24, 1819, in Beveridge, IV, 312.
[4] *Columbian Centinel,* March 6, 1819.
[5] *New Hampshire Patriot,* June 22, 1819.
[6] *Ibid.,* Feb. 16, 1819.

Yet even these gains had to be put in perspective. Madison's proposal to end circuit riding passed the Senate but failed in the House, for there had been strong protest against permanently exposing the Justices to the "dangerous influences and strong temptations"[7] of the capital. The judicial-pay augmentation succeeded only when an amendment attached it to a pay raise for the Cabinet. And, from the standpoint of the Federalist opposition, New York's revised insolvency law still displeased the archconservative Chancellor Kent, who grumbled that even the prospective law constituted an impairment of contract in the very necessity of the case.[8]

Kent's observation was a confidential one, and he had placed this character on his remarks in significant deference to the burgeoning jurisdiction of the federal Supreme Court. It was also significant of how widespread national dissatisfaction was that some portion might come from a dissatisfied conservatism. Nonetheless it was a combination of an old states'-rights rigidity with a new leveling and reforming spirit that raised the loudest hue and cry and produced an extrajudicial counterreaction from both Marshall and Story.

Interestingly, the two were not agreed on what case of the Great Term's trilogy was the most important, or at least required some further explication. Despite the reporter's indication of widespread public interest in the insolvency decision, both passed it over, to divide on the remaining two. Story thought there should be a popular exposition of the *Dartmouth* opinion, "not for the purpose of commending the Court," but from a higher motive—to lay before the public in a popular shape "the vital importance to the wellbeing of society, and the security of private rights, of the principles upon which that decision rested."[9] He had hoped to secure Kent for the expositor, but the Chancellor declined, an-

---

[7] *Annals of Congress*, XXXII (1819), 130.
[8] "[T]he idea of a contract made with a view to a law which impairs the obligation of contracts is as incomprehensible to him [Kent] as it is to me." (Wheaton to Story, June 14, 1819, Wheaton Papers.)
[9] Letter from James Kent, Aug. 21, 1819, in W. W. Story, I, 331.

ticipating that the same points might come before his bench. The apologia accordingly devolved upon a lesser tract written by the relatively undistinguished Timothy Farrar, one of the college counsel.[10] On the other hand, Chief Justice Marshall saw the critical issue in the *McCulloch* decision. Provoked by Virginia criticism, he followed his powerful court opinion with a tedious and anonymous postscript in the *Philadelphia Union*, but so covertly that even Story and the Court's reporter were in doubt as to the authorship of the polemic.[11] Although ignorant of the source, the reporter welcomed the articles. "It must by no means be left doubtful even for an instant whether the ground assumed by the Court is to be maintained at all costs."[12]

While Mr. Wheaton's initial declaration was concerned with the litigation between Maryland and the federal bank, before the year was much further along, his concern extended to what he called "the disgraceful and dangerous conduct of Ohio."[13] The latter concerned a controversy which began almost at the very time the *McCulloch* opinion was delivered. It centered upon the enforcement of an Ohio tax statute which was quite similar to

[10] See Shirley, 279-98. See also a letter from Daniel Webster to Charles Marsh, April 10, 1819 (*ibid.*, 211): ". . . Judge Story is strongly of the opinion that [Farrar's work] would be a useful work, that Wheaton's reports go only into the hands of professional men, but that this book might be read by other classes . . ."

[11] Albert Beveridge states (Beveridge, IV, 318-19) that Marshall was the author of the *Union* articles, and Charles Warren initially agreed (Warren, *Supreme Court*, I, 515 n.1) but later suggested reporter Wheaton as the author (Warren, *The Story–Marshall Correspondence* [1942; hereinafter cited as Warren, *Correspondence*].) Wheaton had his own candidate: "I suspect you are right in your suspicion that the Chief has had a hand in the defense of the Bank argument for he has evinced an unusual degree of solicitude on the subject of that argument by writing me several times to make some slight verbal alterations. But I had understood that the articles in the 'Union' were from the pen of Mr. Sargeant. I will look them up, not having seen them, & will (if I have room) put them into the appendix upon your recommendation which I have no doubt my own judgment will satisfy." (Wheaton to Story, June 14, 1819, Wheaton Papers.) Prof. Gerald Gunther has set the entire matter at rest with his definitive *John Marshall's Defense of McCulloch v. Maryland* (1969).

[12] Letter from Wheaton, June 14, 1819, Wheaton Papers.

[13] Wheaton to Story, Oct. 22, 1819, Wheaton Papers.

the just-voided Maryland law but which nonetheless was being enforced by the state auditor in the teeth of a restraining order of the local federal circuit court. There had been some question as to the efficacy of service, but even more serious was the power of the Court to issue the order at all. True enough, an ambiguous clause in the bank's charter authorized it to sue the federal circuit courts, but this was really the beginning rather than the end of inquiry. Whether Congress meant to give the bank a carte-blanche entry to the federal courts or, indeed, whether it could do so—that is, make the very act of getting into court a basis of the national jurisdiction of a controversy, whatever its character otherwise—presented subtle and complex questions. These were further complicated by the issue of whatever jurisdiction might be given in the ordinary case; this controversy involved not a suit between private parties, but rather the direct imposition of a federal judicial writ upon a state officer acting directly under the authority of his sovereign and the color of his office.

The consequences of this confrontation had occurred before. The Supreme Court's early effort to bring sovereign Georgia to its bar produced instead the Eleventh Amendment, stripping the Court of the very jurisdiction it asserted. Along a somewhat different line of historical precedent, the demand in Virginia for republication of the Resolutions of 1798 could also be seen as ominously prophetic. Two decades earlier the initial proclamation of these doctrines of states' rights and strict construction had been the overture to the demise of the national power of the Federalist Party, historic protector of the federal courts. Indeed, a man with a sense of history might well fear the backswing of the pendulum as reaction to the centralizing decisions of 1819 began to be felt. Perhaps that very apprehension accounted for the stiff pose in the Stuart *Story*.

Or, perhaps, any apprehension underlying the stiff pose came from yet another constitutional controversy, the Missouri question.

CHAPTER XVI

New Arrivals, Old Survivals

FIREBELL IN THE NIGHT

Midway between the decisions in the Dartmouth College and Crowninshield cases, on February 13, 1819, the Missouri statehood bill was called up in the House of Representatives. On that same day, Congressman James Tallmadge, Jr., of New York proposed an amendment providing for the emancipation at twenty-five of all slaves thereafter born in the newly admitted state. Tallmadge followed a New York precedent, but the mere hint that such procedure might be recast in national law as a positive instrument of emancipation provoked a fresh constitutional crisis.

From the standpoint of states' rights and strict construction, any such action by the federal government was an impermissible usurpation. Yet from the standpoint of countervailing national-istic–natural-law logic, the proposal was not only legitimate but proper and even inevitable. Moreover, from the imperative of history, it seemed difficult to avoid the inference of such power the moment the federal government ceased to be a creature of the states and became, whether *de jure* or *de facto*, their creator. Springing from these tangled roots, the confrontation shook the country and seemed to prove that the irenic years which had preceded it were not the era of good feelings but, rather, the calm before the storm.

Over those years, a group of factors had developed, and these lent the struggle its bitter and turbulent character. Part was economic, as national growth and development proceeded in the South in the form of an expanded and invigorated plantation system, while its Northern face took the form of an industrial revolution. Slavery, indispensable to one system, useless to the other, contributed powerfully to the estrangement. "It is very easy," protested Senator William Smith of South Carolina, "for those who have their fortunes secured in bank stock, or stock of the United States, or money at interest, or money in their coffers, deliberately to proclaim a jubilee to our slaves, in which they have neither interest to lose nor danger to fear."[1]

There was more to the alienation than economics. Perversely, the growing nationalism exacerbated the breach, as it gave a new sense of accountability in each part of the country for that which happened in every other part. Coexisting with the new nationalism, at odds with it and still a part of it, was a new sectional rivalry in which North and South eyed the trans-Mississippi West and each sought to cast the new area in its own image. Basically, however, irreconcilable cast was given the controversy by the rise of a new ethos stressing perfection, rationality, and philanthropy. Certainly it was no coincidence, but, rather, an interesting sequence of events when early 1819 saw not only the great centralizing decisions of the Supreme Court and the emergence of the Missouri controversy, but also a new theology as Story's Harvard classmate William Ellery Channing took his text from I Thessalonians 21 ("Prove all things; hold fast to that which is good") and preached his landmark sermon, "Unitarian Christianity."

For all his growing political conservatism and perhaps because of it, Story was in the mainstream of the Unitarian reform movement in an ethos which combined a rational and reforming theology with lingering traces of a youthful concern with the philosophers of the Enlightment and a deep sense of national pride. In

Annals of Congress, XXXV (1820), 378.

fact, it would not be too much to say that Story's nationalism involved a mystical, almost religious, strain in an exulting nationalism.

Politics, patriotism, and theology, accordingly, could be seen in his charges to federal grand juries during his winter swing around New England in late 1819. Nominally, his subject was the anti–slave-trade statute, and, no doubt, his earnest exhortation to enforce this law was in part prompted by his concern at the past—and present—part played by New England shipping in fastening slavery on the South. His major motivation, however, was plainly the Missouri controversy and his target slavery itself, for his remarks drew no line between the trade and the institution, whose "existence . . . under any shape is so repugnant to the natural rights of man and the dictates of justice, that it seems difficult to find for it any adequate justification."[2] At least one Southern member of Congress bitterly protested that such "preaching to grand juries"[3] was reminiscent of the anti-Jeffersonian political harangues before those bodies for which Justice Samuel Chase had been impeached almost twenty years before. In private correspondence, Story virtually admitted the truth of the charge: "We are deeply engaged in the Missouri question. I have fought against the slave trade in Rhode Island, *pugnis et calcibus*. My charge was well received there."[4]

As the controversy unfolded, it became increasingly plain that the national judicial power, as developed in the Great Term of 1819, was inescapably bound up in the Missouri question. The arch-Federalist Rufus King had recognized both the power and the potential when he insisted that the contest "settles forever the dominion of the Union. Not only the Presidency, but the Supreme Judiciary, at least a majority . . . will forever hereafter come from the Slave region."[5] From the opposite side, John Randolph likewise saw the connection when he denounced Marshall's for

[2] Charge to the grand jury, in W. W. Story, I, 336.
[3] *Annals of Congress*, XXXVI (1820), 410.
[4] Letter to Jeremiah Mason, Nov. 26, 1819, in W. W. Story, I, 366.
[5] Rufus King to J. A. King, Feb. 6, 1820, in Warren, *Supreme Court*, I, 54

mulary in *McCulloch v. Maryland* as giving Congress power to "emancipate every slave in the United States."[6]

An indication of the mixed political and judicial nature of the controversy was suggested by that part of Story's correspondence with Marshall in the summer of 1819 which dealt with the somewhat technical admiralty question of whether "the ports of the different States are to be deemed foreign ports"[7] with respect to certain aspects of admiralty jurisdiction. Noting that the English precedents so denominated Irish harbors notwithstanding a supervening political hegemony, Story suggested that the point applied "with greater force in the United States, where each State is really a distinct sovereignty."[8] Yet he was unable to speak in these self-denying aspects very long, and he followed up this statement with an activist proposal on the merit of ignoring British precedent and adopting "a rule in the United States [from the] maritime law of the continent."[9]

And the basically nationalist cast of his constitutional view was more spectacularly manifested when at the Salem town meeting in early December, 1819, he broke his political silence, for the first and only time in his years on the bench, with a long and passionate speech insisting "that the spirit of the Constitution, the principles of our free government, the tenor of the Declaration of Independence, and the dictates of humanity and sound policy, were all directly opposed to the extension of slavery."[10] Certainly the national atmosphere, where resolution and counterresolution were the order of the day, helped justify his action. Moreover, an institutional concern for the Supreme Court was also involved, for Virginia had issued its protesting resolutions and by them linked the delay in admission of Missouri and the nationalizing decisions of the Supreme Court's 1819 term as essentially related grievances.

But not all of his listeners pretended to understand or appreciate

[6] Quoted in Beveridge, IV, 309.
[7] Story to John Marshall, July 26, 1819, in Warren, *Correspondence*, 4.
[8] *Ibid.*, 5.
[9] *Ibid.*
[10] *Salem Gazette*, Dec. 11, 1819, quoted in W. W. Story, I, 361.

his position. His old adversary, the Reverend William Bentley, went home and diaried: "Town meeting upon the Missouri Slavery. The question would be more interesting if it could be believed from the persons busy in it that they did intend only the humanity professed in it . . . Judge Story talked long. . . . I love to see how these spoutings are managed by political address."[11] Dr. Bentley shared the reactions of many old-line Republicans who saw the Missouri controversy merely as an attempt by the dying Federalist Party to gain a new lease on life with a note of moral uplift. To be sure, the Federalists, their backs against the wall, might well look at the centralist trends in their opponents and assume that a certain turnabout criticism was fair play. On the other hand, the old-line Republicans saw the Federalist views of humanitarianism shown best by endemic diatribes against Thomas Jefferson's philanthropy, and true Federalist views on state sovereignty and national power by the resolves of the Hartford Convention. Indeed, to many Jeffersonians of Dr. Bentley's view, the Missouri controversy seemed a reprise of the old Yazoo land fraud controversy when outright Federalists and conservative Republicans forged an alliance to promote Northern self-interest. Story had risen to prominence in that earlier coalition, and his extensive lobbying travels back and forth to Washington had included collaboration with Rufus King. Now the collaboration seemed renewed as King's powerful polemic protesting the spread of slavery became the constitutional armory of the anti-Missouri forces. Doubtless it formed the basis of Story's Salem speech, and Story himself admitted that the memorial which he drew up and which was adopted "by a large and very respectable meeting of citizens" in Boston was taken almost wholly from it.[12]

Still another Northern protest came from Washington, where the second session of the Sixteenth Congress had already convened with the battle lines still drawn from the first. Congressman

[11] Bentley, IV, 634.
[12] Niles' Weekly Register, Dec. 11, 1819; see also Jeremiah Mason to Christopher Gore, Jan. 16, 1820, in Hillard, Memoir and Correspondence of Jeremiah Mason (1873; hereinafter cited as Hillard, Mason), 236.

John Holmes of Massachusetts, anxious to become Senator Holmes of Maine, shared Dr. Bentley's sentiments, bitterly complaining that an inflexible antislavery position on the Missouri question "had been pushed on by Judge Storey [*sic*] . . . & all the intrigues of Mr. Webster."[13] The complaint was not without basis. In terms of purely political accommodation, northern Maine, like western Missouri, had grown both economically and governmentally into a sense of self-dependence, and in both the desire to cut the leading strings—in one case as a Massachusetts province and in the other as a federal territory—was exceptionally strong. Joint admission by way of compromise seemed an obvious answer, but this reckoned without the association of Congressman Daniel Webster and Mr. Justice Story, which had been in effect since 1813 on matters ranging from federal judicial jurisdiction to bankruptcy, and which amounted almost to a partnership.

On the Missouri question, however, Story was something less than a silent partner and he had little taste for compromise. The same sense of urgency which prompted the speech at the town meeting and the drafting of the Boston memorial induced him to go beyond serving as Webster's speech writer and take to the lobbies of Congress. Or so at least some reports suggested "[T]here was a story in circulation," protested a South Carolina Senator who doubtless intended no pun, ". . . that one of your judges had descended from his high station . . . mingled in the strife; and endeavored, with no little zeal, to influence, by his arguments, both within and without the Congress, the decision of a political question to a result that would shake this Union to its centre."[14] Senator Smith did not identify his judge by name, but his reference to the errant jurist's "vanity or ambition"[15] marked out his target clearly enough. The target, however, also had significant words of his own, in a changed vocabulary. Back in the Jefferson administration, young Joseph Story signed himself "really at bot-

---

[13] John Holmes to William King, Dec. 25, 1819, in Glover Moore, *The Missouri Controversy* (1953), 106.
[14] *Annals of Congress*, XXXVI (1820), 410.
[15] *Ibid.*

tom a Virginian."[16] Now, however, a portion of the Northern Republicans united with their Southern copartisans to stave off the irrepressible conflict and bring in Missouri as a slave state, with Maine admitted as bargain-counterweight. Story would have no part of the Missouri Compromise, and he fulminated that "Virginia has ruled us by the old maxim, 'divide and conquer.' "[17]

Yet Story was too close to the scene to appraise events. Union, not division, was the fundamental order of the day. Already the consequences of the Missouri controversy were reshaping reaction to the Great Term, as two isolated and seemingly dissimilar episodes plainly showed. Ohio, notwithstanding its concern over the federal bank, saw its Congressmen vote *en bloc* to uphold federal authority in the form of the Tallmadge amendment. More significant was the reception that greeted the resolutions issuing out of Virginia, which specifically forced the question by linking as a single constitutional issue the Supreme Court's decisions and the delayed admission of Missouri. In New Hampshire as in Ohio, the new ingredient of the national power vis-à-vis slavery provoked a new reaction. The legislature, still smarting over its reversal in the Dartmouth College case, felt impelled to virtually restate the Supreme Court's rule of decision in that very controversy when it rejected the Virginia protests and framed a counterresolve that the Virginia views "contend for an erroneous construction of the Constitution of the United States . . . which if adopted will prove highly injurious to the best interest of the Nation."[18]

A FEUD CONTINUED

For Story, the 1820 term was marked not only by the historic double compromise of the Missouri controversy, but also by judicial developments, some routine and some not. Paralleling his

[16] Letter to Jacob Crowninshield, Jan. 4, 1806, Crowninshield Papers.
[17] Letter to Edward Everett, March 7, 1820, in W. W. Story, I, 367.
[18] Resolve of the New Hampshire legislature, in Hillard, 243.

opposition to the extension of slavery and drawing on much the same instinct was his unavailing protest at Pennsylvania's punishment of one of its federalized militiamen,[19] wherein his sensitivity for federal prerogative reinforced a humanitarian apprehension of double jeopardy. To be sure, there was more here, for his remonstrance was really directed against the fortification of the doctrine of concurrent powers in an area where he felt that canon had no place. Along the same centralizing line but cast toward commercial objects was an opinion he wrote for the Court in *Mandeville v. Welch*[20] emphasizing the unique character of negotiable instruments by presuming their issuance for value. But most provocative, at least in terms of interjudicial relationships, was an admiralty question which was argued but not decided in that term, and which was to split the Court by the narrowest of margins on whether British cargo might be transformed in national character by the issuance of Spanish documents. This was *The Amiable Isabella*, about which the Court's reporter, who doubled as advocate at its bar, later wrote him: "I shall expect you will give a *great* opinion in the case of the Isabella. Of course, I cannot even *guess* whether it will be for or against us."[21]

Mr. Wheaton made no secret of his duality of callings. On the contrary, his announcements advertised the availability of his professional services in New York as well as "at the Supreme Court of the United States at Washington, which Mr. Wheaton regularly attends as a Counsellor, and the Reporter of its decisions."[22] Doubtless he and Story were a little more circumspect about their relationship, which seemed to go to the edge of propriety in an age considerably more indulgent than its successors in such matters. For Mr. Wheaton was free in his requests not only for Story's assistance in his reports ("Will you have the goodness to take the trouble to draw up a short marginal note of the principal points

[9] *Houston v. Moore,* 5 WHEATON 1 (1820).
[20] 5 WHEATON 277 (1820).
[1] Letter from Henry Wheaton, Oct. 10, 1820, Wheaton Papers.
[22] Announcement of Henry Wheaton, Oct. 8, 1819, Wheaton Papers.

decided in Dartmouth College v. Woodward?"[23]), but also for professional employment ("I pray you to bear me in mind on the Circuit for retainers"[24]).

Obviously, this relationship also provided an avenue of communication in special circumstances, and one of these occurred when Story left Washington before the formal close of the 1820 term. As Wheaton wrote him, in leaving the last act early he had missed the best of the play:

At 12 o'clock the judges here came into Court, & the Chief Justice expressed their regret that they were obliged to continue the case of the Amiable Isabella to the next Term. Immediately, Mr. Justice J. announced, with great emotion, his determination to fire off,—stating that as his mind was unalterably made up, & as the last argument, so far from shaking, had confirmed his first impressions, he thought the party entitled to the benefit of his vote which might be lost in case death or *any other cause*, should prevent his being present . . . next Term. He then proceeded to read the same opinion which he drew . . . and when that *ended* read on: "Thus far was written before the last argument, which has strengthened me in my former opinion." He then proceeded in a style which beggars all description, to ridicule Pinckney's argument, treating it with the utmost contempt as a flimsy declamation of a venal advocate for privateersmen masked under the appearance of the sanction of the Government. "If," said he, "I thought the Government had authorized the use of such argument I should blush for my Government."—Pinckney was so enraged that it was with difficulty that Wirt and myself could keep him from getting up and discharging his resentment in open Court. Every person present was equally struck with the extraordinary want of dignity, or rather of Decency, in the learned judge's conduct—and nothing is talked of but his *tirade*—I suffer them to speculate upon what may be the cause

[23] Letter from Henry Wheaton, Aug. 2, 1819, Wheaton Papers. As to the notes in the Wheaton reports; see also W. W. Story, I, 283.
[24] Henry Wheaton to Joseph Story, Oct. 10, 1820, Wheaton Papers.

tantae irae, professing to be quite ignorant of the whole matter. The general impression seems to be that *he* has lost *his* cause, but what has made the loss so bitter no person pretends to understand.

The judges lament this extravagant sally, which was the more unfortunate as great numbers of persons were assembled for the purpose of hearing the decision of the Court. Judge Washington assures me that everything was done that *could be done*, to prevent it, but in vain. *Quem deus vult perdere &.*

I pray you not to quote me for any thing of this even to any of your friends. Please to say you have heard so & so.[25]

There was far more to Justice Johnson's outburst than the fairly narrow point of prize law at issue in the *Amiable Isabella* case. More likely it was another outburst of his dislike of Story which had intermittently flared since the latter took his seat on the Court. Johnson also disliked Henry Wheaton, both as reporter and as advocate. And he seems to have known about the Story–Wheaton collaboration and disliked that too. However, it is also possible that the outburst and his indicated intention to get his views on record may have been due to an impending resignation, for it was an open secret that Johnson was angling for appointment to a collectorship, and Webster was surprised that he even sat for the 1819 term. On the other hand, it is equally possible that the appointment had been tendered and declined earlier,[26] and that Johnson's remarks merely were the consequence of the complex character described by Wheaton in sending a volume of the reports:

I am sorry there are so many of our friend's crudities in this volume. There are some things quite above my comprehension, & others in so bad a taste that I lament it very much. . . .

[25] Letter from Henry Wheaton, March 17, 1820, Wheaton Papers. The year does not appear in the letter, but seems obvious from internal evidence.
[26] "Judge J's letter to Secretary *declining* to resign is a queer thing & a perfect key to his character." (Wheaton to Story, April 30, 1819, Wheaton Papers.)

He has great strength of mind, but the defects of his early education predominate and he has unfortunately most conceit where he is most deficient—But what can't be cured must be endured.[27]

[27] Letter from Wheaton, July 2, 1820, Wheaton Papers. Story seemed of the same mind: ". . . I think some of Judge Johnson's opinions in the 3rd volume of your Reports are very uncourteous to some of his brethren. It is surprising that he is not sensible that he errs most strikingly . . . where he is so very jealous himself. I mean in respect to a tenderness for the judgment of others." Letter to Wheaton, Aug 12, 1818. *Ibid.*

CHAPTER XVII

An Election at Forty-one

OLD INSTITUTIONS,
NEW APPREHENSIONS

The many currents of change which had shaken the country
during the Missouri controversy were reflected in Story's Massachusetts in a growing dissatisfaction with the state constitution
of 1780. Considered a landmark of its time, when church, college,
and commonwealth still merged in an almost seamless polity, the
constitution was increasingly criticized in an age of economic
change, religious dissent, and social unrest. A proprosal for organic revision accordingly received an overwhelming passage at
the polls. In the selection of convention delegates from Salem,
Story led one party ticket and ran second on the other, and a
local paper reporting the results indicated the changing times with
a new name for the Republican Party: of those who were chosen,
it said, "five are Democrats and four Federalists. We hope other
towns have set a like good example of harmony and freedom from
party spirit."[1] It did not occur to the editor to comment as to
the meaninglessness of the old party divisions, underscored on a
nationwide scale when the country which had been almost torn
asunder in the Missouri controversy returned James Monroe to
the Presidency in an electoral vote only one short of unanimity.

Salem Gazette, quoted in Boston Columbian Centinel, Oct. 18, 1820.

As one acute observer of the crisis of 1819–20 noted, the post-compromise mood of the country drew heavily upon a readiness, indeed an eagerness, to react and accept a half-satisfactory settlement as a release from the emotional confrontations. And certainly the Monroe reelection seemed to typify a national determination to treat the problem of slavery as nonexistent, for the Northern chorus of critical hostility previously raised by King, Webster, Story, *et al.* suddenly lapsed into virtual silence.

Hence, the *Gazette*'s prim comment was not without substance. Indeed, only the previous year George Ticknor, newly returned from Europe, was startled to see Federalists Daniel Webster and George Sullivan having dinner with Democrats Joseph Story and George Blake. Yet beneath the calm, and notwithstanding the bipartisan elections and bipartisan dinner, novel and surging forces were struggling to emerge, and it was this half-hidden turbulence which gave an extraordinary character to the Massachusetts constitutional convention. For the body was brilliant in composition, mediocre in products, alternately optimistic and apprehensive, acute and obtuse.

The ambivalence of the convention's tone and temper seem presaged in Story's correspondence of the preceding summer with Sir William Scott. Expressing apprehension of the burgeoning American industrialization and particularly of the rise of "great manufacturing cities, apparently the seats of great vices, and great political fermentation,"[2] he enclosed a copy of the *Dartmouth College v. Woodward* report in his letter to the English judge. His action was not without a certain irony, for notwithstanding Story's view of the Dartmouth case as a legal and polemical contribution to the cause of institutional conservatism, it was his concurring opinion in that controversy which explicitly extended the principle of charter inviolability to business corporations and thereby became the legal cornerstone of the ongoing American industrialism. (Typifying his own lack of comprehension concerning his contribution to the disintegration of the older com-

[2] Letter to Sir William Scott, May 20, 1820, in W. W. Story, I, 385.

mercial order was his action in drafting—almost concurrently with the Scott letter—a memorial for Salem shipping interests pleading for a continuation of favorable federal legislation and insisting that commerce had claims no less pressing than manufacturing.) There were some other anomalies in the letter to Scott. One was some florid praise of the latter's prize decisions, which, back before the War of 1812, had been a thorn in the American side comparable only to the press gangs and the Orders in Council; young attorney Story then was writing that Scott's judgments were "untenable in principle and . . . rest merely on vague conclusions of commercial interest."[3] Yet the new transatlantic judicial rapport was also a symbol of significance of a reaction to new times and new conditions in which the legislature was becoming the engine of change and the judiciary the citadel of conservatism.

The view received a particularly topical application when Story and the Commonwealth Chief Justice, Federalist Isaac Parker, turned out to be the principal competitors for the honor of presiding when the Massachusetts constitutional convention assembled in late 1820. Parker won, 195 to 130. For Story, defeat was victory. It gave him a voice in debate which he could never have had as presiding officer, and it also made him the logical choice as chairman of the committee on the judiciary. Moreover, for the first time since leaving the Massachusetts legislature a decade earlier, he was free to engage in the cut and slash of public controversy, and he accordingly challenged Webster in a friendly rivalry to be the dominating spirit of the gathering. Even here, however, the mixture of public triumph and private sorrow which characterized most of his life appeared, and he went through the convention beset by concern over the serious illness of a small daughter. Notwithstanding this continuing apprehension and an occasional emergency departure to make a worried trip back to Salem, he seemed to have something to say on almost every matter, starting with opening remarks on seating the Plymouth dele-

[3] Letter to Jacob Crowninshield, Jan. 4, 1806, Crowninshield Papers.

gation and closing with a motion on printing copies of the convention report.

Principally, however, his activities were directed along three closely related fronts—the rights of property, the privileges of Harvard, and the power of the judiciary—where he forcefully expounded a philosophy which saw the institution of property as not only one of the natural rights of men, but encompassing their highest exemplification:

> Gentlemen have argued as if personal rights only were the proper objects of government. But what, I would ask, is life worth, if a man cannot eat in security the bread earned by his own industry? [I]f he is not permitted to transmit to his children the little inheritance, which his affection has destined for their use? What enables us to diffuse education among all the classes of society, but property? Are not our public schools, the distinguishing blessing of our land, sustained by its patronage?[4]

It was concededly difficult to fit the rising industrial capitalism into this simplistic and almost pastoral model; Story, however, seemed to feel no difficulty but, rather, appeared to make a virtue out of necessity as he pleaded for virtual disenfranchisement of the urban working classes: "Take . . . Manchester in England . . . where there are five or ten thousand wealthy persons, and ninety or one hundred thousand of artizans reduced to a state of poverty and vice and wretchedness . . . Who would found a representation on such a population, unless he intended all property should be a booty to be divided among plunderers."[5]

As Henry Commager has noted, Story made no inquiry into the cause of the artisans' degradation and no suggestion for a cure.[6] Indeed, the speech is at anomalous variance from the compas-

[4] *Journal of Debates and Proceedings in the Convention of Delegates, Chosen to Revise the Constitution of Massachusetts* (1853; hereinafter cited as *Journal of Mass. Convention*), 286.
[5] *Ibid.*, 288.
[6] "Joseph Story," in *Gaspar Bacon Lectures* (1953), 61.

sionate ethic which ruled him in all private relationship, where he persistently showed a sympathy "with the poor, the lowly, the humble."[7] Individuals, however, were one thing, institutions quite another. Story saw no conflict here between his private and social views, nor, for that matter, any contradiction of his anti-slavery polemics. In fact, he selected the speech for inclusion in his collected writings.

Manifesting the same sense of institutional concern were his efforts on behalf of the judiciary. Perhaps his greatest single triumph came when he persuaded the convention to reverse itself on a previous vote empowering the legislature to cut judicial salaries. He did more than defend, however; he secured convention approval (though not without becoming "aware of the impatience of the House"[8]) of a four-point program of judicial reform—increasing to two thirds the legislative majority required for judicial removal, installation of equity jurisdiction (but with a fact-finding jury), elimination of advisory opinions, and transfer of divorce proceedings from the Governor's Council to the regular courts.

Even closer to his heart, was his defense of Harvard against suggestions that a major reordering was necessary to prevent the college from becoming "a powerful engine of politicians and polemical divines."[9] Here the debate doubtless left him with mingled emotions—pleasure on hearing encomiums heaped upon the *Dartmouth College* opinion and shock at George Blake's anachronistic Jeffersonian rhetoric that it was at least an open question whether the convention had "the right to mould the government" of Harvard "into whatever form they pleased."[10]

The convention seemingly overwhelmed any thought of fundamentally changing Harvard's status, although Story's subsequent comment on the presence of "a pretty strong body of Radicals . . . still the lovers of the people, alias the lovers of

[7] Joseph Story to W. W. Story, Jan. 23, 1831, in W. W. Story, I, 33.
[8] *Journal of Mass. Convention*, 523.
[9] J. Q. Adams, *Writings*, VII, 90, note 1.
[10] *Journal of Mass. Convention*, 86.

popularity" suggested that the issue had been closer than the printed record revealed. In a revealing comment, he defended the results as "the best we could obtain, and in some respects we were triumphant, as to the judiciary and Harvard College."[11] He could have been a little more positive on the convention's achievements, for the demands of the religious establishment were loosened and the franchise was expanded.

Yet the Massachusetts electorate carried the ambiguous convention proceedings to their logical conclusion by passing ten and defeating five of the proposed amendments. Among the casualties were Story's judiciary amendments. The rejection could scarcely be called an encouraging sign for the judicial process. In fact, the combination of the convention and the election seemed to leave him with a heavy sense of pessimism:

> . . . [C]onsidering the popular cant & popular prejudices, I have some fears that we shall not have wisdom enough to maintain ourselves upon the present decided basis that protects property. The truth is that we have yet much to learn as to the nature of free governments; & it will be a matter of surprise if in our rage for experiments to ascertain with what weakness in its institutions the government may possibly go on & stop & go on—we should not shipwreck the cause of liberty. I endeavor to hope for the best—but there are many painful forebodings about us.[12]

There seemed to be only one ray of light in the gloom. Harvard awarded him its LL.D. at the 1821 commencement.

SOME NEW RESOLUTIONS

The judicial process, failing of vindication in Massachusetts in its capacity as guardian of vested right and private property, came under counterpart positive attack elsewhere in its aspect as an

---

[11] Letter to Jeremiah Mason, Jan. 21, 1821, in W. W. Story, I, 394-95.
[12] Letter to John Marshall, June 27, 1821, in Warren, *Correspondence*, 13-14.

instrument of national sovereignty. The venerable Jefferson, writing as though the year were still 1798 and his own Presidential administration had never occurred, joined the assault, and the Ohio legislature, recalling his election of 1800, insisted that that event had settled the question of "whether the Federal Courts are the sole expositors of the Constitution . . . against the pretensions of the Federal judges . . ."[13]

South of the Ohio River, the nationalist and conservative faces of the judiciary became increasingly embroiled in a multifaceted controversy. The commonwealth of Kentucky, reiterating its own Resolutions of 1798, successively challenged federal jurisdiction in three areas. One argument challenged the assertion of admiralty powers over Kentucky rivers. A second assailed federal process and execution inconsistent with Kentucky relief laws. Particularly attacked was federal consideration of the possible infirmity of Kentucky's occupying-claimant statute, a law which required that a good-faith occupant of land, ousted under superior title, be given the value of his improvements and released from a liability for rents. Yet even here the process of ultimate vindication was already at work.

The occupying-claimant statute was at issue in the 1821 term of the Supreme Court, in the case of *Green v. Biddle*,[14] and Story wrote an opinion striking it down as unconstitutional. Back in 1814 while on circuit, he had invalidated a New Hampshire law to much the same effect, although he had then based his opinion wholly on a state law and explicitly rejected the federal constitutional issue.[15] Now he resorted to that ground, using the contracts clause as a formal base, although the natural-law character of his rationale was dominant in an indignation which treated the Kentucky statute as a program of legalized extortion.[16] To be sure, he had more to work with in the Kentucky case, for the

[13] *State Documents on Federal Relations*, ed. Ames (1911), 96.
[14] 8 WHEATON 1 (1823).
[15] *Society for the Propagation of the Gospel v. Wheeler*, 22 FED. CASES 756 (1814).
[16] 8 WHEATON at 10-18 (1823).

"contract" was the compact whereby Kentucky was severed from Virginia and in which the mother state had attempted to insure the security of her western land grants. Yet the entire subject was one of immense controversy, involving not only chaotic frontier titles but a Virginia liberality which had assertedly granted Kentucky away several times over. Given this character of the case, it was no surprise when, within a few days of Story's opinion, Henry Clay appeared on behalf of his state and successfully moved that the matter be reargued.

Hence, the key case of the 1821 term was another and somewhat unusual proceeding which came up with suspicious speed from the Mayor's Court of Norfolk. The case, *Cohens v. Virginia*,[17] framed a new confrontation of state and federal authority in an asserted conflict between an act of Congress authorizing a lottery in support of the District of Columbia and a Virginia statute prohibiting the sale of any save domestic lottery tickets within the state. If the constitutional theories latent in the Missouri controversy and the *McCulloch v. Maryland* opinion roused the sleeping spirit of Virginia in 1819, the impact of the Cohens case excited it to a new sense of concern. Theory suddenly became reality as the Old Dominion found herself summoned as a respondent to the bar of the Supreme Court in a criminal proceeding involving two of her own citizens.

Down in Richmond, in what seemed to be a routinized and annual solemnity, the General Assembly assailed federal pretensions and resolved that the Eleventh Amendment merely clarified the original constitutional intent of forbidding a state from being made a defendant in federal judicial proceedings save as expressly authorized by the constitutional text. Counsel for the Dominion was accordingly instructed to argue only the point of jurisdiction, and extrajudicially a note not heard since the Hartford Convention reappeared in the national debates. The son of one of Story's old friends wrote his father of both the reborn attitude and its possible consequences:

[17] 6 WHEATON 264 (1821).

Many of the Southern people, & particularly the Virginians, talk coolly & deliberately of a separation of the States, or at least of an attempt to deprive the General Government of some portion of its powers—Besides this business in Missouri, they say the General Government is every year setting up new claims & pretensions—They mention the establishment of the Bank; the jurisdiction in so many incroachments [sic], as they deem them of the Government generally—Virginia is at the moment before the Supreme Court, as a party in her sovereign capacity as a State, notwithstanding the provision of the Constitution that no state shall be sued—She has pled to the jurisdiction—& if this is decided against her, as it probably will be, she means not to answer to the merits of the case, but resist judgment if it goes against her—Ohio still has a violent quarrel with the Court—. In the Virginia case (that of lotteries authorized by Congress, & prohibited by her laws) the Court will probably decide in favor of Jurisdiction, thus securing their own power, & on the merits, in favour of Virginia . . ."[18]

The prophecy was fulfilled when Chief Justice Marshall wrote an opinion which one acute observer[19] noted was as much a reply from the bench to the Virginia pamphleteers as it was a resolution of constitutional controversy. Following his own tactic in *Marbury v. Madison*, Marshall thrust a favorable adjudication on the party who assailed his power to render it. While conciliatory in tone, it was nonetheless an uncompromising restatement of the theses earlier asserted in Story's *Martin* opinion—that American nationhood antedated the Constitution, that the national government was supreme within its powers, and that the judicial expression of that supremacy compelled review of the state tribunals, the latter result obtaining as fully from necessity as it did from the constitutional text.

[18] William Plumer, Jr., to William Plumer, Sr., Feb. 25, 1821, in Brown (ed.), *The Missouri Compromise and Presidential Politics* (1926), 41-42.
[19] Andrew C. McLaughlin, *A Constitutional History of the United States* (New York, 1935), 396.

Predictably, the opinion fanned new fire into the spirit of Virginia, and on returning home the Chief Justice wrote Story that it was "assaulted with a degree of virulence transcending what has appeared on any former occasion."[20] Replying as if the Hartford Convention never took place, Story reported: "[T]he decision . . . meets with general approbation among our professional gentlemen . . . Massachusetts is attached to the Union & has no jealousy of its powers . . . We should dread to see the government reduced, as Virginia wished it, to a confederacy."[21]

He did, however, find disquieting possibilities in Virginia polemics and polemicists. Asserting that it was Virginia's example which had already led Ohio astray, he expressed deep concern over Mr. Jefferson's continued proclamation that the judiciary was not the ultimate arbiter of all constitutional questions. To be sure, Story might well be concerned that contradiction of his *Martin* doctrine proceeded from so high a source. He was, however, on somewhat questionable ground, at least in a letter to the sixty-five-year-old Marshall, in referring to the ex-President's sunset years: "There never was a period of my life when these opinions would have not shocked me; but *at his age* & in these critical times, they fill me alternately, with indignation & melancholy."[22]

There was another venerable Virginia statesman whose views were besought in the current crisis. This was James Madison, and the quest was well worth the effort, for Madison's pen could invest the current Virginia resolves with the brilliance it had put into the original ones of 1798. Yet that same pen had also been dedicated to the ratification of the Constitution, and it was characteristic of Madison's cautious thought that he evaded a commitment and reserved his position. What he did say, however, forecast a conclusion far closer to that of the co-author of the Federalist Papers of 1788 than to the draftsman of the Virginia Resolutions of a decade later:

[20] Letter from John Marshall, June 15, 1821, in Warren, *Correspondence,* 7.
[21] Letter to John Marshall, June 27, 1821, *ibid.*
[22] *Ibid.,* 9.

The Gordian knot of the Constitution seems to be in the problem of collision between the Federal and State powers, especially as eventually exercised by their respective tribunals. If the knot cannot be untied by the text of the Constitution, it ought not certainly to be cut by any political Alexander.[23]

TWO RIVERS

If by late 1821 the Ohio River seemed to be an axis of resistance uniting the Old Dominion with her daughter commonwealths of Kentucky and Ohio in hostility to the nationalizing edge of the federal judicial power, the Hudson seemed to be a stream of perplexity and gave a new direction to the set that power might possibly take. In virtually every confrontation thus far, that power had been invoked, directly or collaterally, on the side of vested and preexisting rights of private property. Coming out of Albany, argued once inconclusively and finally docketed for the 1822 term was a case which sought to summon that power to the opposite effect. Here the state-granted Fulton-Livingston steamboat monopoly on New York waters was assailed as invalid for traversing the federal coasting statutes and the federal power over interstate and foreign commerce.

Yet the case, *Gibbons v. Ogden*,[24] arrived in the Supreme Court with the federal claims having the particular disadvantage of having been weighed and found wanting, once by Chancellor Kent in the Supreme Court of New York and again by that state's Court of Errors.[25] To be sure, there was some regret that it arrived at all. Notwithstanding a decided appetite for jurisdiction, Story seemed to feel that, atop the unsettled Ohio and Kentucky controversies, the New York proceeding was an embarrassment of jurisdictional riches:

[23] Letter to Spencer Roane, June 29, 1821, in Warren, *Supreme Court*, I, 554.
[24] 9 WHEATON 1 (1824).
[25] 4 JOHNSON CH. 150 (1819), and 17 JOHNSON 488 (1820). Suit was first filed in the U.S. Circuit Court for New York, where Justice Livingston dismissed it for lack of jurisdiction; see *Livingston v. Van Ingen*, 15 FED. CASES 697 (1811).

It is . . . matter of regret to me that the constitutionality of the Act of New York is about to come before the Supreme Court. We have already had our full share of the public irritations, & have been obliged to decide constitutional questions, which have encountered much opposition—I had hoped for a little repose; but I perceive it is not to be allowed us. Whichever way we decide the Steamboat case, it will create a great sensation—We must content ourselves however in doing our duty & leave to time to decide the consequences."[26]

Yet if it had to be decided at all, as far as Story was concerned, there was every predisposition to defer to Kent's judgments. This was true in ordinary times. Now the sentiment was overwhelming. Kent approached the end of his career, being swept from the bench without thanks or pension by the New York constitutional convention of 1821.

Coming hard on the heels of the Massachusetts convention, the incident struck Story with dismaying force. Yet, typical of his complex personality, his public utterances struck a cheerful and optimistic note; in fact, the summer of 1821 saw what was perhaps his greatest declamation, delivered before the Suffolk bar on September 4, 1821.[27] Nonetheless the strongest impulse seemed to be that of his hardening conservatism as he wrote to the Chancellor's reporter that Kent's enforced retirement could be ascribed only to political madness; and to another confidant he went even further in a bleak confession:

The truth is and cannot be disguised, even from vulgar observation, that the Judiciary in our country is essentially feeble, and must always be open to attack from all quarters. It will perpetually thwart the wishes and views of demagogues . . . Its only support is the wise and the good and

[26] Letter to Brockholst Livingston, June 4, 1822, in Story Papers, Massachusetts Historical Society.
[27] "The Progress of Jurisprudence," in *Miscellaneous Writings,* 198. See also Miller, *The Legal Mind in America* (1962), 63-75.

the elevated in society; and these . . . must ever remain in a discouraging minority in all Governments.[28]

Certainly Story noted little of the wise, good or elevated when, shortly before the convocation of the 1822 term, the outline of a two-pronged Kentucky counterattack on the Court began to emerge. The opening gun was a bitter remonstrance of the Kentucky legislature, and salients of attack opened in Richmond and Washington. On the first front, an effort was made to cut the underpinnings of the occupying-claimant decision by revision of the Virginia–Kentucky compact of 1789. On the second, Senator Richard Johnson of Kentucky rose in the newly assembled Seventeenth Congress and launched a witty, powerful and comprehensive attack against the federal judiciary, with his targets ranging from the assumption of admiralty powers on the Ohio River to the anomaly of a federal government being the final judge of the nature and extent of its own powers. By way of remedy for the first grievance, he proposed a statute limiting admiralty jurisdiction to the ebb and flow of the tides; for his second, a constitutional amendment making the Senate a supercourt of appeals in federal–state controversies.

Johnson's admiralty bill passed the Senate only to fail in the House. There was little of novelty here. In fact, the proposed statute did no more than restate the historic limits on admiralty jurisdiction clearly marked out seven years before in Story's landmark opinion of *De Lovio v. Boit*.[29] The real thrust of the congressional attack came in the proposal to reverse not only the occupying-claimant case, but also the *Martin* opinion and the decisions of the 1819 term by establishing the Senate as an American House of Lords. Yet already countervailing forces began to exert their influence, and Webster wrote Story of the quickening developments:

[28] Letter to Jeremiah Mason, Jan. 10, 1822, in W. W. Story, I, 411.
[29] 7 FED. CASES 418 (1815). See *supra*, pages 129–32.

Mr. Johnson of Kentucky has to-day, I learn, made a long speech in favor of his proposed amendment. He has dealt . . . pretty freely with the supreme court. Dartmouth Collége, Sturgis and Crowninshield, *et cetera* have all been demolished. To-morrow he is going to pull to pieces the case of the Kentucky betterment law. Then Governor Barber [of Kentucky] is to annihilate Cohens v. Virginia. So things go; but I see less reality in all this smoke than I thought I should, before I came here.[30]

Webster, as prophet, correctly estimated the situation, as Johnson's efforts turned out to be love's labor lost. Nothing came of the suggested amendment in the Senate, while on the opposite side of the Capitol the proposal of a Virginia Representative to repeal the statutory base of the Supreme Court's appellate jurisdiction over state tribunals wound up on the table. And even the limited cooperation Kentucky received in Washington was deceptive. For if the seeming Virginia–Kentucky rapport in the national capital suggested a revival of the partnership of 1798, Virginia–Kentucky differences in Richmond began to indicate that the senior member might have second thoughts on any such renewed liaison. For beyond question there was growing Virginia recognition that the Supreme Court's occupying-claimant decision as the bulwark of Virginia titles to Kentucky lands made it incumbent on her legislature to postpone indefinitely proposals to emit a new set of resolutions denouncing the *Cohens* decision in particular and the national judiciary in general.

[30] Letter from Daniel Webster, Jan. 14, 1822, in Webster, *Private Correspondence*, I, 320.

CHAPTER XVIII

A Question at Forty-two

THE CUMBERLAND ROAD

There were other indications that the nationalist sentiments of the Old Dominion drew on more altruistic motives. Madison's restrained refusal to join the attack on the Supreme Court was paralleled by the action of another old Virginian in acknowledging the tribunal's authority. This came from President James Monroe, and it began with unpromising accents of strict construction when, on May 4, 1822, he vetoed a bill to construct the long-proposed Cumberland Road. However, the 27,000-word veto message was far more a statement of political philosophy and a mirror of the national mood than it was a disapproval of a legislative proposal.[1] Tracing American political institutions from the foundation of the colonies through the Revolution and the Articles of Confederation, Monroe delivered his own constitutional exegesis with two obvious targets in view. One was the strict-constructionists in Kentucky and Virginia; the other was Marshall's soaring vision of national powers in *McCulloch v. Maryland*. Characteristically, the President, who had kept the confidence of North and South, pointed to a middle ground. On his general premise, he insisted that the Constitution was the creation of neither the people nor the states but, rather, the people *in* the

[1] Veto message of May 4, 1822, in Richardson, II, 144.

217

states. On this particular conclusion, he insisted, contrary to the *McCulloch* doctrine, that there were indeed limitations which attached to congressional means of executing its delegated powers, and that one of these cut down the bill before him—namely, that no cumulation of local benefits could transform such a proposal into one serving the *general* welfare. However, on Story's *Martin* view of the Supreme Court he said nothing, but, in an action which spoke louder than words, he sent a copy of the message to the Court with a request for the comments of the justices.

It was an illuminating exercise on both sides for Monroe's *de facto* recognition of the unique constitutional competence of the Court was paralleled by the wariness with which Story evaded the Presidential request. He too pointed for a middle ground as he responded that the federal power to undertake internal improvements "is a subject on which many are divided in opinion, but all will admit that your views are profound and that you have thought much on the subject."[2] The response marked the transition which his own reflections and jurisdictional appetite had covered over a ten-year span. Back in the War of 1812, on the constitutional issue of nationalization of the state militia, he had felt that the ideas of the members of the Supreme Court should be aired and "regretted that neither the President nor the Congress had required their opinion."[3]

But 1812 was not 1822, and doubtless the assault on the federal judicial power and indeed the emerging dimensions of that power produced a sense of cautious restraint. Paralleling his regret that the necessity of decision in the steamboat case was being thrust on the Court was his changed viewpoint on advisory opinions. His remarks at the Massachusetts constitutional convention showed both the change and the basis. "The power of calling on the judges for their opinions," he pleaded, "may be resorted to in times of political excitement, with the very view to make them

[2] Quoted in William P. Cresson, *James Monroe* (Chapel Hill, N.C., 1946), 395.
[3] Plumer, 431.

odious, and to effect their removal from office. A better opportunity could not be afforded to an artful demagogue."[4]

Significantly, however, one member of the Court did not follow Story's example. In a revealing manifestation reflecting the ambiguity and ambivalence of the entire national reaction to the changing times, Justice William Johnson drew on the 1819 term as he categorically replied to the President that all members of the Court were "of the opinion that the decision on the bank question completely commits them on the subject of internal improvements."[5]

A MATTER OF SELF-INTEREST

It was also characteristic of Johnson's eccentricity, or so Story doubtless thought, that the South Carolina judge who had gone to one extreme in revealing judicial solidarity went to another in revealing the Court's internal conflict when, a half year later, the Supreme Court finally disposed of the Kentucky claimant law at its 1823 term. On the face of the case, there seemed some puzzle as to the need for haste, as Kentucky's Justice Todd—the member of the Court able to make a unique contribution to the case—was absent, Justice Livingston was on his deathbed, and Chief Justice Marshall self-disqualified. Outside the record, however, another circumstance emerged; possibly a matter of causation or possibly an irrelevant coincidence, it occurred only a matter of days before the action of the Court. This was the failure of Kentucky efforts to secure revision of the statehood compact as the amendatory proposals sputtered out in an impasse between the two houses of the Virginia Assembly.

The suspicion that the Court's action was taken with an eye cocked on Richmond was heightened by a shuffling of opinions. For, while the Court reiterated its invalidation of the Kentucky statute, Story's opinion reaching the goal largely on a natural-law logic was withdrawn and replaced by one of Justice Washington, which was explicitly keyed to the contracts clause and the statehood compact. All the Justices concurred, but Justice Johnson joined only on the ground that federal process did not incorporate the state procedural statute. Certainly there was reason for placing the decision on the least provocative ground, and Justice Johnson stated why as he parted company from the opinion and announced from the bench that the opinion of the Court actually embodied the constitutional views of but a minority of the Justices in a result that carried by a division of three to one. The tactic was doubly calculated to be a thorn in Story's side, since this public revelation of the inner workings of the Court, distressing enough in the contemporary context of the controversy, came at a moment of particular concern over the tribunal's institutional well-being. For in Justice Livingston's last illness Story was beset with more than the loss of a friend.[6] Rather, the first breach in the ranks since he took his seat on the Court threw the question of Livingston's succession into sharp relief, particularly as rumors grew that the new Justice might come from the old-line school of states' rights and strict construction.

If Story's reaction to Johnson's remarks from the bench partook more of sorrow than of anger, Henry Clay's response reversed the order of the emotions. Furious at both the outcome and the margin, Clay sought still one more argument, and his wrath was unquestionably exacerbated when his effort was denied, Story demurring on the view that "he (Story) could not conceive it possible, that his mind could be further informed on the subject."[7] For to Clay, the dispatch with which the Court disposed of the case was but Virginia's obvious and shabby sacrifice of constitutional theory to immediate self-interest:

> . . . [O]n this subject of the Federal Judiciary and State rights I mean to say a few words . . . Has not Virginia ex-

[6] See Dunne, "The Story-Livingston Correspondence," *American Journal of Legal History*, X (1966), 224.
[7] Clay, Report to the General Assembly, Nov. 4, 1823, in Clay, *Papers*, ed. Hopkins (1959-63; hereinafter cited as Clay), III, 514.

posed herself by . . . her conduct . . . ? When in the case of *Cohens* and *Virginia,* her own authority was alone concerned, she made the most strenuous efforts against the exercise of power by the Supreme Court. But when the thunders of that Court were directed against poor Kentucky, in vain did she invoke Virginian aid. The Supreme Court it was imagined would decide on the side of . . . Virginia. It has so decided; and, in effect, cripples . . . Kentucky moore [*sic*] than any other measure ever affected the Independence of any state in this Union, and not a Virginia voice is heard against the decision.[8]

The Johnson disclosure aside, Story was almost as displeased with the case as Clay. He was obviously irked with the substitution of the Washington opinion for his own effort. "I see no reason to take back our opinion," he wrote the absent Justice Todd, "though for one, I felt a solicitude come to that result, if I could have done it according to my views of great principles."[9] And even on the merits of Johnson's dissent, he indulged in a rare display of testiness: "[Y]ou will see what his peculiar opinions were."[10]

Yet if peculiarity of opinion—or at least the holding of opinions of questionable consistency—were to be the gauge, Henry Clay took a place alongside Justice William Johnson. Certainly Clay, as counsel for the commonwealth of Kentucky, suggested a view of the national judicial power which stood at some remove from the view taken by Clay as counsel for the federal bank. Indeed, reminiscent of the Virginia behavior after the occupying-claimant decision, which prompted Richmond to stifle its wrath over the *Cohens* decision, Clay had another view of the same judicial power when he sought to stiffen the federal bank's spine as the waning character of the Ohio controversy prompted the state to suggest a compromise settlement. "By a recent decision of the

[8] Henry Clay to Francis T. Brooke, Aug. 28, 1823, in Clay, III, 478-79.
[9] Letter to Thomas Todd, March 14, 1823, in W. W. Story, I, 423.
[10] *Ibid.*

Supreme Court," he wrote the bank's president, "jurisdiction is affirmed in the Federal Judiciary in all cases, criminal as well as civil, in which it may be necessary to maintain the inviolability of the Laws of the U States, against the laws of any of the States."[11]

Clay's effort to walk both sides of the street had not escaped notice or criticism. Indeed, almost a year before, an acute observer, focusing on the failure of the federal courts to give effect to state relief legislation, called him to account:

> I see you have been putting forth some more high handed doctrines in behalf of the Bank of the United States. Do you really think that it is competent for Congress to give to suitors in the federal courts remedies unknown or contrary to State laws upon the same subjects—God-a-mercy upon us if the federal courts once decide this may be done . . .[12]

A FEW PROPOSALS

Predictably, Justice Johnson's disclosure of the minority character of the occupying-claimant opinion roused Kentucky to a fresh fury, and the legislature petitioned Congress to require that at least two thirds of the full bench of the Supreme Court be required for an invalidation of state legislation. The Kentucky delegation in Congress took up the cry, and a flood of suggestions for judiciary reform poured forth from the newly convened Eighteenth Congress: reduce the Supreme Court to five; enlarge it to nine or ten; confine it to Washington; establish organic circuits after the mode of the Judiciary Act of 1801; establish Western circuits whose judges would not sit on the Supreme Court and so on, almost infinitum.

Much of the pressure came from Western expansion, which had already undone the initial design of a star and a stripe for each state in the national flag. Much the same force was unraveling the initial plan of the judicial system fashioned as a kind of American assizes with the same group of men trying cases individually

[11] Letter to Langdon Cheves, March 10, 1821, in Clay, III, 61.
[12] Letter from Charles Hammond, July 1, 1822, *ibid.*, 245.

and serving *en banc* as an appellate tribunal. Unhappily, there were not enough justices to go around for circuit duty as the states expanded, and the limited number of Supreme Court seats was itself a source of irritation to local pride. "[S]ix of the original states and eleven since admitted into the Union, have not yet been honored with an appointment of a judge of this Court," reported *Niles' Weekly Register*.[13] And the expedient largely followed in the West, having a federal district judge double as circuit judge, compounded the basic injustice of the general circuit system in which the same men sat on trial and appeal. It also led to protracted delays when the composite court could not meet. "[T]here has been another failure of the Federal Court at Columbus in Ohio," wrote Clay that January of 1824, "owing to the non-attendance of both the Judges. This makes three successive failures of the January term of that Court."[14]

Hence, there seemed abundant motives for judicial reform when Kentucky's Senator Johnson took the floor of the Senate on December 10, 1823—almost two years to the day since he launched his first attack on the Supreme Court—and asserted that the minority claimant opinion provided the strongest argument for his earlier proposal to give the Senate final appellate jurisdiction over state legislation. He chose, however, to abandon this previous suggestion in favor of the two-thirds-majority rule proposed by his legislature. On the House side, Congressman Charles A. Wickliffe, also of Kentucky, made a parallel attack in proposing repeal of the statute providing for an appeal of state decisions to the Supreme Court.

Yet again Webster was more concerned with proposals for change which came from other sources and seemed more fearful of suggestions that the Supreme Court be reduced in number and confined to Washington: "Suffice it . . . to say, that if we separate your bench from the circuit, and reduce it to five, I should expect to see it, in a very few years, the most unpopular tribunal

[13] April 16, 1825.
[14] Letter to Nicholas Biddle, Jan. 20, 1824, in Clay, III, 596.

which ever existed."[15] Story was inclined to agree in endorsing the proposal to enlarge the tribunal only because of "more formidable evils, resulting from diminishing the number to five, or taking the Judges from the salutary and stirring influence of the Circuit business."[16] He soon, however, reluctantly moved to change his position to one of support for permanent circuit courts. Probably his basic reason was recognition of the need of the Supreme Court's giving permanent Washington attendance to its ever-mounting judicial business. Nevertheless, he disliked the prospect of ceasing to dispense firsthand justice in the circuit trial court, even though the burden of travel was immense and the addition of Maine—admitted as part of the Missouri Compromise— had virtually doubled the length of his annual trips through New England.

The split system also imposed what a contemporary observer labeled a "rough . . . and tumbling journey . . . from the Atlantic to the Potowmack,"[17] and Story must have made the ten-day winter trip to the 1824 term with the legislative rather than judicial developments the major item of his concern. The prospective docket provided a number of major cases, for in posture for final consideration was Ohio's controversy with the federal bank and so likewise was the steamboat case, but the congressional front was primary, and here some of the tension was relieved when an early enactment reformed certain Western circuits. Doubtless this development accounted for the fact that the first actual pass at arms on judicial power ended in a victory for the proponents. This came on January 20 when the bill of Representative Wickliffe of Kentucky for outright repeal of Supreme Court jurisdiction over state judgments received a *coup de grâce* in a committee recommendation that passage was "not expedient."[18]

[15] Letter from Daniel Webster, Jan. 4, 1824, in Webster, *Private Correspondence*, I, 338-39.
[16] Letter to Daniel Webster, Jan. 10, 1824, in W. W. Story, I, 438.
[17] George Blake to John Brazer Davis, Feb. 10, 1824, in *Proceedings of the Mass. Historical Society*, XLIX (1916), 187.
[18] *Annals of Congress*, XLI (1824), 1291.

This was an auspicious beginning but by no means the end, and probably Story was not aware of the development as he traveled south to give battle. "I saw our friend Judge Story," an informant wrote Webster from Philadelphia, ". . . and was delighted to find him in high health and spirits. He is ready for a tough campaign; but on his return I shall look for paler cheeks and dimmer eyes."[19] The prediction was almost fulfilled, although not along the lines suggested, for Story narrowly escaped injury when his stage was in an accident out of Baltimore.

A fresh legislative assault came almost coincidentally with the opening of the Court's new term when, on February 9, Representative Robert P. Letcher of Kentucky presented his commonwealth's legislative remonstrance to the House of Representatives, and as this appeal to states' rights came in the halls of Congress a counterpart appeal opened in the Supreme Court with arguments on the steamboat case. In it there was reason to assume that Kent's powerful opinion could well be adopted on the national level, for the specific facts of the case afforded only a tangential collision between state and national power, and the impact of the nationalist view shook a vested property right to its foundations. Nonetheless, the collision, however slight, was there, and Webster predicted the consequence: "I have no doubt the Court will decide that . . . the New York law is inoperative."[20]

On March 2, 1824, in a characteristically hammer-stroke opinion, Chief Justice Marshall vindicated Webster's prophetic sense and pronounced the New York steamboat monopoly offensive to the federal coasting statutes and implied that the result would have been the same had the congressional power over interstate commerce remained completely unexercised.[21]

The reaction seemed diametrically opposite to that which followed the 1819 term. From one end of the country to the

[19] Letter from Francis Hopkinson, Feb. 1, 1824, in Webster, *Private Correspondence*, I, 344.
[20] Letter to Jeremiah Mason, Feb. 15, 1824, in Hillard, *Mason*, 276.
[21] *Gibbons v. Ogden*, 9 WHEATON 1 (1821).

other the Court was acclaimed, particularly in the states which had been immediately affected by the New York statute and which had passed retaliatory laws of their own. Indeed, applause came from within New York itself, where the monopoly had produced a powerful and tenacious opposition. It was against this background that, on March 11, Representative Martin Van Buren brought in a brace of bills from the House Judiciary Committee which were designed to be all things to all men. One of them proposed resurrection of the Judiciary Act of 1801 in the establishment of organic circuit courts; the other, an anodyne to Kentucky grievances, proposed requiring the concurrence of at least five Supreme Court Justices in order for any state legislation to be invalidated by the Court.

Yet even had the five-sevenths proposal actually been law at the 1824 term, it would have saved neither the New York monopoly nor Ohio's attempted repression of the federal bank. For it was scarcely a week after the bill had been brought from committee that Chief Justice Marshall handed down a powerful reiteration of the *McCulloch* opinion. Passing from defense to offense, he upheld the power and the intention of Congress to expand federal jurisdiction to all federal matters and, further, asserted the power of the national courts to subject the officers and agents of the states to that jurisdiction, the Eleventh Amendment notwithstanding.[22]

Particularly illustrative was Johnson's position. In lieu of his previous efforts to synthesize the old Republican doctrine and the new nationalism, he now adopted a centralizing tendency in advance of that of Marshall. Not that he completely changed his position; while one of his dissents referred to "my brother Story,"[23] he accompanied it with a thrust at both Story and Wheaton in a reference to "the reporter who seldom lets an opportunity escapes him" to display his erudition.[24] However,

---

[22] *Osborn v. Bank of the United States,* 9 WHEATON at 738 (1824).
[23] *Miller v. Stewart,* 9 WHEATON at 718 (1824).
[24] *Ibid.*

Johnson delivered a concurrence in the steamboat case whose nationalism surpassed that of Marshall, and his procedural disagreement in *Osborn* left it perfectly clear that he would have voted to strike down the substantive Ohio law had it come up by writ of error from an Ohio court.

Again, the reception of the decision stood in stark contrast to its *McCulloch* predecessor. Here, however, the reaction drew more from the passage of time than from positive acclaim. Indeed, the Ohio crusade against the bank had lost most of its momentum on its home ground, and the state, one of those which had passed retaliatory legislation against the New York steamboat monopoly, was far more interested in the Supreme Court's disposition of that enterprise. And, even more indicative of the potential of new issues to force policy changes, the concurrent session of the Ohio legislature had abandoned states'-rights resolves in favor of some which urged the end of slavery in other states by emancipation and colonization.

Notwithstanding the disintegration of what once seemed a states'-rights phalanx, the Court adjourned the 1824 term overshadowed by the distinct possibility that it would be harnessed by the five-sevenths rule, and even Webster seemed to look on it as the minimum concession. "Do you see any great evil in such a provision?" he wrote Story.[25] The Justice apparently did, for Webster rose in opposition but with a mood to compromise when the proposal was presented in the committee of the whole, and all his talents seemed needed to face the storm. "[D]ebate . . . lasted all day," he wrote Story on May 4. "*Cohens v. Virginia*, Green and Biddle, etc. were all discussed."[26] More important, however, was his estimate of the tactical situation. "The proposition for the concurrence of five judges will not prevail."[27] As usual, he was right. On May 14, the committee rose and had leave to sit again. On this particular issue it never did, although Kentucky

[25] Webster to Story, April 10, 1824, in Webster, *Private Correspondence*, I, 349.
[26] Webster, *Private Correspondence*, I, 350.
[27] *Ibid.*

hostility had one gasp left. Three days later, Kentucky's Representative Thomas Metcalfe attached the five-judge proposal as an amendment to a routine judiciary bill. It drew fire from a variety of sources, one of which, while already waning, still held enough power to help carry the day for the Supreme Court and judicial federalism. This was the school of Southern nationalism, already in retreat and soon to be in rout. Nonetheless its waning force was powerfully expounded in the judiciary debate by Representative George McDuffie of South Carolina, who insisted that what the Cohens case really decided was "whether the United States have or have not a Government."[28] The comment epitomized the mood of the House, and sensing the fate which awaited his amendment if put to the test, Representative Metcalfe withdrew it.

The abortive and unspectacular demise of the Kentucky proposal to curb the Court did not mean that criticism of the national judicial power either inside or outside Congress, was at an end. Nonetheless, it did provide a recognizable and significant bench mark in the sequence of events, manifesting generally at least a minimal consensus of satisfaction with the tribunal and the basic consonance of its decisions to the national mood. And the consensus had powerfully vindicated the view which Story expressed in *Martin*—that practical necessity fully as much as textural theory demanded that an operative power of last decision reside somewhere within the constitutional design. And certainly the sweep of events had underscored the invalidity of the old Republican view of a self-equilibrating Constitution in which state and national power, like the heavenly spheres, swept through their orbits in never-touching paths. Rather, the very clash of local interests provided a new principle of constitutional growth.

And indeed nowhere was the transitional process better shown than in Virginia itself, where the rhetoric of protest began in

[28] *Annals of Congress*, XLII (1824), 2646.

1812 with a reiteration of the Resolutions of '98 and then lapsed, diminuendo, into the somewhat abashed silence of 1822. And in a significant parallel manifestation, the very author of the original Virginia Resolutions finished his reflections upon "a trial of strength between the Posse headed by Marshall and the Posse headed by the sheriff," and concluded that the Constitution "intended the Authority vested in the Judicial Department as a final resort in relation to the States for cases resulting to it in the exercise of its functions."[29] A powerful seconding Virginia voice to Story's *Martin* opinion was added when President James Monroe in his last message to Congress finally asserted what had been implied in his request for the Justices' views on his Cumberland Road veto as he proposed that the Supreme Court spend its entire time in Washington, because "this court decides, and in the last resort, on all the great questions which arise under our Constitution."[30] Finally, an ironic Northern counterpart to those Virginia sentiments on the Supreme Court came when the oracle of Federalism, James Kent, said much the same thing. Concerning his forthcoming *Commentaries on American Law*, he wrote Story as 1824 approached its close that on the Supreme Court decisions, "I almost uniformly agree with you . . . I shall find some fault with the steamboat case, but most decorously."[31]

[29] Madison to Jefferson, June 27, 1823, in Madison, *Writings*, ed. Hundt, IX (1910), 141-42.
[30] Richardson, II, 261.
[31] Letter to Story, Dec. 18, 1824, in *Proceedings of the Mass. Historical Society*, 2nd series, XIV (1901), 414.

PART SIX

The Lowering Storm

CHAPTER XIX

Two Men from Massachusetts

THE AMERICAN DREAM

"After two successive sleepless nights," diaried the newly inaugurated John Quincy Adams, "I entered upon this day with a supplication to Heaven, first, for my country, secondly, for myself and those connected with my good name and fortunes . . ."[1] The President did not go into further detail, but if connection with his good fortunes was the test, Justice Joseph Story had a formidable claim to remembrance. In fact, had it not been for Story's extrajudicial efforts, Adams might not have taken the Presidential oath on March 4, 1825. The Judge's activity began in the winter of 1816–17 when he urged the newly elected James Monroe to make Adams Secretary of State. It became decisive shortly after Monroe's inauguration. Henry Clay and several lesser lights, well aware that the State Department had been the springboard to the Presidency, objected to the proposed appointment by questioning the sincerity of Adams' conversion to the political party still called Republican, but Story carried the day with a forceful endorsement which, in Adams' words, "undertook to answer for my Republicanism."[2]

[1] J. Q. Adams, *Memoirs,* VI, 518.
[2] *Ibid.,* IV, 131. See also VIII, 98.

Yet, in going political surety, Story was but paying off an old debt, for, in a sense, the man he proposed for the Cabinet had been nominated and confirmed for the seat he held on the Supreme Court. The careers of the two men had been episodically intertwined long before that. It was unquestionably at Adams' recommendation that, upon his appointment as minister to Russia, the thirty-year-old Story took over the direction of *Fletcher v. Peck*, and earlier allegiance linked them in the overthrow (undertaken with varying degrees of enthusiasm) of Jefferson's embargo of 1808–9. Moreover, they were united by attitude as well as history, for they shared a stiff-necked obduracy to partisan discipline. "[W]hile young Adams is working into political favor," a Jeffersonian partisan had noted in early 1808, "young Story of the Law . . . is working out."[3]

The observation mixed fact and hope. True enough, Story bolted the party line time and again when a specific position did not suit him, but never did he dream of emulating young John Quincy Adams, who apostatized from Federalism and crossed over to the enemy camp. In part the differing political behavior was rooted in polar differences in temperament. Story, while never formally breaking with the party of Jefferson, early made his peace with New England's pro-British Federalist elite. Some of its members sourly regarded his affable bonhomie, but their reservations were pale compared to the hatred they bore for that political Ishmael, John Quincy Adams. For his part, Adams, detested in the party of his birth and suspect in the party of his adoption, testily reciprocated the antipathy he excited in both opposing camps and viewed virtually all men with a misanthropy which bore most heavily upon himself.

The values which Story and Adams shared far overshadowed their temperamental differences, and what the observation of one man "working out" and the other "working in" really perceived was a nationwide gravitation from opposite partisan extremes to a central ground of enlightened nationalist conservatism. Equally removed from the old tie-wig Federalism and Jeffersonian phi-

[3] Bentley, III, 346.

lanthropy, the new movement took root within the Republican Party, and though it lacked a name, it had a creed and a symbol. The creed could be found in the opinions Story wrote in *Terrett v. Taylor* and the Dartmouth College case, which interwove the ancient natural law and the new constitutional dispensation into an exposition of the institution of contract as the indispensable prerequisites and, indeed, the very embodiment of life and liberty. And the symbol on the national political scene, for the new conservatism could scarcely be said to have a leader, was John Quincy Adams.

Paralleling this evolution was another movement, also authentically American in its temper and also reposing in the bosom of the Republican Party. If the new conservatism suggested that the nuclear spirit of the dying Federalist Party was taking a new lease on life, so did the new egalitarianism indicate that the old-time Jeffersonian philanthropy was not dead but sleeping. Composed of ambiguous and cross-purposed elements, the unfolding movement also had a creed and a symbol. Its creed was the Jeffersonian dictum that the earth belonged to the living. Its symbol —and more leader than symbol—was Andrew Jackson, whose heroic and simplistic image, sharply contrasting with Adams' fastidious intellectual hauteur, fired and united a diverse following in their restive dissatisfaction with the status quo and a determination to change it.

Story had observed the development of these restless forces well before they had taken on a Jacksonian coloration, and their pace and development had prompted the hardening of his own conservatism. As early as 1818 he had apprehensively noted "a new race of men springing up to govern the nation . . . the hunters after popularity . . . the demagogues . . ."[4] And the pattern of the next several years—particularly the leveling and democratizing constitutional conventions of Massachusetts and New York—deepened his initial apprehension and produced a lively concern with the election of 1824.

Apparently so did everyone else as the Virginia Dynasty and

Letter to Ezekiel Bacon, March 12, 1818, in W. W. Story, I, 311.

with it the orderly transfer of Presidential power ended in a scramble to succeed James Monroe. Within the Cabinet, William H. Crawford, John C. Calhoun, and even the lackluster Smith Thompson (soon to sit beside Story on the Supreme Court) maneuvered with Adams in an ongoing contest for the succession. Outside, Andrew Jackson and Henry Clay joined in the quest. "The great business in Washington," Story wrote a Baltimore classmate in early 1823, "seems to be speculation as to the next President. I am glad . . . Maryland will be for Mr. Adams."[5] Yet concern seemed to mount, and by the beginning of 1824 his reports home apparently prompted his brother-in-law to complain over the "uncertainty as to the success of Mr. Adams in the presidential race."[6]

The uncertainty, however, continued through the year, past Election Day, and almost to the verge of the inaugural itself. It was resolved only when Adams reached the Presidency in the way his father left it—a constitutional crisis, and the succession determined by the House of Representatives. This time the deadlock was broken when the third-finishing Henry Clay threw his support to Adams, and the victory was secured completely when Daniel Webster, a letter from Adams in his pocket promising to be mindful of right-thinking Federalists, secured the support of critically important Congressmen. The double maneuver effectively undid the front-running Andrew Jackson, and the wrath of the Jacksonians exploded in cries of bargain and sale when Adams asked Clay to become Secretary of State in the new Cabinet.

The bargain may not have been as firm as some suggested, for Washington gossip had it that if Clay declined, Justice Story would receive the State portfolio.[7] In all probability the rumor merely reflected the long-time association of the two men from Massachusetts. Conceivably it could have reflected Story's thir

[5] Letter to Nathaniel Williams, Feb. 28, 1823, *ibid.*, 424.
[6] Letter from Stephen White, Feb. 16, 1824, in Story Papers, Library Congress.
[7] See letter to Mrs. Story, Feb. 20, 1825, in W. W. Story, I, 482.

extrajudicial intervention in the Adams cause, for the Justice was reputed to have invaded the halls of Congress before, and he would hardly have shrunk from a discreet contact with his friends at a time when every Representative's vote might tip a state delegation or even mean the Presidency itself. In terms of content and distinct from cause, however, the rumor was totally false, for Story had no intention of accepting a Cabinet post even were it offered. Rather, he had found his settled purpose on the bench of the Supreme Court, and from it he intended to join, both by aspiration and by accomplishment, in the structuring of an American constitutional state for which Adams' inaugural prayer had been offered and in which he shared even without knowing—"that the last results of its events may be auspicious and blessed."[8]

THE AMERICAN LAW

Implicit in Story's delighted comment on the Adams inaugural —"strong, sustained, correct and liberal, beating down party distinctions, and leading the way to a manly exposition of the Constitution"[9]—was his preference for his judicial office to the senior post in the Cabinet. Already his own judicial work had foreshadowed the Adams declarations in expounding the Constitution as the organic law of a nation-state, with the Supreme Court its ultimate expositor.

But there was more to the emerging configuration of law than its constitutional division between state and federal forms. The law itself was changing. A burgeoning commercial and industrial revolution was enormously enlarging and complicating its corpus. So, too, were the manipulative techniques. The lawmaking center of gravity was slowly shifting from the court to the legislature. Yet even as the statute books acquired an unprecedented length and detail, the term reports themselves achieved a new distinctive

[8] J. Q. Adams, *Memoirs*, VI, 518.
[9] Letter to Mrs. Story, March 4, 1825, in W. W. Story, I, 484.

form, passing from fragmentary notations *ad hoc* to—as the typical Story opinion showed—systematic and comprehensive restatements of topical law. And, acting as both leaven and overlay, the burgeoning American nationalism was putting its own distinctive impress on law as it was already transforming literature, letters, painting, and theology. Titles alone afforded an illuminating viewpoint to the nationalizing cultural transformation. At the turn of the century, a legal *summa* might consist of a reissue of the traditional Blackstone, supplemented by an index captioned "A Connected View of the Laws of Virginia as Member of the Federal Union." By the time of the Adams administration, however, organically transformed works entitled *Commentaries on American Law* and *General Abridgment and Digest of American Law* were in process of appearance.

Yet the whole process was a slow, tedious one, inevitably beset with both political and constitutional difficulties. Nor was it all along the lines the neo-conservatives desired, as developments from Kentucky illustrated. For the course of events in Kentucky included abolishing imprisonment for debt, establishing a comprehensive pattern of debtor relief, and then attempting to oust the entire state appellate bench for failure to give the relief laws effect. And Kentucky felt particularly outraged by the federal courts which sat beyond its wrath but on its soil and which likewise refused to enforce the state's ameliorative legislation in its own process and execution. As we have seen, Kentucky had two other grievances against these tribunals. One was the invalidation of the so-called occupying-claimant law which gave good-faith occupiers of land the value of their improvements. The other was an outraged discovery that it was a maritime state, with federal admiralty jurisdiction being asserted over the Ohio River, a stream entirely within its boundaries.

At the 1824 term by a minority vote, the Supreme Court upheld the invalidation of the occupying-claimant statute, and it was just one year later that the two other Kentucky questions came before the Supreme Court for final adjudication. Chief Justice Marshall, predictably, and the recently appointed Justice Smith Thompson, not so predictably, wrote a pair of matched opinions which avoided the constitutional issue and simply held that the federal process statute did not incorporate the ameliorative Kentucky legislation.[10] Even less predictably but more significantly, perhaps, Justice Story spoke for the Court and denied that admiralty jurisdiction extended to Kentucky waters.[11]

A cynic might see Story's uncharacteristic denial of jurisdiction as an attempt to placate the frontier state by resolving at least one controversy in her favor. And certainly there was other circumstantial evidence to that effect, both in the Kentucky fury consequent upon the disclosure of the minority character of the occupying-claimant decision and in a strong contemporary effort in the halls of Congress to curb the Supreme Court's powers over state legislation. Yet the evidence was misleading; Story had no option on the admiralty question, for the very historical exegesis which had sustained him in *De Lovio* explicitly foreclosed an inland jurisdiction which English admiralty never had. But also characteristic of his judicial ability to make a virtue of adversity was the truly significant reference in his apparent disclaimer—that Congress might, under its commerce powers, extend the admiralty to American inland waters ("If the public inconvenience . . shall be extensively felt, the attention of the legislature will doubtless be drawn to the subject"[12]).

Indeed, a luminous lesson in the ability of legislative action to fulfill judicial inadequacy had just been provided by the closing session of the Eighteenth Congress. The subject matter was criminal jurisdiction, an area in which Story seemingly had been not only defeated but routed. For his colleagues' early rejection of his idea for a self-declared criminal jurisdiction of common-law

Wayman v. Southard, 10 WHEATON 1 (1825), and *Bank of the United States v. Halstead, ibid.*, 51.
The Thomas Jefferson, ibid., 428. See also "From Judicial Grant to Legislative Power: The Admiralty Clause in the Nineteenth Century," *Harvard Law Review*, LXVII (1954), 1217.
10 WHEATON at 430 (1825).

crimes was reiterated in 1818 in *United States v. Bevans*, where the Supreme Court quashed a federal indictment for a murder committed aboard the *U.S.S. Independence* while she was anchored in Boston harbor.[13] Story appeared to acquiesce in the Court's disclaimer of jurisdiction in the absence of a specific statute and thereby to disown the position he had taken in the circuit court below. Appearances, however, were deceiving, for his silence was prompted by the capital nature of the case, and he subsequently published his unchanged views in an appendix to Mr. Wheaton's reports.[14]

A more positive statement of his views appeared in the *United States Statutes at Large*, in a section sponsored by Daniel Webster and passed by the Eighteenth Congress, and popularly known as the Federal Crimes Act of 1825.[15] If the new criminal code had any deficiencies, Justice Story could blame only himself, for he was the draftsman. To be sure, the enactment fell short of affording the amplitude a common-law jurisdiction would have given, but it was nonetheless a comprehensive and systematic measure and also a promising omen on the books, for he had written the first draft back in 1818, the same year that the Supreme Court had turned him back in the Bevans case. Mr. Justice Story had plans for other statutes, and presumably the schedule should improve, for as a draftsman he might now count on a sympathetic President and an understanding Congress. And, notwithstanding *Bevans*, he could continue to count on a group of colleagues who, with one conspicuous exception, were more a band of brothers than a bench of judges.

THE AMERICAN TRAGEDY

The exception was, of course, Justice William Johnson of Charleston, South Carolina, whose long-standing differences with

[13] 3 WHEATON 336 (1818).
[14] See 5 WHEATON, 103 n. (1820).
[15] *United States Statutes at Large*, IV, 115 (1825).

Story had included the question of the legality of the maritime slave trade under international law. Not unsurprisingly, Johnson and Story, sitting on circuit, had previously returned different answers to the question.

In Savannah in 1821 in *The Antelope*[16] Johnson ruled for legality; the following year in Boston Story in *La Jeune Eugénie* held to the contrary.[17] Johnson rendered judgment without opinion, and well he might, for legal precedent as well as politics both domestic and international supported his position. Story, on the other hand, claiming a jurisdiction which no court in the world had so far asserted, delivered a towering twelve-thousand-word opinion which followed the grand style he had developed in *De Lovio v. Boit* and *Martin v. Hunter's Lessee*.

The difference between Story and Johnson was, in fact, the knife edge that sometimes separates international law from purely municipal enactments. As far as the latter point was concerned, virtually every civilized nation had in one way or another condemned the maritime slave trade. Typical was the American action which declared it to be piracy and forbidden to American citizens under pain of death.[18] Yet the trade persisted, for enforcement of the formidable array of statutes, conventions, treaties, and international conferences remained a matter between sovereign and subject, save in the few instances where a reciprocal right of stoppage, search, and seizure had been negotiated by treaty. A beginning at international enforcement had been made when the British Lords Commissioners of Appeals in 1811 looked to their parliamentary statutes and declined to remand slave ships to claimants once possession had been broken by the Royal Navy.[19] But that holding had been reversed in successive decisions of Admiralty and King's Bench,[20] Sir William Scott in the initial

[16] Unreported. See Morgan, 137 (1954).
[17] 26 FED. CASES 832 (1822).
[18] *United States Statutes at Large,* III, 600 (1820).
[19] *The Amédie,* 1 DODSON 84 (1811).
[20] *Le Louis,* 2 DODSON 210 (1817); *Madrazo v. Willis,* 3 BARNEWELL & ALDERSON 353 (1820).

reversal noting that any truly international jurisdiction, as in the case of piracy, could rest only on statelessness, and that as long as a sovereign power chose to regard the slave trade (or any other matter) as a matter between its citizens and itself the same result could not follow.

To many suspicious Americans, and their number often included John Quincy Adams, Scott's admiralty court was the weathervane of the British Foreign Office, and the judicial demarche simply a retreat from the searches, seizures, and impressments which the Royal Navy had imposed on ships of all flags during the Napoleonic Wars. Resentment of British highhandedness, however, had left its mark in the perverse circumstance that the rising revulsion to the slave trade was accompanied by a bitter resistance toward the only practical means of ending it—the world-ranging patrols of the Royal Navy. And nowhere was this anomaly better shown than in Adams himself, who, while abhorring the trade, was nonetheless able to respond to a British inquiry whether anything could be worse: "Yes, admitting the right of search by foreign officers of our own vessels . . . for that would be making slaves of ourselves."[21]

And this was precisely the reaction of the French Foreign Ministry when the *Jeune Eugénie* was captured off the coast of Africa and brought before Story's Boston circuit court. The ship had no cargo at the time of seizure, but the long lower deck, the chains and manacles, and the many water casks gave her sinister character away. American-built, she had passed to a nominal French ownership in an ambiguous transfer in the West Indies. Her true ownership and the consequences of her illegal voyage—for it stood condemned by both French and American law—were argued in three separate but related proceedings: in the bitter protests of the French minister to Secretary of State Adams, in a spirited debate within the Monroe Cabinet, and by counsel for the interested parties in Boston.

The resulting transformation of the *Jeune Eugénie* incident

[21] Quoted in Mannix, *Black Cargoes* (1962), 205.

from a dispute over a squalid ship to an affair of state was material
for a great opinion, and Story responded accordingly. He began
in a usual mode, by emphasizing the gravity of the issue and half
apologizing that the inescapable dissection of the technicalities of
the *in rem* proceeding, in which he sifted the evidence of ownership and found it lacking one way or the other. This seeming
workaday calculus was in fact the critical first stage toward his
ultimate goal: proving that ownership, whatever it might be, was
irrelevant to his jurisdiction. The significance of the finding became apparent as the next two steps of the opinion unfolded.
One was an appeal to history in a recounting of the magnitude
and horrors of the slave trade as shown in recent congressional
reports. The other was a luminous exposition of a naturalistic
theory of international law—immanent in principle and ascertainable in rationality—which provided the context in which the consensus of condemnation of the slave trade had unfolded. Both the
state and the logic of British precedent gave him difficulty, but
he pressed through it, passed beyond the early British ruling, and
reached the expansive conclusion which attempted to radically
transform what had been but a series of purely municipal crimes:

> It appears to me, therefore, that in an American court of
> judicature, I am bound to consider the [slave] trade an of-
> fense against the universal law of society and in all cases,
> where it is not protected by a foreign government, to deal
> with it as an offense carrying with it the penalty of con-
> fiscation.[22]

By this logic Story meant that the *Jeune Eugénie*, whatever
her ownership, was forfeit unless it could be proven that her business was protected by the French government, which it obviously
was not. Yet this very logic also roused the French to threaten
counterseizures of American ships and even stronger measures.
Snatching the rose of safety from the nettle of danger, Story responded in a double tour de force. Following the suggestion of

26 FED. CASES at 847.

the executive branch while declaring his judicial independence of it, he granted the French claim—a remand of the ship to the French consul, ostensibly for further proceedings under French law.

It could have been a much shorter exercise. Story might have found the initial transfer colorable, declared the *Jeune Eugénie* American (indeed, she had been captured on such assumption), and condemned her. But Story was far more interested in condemning the trade than in condemning a ship, and the pattern of contemporary circumstances suggested why he went to such lengths to strengthen the hands of those who shared his views. One target was American public opinion. "Everybody is in expectation here," wrote Webster from Philadelphia in early 1821, "of receiving your opinion in the case of the Young Eugenie. It must come out, and that soon."[23] But beyond Philadelphia was Washington, where a strong group in the House of Representatives was seeking to pass a resolution proposing an Anglo-American treaty which would provide for bilateral search and seizure of slavers flying either country's flag. And across the Atlantic lay the ancient city of Verona, where later that year yet another international conference was to seek practical means of suppressing the trade.

If this was Story's design, it met a mixed and ultimately abortive fate. On the American side of the Atlantic, things began well enough. In January of 1823 the House overwhelmingly approved the resolution, and Secretary Adams moved to negotiate accordingly. He found the British to be cooperation itself, largely because on the other side of the Atlantic things had gone badly. At Verona the British had sought to have every participant denounce the slave trade as piracy "with a view to finding upon the aggregate of such separate engagements . . . a General Law to be incorporated into the Public Law of the Civilized World."[24] The

[23] Letter of Jan. 3, 1821, in Webster, *Private Correspondence*, I, 314.
[24] The Duke of Wellington to Secretary Canning, Nov. 29, 1822, in *British and Foreign State Papers, 1822–1823* (London, 1850), 99.

parallelism with Story's *La Jeune Eugénie* logic was obvious, and a friend wrote him joyfully that the opinion was "about to receive the efficient support of the British Government."[25] The optimism was premature. Possibly as a direct result of the *Jeune Eugénie* controversy, and certainly as its indirect consequence, French opposition shattered the British proposal. In place of the binding treaty which the British had sought, all that the Verona Conference produced was paper resolutions, empty of force, power, or legal effect.

At home the tide was also flowing the other way, for almost at the moment Story delivered his *La Jeune Eugénie* opinion in Boston, discovery of an incipient slave revolt rocked Charleston to its foundations and sent a shock wave through the entire South. Unquestionably, the hardening of Southern attitudes on slavery took its toll when, in early 1824, the Senate took the reciprocal search and seizure which Adams had so painstakingly negotiated and gutted it with a host of reservations and exceptions, so that the British washed their hands of further cooperation with the United States.

It was against this background that *The Antelope* came out of Justice Johnson's Georgia circuit for final decision at the Supreme Court's 1825 term. Possibly three years earlier the decision, which refused to condemn the trade as a matter of international law, might have been reversed. For at that time Story had circulated his newly written *La Jeune Eugénie* opinion among his colleagues and had written home, "[T]he Chief Justice . . . says that he thinks that I am right, but the questions are new to his mind."[26] The momentum of events, however, resolved the questions the other way. Indeed, after the Verona impasse and the treaty debacle, all that the Supreme Court had for decision was whether it would rush in where the combined talents of the British Foreign Office and John Quincy Adams had failed, by assert-

Letter from William Johnson, May 11, 1824, Story Papers, Library of Congress. The writer was Chancellor Kent's reporter and not the Supreme Court Justice.
Letter to Jeremiah Mason, Feb. 21, 1822, in Hillard, *Mason*, 256.

ing an American right of search and seizure against the world and correspondingly granting to all comers the same right as to American vessels. The Court, speaking through the Chief Justice, upheld Justice Johnson, and not even Story formally dissented, although he never conceded the point.[27]

There was another and peculiarly domestic consideration in the case which had been suggested by the newly elected Senator John M. Berrien of Georgia—that if the slave trade was the equivalent of piracy, then Americans, as a nation, were "robbers . . clinging to your plunder."[28] But this conclusion could not obtain in a country where the protective covenants of slavery, the Fugitive Slave Law, and even slave representation were indispensable elements of the Constitution. Perhaps the argument accounted in part for Story's silence. In any event, he apparently found it impressive, for years later he cited it in validating the federal Fugitive Slave Law in *Prigg v. Pennsylvania*.[29]

---

[27] *The Antelope*, 10 WHEATON 66 (1825). In a letter to Ezekiel Bacon, Nov 19, 1842 (W. W. Story, II, 431), Joseph Story wrote: "My decision was overruled . . . in the case of the Antelope, but I always thought that was right, and continue to think so."
[28] 10 WHEATON at 86.
[29] 16 PETERS 539 (1842).

CHAPTER XX

The Glorious Year of 1825

FAIR HARVARD

While the *Antelope* decision symbolized the fault line which the institution of slavery had shot through the American constitutional structure, its significance in early 1825 seemed overshadowed by the restrained optimism of the Adams inaugural, and Story rode north from the 1825 term into what probably was to be the happiest year of his life. And certainly his cup must have filled to overflowing when, on June 4, 1825, a brief item in the Boston papers noted that the Harvard Corporation had "selected the Honorable Joseph Story to fill a vacancy in its number."[1] The selection both crowned an association begun thirty years earlier with Story's belated enrollment in the class of 1798 and vindicated the prophetic character of the second honors he won on graduation. Recognition began in 1815 when Story was named to assist the school of theology, was underscored in 1819 with appointment to the board of overseers, and was seemingly crowned in 1822, with the grant of Harvard's doctorate of laws *honoris causa*.

Unhappily, however, a touch of blight marred the unfolding

[1] *Columbian Centinel*, Jan. 25, 1825.

laurels and provided some criticism in an age more tolerant than its successors in such matters. There had been comments on the overseer appointment, which came while the question of state control over private colleges was under advisement before the Supreme Court in *Dartmouth College v. Woodward*. The same nuance touched his defense in the Massachusetts constitutional convention of Harvard's prerogatives, and the subsequently awarded LL.D. And now, in becoming a fellow of the Harvard Corporation, Story came uncomfortably closer to violating the Blackstonian maxim that no one should be a judge in his own case, for only six months earlier he had taken the lead in rebutting the proposition that such appointment could be made only from the resident professors of the university.

The "fellow" controversy was the focus of an even more basic one over the future of Harvard itself which began in 1819 with the appointment of George Ticknor as Smith professor of French and Spanish literature. Spurred by an inspiring European view of what a university might be, and appalled at the intellectual inertia and the misapplication of funds he found at Cambridge, Ticknor fruitlessly appealed to the university president, to the resident professors, and, in 1821, to William Prescott, fellow of the Harvard Corporation, onetime member of the Salem bar, and Story's close friend and mentor. From this it was the shortest of steps to Overseer Joseph Story, whose collaboration in the proposed reform rapidly reached the point where Ticknor was writing Story of "your plan" for Harvard and of making the university "what you desire."[2]

The reformers got their chance in May, 1823, when forty out of seventy-six seniors (including a son of Secretary Adams) were expelled in what was subsequently known as "the Great Rebellion." Undergraduate unrest at Harvard was not new. In fact, in Story's own undergraduate days Watson's *Apology for the Bible* was distributed as an antidote for Paine's *Age of Reason*, and students were cautioned against "riotous actions within the walls

[2] Letter to Joseph Story, Jan. 6, 1823, in Story Papers, Library of Congress.

of the college, or . . . indecencies in the hall and the chapel."[3] The difference lay in the indisposition of the students—and of the country—to bear a rule which was increasingly regarded as unjust and anachronistic. Whether the Harvard reformers saw the parallel was another question. In any event, by July of 1813 the Story–Ticknor program (although it was never called that) had been finally reformulated. It called for a general overhaul of the university's teaching and admission policies—a reinvigorated presidency, departmental orientation, instruction by proficiency, and a broad elective program.

Tactically, the reformers sought preliminary approval of their plans through committees from the overseers and the fellows. The committees were duly appointed—Story headed that of the overseers—and thereafter held a seemingly interminable series of joint meetings. The overseers' committee finally drew up an approving report of the Story–Ticknor proposals which the Justice sent to President Kirkland. In his turn Dr. Kirkland held the document over two months, then returned it, and in due course the report was presented to a meeting of the full board of overseers in June, 1824.

By this time the forces opposing change—largely the resident faculty—had rallied sufficiently to mount a defense, headed by Andrew Norton, professor of Scripture. Their tactics involved a vigorous personal, if anonymous, attack on Story and Ticknor as bungling intermeddlers ("unauthorized, unapparent, irresponsible individuals, however respectable they may be."[4]) The defense was temporarily successful, at least to the extent of inducing the overseers to appoint yet another committee under Overseer Lowell to appraise the recommendations of the one headed by Overseer Story. The resident faculty members did more than defend. They counterattacked by framing a memorial which insisted that the Harvard Corporation could come only from their

John Clarke, *Letters to a Student in the University at Cambridge* (Boston, '96), 31.
Quoted in D. Tyack, *George Ticknor and the Boston Brahmins* (1967; hereinafter cited as Tyack), 117.

number. Originally this had indeed been the practice, but over two centuries the "corporation," as the fellows were called collectively, had increasingly been taken from the ranks of the merchant-lawyer establishments of Massachusetts.

While the twin controversies were supposedly fought out in secret within the university structure, the news that something was afoot could not be completely suppressed. "It is generally known," reported a Boston paper as the two issues came before the overseers' meeting in early 1825, "that, for a year or two past, something or other had been negotiating among the Overseers of Harvard College."[5] The issue was first joined on January 6 on the issue of university reform, and the Story–Ticknor proposals won decisively. By midyear the program had been given final legal effect, which not only included structural changes but also emphasized improving student conditions and, "if possible, avoiding trespass on the real or imaginary rights of the Professors."[6]

The reference to faculty sensitivity was not accidental but closely related to the "fellow" controversy, which was also resolved at the January overseers' meeting. This too had followed trail of committee recommendations, which, in this case, found adversely to the faculty position. The committee report, however, was but the overture for an overkill of extraordinary proportion.

> The Hon. Judge STORY rose and in a speech of over three hours . . . highly eulogized the character of the Memorialists . . . [but] remarked that the question . . . was a law —and distinctly a law question, and as a lawyer, he did not hesitate to say that the Memorialists had mistaken the law.[7]

Doubtless the protesting professors never dreamed what an almost inexhaustible quarry of legal learning was afforded by the single word "fellow." For literally hour after hour its content was ex-

[5] *Boston Recorder and Telegraph,* Jan. 22, 1825.
[6] *Columbian Centinel,* June 6, 1825, quoting the *Commercial Advertiser,* May 10, 1825.
[7] *Ibid.,* Jan. 15, 1825.

pounded and its background explored in a Story opinion cast in the form of a board-meeting address. Whether the speaker knew he was also establishing his own qualifications for the office can only be surmised, but a suspicion is at least permissible. In any event, Story delivered his point of view not only as a lawyer talking down laymen, but as a virtually unique specialist in the legal point involved. For the subject, he began, "was quite remote from the ordinary occupations and studies of lawyers in this country,"[8] and from this prelude he swept through an exhaustive and exhausting survey of British precedent to the triumphal conclusion that no tutorial qualifications attached to the office of fellow. The judge, turned advocate for the defense, shattered the professors' case. A few follow-up speakers completed the rout.

Insofar as Story was personally concerned, his double academic triumph was especially significant for the lengths to which he went in maintaining good relations with the remonstrating professors . . . "I have not the slightest desire," he wrote one, ". . . to triumph over your argument even if I could. Far from it. I shall present my views . . . as a lawyer, and with the constant recollection that doctors may, and lawyers do, often disagree."[9] There was far more here than a tendency to be, at least as far as civility went, all things to all men. Rather, there was an immense respect for the office of teacher in general and, quite possibly, an intuitive apprehension that his own affinity for the law as a taught tradition might someday bring him to the Harvard faculty.

Certainly the law at Harvard had already touched his own career in several ways. In 1815 the foundation of the Royall professorship had prompted him to abandon his plans to give some lectures in Boston. On a more positive note, a year later he used a book review to give his ideas on what legal education should be and to salute, somewhat anticipatorily, the expansion of the Royall

[8] "Rights of the Fellows of Harvard University," in *Miscellaneous Writings*, 295.
[9] Joseph Story to Edward Everett, Jan. 8, 1825, in W. W. Story, I, 448.

chair to the law school which "the Government of Harvard College have, so honorably to themselves established at Cambridge."[10] Recognition was a two-way street, and Harvard early saw the professorial bent of its distinguished alumnus—for Story's speeches, opinions, book reviews, and lectures from the circuit bench were all forms of teaching—and sought his services as law professor in 1820 and again in 1825. In both instances he declined after much thought and genuine regret, but shortly after the first incident the Supreme Court's reporter passed through Cambridge and wrote a prophetic comment:

> I was happy to find, when at Cambridge, that great solicitude was felt that you should accept their call. Indeed I expected that such would be the feeling: but I don't see how you can break off your Salem associations. I hope however that you may yet be fixed at Cambridge.[11]

CIRCUIT JUSTICE

Reporter Wheaton was certainly correct about the nature of Story's ties in Salem. An officer in its banks, a long-time member of its school board, and a frequent and honored speaker at the town meeting, Story had lived there twenty-five years and had come a long way from the early days when his oratorical efforts drew a collective Federalist hiss. He had held the brilliant reception when President Monroe visited the city in 1817, and he had been the obvious choice to serve as president of the day when the venerable Lafayette visited the city in late 1824. "Our gratitude," Story then noted in combining his constitutional theory with the popular mood, "will not perish until America ceases to be a nation."[12]

Lafayette might well have thought Story the most mobile member of a highly mobile race, for not only did they meet in

[10] Book review of *Course of Legal Study* in *Miscellaneous Writings*, 66, 90.
[11] Letter from Henry Wheaton, Oct. 10, 1820, Wheaton Papers.
[12] *Columbian Centinel*, Sept. 24, 1824.

Salem in the fall of 1824, but they met again in Washington after the turn of the year, in Boston in June of 1825, and at Albany the following July. The July encounter was occasioned by a trip that Story and his wife made to Niagara Falls in company with the Daniel Websters. It was a rare enough excursion, and the fact that Mrs. Story felt well enough to travel was in itself a circumstance of congratulation significant enough to make the year a memorable one. Usually the reverse was true, and one suspects that Mrs. Story rather enjoyed her poor health, wearing the martyr's crown in her frequently husbandless parlor. The absent husband made amends of a sort with frequent, lengthy, tender, chatty letters home, but perhaps doing just a trifle too good a job of it.

The trip was also something of a novelty because Story's judicial commitments left little time for such excursions. It was not the Supreme Court service as such which interfered. Actually, duty in Washington accounted for a minor portion of Story's absences. A great bulk of his time was spent away from home riding circuit under a system which sent him around New England twice a year to preside at the trial level alongside the local federal-district judge. Bad enough to begin with, the arrangement came under increasing strain as the country expanded territorially and the law explosion piled up the federal judicial business at both the circuit and Washington levels. It was characteristic of the system that in early spring of 1825 Story rode north to his delay-ridden circuit dockets from a term of the Supreme Court which saw but thirty-eight cases decided out of four times as many argued, and that prospects for the following year suggested an even greater imbalance.

President after president had already asked Congress to confine the Supreme Court to Washington so that its ever-growing docket might have its exclusive attention. President Adams did likewise in his first message, which was read to the newly convened Nineteenth Congress in early December of 1825. Yet the proposal, like its predecessors, had a special gantlet to run, for each attempt at judicial reform had inevitably become entangled in the efforts of disgruntled litigants to bridle the Court for its decisions. As a result, the fact that nothing had been accomplished in the past was in itself almost a triumph, and nothing in the present suggested that the hazardous potential had diminished. In fact, Webster, in discussing the possibility of expanding the federal judiciary—a necessary adjunct of the Presidential proposal—cast his eye at restive Kentucky and expressed a doubt that "the judge-breaking temper now prevailing in some parts of the Western country"[13] would permit the selection of any candidates from that region.

Adams' proposal provoked yet another full-length debate on the federal judicial process, and proceedings opened in the House at the turn of the year. Circuit riding was alternately praised and assailed. So were the Court's decisions. The overloaded dockets were uniformly criticized. Sectional sentiments were expounded ("And so, sir, in this matter of the Supreme Court: the People of the West want to have a finger in the pie"[14]). The changing nature of business enterprise and business litigation was noted (". . . a large portion of the business in the Federal Courts of the West, consists of suits brought by Corporations . . ."[15]). There were pleas for the status quo ("I am not one of those, Mr. Chairman, who believe that a frank and liberal association, by our judges with the honest Republicans of the country, will taint the judicial ermine"[16]).

And doubtless most pleasing to Story were the accolades. One Congressman lauded the justices for impartiality in the face of local associations:

> Let us travel . . . North—have we not seen Judge Story uniting with the Supreme Court . . . declaring to the People of New Hampshire: You have violated the provisions of the Constitution by attempting to divest Dartmouth College of her vested rights. Yet Judge Story had a Circuit in that State, and was connected by all the ties of party and personal

[13] J. Q. Adams, *Memoirs*, VII, 84.
[14] *Register of Debates*, II, Part 1, 914 (1826).
[15] *Ibid.*, 934.
[16] *Ibid.*, 952.

considerations, with the members of the State Legislature who passed the unconstitutional law.[17]

Webster picked up the tribute and turned it into an endorsement of circuit riding:

> And I would ask the honorable member . . . since he had referred to the Judge of the first Circuit . . . if, fifteen years ago, on receiving his commission, he had moved to this City, had remained here . . . with no other connection with his profession other than an annual session of six weeks in the Supreme Court, would he have been the Judge he is now?[18]

Almost miraculously, the House passed the reform bill which abolished circuit riding. Unbelievably, so did the Senate, but with amendments. Each house then refused to recede from its position, and, after an extended season of effort, the measure fell between two stools. All that came from the debates was a statute advancing the beginning of the Supreme Court's term from the first Monday in January to the third Monday in January.

And Mrs. Story had even more time alone in her Salem parlor, and the Justice was away from home more than ever.

DAY OF JUBILEE

In all probability, Story was not too disappointed as he left Washington after the 1826 term to undertake circuit duty in New England. The term itself held little of importance, and the contemporary judicial history was written on the floor of Congress. By appropriate coincidence Story's only significant opinion at that term exemplified the very shortcomings in the federal judicial system which had prompted the extended, if indecisive, legislative review. The opinion came in *The Marianna Flora*.[19] It was the second opinion Story had written in the case, the first having been done when he tried the case at circuit. But the case did more

[17] *Ibid.,* 958.
[18] *Ibid.,* 1145.
[19] 11 Wheaton at 1 (1826).

than typify a procedure wherein appeals went from Story to Story; it also afforded a vehicle for fortifying two points previously made in *La Jeune Eugénie;* it insisted that the courts of all civilized states held a common jurisdiction over the common enemies of mankind, and it strengthened the anti–slave-trade patrols by substantially narrowing the liability of American commanders for erroneous seizure.

The absence of other important judicial decisions did not, however, mean the absence of important judicial business. On the contrary, there was on the docket of the Court, where it had been since 1823, the critically significant issue of the state insolvency laws. Absence, illness, and deep internal division had repeatedly postponed decision, and these causes of delay were compounded in 1825 with the death of Justice Todd and the consequent reluctance of the Court (understandable in view of the uproar following the occupying-claimant case) to decide a constitutional point without a full bench.[20] Yet here the very legislative debate, itself full of criticism of judicial delay, caused still more delay. President Adams, uncertain as to whether Congress might enlarge the Court, delayed nominating Todd's successor until the legislative situation had clarified itself, but by that time adjournment of the term had come and gone.

The legislative impasse did more than shift the insolvency question to the 1827 term. It also marked a brief and misleading lull in the widespread, ongoing movement of legal reform, which included not only the tribunals by which the law was decided, but the substance of the law itself. One facet concerned a drive to systematically classify and collate statutes, for the law explosion had passed the point where legislation could be readily found in a jackstraw pile of session acts. And, in fact, Story himself was working along this line, for he had in preparation *The Public and General Statutes of the United States,* designed to winnow

---

[20] While this principle appears to have been first announced as a rule of court in *Briscoe v. Bank of the State of Kentucky,* 9 PETERS 85 (1835), it may have been initially suggested by Thomas A. Emmett of the New York bar. See his letter to Story, Feb. 3, 1824, in Story Papers, Library of Congress.

the "unwieldy, voluminous, and expensive" *United States Statutes at Large*, to add "a copious verbal index" and thereby make "the facility of reference as complete as possible."[21]

It was not the first time he had put his hand to such a project. Back in 1814 he had served on a commission to codify, as the phrase increasingly had it, the provincial and colonial laws of Massachusetts; his work with the federal statutes came as a natural continuation of this effort. Another commissioner, the venerable Nathan Dane of Beverly, had turned to another line of development—a systematic, comprehensive, and topical exposition of a body of law shorn of irrelevant English elements and fitted to a distinctively American framework. Dane's undertaking was a nine-volume effort (the last volume, significantly, an index) entitled *A General Abridgement and Digest of American Law*, and the author's onetime colleague was kept apprised of its progress. In fact, Dane arranged to have Story sent the first volume for deposit with the Secretary of State under the Copyright Act,[22] and Story responded with a favorable, if somewhat restrained review of Dane's work in *The North American Review*.

While Story associated himself in Dane's quest for "one collected body of American law," he carefully balanced admonitions for "the exclusive admirers of the common law" and "the extravagance of some of the advocates of codes."[23] This manifest reservation of position was significant. There had been a time when he was in the vanguard of the movement to give the law simplicity, accessibility, and precision. But now these very demands were coming with increasing frequency and volume from the Jacksonian camp, which restated the old Jeffersonian dictum that a plowman was fully the equal of a professor in matters of judgment, in the thesis that there should be no law other than that explicitly adopted by the popular assembly.

[21] Preface, *The Public and General Statutes of the United States*, ed. Story (1827).
[22] Letter from Dane to Story, Jan. 14, 1824, in Story Papers, Library of Congress.
[23] Story, "Digests of the Common Law," in *Miscellaneous Writings*, 394, 405.

Certainly Story's early work carried credentials which should have gratified the Jacksonian codifiers. His first work, *American Precedents of Declarations*, had been sarcastically criticized for having "saved many an indigent student or careless practitioner from the intolerable evil of thinking," and *A Selection of Pleadings in Civil Actions* (1805) had been skewered for the same reason.[24] If the codifiers and Story drew on the same early roots, profoundly different attitudes between them became increasingly apparent. For what the codifiers sought as an ultimate triumph Story saw as ultimate tragedy—the reduction of the judiciary to triers of a fact.

Unquestionably, the hardening of attitudes on both sides of the discussion took its toll in the ever-increasing qualifications which Story attached to an initial enthusiasm for codification. Thus, in early 1825 the Court's reporter recalled a Story pronouncement "very decidedly in favour of reducing the whole of our Law to a written text."[25] Story, however, quickly amended the declaration. "I have long been an advocate of codification of the common law," Story conceded in a reply limiting the categorical nature of the original assertion, "at least of that part, which is most reduced to principles & is of daily & extensive application."[26] He could still wax enthusiastic in some areas, however. "What would be our gain," he continued, "if our principles of shipping, insurance, and bills of exchange were reduced to a code, as they are in a most admirable form in the French code of Commerce?"[27] He closed by cautioning the reporter not to show the letter at large, as he had not stated his ideas in satisfactory form.

Doubtless this difficulty of articulation accounted for the ambiguous treatment of the subject in what was one of his greatest speeches, the Phi Beta Kappa oration entitled "Characteristics of the Age" which he delivered at Harvard in August of 1826. He

[24] Anonymous reviewer in *Monthly Anthology and Boston Review*, II (1805), 483. I am indebted to Prof. James McClellan for this reference.
[25] Letter from Henry Wheaton, Sept. 19, 1825, Wheaton Papers.
[26] Letter to Henry Wheaton, Oct. 1, 1825, Wheaton Papers.
[27] *Ibid.*

seemed to lean toward the reformers when he noted that "jurisprudence, which reluctantly admits any new adjunct and counts
in its train a thousand champions ready to rise in defense of its
formularies and technical rules, [has] adopted much which philosophy and experience have recommended."[28] Perhaps his light
note came from an essentially ephemeral sense of security, for the
address was a formidable exercise in optimism. While he quoted
Burke's admonition that innovation was not necessarily reform, he
found the general progress of events to his liking and even had a
few good words to say about the French Revolution. He approvingly surveyed almost the entire range of contemporary institutions and conditions (omitting completely, however, slavery, sec-
tionalism, and democracy) and passed to a vivid nationalist panegyric:

> To us, Americans, nothing can or ought to be indifferent,
> that respects the cause of science or literature . . . There
> is that in the American character, which has never yet been
> found unequal to its purpose. There is that in American
> enterprise, which shrinks not, and faints not in its labors.[29]

Then, drawing on the concurrent passing of John Adams and
Thomas Jefferson a few weeks earlier on the fiftieth anniversary
of the Declaration of Independence, he passed to his triumphal
close:

> [We are] wholesomely conscious of our own powers and
> our destiny. We have just passed the jubilee of our inde-
> pendence, and have witnessed the prayers and gratitude of
> millions, ascending to heaven, for our public and private
> blessings . . . We have been privileged yet more; we have
> lived to witness an almost miraculous event in the departure
> of the great authors of our independence on that memorable
> and blessed day of jubilee.[30]

[28] "Characteristics of the Age," in *Miscellaneous Writings*, 353.
[29] *Ibid.*, 369-70.
[30] *Ibid.*, 373.

CHAPTER XXI

The Turn of the Tide

ELECTIONS, BANKRUPTS, AND REPORTERS

The glorious year which could be roughly measured from the accession of the John Quincy Adams Administration to the golden anniversary of American independence, and which included a consequence of signal successes both on and off the bench, came to an abrupt close as the off-year elections of 1826 returned an anti-Adams Congress and cast the long shadow of Andrew Jackson across the land. "There is," wrote the President, "a decided majority of both houses of Congress in opposition to the Administration—a state of things which has never before occurred under the Government of the United States."[1] And this event was closely followed by another event which had never before occurred under the government of the United States: Chief Justice Marshall was overridden by his own Court on a constitutional question.

The occasion was the long-drawn-out insolvency case *Ogden v. Saunders*,[2] wherein the hour of decision had been fixed by two seemingly unrelated events. One was the appointment of District Judge Robert Trimble to what was becoming the Kentucky

[1] J. Q. Adams, *Memoirs*, VII, 367.
[2] 12 WHEATON 213 (1827).

seat on the Court, an appointment which brought the tribunal to
the full strength appropriate to the deciding of a constitutional
question. The other was the termination of the minuetlike pattern
of maneuver in which Court and Congress sought to evade responsibility for resolving the issue in the face of what Story had
called a strange medley of opposite views in describing a powerful debtor-creditor coalition. The coalition fought hard to preserve its variegated advantages in the patchwork status quo, and
was particularly opposed to the changes implicit in a national
bankruptcy act. Yet, conceivably, the Court might overcome even
this powerful opposition, for if it invalidated prospective state
insolvency laws as an unconstitutional impairment of contract, its
judicial veto would have logically complemented the one previously pronounced in 1819, of retrospective statutes. All such
legislation would be swept from the board, and Congress given
the sharpest of spurs to fill the void. Yet there was no guaran-
tee that Congress would do so, and doubtless this possibility of
legislative *fainéance* gave considerable pause to judicial activism.

Yet Mr. Justice Story was nothing if not a judicial activist. He
had done his best in 1819 to speed judicial decision with the pur-
pose of impelling Congress to act in bankruptcy, and in the in-
tervening years he had lost none of his energetic enthusiasm.
"What hope of a bankrupt act?" he wrote Webster in 1824.
"Why will you not ask me to put one in the shape of a Code.
. . . I want to try my hand at codifying a bankrupt ordinance."[3]
He did so, but, in sharp contrast with his success in the Federal
Crimes Act, Congress failed to act. The consequence sharply underlined the significance of the Ogden case, and one of Story's
Baltimore classmates saw no impropriety in writing him that it
had become "a most momentous question . . . now especially
since Congress will not extend any relief through a bankrupt law
to 100,000 of the most enterprising of our citizens."[4] Yet even

[3] Letter to Daniel Webster, Jan. 1, 1824, in Webster, *Private Correspondence*, I, 437.
[4] Letter from Nathaniel Williams, Mar. 2, 1824, Story Papers, Library of
Congress.

though Congress did not act, it was obviously concerned, and on the eve of Adams' inaugural, Webster told the attentive House in the closing moments of the Eighteenth Congress that "up to this moment he had not learned that [the Supreme Court] had pronounced its judgment in the [Ogden] case."[5]

Two years and a new Congress did nothing to change the legislative impasse, and Story had scarcely arrived for the 1827 term when he learned with dismay "the bankrupt bill has been lost, and under circumstances which will forbid any attempt to revive it for many years."[6] The legislative development did, however, fit in as the last factor in precipitating the decision of the Ogden case, and the resulting profusion of views from the Court suggested the tensions which the question had produced among its members.

Most noteworthy, perhaps, was the concurring majority opinion of Mr. Justice Washington, who tipped the balance on an otherwise divided Court. A one-eyed, snuff-bespattered little man, Washington's nondescript appearance belied both his distinguished name and his flintlike inflexibility. Curiously, it was Washington who, on circuit in 1814, wrote a ringing opinion which held the federal bankruptcy power to be both exclusive and preemptive. When these views were modified in *Sturgis v. Crowninshield*, Washington's deep concern for the logical integrity of the law led him to abandon his heartfelt initial views and apply what he regarded as the *Crowninshield* rationale—that existing insolvency law formed part of every contract when made—to a conclusion that there could be no impairment of contract by a prospective insolvency law. And, significantly, this concern for formal logic led Washington, who detested dissent and who on at least one occasion dissuaded Story from it, to enter his only formal dissent in his thirty-one years on the Court in a related case on the 1827 docket, *Mason v. Haille*.[7] In this dissent Wash-

[5] *Register of Debates*, I, 741 (1825).
[6] Letter to John Brazer Davis, Feb. 4, 1827, in W. W. Story, I, 514.
[7] 12 WHEATON 370 (1827).

ington stood alone and insisted that states could not constitutionally effect a retroactive abolition of imprisonment for debt.

The *Ogden* dissenters—Marshall, Story, and Duvall—were certainly unprepared to carry their canonization of contract to this
extent, and quite possibly their hesitancy produced the sarcastic
nuance in Justice Johnson's majority opinion in *Ogden* that absolute enforcement of contracts required insolvent debtors to be
sold into slavery. If it was a satiric thrust at Story and Marshall,
it might be said that Justice Johnson at least motivated some of
the more hot-tempered outbursts which shocked the Court a few
years earlier. But whether his reference was deliberate or coinci-
dental, there was no doubt that his opinion propounded a new
and tempered view of the constitutional protection of contracts,
although it was one that Johnson had expressed as early as his
concurrence in the Yazoo land-fraud case of *Fletcher v. Peck*.

The Ogden case also afforded Justice Johnson the opportunity
to revert to his occasionally latitudinarian concept of concurrent
powers. For in an extraordinary display of the power of a majority of one, Johnson changed sides on the issue of scope and
joined Story, Marshall, and Duvall (all three of whom were
doubtless making the best of a bad situation) to hold, in effect,
that state insolvency laws were operative only in the courts of
the enacting jurisdiction to contracts framed within that state
and could not be pleaded in the tribunals of the federal government or of sister states.

But perhaps of all the cases at the 1827 term, Johnson found an
even more formidable vehicle of counterattack against Story's
activism in *Ramsay v. Allegre*.[8] Here in a concurring opinion
Johnson used blunt reprimand and subtle reproof to attack both
Story and reporter Wheaton. The case involved the subordinate
(and, in the view of the majority, irrelevant) point of whether
admiralty had personal jurisdiction in the suits of materialmen,
and an argument of a distinguished lawyer to this effect had been
reported by Wheaton at the 1819 term. Johnson questioned the

[8] 12 WHEATON 611 (1827).

accuracy of the quotation and then passed to substantive attack in questioning whether American admiralty held a jurisdiction measured by that of its original English counterpart. It was, of course, an attack on Story's opinion in *De Lovio v. Boit,* and Johnson opened it with a mock inquiry as to where "the idea originated, that the admiralty . . . jurisdiction vested by the Consituation" was the one possessed "before the time of Richard II."[9] Proving that he knew the answer by citing *De Lovio* as a nameless "opinion in the first circuit,"[10] Johnson opened a counteroffensive in scholarship by blandly noting that in the third American edition of Abbott's *Ships and Shipping* the "learned editor"[11] had stated that no American cases existed on this particular aspect of jurisdiction. Obviously relishing his find, Johnson cited cases—all adverse to jurisdiction—which did exist. What he did not say, in exquisitely exasperating forbearance, was that Story was the editor of the first American edition of Abbott, that the third edition advertised its incorporation of Judge Story's notes, and that these notes did not advert to the cases in point.

Johnson's wrath was probably also kindled by his irritation over the Wheaton succession, for he seemed to feel that his colleagues on the bench had combined to rule the choice. Or at least such is the implication in a sour note he sent an unsuccessful aspirant to the job. "I presume you know," he wrote, "that even in a Supreme Court there may be Parties & cannot be uninformed of the Triumvirate that is supposed to exist in ours."[12] Unquestionably, the triumvirate was Marshall, Story, and, notwithstanding his *Ogden* position, Washington; and the available record shows that the three were most capable of acting under seeming individual capacities to effect a common design.[13]

Perhaps Johnson should have added one more member to the

[9] *Ibid.,* 638.
[10] *Ibid.*
[11] *Ibid.,* 626.
[12] Letter to Henry Breckenridge, Dec. 5, 1827, in William F. Keller, *The Nation's Advocate* (Pittsburgh, 1950), 327.
[13] See Burton A. Konkle, *Joseph Hopkinson* (Philadelphia, 1931), 253.

triumvirate, for in the very nature of the case reporter Wheaton had the last word on the *Ramsay* opinion, and he took it in an extended note in his final volume. ("The editor . . . feels it to be a duty which he owes to self-respect, and to the independence of the bar, to take some notice of the comments made in the above opinion."[14]) Nominally respectful and patient in tone, it was in fact a stinging rebuttal to Johnson's position. ("In making these remarks, the editor has certainly not been influenced by any feelings of disrespect towards the learned judge by whom the above opinion was delivered, nor even by a desire to controvert the peculiar doctrines maintained in that opinion."[15]) And any question as to the sarcastic character of the reporter's epilogue was resolved by its repetition in his private correspondence: "I left Judge Johnson my compliments at the end of the Reports."[16]

COURTS, COMMERCE, AND CORPORATIONS

Another rejoinder to Justice Johnson appeared shortly before the close of 1827 with the publication of the third volume of Mason's reports of Story's opinions in the first circuit. Included in the book was a terse reprise of his elaborate *De Lovio* judgment: "Upon the subject of [admiralty] jurisdiction I have no more to say, than that I have seen no reason to change the opinion which I expressed several years since . . ."[17] Yet there was a double irony in the Story–Johnson confrontation which emphasized both the rising importance of the law reports and the waning importance of their differences.

On the first point there was the fact that the issue of the nature and extent of American admiralty jurisdiction had already been decided by the Supreme Court when it sat at Philadelphia in the

4 12 WHEATON at 640.
5 *Ibid.,* 642.
6 Letter to Daniel Webster, Nov. 20, 1827, Wheaton Papers.
7 *Peele v. The Merchants Insurance Co.,* 19 FED. CASES at 99 (1822).

very beginnings of its history. "I heard the argument and the decision," Peter Du Ponceau of that city's bar wrote to Story, "but it is forgotten. . . . There was no reporter at that day, & all who were present at the argument, are, I believe, dead, except myself . . ."[18] But the second was even more important, and concerned the gradual transformation in American enterprise from its simple, sea-trading, mercantilistic forms to complex financial and manufacturing aggregates. The legal consequences appeared in the dwindling proportion and importance of maritime litigation, on one hand, and, on the other, the emergence of a new body of law fitted to the demands of the new economic age. And it was here, in a brilliant series of opinions which both furnished a rebuttal to the codifier's insistence that all law come from the legislature and brilliantly exemplified the capacity of the common law to reshape and refine its precedents that Story combined past and present to forge the legal framework of the new industrial and finance capitalism.

The focus of his work was the corporation, and he had already pointed the way in his concurring opinion in the Dartmouth College case, wherein he boldly substituted public right and private property as the new basis of division of corporate organization and explicitly extended the protection of the contracts clause of the Constitution to entrepreneurial enterprise. Friend and foe recognized the germinal novelty of his approach. Chancellor Kent applauded these "new and interesting views,"[19] while David Henshaw, Jacksonian leader of Massachusetts, bitterly complained that "Judge Story, in the [Dartmouth] case, was much more explicit, and develops the doctrine of the Court . . . more boldly than John Marshall."[20]

The Dartmouth analysis was but the defensive beginning of a sequence of twin developments in which Story profoundly transformed corporate form and corporate function, producing no

[18] Du Ponceau to Story, July 19, 1824, Story Papers, Library of Congress.
[19] Kent, *Commentaries on American Law* (1826), 391.
[20] Henshaw, "Remarks on the Rights and Powers of Corporation," reprinted in Blau (ed.), *Social Theories of Jacksonian Democracy* (1947), 172-73.

only a new vehicle of business enterprise, but a new environment for its institutional development. On the first line, he boldly fused the ancient law of trusts with the equally ancient law of corporations to produce a mutation which was unprecedentedly modern—a business firm chartered by the state, yet largely removed from its control, in which capital was in the nature of a trust fund, directors were analogous to trustees, and the organization itself was distinct and separate from the people who provided its resources.[21] Paralleling this renovation of structure was vitalization in methods with the abrogation of the medieval doctrine which empowered a corporation only by deed under its common seal. For here, over Marshall's objection (and, significantly, at the 1827 term), Story propounded a rule of law permitting corporations to conduct their affairs on the same basis as individuals and other organizations.[22]

Story's keen instinct for the practical in commercial and corporate law drew heavily on firsthand experience. The transition of enterprise from a maritime to a manufacturing base occurred, literally, at his front door as a drab and half-successful industrialization began to supplant seafaring as the principal business of Salem. The town meetings, which had previously been concerned with news from Calcutta and Copenhagen, now talked of "the

21 *Wood v. Dummer*, 30 FED. CASES 435 (1824). See also Handlin, 158-59.
22 *Bank of the United States v. Dandridge*, 12 WHEATON 64 (1827). See also *Bank of Columbia v. Patterson's Administrator*, 7 CRANCH 299 (1818). When Chief Justice Marshall tried the Dandridge case on his Virginia circuit, Story, in a letter to him June 22, 1823 (Warren, *Correspondence*, 19), seemingly applauded Marshall's insistence that corporate contracts be cast in the elaborate, traditional rituals as having "a salutary tendency by inducing greater caution." Marshall, undeceived, responded (July 2, *ibid.*, 19-20) that "the case . . . will probably be reversed . . . [as] . . . the practice of banks has not conformed to my construction of the law," and good-humoredly predicted Story's ultimate authorship of the predicted reversal: "The Judge, however, who draws the opinion must have more ingenuity than I have if he draws a good one." And, in a curious reversal of roles, in *Dandridge* Story wrote a crisp and lucid opinion, while Marshall went through many pages of citation-studded dissent. "We have got on with the Virginia cause famously . . . ," wrote Webster to Jeremiah Mason on April 10, 1827 (Webster, *Private Correspondence*, I, 417), "Judge Story laid out his whole strength and made a great opinion."

importance of bringing into the greatest activity, the industry, capital resources of this town . . . with a view to the establishing . . . [of] branches of Manufactures."[23] The specific response to the problem was a besetting concern for creating a favorable climate for investment and making physical energy available for the new technologies. Needless to say, Story's judicial responses reflected these experimental roots,[24] and to the extent that time permitted he was in the forefront of local efforts on both fronts. He cast his vote in the town meeting in favor of a resolution that the local legislators modify stockholders' liability in manufacturing corporations, and was appointed to a seven-man body which was charged with the town's industrial development.

It was typical of the ever-quickening pace of American life in general and of Story's fantastically crowded schedule in particular that he found it necessary to be excused from the Salem industrial committee. Another example was shown in his presidency of the Merchants' Bank. Back before the War of 1812, in the bank's early beginnings, its affairs had been a combination of leisureliness and formalism. The president truly presided, directors directed, and no item, however small—whether directing the clerk to start an early fire on meeting days or purchasing a secondhand lock from the state prison—could escape the formalities of motion, second, and entry in the record. But by the mid-1820s it was the cashier who discharged the workaday business of the bank, while President Story and the other directors gave it gradually lessening amounts of their attention. Notwithstanding the great value of his banking connection as a window on the world of affairs—and by the standards of the day it involved no conflict with his judicial duties—Story found himself increasingly pressed to give it what attention he did, and the demands which formal minutiae imposed on his time doubtless underlay his position in

---

[23] Salem town meeting, Jan. 24, 1826, Records of the Town of Salem.
[24] *Tyler v. Wilkinson*, 24 FED. CASES 472 (1827). See also Lauer, "The Common Law Background of Riparian Doctrine," *Missouri Law Review*, XXVIII (1963), 60.

the Dandridge case. He was required to sign the Merchants' bank notes—under the charter there was no escape from this onerous chore—and there seemed to be a predisposition to cling to the old rubrics in exceptional cases. Thus, as late as the summer of 1827, Story's loopy, left-handed scrawl was apparently deemed essential to validate a director's resolution at the Merchants' Bank, authorizing appropriate cooperation to discharge "Henry D. Sewall of the city of New York, merchant, an insolvent debtor . . . according to an act of . . . New York . . ."[25]

The action was something of an *amende honorable*, for under the *Ogden* decision the bank could probably have sued in the Federal Circuit Court for New York and collected its debt without being impeded by the state statute. Yet if this was ever its intention, the events following the commencement on December 3, 1827, of the first session of the avowedly anti-Adams and pro-Jackson Twentieth Congress suggested that forbearance was well-advised. For the first time in years, there was no serious talk of the proposed bulwark of the out-of-state creditor, a bankruptcy bill. Instead, what was proposed was outright legislative reversal of the Kentucky debtor-relief decisions in *Halstead* and *Wayman*—and the possible repeal of the "local court" limitation in *Ogden*—by a bill which might carry the doctrine of concurrent powers to an unprecedented level by making federal process the mirror image of its state counterpart. The bill passed the House and was turned in the upper chamber almost at the last minute by the action of Daniel Webster, now the newly elected Senator from Massachusetts, who came late to Congress by reason of the death of his wife, and who informed the President of the state of the matter in an early visit to the White House.

We had much conversation [diaried Adams] . . . upon a bill before the Senate relating to the forms of process in the Courts of the United States, under cover of which there was a project in operation for annihilating the most essential

25 Minutes, Merchants' Bank, Nov. 10, 1827.

parts of their jurisdiction. It was creeping along almost "sub silento," and had arrived at its last debatable stage on the day when he resumed his seat.[26]

Better late than never, and, notwithstanding a heavy load of Supreme Court cases in his capacity as private lawyer, the new Senator threw all his parliamentary skill into a last-ditch stand. As a consequence, the bill was successively read, tabled, reconsidered, retabled, and finally passed in a compromise form which left the character of a federal process still subject to the rule-making power of the Supreme Court.[27] "It was a triumph of the most gratifying nature," wrote Story, "and taught [Webster's] opponents the danger of provoking a trial of his strength, even when he was overwhelmed by calamity."[28] And it was also quite possible that Webster was assisted in his triumph by a thorough briefing by Justice Story.

The narrow Webster–Story legislative triumph in the face of the rising Jacksonian tide suggested that the outcome was more reprieve than victory. Yet there was also at work in the imperceptible yet ever-growing institutional security of the Court another and countervailing element, which could be better seen in the comments of critics than in those of friends. Thus in the debates on the process bill, a Virginia Senator assailed Marshall's implication that there were limits on what judicial powers Congress might delegate to the states. The criticism, however, was cast in tones of extraordinary respect: "I am sorry to see an argument . . . so fallacious, so deceptive . . . proceed from that exalted jurist."[29] And in this he only echoed the sentiment contemporaneously expressed in the pro-Jackson pages of *Niles' Weekly Register:* "Though the constitutional construction of this lofty tribunal, is not wholly conformable to our humble opinions of right,—we have often thought that no person could behold this

[26] J. Q. Adams, *Memoirs,* VII, 455.
[27] *United States Statutes at Large,* IV, 278.
[28] Letter to George Ticknor, March 6, 1828, in W. W. Story, I, 536.
[29] *Register of Debates,* IV, Part I, 358 (1828).

venerable body without profound respect for the virtue and talents concentrated on its bench."[30]

Indeed, the 1828 term seemed significant for its nonjuridical events. One was the accession of a new reporter, Richard Peters of the Philadelphia bar. Another event was that Mrs. Story accompanied the Justice to Washington. Apparently her trip was somewhat short of an unqualified success, for she complained of dyspepsia shortly after her arrival and went home before her husband. She was, however, seen by one observer during her stay as apparently enjoying Washington society with reasonable relish.

CHURCHES AND CHOICES

One element in the ongoing revolution was neither Jacksonian nor particularly democratic in terms of its proponents. This was the rising sense of religious tolerance, which, if anything, had an upper-class adherence. Therefore, it was especially apposite that Story show it an especial exemplification. One came in his effort to obtain the Harvard LL.D. for William Gaston, Catholic and Southerner, in order that "a Protestant University should shew its liberality by doing homage to a gentleman of a different faith."[31]

Along the same line he was at his witty and urbane best when, on his forty-ninth birthday, September 18, 1828, he spoke at the bicentennial celebration of the Puritan settlement of Salem. (In private correspondence, he was almost insouciant in describing his speech: ". . . I have made up all my affairs with our forefathers, and we are quite good-humored and at our ease. I have abused them reasonably and praised them fairly, and they are contented to settle the account on this footing."[32] But he was also eloquent:

[30] Jan. 19, 1828.
[31] Letter to William Sullivan, Oct. 22, 1826, in Connor, "William Gaston," *Proceedings of the American Antiquarian Society*, new series, XLIII (1933), 429.
[32] Letter to Samuel P. P. Fay, Sept. 10, 1828, in W. W. Story, I, 551.

I stand not up here the apologist for persecution, whether it be by Catholic or Protestant, by Puritan or Prelate, by Congregationalist or Covenanter, by Church or State, by the monarch or the people. Wherever, and by whomsoever, it is promulgated or supported, under whatever disguises, for whatever purposes, at all times, and under all circumstances, it is a gross violation of the rights of conscience, and utterly inconsistent with the spirit of Christianity. I care not, whether it goes to life, or property, or office, or reputation, or mere private comfort, it is equally an outrage upon religion and the unalienable rights of man.[33]

Unhappily, even as he spoke, little of the lofty and ethical note could be seen on the national political scene. On the contrary, the most appalling political campaign in the history of the republic was unfolding. The Jacksonians appealed to the ever-widening electoral rolls to undo the bargains of 1824, whose corruption, they insisted, had been proven by Adams' installation of billiard tables. The Adams supporters responded in kind by retelling the story of Mrs. Jackson's illusory first divorce and the technically bigamous origin of Jackson's marriage.

Story was deeply concerned about the election, and the letters of his relatives freely used the first-person plural in exhortations that "we shall beat the Jacksonians by a triumphant majority in the next Pres't. election."[34] In a direct and immediate sense, there was little Story could do to assist. More subtle approaches were available, however, and Story accordingly unlimbered a powerful pro-Adams polemic in the form of a book review. Ostensibly taking a republication of Chief Justice Marshall's *Washington* for his subject, Story gave book and author a few pages and then turned to his main theme, the necessity of preserving the great national institutions through the finality of judicial power. Spe-

[33] "History and Influence of the Puritans," address to the Essex County Historical Society, Sept. 18, 1828, in *Miscellaneous Writings*, 440.
[34] William Fettyplace to Story, Feb. 6, 1828, in Story Papers, Library of Congress.

cifically, he wrote in terms of the ratification struggle of 1788, but his choice of that event only sharpened, the better to defend, the power of the central government, the security of property rights, and the "delicate relation of debtor and creditor."[35] (And, on the latter point, he worked in a commendation for the *Ogden* minority as he noted that in the dissenting opinion Chief Justice Marshall's powers were "never exhibited in a more impressive manner."[36]

There was no doubt in many of his readers' minds as to his allusions, and, in fact, George Ticknor wrote to Story that "the political facts" in the article "were new to the present generation."[37] Nonetheless Story felt that he had done very little:

> It has cost me much forbearance to refrain from engaging in the struggle now going on in the Union, because I think it is momentous, both in principles and consequences. I am sincerely anxious for the re-election of Mr. Adams, because his purity and intelligence and public talents and public virtues deserve it . . . But it is one thing to hold a private opinion . . . and quite another to avail myself of my judicial station . . . to affect the opinions of others.[38]

It was just as well that he stayed as aloof as he did; nothing could have stayed the Jacksonian tide which swept the country in the November elections.

TWO PRESIDENTS

"I doubt not he will make an energetic, firm, and honest President . . . ," Story wrote a Harvard professor. "He has my heartiest wishes for every success."[39] The congratulations were not for

[35] Book review, "A History of the Colonies," in *North American Review*, XXVI (1828), 10.
[36] *Ibid.*, 36.
[37] Letter from George Ticknor, Feb. 21, 1828, Story Papers, Library of Congress.
[38] Letter to Ezekiel Bacon, Aug. 3, 1828, in W. W. Story, I, 538.
[39] Letter to George Ticknor, Feb. 11, 1829, in W. W. Story, I, 565.

Andrew Jackson, but were intended for another incoming president, Josiah Quincy. Quincy, a Boston lawyer, early in 1829 had
been selected as head of Harvard, and Story's good wishes merely
put a good face upon a lost cause.

It was not that Story had anything against Quincy, with whom
he had served in the House of Representatives back in the Tenth
Congress. Rather, he had been in the thick of a losing fight to
advance Professor George Ticknor, his ally in the struggle for
university reform, to the Harvard presidency. The succession
was necessitated by the resignation of Dr. Kirkland in early
spring of 1828, an event which a young minister reported had
been compelled "by some slights, if not insults, put upon him by
the Salem junta in the [Harvard] Corporation."[40] This obviously
included Story, but the immediate thrust of the reference was to
Nathaniel Bowditch, hardheaded author of *The American Practical Navigator*, who, like Story, not only had come out of Salem
(still the second city of the commonwealth) but was a former
—and resigned—member of Dr. Bentley's East Church. Bowditch
was serving as chairman of the committee on retrenchments and
was slowly bringing order in the university finances. This tender
subject was itself cause enough for friction between Dr. Kirkland and his superiors, but the still explosive subject of the educational reforms and the state of Dr. Kirkland's health—or possibly
his medical treatment—made a change in the presidential office inevitable.[41]

With the ink scarcely dry on Kirkland's resignation, Story
pushed Ticknor's cause vigorously and in a matter of days picked
up significant support from Webster, who mixed the secular spirit
of the age with its fading maritime associations in taking a stand:

[40] Ralph Waldo Emerson to William Emerson, April 3, 1828, in *Letters of
Ralph Waldo Emerson,* ed. Rusk (6v., 1939; hereinafter cited as Emerson,
Letters), I, 230.
[41] "For weeks he (Dr. Kirkland) has suffered the most agonizing pains in
the head. . . . It has been necessary to reduce him in every possible way,
by bleeding, medicine, and starvation." (Letter of May 20, 1827, in *Letters
of Ann Gillam Storrow to Jared Sparks,* ed. F. B. Blanschard (1921; hereinafter cited as Storrow), 227.)

"I confess I think of no one so likely to do good as Mr. Ticknor. I presume you will take some time to deliberate, on so important a matter. *I am against a clergyman.* . . . He is not to soar up the shrouds, nor to go out in the Boat, but to stand at the helm & look at the needle."[42]

Webster's reference outlined one line of cleavage in the succession struggle in which the tradition of a clergyman president was countered by the assertion that only a businessman could bring harmony into the university's administrative and financial disorders. Another confrontation revived the old controversy between orthodox and Unitarian, and a third brought up again the struggle between the old-line resident instructors and the educational reformers.

The resulting stalemate dragged through summer, "giving the new and startling spectacle of a body without a head,"[43] and finally in 1828 came to a close when the defeat of Josiah Quincy for reelection as mayor of Boston provided a compromise solution. Story had tried vigorously to advance Ticknor, but the opposition proved too formidable. ("[T]hey could not choose Mr. T," ran one report, "for the public would not swallow such a portion . . . and so they saw fit to choose a middle man."[44])

In a significant coincidence, the recent advancement of the Supreme Court's annual term precluded Story from having a formal part in the final proceedings, and the tone of his comments to Nathaniel Bowditch suggest that he had been overtaken by the speed with which events finally came to a head:

> Since we last met Mr. Quincy has been named as a candidate. If our friend Mr. Ticknor is to be passed by, I am ready to vote for Mr. Quincy. I think he has more qualifications than any other candidate. If you should come to a choice, I authorize you to give my vote to Mr. Quincy, if the Board will allow my vote when I am absent.[45]

Webster to Story, April 18, 1828, Story Papers, Library of Congress.
Storrow, 233 (Aug. 30, 1828).
Ibid., 236 (Jan. 23, 1829).
Story to Bowditch, January, 1829, in Warren, *Harvard*, 364 n.1.

The touch of apprehension was justified. Notwithstanding Story's success in installing proxy voting over twenty years before at the Merchants' Bank, and notwithstanding the *Dandridge* opinion loosening the bonds of corporate formalism, Harvard stood by the old dispensation. Story's tendered vote was refused and Quincy chosen without it.

Quite possibly there was still another strand which ran through the presidential impasse and its ultimate resolution. This was the state of the law school, which had been afflicted in an extreme form by the general troubles besetting the university, and which the key figures in the university establishment probably had marked out for thoroughgoing reform. Indeed, as early as November, 1827, Isaac Parker, who doubled as Chief Justice of the commonwealth and as Royall professor of law, left the latter office with a letter of resignation whose tone indicated it had been requested. The professorship was then tendered Story with an explanation that far more than a teaching assignment was involved. For as Judge Charles Jackson, a fellow overseer, wrote in early 1828: "My object in writing you was, to get authority from you to announce you (at least unofficially) as the head of our law school—& to know who we should appoint as College Professor [of Law] in event of a resignation by Mr. Stearns."[46]

Story seriously weighed the offer and, much to the approval of his relatives, but with considerable personal reluctance, declined. Yet even here his action merely forestalled, rather than precluded fulfillment of the prophecy Henry Wheaton had made several years earlier. Before the summer was out, the venerable Nathan Dane was launching the last, and this time successful, gambit to obtain his services, with a seemingly innocuous request "for a few minutes respecting the Law Branch in Harvard University."[47]

[46] Letter from Charles Jackson, Feb. 25, 1828, Story Papers, Library of Congress. This letter bears out Prof. Sutherland's surmise that Prof. Stearns' "resignation" had been in the making considerably before its occurrence; see Sutherland, *The Law at Harvard* (1967; hereinafter cited as Sutherland), 8.
[47] Dane to Story, Sept. 6, 1828, in Sutherland, 92.

Story proceeded to the 1829 term with a sharp sensitivity for the critical nature of the times, yet unaware of the personalized and shaping nature of events already in process. From Tennessee Andrew Jackson was on his way to Washington, bringing with him a constitutional and political revolution of extraordinary proportions. Yet already in New England a reconstituted university was arising which would provide both haven and citadel for the tempering response that new American law would impose on the turbulence of the age. Washington remained unchanged in one sense. President Adams, who changed his parties but never his enemies, was preparing to launch a polemic against his New England enemies. ("Another pamphlet!!" wrote Webster to his sister-in-law."[48])

The presidential project came up on the afternoon of Washington's Birthday, when Story went by the White House. It was a nostalgic, expansive meeting as the two old friends talked about the extrajudicial intercession with Monroe twelve short—and long—years earlier. And then the President brought the conversation back to the present by showing his visitor the screed prepared against his old enemies, the New England Federalists. Story, startled and expressing "his friendly regard"[49] for some of the presidential targets, besought Adams to change his mind, but the President reserved his position.

Story returned that evening to the ball in honor of George Washington. It was a depressing affair. "[T]he company, though highly respectable and brilliant in dress, was small . . . ," he wrote his wife. "Mr. Adams has no more favors to bestow."[50] Rather, continued Story with regret, all were ready to hail the rising sun. A few days earlier Webster too had used a simile drawn from the weather and had done it better:

Letter to Mrs. E. Webster, Feb. 19, 1829, in Webster, *Private Correspondence*, I, 471.
Adams, *Memoirs*, VIII, 98. Apparently Story's advice was taken, for Adams did not publish the pamphlet; see S. F. Bemis, *John Quincy Adams and the Foundations of American Foreign Policy* (New York, 1949), 576.
Story to Mrs. Story, Feb. 25, 1829, in W. W. Story, I, 562.

General Jackson will be here about 15th February.

Nobody knows what he will do when he does come. . . .

My opinion is, that when he comes he will bring a breeze with him. Which way it will blow I cannot tell.[51]

[51] Enclosure in a letter probably written on Jan. 17, 1829, in *Private Correspondence*, I, 467.

PART SEVEN

The Age of Jackson

CHAPTER XXII

Two Inaugurals

KING MOB

One Justice had been injured in an upsetting of a stagecoach, another was ill, and a third was beset by the infirmities of age. As a consequence of these and other mishaps, the 1829 term of the Supreme Court got off to a belated start. Those who sought omens might well see in such individual misfortunes the foreshadowing of an institutional adversity, and certainly nothing in the approaching inauguration of Andrew Jackson offered much comfort to the philosophy of the Marshall Court. Indeed, a deep sense of judicial apprehension had already been suggested by the unavailing efforts of the individual members of that Court to ward off the Jacksonian victory.

Thus, Chief Justice Marshall in a well-publicized action voted for the first time in twenty years, and his ballot obviously was cast for John Quincy Adams rather than for Andrew Jackson. Justice Smith Thompson had been even more overt. Remaining on the Court, he had run for governor of New York with the vowed purpose of carrying the Adams ticket to victory and had come within a hairbreadth of doing so. Justice Bushrod Washington had openly participated in a convention of Adams men in Virginia. Alongside this activism, Story's pamphleteering book review seemed almost proper. Yet he did assert in print that the forthcoming election merely carried into a new battleground the struggle which the forces of rationalism and order had won—but only temporarily—in ratifying the Constitution some forty years earlier. He thus formed part of a pattern in which, of the six incumbent Justices—for one ailing member of the seven-man bench died during the campaign—only the maverick South Carolinian, William Johnson, supported Jackson. And of the entire Court, only the venerable Gabriel Duvall exhibited a truly judicial impartiality.[1]

Justice Duvall's aloofness was far more the infirmity of age than the abstinence of choice. In the full vigor of his faculties he could well have joined his associates in an extrajudicial electoral activity which itself mirrored an unprecedented nationwide involvement. The mirror, however, inverted the image between Court and country, for the choice of the Justices was not that of the people. Appropriately, the crowds poured into Washington to celebrate their victory, and the upshot was a democratic bacchanal on Inauguration Day. One observer said that "it was a proud day for the *people*—General Jackson is *their own* President."[2] However, Justice Story saw only "the reign of King 'Mob' . . . triumphant."[3]

Even had the Justices the inclination, the state of their docket precluded an extensive participation in the inaugural festivities. The Chief Justice, no complainer even at the threshold of seventy-four, found the 1829 work of the Court "a laborious Term,"[4] and

[1] For the extrajudicial electoral activity and attitudes of the members of the Supreme Court in the election of 1828, see, as to Chief Justice Marshall, *Proceedings of the Mass. Historical Society*, 2nd series, XV, 336; as to Justice Thompson, J. Q. Adams, *Memoirs*, VII, 404-05; as to Justice Washington, *Proceedings of the Anti-Jackson Convention Held at the Capitol in the City of Richmond with Their Address to the People of Virginia* (1828) copy in the Virginia Historical Society, Richmond (my thanks to Mr. William M. E. Rachal of the Society for this item); and as to Justice Johnson *Niles' Weekly Register*, Oct. 9, 1830.

[2] Amos Kendall, quoted in Chambers, *Old Bullion Benton* (1956), 156.

[3] Letter to Mrs. Story, March 7, 1829, in W. W. Story, I, 563.

[4] Letter to Thomas Marshall, March 20, 1829, in Marshall Papers, Virginia Historical Society, Richmond.

it was singularly appropriate that the ever-increasing number and complexity of cases awaiting final decision should so sharply underline the elements at work in the Jacksonian revolution, and particularly an entrepreneurial revolt against a mercantilist-agrarian status quo. Justice Story himself was especially involved in this ongoing pattern of change, and the 1829 docket showed him significantly contributing to breaking the cake of custom. Thus, his opinion in the patent controversy of *Pennock v. Dialogue*[5] provided a powerful stimulant to the new industrial technology. Similarly, his views in *Van Ness v. Pacard*[6] broke new ground in treating fixtures in terms of an increasingly mobile, business-oriented economy rather than a static agricultural one. And perhaps the most illustrative example of the interplay of law and life was *Inglis v. Sailors' Snug Harbor*,[7] an immensely complicated equity case down from New York, which was argued but not decided at the term.

Not all states had equity. It was completely absent from native New England, whose Puritan inheritance, Dean Pound subsequently observed, detested its personalized and highly eclectic jurisdiction which could relieve fools of some bargains and force sharp men to specifically perform others. In addition, there was a widespread and popular suspicion of its juryless procedure, of the enormous range afforded judicial discretion, and of its roots in ancient English doctrine. Yet notwithstanding an ancient lineage which caused an American case to stand or fall on a forgotten statute of Queen Elizabeth, equity provided an immensely congenial vehicle for settling the disputes of a commercial age by its flexibility, speed, and capability of cutting to the heart of any issue. "[L]aw," Story noted a few years earlier, "working as it does into the business of a nation crowded with commerce and manufactures, must be forever in search of equitable principles

[5] 2 PETERS 1 (1829). See also F. Prager, "The Changing Views of Justice Story on the Construction of Patents," *American Journal of Legal History*, IV (1960) 1.

[6] 2 PETERS 137 (1829).

[7] 3 PETERS 99 (1830).

to be applied to the new combinations of circumstances, which are springing up daily to perplex its courts."[8]

Inglis was not a business dispute but a contest for a legacy. The stakes were high, and Daniel Webster said he had made a greater exertion in it than he had in any case since *Dartmouth College* or than he would ever make again. The case involved the nature of American nationality, the character of equity powers, New York's anti-Tory legislation, and the consequences of the Anglo–American treaties. Story was deeply familiar with each facet. His *Martin v. Hunter's Lessee* opinion had dealt with the impact of treaty rights on anti-Tory expropriations. He had been a lifelong student and champion of equity jurisdiction. His was perhaps the strongest and most eloquent voice on the juridical consequences of American nationality. And by singular coincidence this constellation of legal issues seemed to him to be brought into focus by a passage in the work of an old friend.[9]

The old friend was the venerable Nathan Dane, and the work was Dane's *General Abridgment and Digest of American Law*, a legal cyclopedia shorn of irrelevant British precedents and fitted to the new and national legal environment. The work of a lifetime, the *Digest* was nonetheless regarded by Dane as a beginning rather than an end. In an astonishing (or perhaps conscious) parallel to the action by which Sir Charles Viner had brought Blackstone to Oxford a half century earlier, Dane determined to devote the financial fruits of a successful legal abridgment to the establishment of a chair of a truly national law.

Dane cast his net much wider than Viner, for in addition to what he called "Federal law and Federal equity"[10] he wished his bounty to be framed in a Ptolemaic order which set those elements in a construct of natural law, international law, and commercial and maritime law (at this time still virtually one). He had selected both his institution, the near-moribund Harvard Law

[8] Story, "The Growth of Commercial Law, in *Miscellaneous Writings*, 279.
[9] See 3 PETERS at 164, n. 1.
[10] See W. W. Story, II, 4.

School, and he had selected his man—Mr. Justice Story. Following up a play first made in the fall of the preceding year, Dane succeeded where other attempts to secure Story's teaching services had failed, by expressly conditioning his contribution upon the Justice's acceptance.

Much as in the case of Story's elevation to the Supreme Court some seventeen years earlier, agreement was virtually preordained —he was "driven to accept," was the way he put it.[11] To be sure, as in modern negotiations, there were a few abrasively mundane details, centering around housing, but other arrangements went forward looking to his academic induction on September 1, 1829. Probably no one, not even Nathan Dane, saw a connection between this inaugural and that which six months earlier had marked the beginning of Jackson's Presidency. Yet the two events were related and even star-crossed. For in the clash between the exuberant folk nationalism of the Jackson inaugural and the national jurisprudence sought by Dane, King Mob would become, in the most literal sense, a constitutional monarch.

KING LAW

Almost six months to the day after the Jackson inaugural, the civic dinner of the year was held at Hamilton Hall in Salem, Massachusetts. The occasion was Story's removal to Cambridge to accept the Dane professorship. The departure was appropriately scaled for the town's leading citizen, whose honors, even without judicial office, were formidable: presently fellow and formerly overseer of the Harvard Corporation, president of the Merchants' Bank of Salem, vice-president and trustee of the Salem Institute for Savings, vice-president of the Bunker Hill Memorial Association, cofounder of the Essex Historical Society, fellow of the American Academy of Arts and Sciences, member of the Massachusetts Historical Society, member of the Massachusetts

---

11 Letter to Richard Peters, Aug. 1, 1829, in W. W. Story, II, 22. See also Warren, *Harvard*, I, 415-21, and Sutherland, 90-95.

Agricultural Society, and holder of honorary doctorates in law from Brown, Harvard, and Dartmouth.

Everyone of importance and many of unimportance in Salem attended. The Boston delegation included Mayor Harrison Gray Otis and Senator Daniel Webster; that of Cambridge, Probate Judge Samuel P. P. Fay and Harvard's president, Josiah Quincy. Even Governor Howe of Illinois was there. Course followed course, toast followed toast, the Boston Brigade Band played, and Judge Fay expressed the consensus in pronouncing the dinner "a most *sensible* device, by which the *givers* were made to enjoy as much as the receivers."[12] For his part, the guest of honor capped the afternoon of speeches with "a most eloquent and feeling address to his fellow citizens from whom he was about to separate, and dwelt on the circumstances of his residence among them for thirty years and his emotions on parting from his early and fast friends."[13]

Certainly a display of sentiment might be forgiven a man, two weeks away from his fiftieth birthday, who was leaving a home of long and close adoption. "Was a new alms house or schoolhouse to be erected, he was one of the building committee," it would be later written. "To him, we owe more than anyone else the existing excellent condition of the streets of our city. . . . He . . . served, with his accustomed fidelity and zeal, for many years, on our school committees."[14] The passing years had deeply changed the man as well as the town, and, save for his nervous gesture or hearty laugh, it was difficult to believe that this plump and half-bald pillar of the establishment could ever have been the volatile auburn-haired poet who came over from nearby Marblehead back in 1801.

The ensuing three decades had laid a heavy hand on Salem. Story began his practice when the Salem ships still exemplified the town motto with flags carried *divitis Indiae ad ultimum sinum*

[12] *Salem Gazette*, Sept. 4, 1829.
[13] *Ibid*.
[14] John W. Treadwell to William W. Story, Aug. 25, 1847, in W. W. Story, I, 207-8. See also *American Jurist*, IV (1830), 298, 507.

—to the farthest port of the rich East. By 1829, however, the nascent industrialism, itself part and parcel of the Jacksonian revolution, was fast replacing Salem's maritime glories with some drab and half-successful manufacturing enterprises. In a closely related consequence many leading figures were moving. William Gray, the richest merchant, William Prescott, the leading lawyer, and Nathaniel Bowditch, the world-renowned mathematician, had all gone. And now Justice Story was leaving.

He did not go without playing a part in a rear-guard effort to facilitate the transition from commerce to industry. In a move paralleling the legal transformation of the corporation which he was effecting from the bench, Story joined in the town meeting's petition for removal of a stockholder liability in manufacturing corporations. Along the same line he had backed an abortive venture for a municipal mill-dam corporation, planned as a power source for infant industry. The latter effort foundered badly ("Poor Salem remains still down at the heel with her stockings about her feet"[15]), and the town which was once the proud second city of the commonwealth became an exporter of her famous men.

If Salem declined, however, Cambridge flourished, and the difference between them was symbolized in the way the farewell banquet had been outshone by an inaugural feast staged a few days earlier to commemorate the reorganization of the Harvard Law School. The company was impressive, the program was long, and the puns were polished ("*Non timeo Danaos et dona ferentes*"[16]) as Professor Story was formally inducted into office. Assuming academic duties with him was John Hooker Ashmun, a rising twenty-nine-year-old lawyer who was named to serve as Royall professor in a full-time teaching capacity. Story gave a long inaugural address ("in English," noted the program[17]).

[15] Henry Coleman to Joseph Story, February, 1827, Story Papers, Library of Congress. See also *American Jurist*, II (1829), 92 and 104, and Felt, *Annals of Salem* (1845), II, 162.
[16] Warren, *Harvard*, II, 16.
[17] W. W. Story, II, 7.

Eighteen thousand words in length, the lecture was the typical product of an age which liked its oratory by the hour. Exemplifying a stoic naturalism, Story traced law through its foundations in the very order of things to the overstructure of all human effort and, while proclaiming its attainment the proper office of every liberally educated man, pleaded for its involvement with the actual concerns of life by a body of specialists trained to its use. In coming to a conclusion, the new professor hailed Dane as the American Viner and then in an extraordinary denial of the history which was about to unfold noted that "here the parallel must stop."[18]

Neither the modesty of the disclaimer nor the over-all character of the address as the proclamation of a new conservatism served to impress a young minister named Ralph Waldo Emerson, who had come for the Ashmun inaugural and complained that "a good many people wd. rather have heard what he had to say for himself than to hear Judge Story . . . but Mr. A. contented himself with promising to behave well."[19] The subject of the barbed remark was beyond it. He had a new field and was anxious to get on with the work. "We have at present twenty-seven law students . . . ," he exulted. "I perceive that there is a vast labor before me."[20]

THE 25th SECTION

Story's inaugural pictured the American ideal as an essentially transplanted continuation of the great European tradition of civility, order, and rationality. The Jacksonian view, however, was not so much an Americanized transplantation of an old order as the institution of a genuinely new one. Contradicting Story's inaugural oration, this view of a *via media* between aboriginal bar-

[18] Story, "The Value and Importance of Legal Studies," in *Miscellaneous Writings*, 547.
[19] Ralph Waldo Emerson to Anne Lyman, Aug. 26, 1829, in Emerson, *Letters*, I, 432.
[20] Letter to Simon Greenleaf, Oct. 20, 1829, in Warren, *Harvard*, I, 432.

barism on one hand and an overcivilized decadence on the other was asserted about the same time.[21] The latter doctrine appeared, not in the formal Presidential inaugural, but in Andrew Jackson's first State of the Union Message, which went to the newly convened Twenty-first Congress on December 10, 1829. Moreover, it was more implicit than articulate, but it still could be pieced out from two Presidential references. One was a *de facto* ultimatum to the Indian tribes in Georgia and Alabama struggling against repressive state legislation—"emigrate beyond the Mississippi or submit to the laws of those States."[22] The other, somewhat more subtle, concerned the second Bank of the United States. Noting that the bank's charter would soon expire and that its stockholders would seek a renewal, the President ominously commented: "Both the constitutionality and the expediency of the law creating this bank are well questioned by a large portion of our fellow-citizens . . ."[23]

Externally dissimilar, the bank and the Indians were united in being seen as common enemies, one a decadent monopoly, the other a primitive barbarism. Both were marked for a destruction which was seen as an unfortunate, but inevitable, consequence of their very natures, for both stood in the way of a surging laissez-faire sense of enterprise whose seemingly diverse faces—financial, industrial, and agricultural—drew on a singularity of purpose of self-made men to civilize the wilderness and found a new order of things. Thus, the emerging forces in commerce, industry, and finance which found the regulating hand of the second Bank of the United States an increasingly galling constraint shared essentially the outlook of the land-hungry emigrants who saw the Indian enclaves as an intolerable anachronism. If the federal bank and the Indians had common enemies, they also shared a common protection in a federally guaranteed status. Scores of treaties with the United States, some antedating the Constitution itself, con-

[21] See, generally, Ward.
[22] Richardson, II, 458.
[23] *Ibid.*, 462.

firmed the Indians in their tribal lands, and Chief Justice Marshall's landmark opinion, *McCulloch v. Maryland*, had given the federal bank plenary constitutional vindication. Yet the Presidential message called into question the seemingly settled status of both issues, and more: what was really challenged was the Supreme Court's capacity to be the ultimate arbiter of any constitutional issue.

The Presidential message said nothing about the slavery issue, which cut across all others like a sinister fault line. It was in part bound up with the land hunger underlying the Indian question, for the massive new plantation system differed from its pastoral antecedents almost as much as the new industrialism differed from the old commerce. There was one singular circumstance: however much the two new economic orders draw on similarly motivated systems of laissez-faire, the institution of slavery ranged them implacably as opponents. Useless to one system, indispensable to the other, it colored all issues, exacerbated particularly the differences over the tariff, and inevitably manifested itself in bitter sectional and cotitutional controversy.

Thus, the tangled complex of constitutional issues raised by Jackson's first message to Congress was vividly illustrated a few days later when Senator Samuel A. Foot (occasionally spelled Foote) of Connecticut introduced a proposal to restrict the sale of Western lands. Much the way a great battle suddenly develops from the accidental clash of pickets in an obscure village, the Foot resolution quickly escalated into what the Washington press called "the great debate."[24] For, quickly outranging the constitutional propositions in the Presidential message, although in a sense deriving from them, there suddenly surfaced a basic issue of whether the Union was one or many, and on that issue Daniel Webster and Robert Young Hayne, Senator from South Carolina, traded indecisive, if Homeric, blows.

Art, it is said, knows its own truth, and the painter whose hand struck off the heroic canvas *Webster Replying to Hayne* sug-

[24] *Niles' Weekly Register*, Feb. 27, 1830.

gested, wittingly or otherwise, the larger dimensions of the exchange. Presiding and yet depicted almost as one of the principals
is Vice-President John C. Calhoun, now close to resignation as a
consequence of a steadily eroding political relationship with
Jackson. Less prominent but still apparent in the background is
Justice Joseph Story, still unmoved from the nationalism of his
youth. To what extent Calhoun and Story supplied the weaponry
of the actual debaters can only be surmised.

Certainly the two principal spokesmen had outside resources.
Indeed, Webster even made a sarcastic suggestion that Hayne had
"at his elbow . . . some high-minded and lofty spirit . . . ready
to supply . . . every thing, down even to forgotten and moth-
eaten two-penny pamphlets."[25] But Hayne needed no twopenny
pamphlet. Calhoun had already published his *South Carolina Exposition,* which presented a powerful case for the Constitution as
a union of sovereignties and asserted, for each of them, a right of
nullification or, as Hayne preferred to call it, "constitutional resistance."[26] Likewise, Story had preceded Webster as the exponent
of the nationalist interpretation of the Constitution with the opinion in *Martin v. Hunter's Lessee* which validated the legitimacy
of Section 25 of the Judiciary Act of 1789 and made the Supreme
Court the superior of state tribunals in cases of controverted
constitutionality.

This was really what was at issue in the Webster–Hayne confrontation, for paralleling Webster's more famous three-part
credo, "Liberty *and* Union, now and forever, one and inseparable,"[27]) was his threefold canonization of the Supreme Court
as the cutting edge of the blade, "one tribunal, established by all,
responsible to all, with power to decide for all"[28] and the ineluctable recognition of the role of the federal judiciary. After noting
the import of the Constitution's provisions making its own and
derivative provisions the supreme law of the land and providing

[25] *Register of Debates,* VI, 62 (1830).
[26] *Ibid.,* 73.
[27] *Ibid.,* 80.
[28] *Ibid.,* 78.

that the judicial power of the United States should extend to its constitution and interpretation, Webster eulogized their consequence for both the national government and the Union:

> They are, in truth, the key-stone of the arch. With them it is a constitution; without them, it is a confederacy. In pursuance of these clear and express provisions, Congress established at its very first session, in the Judicial Act, a mode for carrying them into full effect, and for bringing all questions of constitutional power to the final decision of the Supreme Court. It then, sir, became a Government.[29]

And all this Story had said in his *Martin* opinion. Whether he played a closer role in the Great Debate is a fascinating question. Relevant of course, is his virtually lifetime service as the "Jupiter Pluvius from whom Mr. Webster sought to elicit peculiar thunder for his speeches."[30] Particularly significant seems Webster's admission that at the time he was in the midst of other pressing engagements and did not make any of his speeches what they should have been. Intrinsic evidence also is indicative, and particularly so is an appendix which was subsequently placed in the record and which obviously came from a researcher rather than an orator—a 1787 report from a committee of the old Confederation Congress concerning public lands, an 1809 resolution of the Virginia legislature characterizing the Supreme Court as the ultimate constitutional tribunal, and (a particularly malicious touch) an 1816 Calhoun speech in favor of a collective tariff.

The judicial issue that was raised in the Webster–Hayne exchange sputtered on indecisively until the end of the session in

---

[29] *Ibid.*

[30] Parker, *Additional Speeches, Addresses and Occasional Sermons* (1855), I, 169. And on the general question of Story's assistance to Webster see W. W. Story, II, 408, and Bauer, *Commentaries on the Constitution* (1952), 160, 161, 178. Of possible significance is Story's absence on account of illness; see Daniel Webster to Jeremiah Mason, Feb. 27, 1830, in Webster, *Private Correspondence*, I, 439. On the other hand, an apochryphal Webster quotation suggests that the orator was self-sufficient: "Give yourself no uneasiness, Judge Story; I will grind him as fine as a pinch of snuff"; quoted in Wiltse, *John C. Calhoun*, II (1949), 58.

late spring, and it overshadowed anything on the Supreme Court's calendar. Story's principal interest seemed to be his new professorship ("I shall be glad . . . to work with the Law Students. I am impatient to prepare some written lectures . . ."[31]). There was, however, an epilogue to the Great Debate which may have made him wish he had stayed in Washington. This concerned the famous exchange of toasts between Vice-President Calhoun and President Jackson at the celebration of Jefferson's birthday on April 13, 1830.

It was, of course, singularly ironic that an event designed to promote solidarity would provide the occasion for a dramatic and spectacular fission. Yet it was no more ironic than the contemporary petticoat controversy which escalated into a major political crisis and brought down the cross-purposed Jackson Cabinet like a house of cards. For when Mrs. Calhoun successfully rallied the ladies of that Cabinet to ostracize Mrs. Eaton, currently wife of the Secretary of War but previously barmaid Peggy O'Neill, she awakened the President's memories of a political villification of his own dead wife, forced via distaff pressures all Cabinet officers save one to take her side, and made the one man who was immune to those pressures, widower Secretary of State Martin Van Buren, the heir apparent of the Administration. Yet here was no random series of events. The heterogeneous Jacksonian coalition, whether mirrored in the Great Debate, the Jefferson Day dinner or the Cabinet, was confronted at every turn by the question of whether the Union was one or many, and the birthday dinner was unique only in providing the forum whereby the President's cannon-shot toast "Our Federal Union—it can and must be preserved!" compressed into a terse imperative the many pages of Story's *Martin v. Hunter's Lessee* and the days of Webster's replies to Hayne.

Story shared the general incredulity ("Are the reports of the Birthday Dinner mere gossip or true?"[32]), for the Presidential as-

[31] Letter to George Ticknor, March 10, 1830, in W. W. Story, II, 35.
[32] Letter to Daniel Webster, April 17, 1830, in C. H. Van Tyne (ed.), *Letters of Daniel Webster* (New York, 1907), 154-55.

sertion was largely unexpected. Yet it had been foreshadowed in a brief note which Jackson sent Webster after the Great Debate: "There is no cause more sound than the preservation of this, our Union, and you have done more to further it in a day than others have achieved in years."[33] Indeed, the private Presidential note constituted a sharp revisionary codicil to the nuances of the first message to Congress, and it would have immense future significance for both the Supreme Court and Section 25 of the Judiciary Act.

[33] Quoted in Noel B. Gerson, *Old Hickory* (Garden City, 1964), 253.

CHAPTER XXIII

The Education of a President

The ambiguities and nuances in the various Jacksonian messages worked themselves out in three singularly sequenced Presidential positions taken as the year 1832 unfolded. In March came a thrusting Jacksonian denial—effected by an inaction which spoke louder than words, although words there were—of the Supreme Court's role as the ultimate expositor of the Constitution. In July, the implied became explicit with the positive denial asserted in a ringing veto. Yet in December came not only an assertion of the Supreme Court's unique constitutional competence but an expressed willingness to defend that status by force and arms, if need be.

NEW ECHOTA

The Indian question which had partially underlain the Great Debate was most acute, not on the territorial frontier, but in the original states, and there with respect to the most civilized tribes. Its specific focus was the Cherokees, who, readily adopting the white men's ways in everything from the alphabet to slavery, had even dabbled in *realpolitik* by taking the American side against the Creeks in 1812 and serving as Jackson's valued allies in his great victory at Horseshoe Bend. In July of 1827 at their tribal capital of New Echota they went further yet. Combining a declaration of independence with the adoption of a constitution, the tribe asserted its complete autonomy save for the supervening sovereignty of the federal government, and explicitly denied any state authority over its lands or people. The constitution was based on that of the United States. There was, however, a possibility that this action violated its very model by setting up one state within the territory of another. Also unclear was the effect of such action upon the federal government's hopelessly conflicting obligations. On the one hand, the United States had promised the Indians to protect their lands. On the other, it had promised Georgia to clear them. The conflict of commitments had been debated indecisively in John Quincy Adams' Cabinet. Jackson, however, saw neither problem nor doubt, and his view was contained in the recommendation in his first message to Congress for Indian submission or removal.

Eleven days after the message, the Georgia legislature took the President at his word by declaring the Cherokee constitution null, extending Georgia's county and court organization to the Cherokee lands, and generally molding a comprehensive pattern of repression and control. Congress moved somewhat more slowly, but by May of 1830 it passed an Indian Removal Act along the lines requested by the President. It did so over the vigorous opposition of Webster on the Senate floor and with the possibility of constitutional challenge from a powerful array of talent, for Webster, former Attorney General William Wirt, Chancellor Kent, and Jeremiah Evarts of Boston, editor of the *Christian Herald*, had been enlisted in the Cherokee cause.

The Indians' advisers began with the doubtful counsel of suggesting that the President be informed "that you wish to have the matter decided by the Supreme Court. . . . You may rest assured that if you will get your case clearly before the Supreme Court, your rights will be defended."[1] The Cherokees' conversations with the President were a dismal failure. Jackson heard the

[1] Jeremiah Evarts to John Ross, July, 1830, in Woodward, *The Cherokees* (1963; hereinafter cited as Woodward).

Indians out and abruptly dismissed them: "Sir, your audience is ended. There is nothing I can do for you."[2] One Cherokee bitterly regretted a lost opportunity: "If I had known Jackson would drive us from our homes, I would have killed him that day at Horseshoe."[3]

Obviously, the Cherokees would have been better advised to avoid talk altogether. The President had already adopted the Georgia position that their tribal government itself was an unconstitutional excrescence and, on a larger ground, had clearly implied in his first message to Congress that he felt himself every bit the coequal of the Supreme Court in construing the constitutional text. Thus, with the executive, the state, and Congress ranged in opposition, Cherokee prospects seemed bleak. However, Wirt thought he found his opportunity in the case of George Tassell, a Cherokee accused of murdering another member of the tribe. By the Cherokee constitution Tassell was subject only to tribal law. By the new Georgia statutes, he was under state jurisdiction. Tried by the Hall County Superior Court, he was convicted and sentenced to death. As Wirt sought to bring the case before the Supreme Court, the comments of the Georgia judge suggested some ominous overtones: "Now, without intending the least disrespect to that [Supreme] Court, to whose constitutional authority this and all other state courts, I hope, will most cheerfully submit, this question can never go from a court in which I preside, until the people of the state yield it."[4] These implications quickly came to pass. When, on December 12, 1820, the Supreme Court issued its citation in response to Wirt's plea, the state responded by executing Tassell forthwith, and the governor wrote Jackson that the Cherokees should by now realize the "utter imbecility of placing any further reliance on the Supreme Court."[5]

The Cherokees, however, had a second string to their bow,

[2] Quoted in Irvin M. Peithmann, *Red Men of Fire* (Springfield, 1964), 61.
[3] *Ibid.*, 72.
[4] *Niles' Weekly Register*, Oct. 2, 1830.
[5] Letter from Gov. Troupe, Jan. 3, 1831, in Woodward, 165.

and an obvious sympathizer in Justice Story as well. Shocked at the intemperate and indecorous execution of Tassell, the Justice noted with obvious satisfaction that unrequested by the Court, the question was presented "in another form."[6] It came by application for an injunction against Georgia's repressive laws which the Cherokees submitted to the Court as a matter of original jurisdiction on the grounds that they were "a foreign nation" entitled by the Constitution to begin proceedings there.

Speaking for a divided Court, Marshall held otherwise. Carefully refraining from any endorsement of the Jacksonian thesis that the Cherokees had formed an unconstitutional substate, the Chief Justice simply read history, precedent, and international law to the effect that the Cherokees were not a "foreign nation" within the contemplation of the Constitution.[7] Story, joining Justice Smith Thompson's contrary reading of the same record, ranged himself in opposition to the Chief Justice—his first constitutional break with Marshall since their disagreements over the prize and confiscation cases of the War of 1812. Nor did return home from the 1831 term and further reflection change his view, as he strongly asserted a sense of being "more and more satisfied we are right. . . ."[8]

He had his chance to assert his position when still another of the Cherokee cases came before the Court next year, at the 1832 term. This time the petitioners were white missionaries who had been jailed under a Georgia repression statute and who sought release through the writ of the Supreme Court. On March 7, 1832, they seemed to have obtained their goal, along with a vindication of Cherokee rights, as the Georgia statutes were invalidated by the Court.[9] "[G]lorious news," went the announcement to the Cherokees. "The laws of the state are declared by the highest judicial tribunal of the country to be null and void."[10]

[6] Letter to George Ticknor, Jan. 22, 1831, in W. W. Story, II, 49.
[7] *Cherokee Nation v. Georgia*, 5 PETERS 1 (1831).
[8] Letter to Richard Peters, June 24, 1831, in W. W. Story, II, 46.
[9] *Worcester v. Georgia*, 6 PETERS 515 (1832).
[10] Elias Boudinot to Stan Watel, March 7, 1832, in Woodward, 168.

Exaltation was premature, however, for it failed to take account of the Presidential reaction. Story had been apprehensive ("I do not believe the President will interfere"[11]), and rightly so. "[T]he Supreme Court . . . have united to embarass me,"[12] exploded the President, and this irate response was mild compared to that of the Presidential supporters both in and out of Congress. *Niles' Weekly Register* reported an allegation that Marshall, Story, Clay, and Webster had "held a *caucus*, at which it was decided that the Cherokee case should be decided 'solely on political grounds.' "[13] Doubtless the allegation produced what Story called "a very strong sensation in both houses."[14] Perhaps he was fortunate that the level of legislative response went no higher than it did. Unquestionably it underlay a cryptic passage contained in a letter from John Randolph to the President: "If I had a seat in the H. of R., I would move an impeachment of the Ch. J. and Story."[15]

PHILADELPHIA

Throughout the Union, the Cherokee repression was seen in different modes. In New Echota it was obviously a prelude to disaster. In Charleston, a city increasingly restive over the tariff, the episode was seen as an admirable example of state self-help in the face of unwarranted federal intrusion. A young French traveler, Alexis de Tocqueville, saw the unfolding of a Greek tragedy ("The success of the Cherokees proves that the Indians are capable of civilization, but it does not prove that they will succeed in it"[16]). In Philadelphia, headquarters of the federal bank and

[11] Letter to George Ticknor, March 8, 1832, in W. W. Story, II, 83. See also Choust, "Did President Jackson Actually Threaten the Supreme Court of the United States with Nonenforcement of its Injunction against the State of Georgia?," *American Journal of Legal History*, V (1960), 76.
[12] Letter to Anthony Butler, March 6, 1832, in Andrew Jackson, *Correspondence*, ed. Bassett (7v., 1926–35; hereinafter cited as Jackson), IV, 415.
[13] April 28, 1832.
[14] Letter to George Ticknor, *supra* (note 11).
[15] Letter to President Jackson, March 18, 1832, in Jackson, IV, 422.
[16] De Tocqueville, I, 359.

still the financial capital of the United States, the fate of the Cherokees seemed an ominous prelude to another proscription.

The city had been uneasy for some time. "Of all the cities in the Union," wrote still another French traveler, "the peaceful Philadelphia is the most troubled by the Bank question, because it is the seat of the mother bank."[17] To be sure, the bank's charter, in addition to its constitutional vindication in *McCulloch v. Maryland,* had several years to run, but the unavoidable nature of the confrontation was clear. The anti-Jackson forces, accordingly, made a virtue of adversity as the bank was deliberately chosen as the campaign issue for the 1832 election. A rechartering bill was passed by Congress and thrust on the President.

Predictably it came back with a sharp veto message, which now explicitly stated what had been implied by the first Presidential message to Congress and next underlined in the Presidential reaction to the case of the Cherokees:

> It is maintained by the advocates of the Bank that its constitutionality in all its features ought to be considered as settled by precedent and by the decision of the Supreme Court. To this conclusion I cannot assent. . . .
>
> If the opinion of the Supreme Court covered the whole ground of this act, it ought not to control the coordinate authorities of this Government. The Congress, the Executive, and the Court must each for itself be guided by its own opinion of the Constitution. Each public officer . . . takes an oath to support it as he understands it, and not as it is understood by others. . . . The opinion of the judges has no more authority over Congress than the opinion of Congress has over the judges, and on that point the President is independent of both. The authority of the Supreme Court must not, therefore, be permitted to control the Congress or the Executive when acting in their legislative capacities, but to have only such influence as the force of their reasoning may deserve.[18]

[17] Chevalier, *Society, Manners, and Politics in the United States* (1966 reprint; hereinafter cited as Chevalier), 55.
[18] Richardson, II, 581-82.

This declaration of Jacksonian independence was accompanied by its application in several specific contexts. One was a subtle and vigorous attack on Marshall's logic in *McCulloch v. Maryland*. A second was a stinging attack on the monopolistic character of the federal bank. And a third came in the conclusion with a stirring restatement of the Jacksonian creed:

> In the full enjoyment of the gifts of Heaven and the fruits of superior industry, economy, and virtue, every man is equally entitled to protection by law; but when the laws undertake . . . to make the rich richer . . . the humble members of society—the farmers, mechanics, and laborers . . . have a right to complain. . . .[19]

Webster delivered a powerful counterattack on the Senate floor and then, with a view to printing an amplified version for the upcoming Presidential campaign, dispatched a marked copy of the veto message to Story:

> Now, my dear sir, the object of this is, to request you to turn to the message, read this part of it, and give me, in a letter of three pages, a close and conclusive confutation, in your way, of all the nonsense in this particular. It will take you less than half an hour. Pray . . . let me have it . . . in two or three days.[20]

In this case Webster had particularly strong grounds for assuming that Story's assistance would be forthcoming. Well before its foundation, Story had been an enthusiastic proponent of the federal bank. Nor was his position solely a legal one. Although he had moved from Salem, Story had continued in the presidency of the Merchants' Bank, and as a conservative banker he was doubtless sympathetic to the federal institution's cause. He also felt personally very close to Nicholas Biddle, the federal bank's president.

19 *Ibid.*, 590.
20 Letter from Daniel Webster, July 21, 1832, in Swisher, *Roger B. Taney* (1938; hereinafter cited as Swisher), 202.

All these factors combined to force the conclusion that Webster's request did not go unanswered. As Professor Swisher notes, the only thing we do not know about Webster's printed attack on the veto message is the extent to which it was the product of a member of the Supreme Court.[21]

CHARLESTOWN

On December 10, 1832, six months to the day after the veto of the federal-bank recharter bill, another Presidential message was delivered from the White House. Equally powerful and stirring, it was profoundly different in content. If the July message chided the Supreme Court's assumption of power, the December message defended it. If the earlier message remonstrated against Marshall's opinion in *McCulloch v. Maryland*, the later one vindicated Story's views in *Martin v. Hunter's Lessee*. If the first pronouncement implicitly criticized the review of state-court judgments by the Supreme Court under Section 25, the second defended that jurisdiction and laid the prestige and, if need be, the power of the Presidency behind it.

The ironic turnabout in the Presidential position not only reversed the July polemics and the spring inaction in the case of the Cherokees but also represented a *volte-face* within the legislative program of the Administration forces themselves, where as early as 1830 a repeal of Section 25 had been under way. One of the principal Jacksonians, Missouri's Senator Thomas Hart Benton, had vigorously attacked the philosophy underlying Section 25 when, in the case of *Craig v. Missouri*, he began his argument with a flourish: "The State of Missouri has been 'summoned' by a writ from this court under a 'penalty' to be and appear before this court. In the language she is commanded . . . Language of this kind does not seem proper when addressed to a sovereign State."[22] The point left a mark. While Chief Justice Marshall wrote a majority opinion striking down Missouri's "loan office

[21] *Ibid.*
[22] 4 PETERS at 419 (1850).

certificates" as the constitutionally invalid bills of credit, he none-theless went out of his way to respond constructively to Benton's criticism. Marshall was also upset by the dissenting opinions. "[I]t requires no prophet," he wrote Story, "to predict that the 25th Section is to be repealed or to use a more fashionable phrase, to be nullified by the Supreme Court of the United States . . . [A]ccomplished it will be at no very distant period."[23]

Marshall had taken the word "nullified" from the lexicon of the Great Debate between Hayne and Webster. That confronta-tion, however, was not a dialogue but a multilateral exchange in which Benton was a participant and wherein his fundamental as-sertion (paralleling his *Craig* argument) was that "power to de-cide on the Federal constitutionality of State laws . . . is a power to govern the States."[24] Benton's hostility toward federal hegemony over state law was not a new position for him. Previously he had used his St. Louis newspaper to attack the concept. Significantly, the journalistic criticism drew on the Missouri admission contro-versy and, using the doctrine of strict construction as a shield for slavery, vigorously denounced the antislavery polemics which Story had delivered before federal grand juries during that epi-sode.[25] Moreover, Benton had strategically placed associates in the Jacksonian camp who shared his antijudicial views. One was Richard Johnson, who, as we have seen, had been a critic for many years of the expanding jurisdiction of the Supreme Court. Another, also a Kentuckian but of Yankee origin, was Amos Kendall, who rose from the so-called "Kitchen Cabinet" to the Cabinet itself and who expressly denied that the Constitution had provided any "common arbiter."[26]

[23] Letter to Joseph Story, Oct. 15, 1830, in Warren, *Supreme Court*, I, 727.
[24] *Register of Debates*, VI, Part I, 112 (1830).
[25] See, e.g., St. Louis *Beacon*, Oct. 17, 1829, and its appraisal of judicial emancipation if "a majority of the judges should be found on the bench of the Supreme Court of the United States, to act on the law declared by Mr. Justice Story in his charge to the grand jury at Portsmouth, N.H., in May, 1820 . . ."
[26] Kendall, *Autobiography*, ed. Stickney (1872; hereinafter cited as Ken-dall), 222.

All this suggests that a half-formed design to clip the Court's wings by repealing Section 25 was afoot within the Jackson Administration almost from its first moments of power. From Richmond, a strongpoint of Jacksonian support, Marshall wrote cryptically in early 1830 of a new disposition to prostrate the judiciary. And sometime prior to 1833—for a variety of reasons—the proposal received Presidential support. Or so went an undenied assertion made on the floor of Congress to a Jacksonian floor leader. "It is well known in the House," said Congressman Daniel of Kentucky to James K. Polk, then presiding in that body, "that the President was in favor of the repeal of the Twenty-fifth Section—this you yourself well know."[27]

Congressman Daniel made his accusation on February 28, 1833. He did not explain how the proposal had lost Andrew Jackson's support. He did not have to. Every one of the listeners knew that the turnabout had been due to the ongoing nullification controversy, which had flared from constitutional disputation to constitutional crisis in November of 1832, when the tariff was declared null and void in South Carolina by a popularly elected convention of that state. Enforcement of the tax was forbidden within the state after February 1, 1833, and details of resistance were left to the legislature. And thus the issue came to a head, not in the soaring rhetoric of the Ordinance of Nullification but in a workaday legislative enactment which forbade appeals concerning the tariff to the federal courts and provided for fine and imprisonment of any state official furnishing a record for federal review. Accordingly, the heart of the confrontation was thrust upon Jackson in the form of a contest on the federal judiciary.

Initially the President seemed mild and even conciliatory, an attitude quite consistent with his position on the Indian question and his initial message carried much of the states'-rights overtones of his July veto. Then, in much the same manner as when his countering toast at the Jefferson Day banquet of 1830 stunned friend and foe alike, the ultimate Presidential response to nullifi-

[27] Warren, *Supreme Court*, I, 739-40, n.3.

cation came in the form of a cannon-shot constitutional exegesis—eloquently asserting the doctrines urged in Story's *Martin* opinion and Webster's reply to Hayne. The President's major premise was the proposition that "the Constitution of the United States . . . forms a government, not a league."[28] The judicial issue was his minor one. Asserting that the federal courts, not the states, held the ultimate right of constitutional construction, he thunderingly denounced the attempted nullification, not of the tariff, but of Section 25 of the Judiciary Act of 1789: "Here is a law of the United States, not even pretended to be unconstitutional, repealed by the authority of a small majority of the voters of a single state."[29]

Story could scarcely believe the turn of events. "The President's proclamation is excellent, and contains the true principles of the Constitution; but will he stand to it?"[30] A like incredulity gripped John Y. Hayne, who was now governor of South Carolina as a consequence of a musical-chairs sequence in which he left the Senate for the statehouse in order to provide a seat and vote in the upper federal chamber for John C. Calhoun, who had resigned the Vice-Presidency. The President himself, Hayne indignantly asserted, "has exercis[ed] as is known to all the world—the right to refuse to execute acts of Congress and solemn treaties, even after these had received the position of every department of the federal government."[31] He then cited Jackson on right he claimed for himself: "That the . . . right of deciding, finally and exclusively, as to the validity of acts of Congress . . . belongs to the judiciary . . . has been denied by none more strongly than the president himself who, on a memorable occasion refused to acknowledge the binding authority of the federal court . . ."[32]

Story need not have been so apprehensive, nor Hayne so out-

Richardson, II, 648.
Ibid., 647.
Letter to Richard Peters, Dec. 22, 1832, in W. W. Story, II, 113.
Quoted in *Niles' Weekly Register*, Jan. 5, 1833.
Ibid.

raged. Jackson, his hand strengthened by an overwhelming victory at the polls, surpassed any of his maneuvers of war with those of politics. In an extraordinary combination of threat and blandishment, he disarmed the nullifiers but permitted them to salvage some vestiges of pride in their defeat, as the tariff was further revised and the offending Ordinance of Nullification repealed. Perversely, the Cherokee controversy contributed to the very vindication of judicial power, for Jackson had stripped South Carolina of her natural allies in the southernmost states.

An extraordinary episode marked the turn of events. Story, amazed, wrote home that he and the Chief Justice were to be counted among the president's "warmest supporters." He even recounted how, at a state dinner, President Jackson "specially invited me to drink a glass of wine with him. . . . Who would have dreamed of such an occurrence."[33]

[33] Joseph Story to Mrs. Story, Jan. 27, 1833, in W. W. Story, II, 119.

CHAPTER XXIV

The American Law

TWO DOCTORS FROM HARVARD

Even more symbolic than the toast in which Story joined the President was the honorary doctorate of laws which Harvard bestowed on Jackson in mid-1833, thereby making the Chief Executive and the senior Associate Justice co-holders of that title. The Harvard honors came as the climax of the President's Northern tour, in which New England's thundering reception more than made up for its previous electoral distaste. To be sure, some stiffnecked Yankee opposition remained. In a gross libel on Jackson's crisp military prose John Quincy Adams protested against Harvard's bestowing her honors on a barbarian who could scarcely write his name, but all in vain. In a tart New England response citing precedents of earlier degrees, the head of the university, Josiah Quincy, replied that if the American people had twice decided Jackson knew enough law to be their ruler, Harvard would not contradict them. Quincy had served with Story back in the Tenth Congress, and he may well have looked to the future as well as the past. For, while John Marshall was still in high intellectual vigor, the Chief Justice also was close to eighty and Quincy had already expressed a public hope of the succession falling to Story. ("The Supreme Court," Quincy had toasted a few years earlier, "in event of a vacancy, may it be raised one Story higher."[1])

Myth, it is said, expresses in its own way a profundity of truth beyond the power of gradgrind facts, and the newfound rapport between Harvard's two doctors of law, upon which Quincy had based his hopes, was best reflected in one myth growing out of the Harvard ceremony. As the tale had it, following the long Latin oration pronounced by Quincy and in response to the cries of some supporters for an appropriate reply, Jackson answered with the only two Latin phrases he knew, "*E pluribus unum, sine qua non.*"[2] And as one historian has noted, the fable—actually invented by Jackson's detractors—merely made a poetic Latin epigram out of the reply with which the old President had previously faced down both Calhoun and the nullifiers.

But Jackson's apochryphal Harvard response did more than restate the Nullification Proclamation and the Jefferson Day toast. It also summarized—indeed, could well have been the epigraph of —a tour de force which his fellow doctor of laws had published six months earlier. This was Story's three-volume *Commentaries on the Constitution with a Preliminary Review of the Constitutional History of the Colonies and States before the Adoption of the Constitution.* Written in nonlegalistic language and appropriately dedicated to Marshall, the work combined appeals to history, utility, and philosophy in a forceful, but irenic, nationalist interpretation of the Constitution. Starting from a close examination of the charters and history of the colonies, working through the abortive Confederation, and then closing with a line-by-line commentary of the constitutional text, the work was at once a towering sequel to the Federalist Papers and an artifact of apprehensive pessismism about the world unfolding around the author.

Schematically, Story's monumental exegesis divided along three

---

[1] Quoted in James S. Loring, *The Hundred Boston Orators* (Cleveland 1852), 269; see also Quincy, *Figures of the Past* (1926), 269.
[2] Ward, 85-86

lines. One was a point-by-point response to the constitutional canon of strict construction which the great Virginia jurist St. George Tucker had appended to an 1803 edition of Blackstone's *Commentaries* under the title "A Connected View of the Laws of Virginia as a Member of the Federal Union." At this level the Story–Tucker exchange was a dignified and intellectual debate in which professors of Harvard and of William and Mary, much like divines of Rome and Geneva, exchanged their solemn disputations. It thus differed from the second level of the work, which was also polemic but philosophical rather than legal and distinguished by a note of personal pique. This was a systematic remonstrance against Thomas Jefferson, whose posthumously published correspondence[3] had gone off in 1829 like a bomb, with reverberations reaching the floors of Congress and striking Story among many others.

Story and Jefferson had never really liked each other since their first, strained meeting in the White House back in 1807, but Story had managed not only to suppress his antipathy but even to accord Jefferson persistent public and private compliments.[4] His forbearance seemed shabbily repaid when from beyond the grave Jefferson pilloried him as a Tory, a pseudo-republican, and a party deserter. Uncharacteristically responding in kind, Story denounced the Jefferson letters as "the most precious melange of all sorts of scandals"[5] went out of his way in his law-

[3] *Memoirs, Correspondence, and Miscellanies from the Papers of Thomas Jefferson* (1829).
[4] The first correspondence between them seems to have been Story's presentation of copies of his books *The Power of Solitude* and *A Selection of Pleadings* to Jefferson in 1806 in "feeble testimony of the high regard which entertain for those talents which from the dawn of the revolution to the present moment have been rigorously employed in creating and preserving an independent nation" (Letter to Jefferson, Jan. 4, 1806, Story Papers, Essex Institute, Salem). Again, in 1816, Story sent Jefferson a copy of his eulogy of Samuel Dexter as a "token of . . . gratitude and respect" (Letter of May 5, 1816, Story Papers, Massachusetts Historical Society, Boston). Also, on the occasion of the deaths of Jefferson and Adams on July 4, 1826, Story gave a powerful and moving oratorical tribute to both; see Records of the Town of Salem, July 28, 1826.
[5] Letter to Samuel P. P. Fay, Feb. 15, 1830, in W. W. Story, II, 33.

school inaugural to denounce Jefferson's views on Christianity and common law ("the specious objection of one of our most distinguished statesmen"[6]), and defended himself in an autobiographical letter to his son (" 'Pseudo-republican' of course, I must be; as everyone was in Mr. Jefferson's opinion who dared venture upon a doubt of his infallibility"[7]). And then, in a final Parthian fusillade, he strung a skein of barbed anti-Jefferson footnotes through his *Commentaries on the Constitution.*[8]

But there was also an anti-Jacksonian theme running through the work, and at this third level Story illustrated his painful alienation from the surging democratic forces in American life. On the new and vigorous party system produced by the fissioning of the old Republicans into Whig and Democratic components, his only commentary was a repetition of Washington's warning on the evils of faction. The new and invigorated Presidency, perhaps best typified in a constantly changing Cabinet, in a coterie of unofficial advisers, and in purposeful use of the federal payroll, provoked only a disquisition on the potential harm of the powers of appointment. And the ever-growing capability of the common man to have some choice in his destiny provoked the brooding reflection with which Story cut short his panegyric on the American destiny and closed his last volume: that all this "may perish in an hour by the folly of its only keepers, THE PEOPLE."[9]

THE *COMMENTARIES*

Story's work on the Constitution was not the first fruits of his Dane professorship. The initial product appeared almost a year before, under the title *Commentaries on the Law of Bailments*

---

[6] *Miscellaneous Writings,* 517.
[7] Letter to William W. Story, Jan. 23, 1831, in W. W. Story, 185.
[8] See, e.g., II, (1833), 40, 159, 163; and III (1833), 164, 169. And see Peterson *The Jefferson Image in the American Mind* (1966), 32-36, 94-97.
[9] Story, *Commentaries on the Constitution* (1833), III, 760.

with Illustrations from the Civil and Foreign Law. Significantly, the title page made no reference to judicial office but described the author only as "Dane Professor of Law in Harvard University." That the topic of bailments—the divided dominion of personal property which contemplated custody in one party and ownership in another—had been chosen as the first work was doubtless due to the suggestion of Nathan Dane, to whom the work was dedicated. Persuasive also to Story must have been the attraction of providing an American counterpart to the English case of *Coggs v. Bernard*,[10] where Lord Justice Holt had reached across the Channel to enrich the drab and scanty common law on the temporary possession of personal property with the rich sophistication of the Roman codes. The instrumental possibilities of such cross-fertilization in an American context were particularly fascinating, for foreign law, Story insisted, "cannot be a matter of indifference to any who study the law, not as a mere system of arbitrary rules but as a rational science."[11] Indeed, providing strength and vitality to Story's views of the law was a nationalist vision—which in its own way echoed Jackson's Nullification Proclamation—"that America may yet be reserved the honor of still improving it by a more intimate blending of each system in her own administration of civil justice."[12]

Exemplifying the thesis, Story's *Bailments* ran in an extraordinary range from the Codes of Justinian to the American frontier —deposits, mandates, loans, powers, postmasters, stagecoach drivers, and bank cashiers. In short, it was the Story opinion expanded to book length. Superbly organized, lucidly written, comprehensive in breadth, and accurate in research, the book both laid out the law as it was and from time to time gave a nudge to what ought to be ("I have . . . availed myself occasionally of the freedom belonging to a commentator to express a doubt or deny a dogma"[13]). The work was immensely popular. To be sure, it

[10] 2 RAYMOND 909 (1703).
[11] Story, *Commentaries on the Law of Bailments* (1832), 394.
[12] *Ibid.*
[13] *Ibid., ix.*

had no competition save the American edition of Sir William Jones's *Essay on Bailments*, a slim outline of scarcely over one hundred pages. More generally, it differed from contemporary and previous works in being neither a purported *summa* of an entire national law (although, following the mode of Blackstone and Kent, it bore the appellation "commentaries") nor an Encyclopédiste topic-by-topic disquisition in the style of Viner or Dane. But it was not so much novelty or lack of competition which made for the book's success, but, rather, its immense practicality as a manual for a milieu increasingly concerned with the complexities of commercial and industrial enterprise.

Appropriately, it was the ongoing convergence in the workaday business of an enterprising nation and an enterprising world that formed the basis of Story's next great work of 1834. Dealing with harmonization of the law in interjurisdictional transactions, it was somewhat misleadingly named *Commentaries on the Conflict of Laws*, or, in full, *Commentaries on the Conflict of Laws Foreign and Domestic in Regard to Contracts, Rights, and Remedies, and Especially in Regard to Marriages, Divorces, Wills*. Dedicated to Chancellor James Kent, and again drawing heavily upon the European civilians, it systematized—the English legal authority Dicey said it almost created—a whole branch of jurisprudence. It also laid the groundwork for a theory of an American private law that would complete the constitutional doctrine of *Martin v. Hunter's Lessee* (itself a conflict-of-laws case) by providing for a consistent framework of commercial rules which the federal courts might, and indeed should, pronounce without reference to aberrant local decisions. One specific base rested upon sheer necessity:

> The whole system of agencies, purchases and sales, credits, and negotiable instruments rests on this foundation; and the nation which should refuse to acknowledge the common principles, would soon find its whole commercial interest reduced to a state like that in which it now exists with savage

tribes, with the barbarous nations of Sumatra, and with the other portions of Asia, washed by the Pacific.[14]

The other, asserted more cautiously, touched on the nature of American nationalism, and had to be read against the background of *Martin v. Hunter's Lessee:*

> To no part of the world is [the subject of conflicts] of more interest and importance than to the United States, since the Union of a national government with that of twenty-four distinct, and in some respects independent states, necessarily creates very complicated relations and rights between the citizens of these states, which call for constant administration of extra-municipal principles.[15]

He closed the work on conflicts on a note of hope, both national and international. Quoting the same line from Cicero which would be the linchpin of his concept of a general commercial law—that true law is right reason in agreement with nature—he asserted the aspiration that "the comity of nations will be but another name for the justice of nations."[16]

Yet, unbelievably, in this series of legal pyrotechnics lightening up an ever-widening sky the best was yet to come, and it appeared late in 1836 with his *Commentaries on Equity Jurisprudence*. This in truth was the masterpiece, encompassing within its systematic framework the extraordinary system whose very plasticity proved at once its own vitality and the despair of its commentators. Even for Story's towering talents the work was formidability itself. Originally he thought he might cover the subject in a book of

---

[14] Story, *Commentaries on the Conflict of Laws* (1834), 202.
[15] *Ibid., v.*
[16] *Ibid.,* 532. See also Lorenzen, "Story's *Commentaries on the Conflict of Laws*—One Hundred Years Later," *Harvard Law Review*, XLIV (1934), 5; Nadelmann, "Joseph Story's Contribution to American Conflicts Law: A Comment," *American Journal of Legal History*, V (1961), 230; and Vallabao, "The Influence of Joseph Story on Latin American Rules of Conflict Laws, *American Journal of Comparative Law*, III (1954), 41.

five hundred pages. Before he was finished, however, this estimate had been exceeded more than twice over. "Think of this . . ." he wrote in April of 1836, "I have published a volume of six hundred and ninety pages last year, and am to write another of the same size this year."[17] The extraordinarily complex job of organization and writing came on top of ever heavier Supreme Court duties, Harvard lectures, and circuit travels. Perhaps one measure will suffice: it takes a modern lawyer, engrossed with a conventional work load, almost more time to read Story's *Commentaries* than it took the author to write them. Yet for all Story's genius it at first seemed that in putting his hand to equity he had overreached himself. "I am overwhelmed by my labors," he wrote in early 1835. "I have three works in the press. My *Equity Commentaries* is going through cut proofs; and the closing part is not yet written. Next week I go on my circuit in Maine."[18] It took all his extraordinary gifts—the photographic memory, the long years of dedicated reading, the superb sense of order and sequence, the ability to write at first draft—to finish the job by November of 1836.

Going through fourteen American and three English editions (the last published in London in 1920), *Commentaries on Equity Jurisprudence* crowned the many efforts Story had undertaken on behalf of equity—his early support in the Massachusetts legislature, his prose efforts in the *North American Review*, his pleading in the constitutional convention. Curiously, in his native New England the assemblies remained unmoved, although litigants changed their domicile to get his jurisdiction.[19] Needless to say, Story was delighted with the result. In part it marked the halfway point of the labors he set for himself. "I have now published seven

[17] Letter to Francis Lieber, April 10, 1836, in W. W. Story, II, 230.
[18] Letter to Richard Peters, Feb. 2, 1835, in Richard Peters Papers, The Historical Society of Pennsylvania.
[19] "It is now almost a matter of course that a citizen of this state, having a cause of any magnitude in amount or principle, steps over the line and becomes a temporary resident of another state, in order to avail himself of the jurisdiction of the United States Court." (*Providence Journal*, quoted in *Niles' Weekly Register*, Dec. 3, 1825.)

volumes and, in five or six more, I can accomplish all I propose."[20] Yet, for the first time in his life an apprehensive sense of *ars longa, vita brevis* crept into his optimistic ebullience: "If my life should be spared a few years longer, I hope to complete the entire series of works which I contemplate."[21]

CODIFICATION: BRIDGE AND BATTLEGROUND

The sharpest collision between the legal nationalism of Story and the folk nationalism of Jackson came in the many-rooted and many-faced codification movement. Formally an effort to cast the law into more systematic and comprehensive forms, the movement both reflected and influenced the circumstances of its environment. At the most elemental, it could be seen as a natural response to the ever-increasing output and complexity of the statutes, court decisions, and legal writings of an increasingly complex society. At a more intellectualized level there was an increasing tendency to transfer the methodology and order of the physical sciences to the universe of law. And on a closely related plane, the evolving humanities, particularly history, emphasized the roots of the common law and its relationship to the great tradition of the Roman codes.

Cutting across these forces was a cleavage which saw the differences between Sir William Blackstone and Jeremy Bentham on the nature of the law transferred to American soil in a controversy whose bitterness obscured the basically reformist cast of both viewpoints. To be sure, the differences were radical enough, for the history-oriented outlook which looked upon the law as the embodiment of the past's best effort and sought to gently prune in order to conserve was a pole away from the quest for an immediate and thorough reordering on the basis of analytic ra-

[20] Letter to John Brazer, Nov. 10, 1836, in W. W. Story, II, 240.
[21] *Ibid.*

tionalism. Thus, Bentham's initial offer to write an American code of laws insisted that varying judicial decisions worked a confusion to justice more dangerous than the abolition of law itself, and a characteristic response was a Bostonian sneer against "this 'Codification,' formed by a closet politician in Europe."[22] Significantly, however, with the inauguration of Jackson the offer was renewed by Bentham, who wrote the President that they had a common mission to free the people from the thralldom of the law; and a subsequent Independence Day speech of a Yankee labor leader showed what a sensitive concern the matter involved:

> The judiciary . . . is the headquarters of the aristocracy and every plan to humble and subdue the people originates there. One of the most enormous usurpations of the judiciary is the claim . . . of common law jurisdiction. Common law, although contained in ten thousand books, is said to be unwritten law, deposited only in the head of the judge, so that what he says is common law, must be common law. . . . Of all the reforms . . . the reform of the judiciary and the law is the most important.[23]

This attitude obviously involved the corollary that the popular assembly was every bit the equal of the judiciary in deciding legal and constitutional questions and thus drew on a preexisting—and appropriately Jeffersonian—hostility to both judicial review and judicial legislation.[24] It also showed itself in long-standing persistent efforts to keep the judiciary on a short bridle through low salaries, short terms, and legislative recall.

[22] *Columbian Centinel,* June 10, 1818.
[23] Frederick Robinson, "A Program for Labor," July 4, 1834, in Blau (ed.), *Social Theories of Jacksonian Democracy* (1947), 320, 328.
[24] Jefferson's hostility toward judicial legislation was evidenced early: "I have added, also, a disquisition of my own on the most remarkable instance of Judicial legislation, that has ever occurred in English jurisprudence, or perhaps in any other. It is that of the adoption in mass of the whole code of another nation, and its incorporation into a legitimate system; by usurpation of the Judges alone, without a particle of legislative will having ever been called on, or exercised toward its introduction or confirmation." (Jefferson, *Reports of Cases Determined in the General Court of Virginia from 1768 to 1772* [Charlottesville, 1839], *vi.*)

While Story had been a defender of the judiciary in his early public career, he also was initially in favor of extensive codification. However, a critical turnabout came in 1836 with his appointment to a commission to consider codification of the law of Massachusetts. The commission report seemed reasonable and balanced, for in a lucid exposition it persuasively pleaded the impossibility of writing out the entire range of statutory law and suggested it do so only with that part "of daily use and familiar application."[25] Yet this seemingly reasonable position was merely an overlay for the hostility and insecurity of an antidemocratic pessimism.

> Much against my will [he wrote] I was placed at the head of the commission. We shall report favorably to the codification of some branches of the Common Law. But the report will be qualified and limited in its objects. We have not yet became votaries of Jeremy Bentham. But the present state of popular opinion here makes it necessary to do something. . . .[26]

Needless to say, he dominated the body,[27] and the way he did it is best summed up by a brief line from the secretary of the commission: "I have taken the pains to obliterate everything in the Report which might seem to harmonize with some of the radical notions of the day."[28]

[25] See W. W. Story, II, 241-50. The report anticipates that modern jurist Jerome Frank: ". . . [T]here has been and still is much criticism of the power exercised by judges in construing statutes, and Bentham, Livingston, and their disciples (some even in our own time) have insisted that all 'law' must emanate solely from the legislature, and tried, through codification, to destroy all 'judicial legislation.' Repeated attempts on the European continent to exploit that nation have invariably proved disappointing." (*Giuseppi v. Walling*, 144 F [2] at 620 [1944].)
[26] Letter to John Williams, Dec. 26, 1836, in *Proceedings of the Mass. Historical Society*, 2nd series, XV (1902), 221.
[27] "You will I am sure pardon my saying that if Judge Story be on the Commission, and of course at its head, the work must be substantially his work." (Theophilus Parsons to Charles Sumner, April, 1836, in Warren, *Harvard*, I, 503 n.2.)
[28] L. S. Cushing to Joseph Story, Dec. 30, 1836, Story Papers, Essex Institute.

The commission episode thus marks a significant point of regression at which Story's political despair began to take its toll on his talents. For it has been well said that the real loss lay in the truly model codes—organic, integrated, comprehensive—which might have been turned out had Story taken the helm of the commission, directed it into areas promising fruitful result, and thrown into the task his instinct for synthesis, his sense of balance and order, and, above all, his feel for both structure and suppleness in the law.

Yet Story's total response was in fact far more constructive than his foot-dragging contribution on the Massachusetts commission. True enough, he more than any other man defeated the extreme proposals of the American codification movement. However, he did so by endowing American law with the very systemization, clarity, and harmony that the most vociferous codifiers demanded. In part, his success was due to the fact that the literal demands of the codifiers were simply impossible to fulfill. Within the bounds of possibility, however, his counterattack developed along two interrelated lines. One was his writing—particularly the *Commentaries*—which itself provided a codification, par excellence, of American law. The other was the Harvard Law School.

A LAW SCHOOL IN CAMBRIDGE

In the struggle between reform and institutionalism, nowhere were the character and consequence of legal education better recognized than by Jefferson himself, who insisted that Blackstone's *Commentaries* were a hornbook of reaction and had turned a whole generation of young lawyers into Tories. "Tory" was also the epithet that Jefferson's posthumously published correspondence applied to Story, and the target of the criticism would have gladly accepted its substance, if not its label. For Blackstone, not Bentham, was the core of the school which Story refounded at Harvard, and it was Sir William's *Commentaries,* supplemented by standard English works and a growing number of

American ones, that formed the basis of the curriculum. Instruction was through recitation from the text, moot courts were held, and dissertations were asserted and defended as a preliminary to graduation.

There were two breaks with tradition. In technique, the rote instruction, the mechanical recitation, the deadening discipline which had hitherto characterized Harvard education vanished with the appearance of a teacher who relished both the subject and the people he taught. He was

> always ready and profuse in his instructions, anxiously seeking out . . . difficulties which perplexed the student and anticipating his wants, leaving no stone unturned by which the rugged paths of the law might be made smoother. . . . [The students] love him more than any instructor they ever had before. He treats them all as gentlemen, and is full of willingness to instruct. . . . The good scholars like him for the knowledge he distributes; the poor (if any there be), for the amenity with which he treats them and their faults.[29]

The sequence of instruction was also altered, in a professional division of labor undertaken to accommodate Story's judicial commitments. Story, absent the entire middle term, concentrated in the other two on the subjects of constitutional, civil, and commercial law. Professor Ashmun made appropriate adjustments so as to carry the work of common-law subjects throughout the entire academic years. The professors complemented each other in their mode of instruction. Ashmun was precise, systematic, and spoke from carefully prepared notes. Story, on the other hand, preferred to rely on his photographic memory and sense of rapport with the class to speak *ad libitem*, often with reference to topical subjects and always with effectiveness.

> I attended [ran one report] on Monday at 12 o'clock in the lecture room of the Harvard Law School a lecture by Judge

[29] Charles Sumner, quoted in D. Donald, *Charles Sumner and the Coming of the Civil War* (New York, 1960), 23-24.

Story on Constitutional Law. He discussed the question "Whether the Constitution was a compact agreement or covenant," touched slightly on the doctrine so popular in South Carolina, and closed with a most beautiful and elegant eulogium on the prospects and happiness of our federated form of government. I was very much pleased with his pleasant and unaffected manners. . . .[30]

The school flourished accordingly. The enrollment crept upward, with students coming from ever-widening geographical origins. The law library, whose low estate matched the low-water mark of student enrollment, was almost completely reconstituted as Story turned over his private collection to the school for a nominal price. And then, in a solicitation of funds which might serve as a model to modern universities, President Quincy persuaded Nathan Dane to match his original bounty by providing a building to house the books and the professors. Dane Hall, "a beautiful Grecian temple . . . the most architectural and the best-built edifice belonging to the college,"[31] was accordingly dedicated in September, 1832.

A serious setback came in early 1833 with the death of Professor Ashmun, and Story felt the loss professionally and personally ("I feel a pride in declaring that we have worked hand in hand with the most cordial fellowship"[32] as he carried the double teaching load through spring. Then he had the great fortune to find a successor who was to be the ideal coadjutor, Simon Greenleaf of the Maine bar. Temperamentally complete opposites, the two men were as one in talent and reciprocal affection. Story was concerned with general principles, Greenleaf with details. "No wonder," later said a colleague, "that such a man as either of these succeeded; no wonder that a School, in which were two such men, succeeded."[33]

[30] Fred Blount to John Byran, June 29, 1831, in *Proceedings of the Mass. Historical Society*, XLII (1910), 74.
[31] Charles Sumner to Mr. Tower, Oct. 22, 1832, in Warren, *Harvard*, I, 477.
[32] Story to Josiah Quincy, Nov. 3, 1829, *ibid.*, 462.
[33] Prof. Parsons, quoted in Warren, *Harvard*, I, 483.

There was far more, however, to success than two men, even with one bringing an immense enthusiasm, a towering national reputation, and an instinctive teaching ability to the aid of an institution in difficulty. In part success was underlain by Story's stated objective of giving the school a decided superiority over every other institution of like nature, and his drive caused Harvard to turn the corner in terms of enrollment and prestige almost from the first moment of his association with it. But it turned the corner not only for itself but as a prototype of a national development, for it did so in a national environment which produced an increasingly complex law and an increasing volume of legal controversies. Accordingly, Harvard's influence was both seminal and critical. Its development of academic and intellectualized training for the legal profession not only sounded the death knell for the old law-office apprenticeship system (which would take a long time in dying and then go down fighting hard), but also ended the codifiers' millenarian dream of a world wherein every man would be his own lawyer.

Insuring both relevance and success of the academic revolution was the commercial orientation which Story brought to the curriculum. It did, to be sure, lay him open to charges that he had vulgarized the majesty of legal education by investing it with a trade-school cheapness. While Story could have answered that a liberal education was the prerequisite, not the product, of legal training, a more historically cogent reply might well be that it was this very workaday concern which involved both the law—constitutional, public and private—and its institutions in the ongoing entrepreneurial revolution and thereby resulted in the quickening vitalization of the one and the tempering restraint of the other.

A perceptive insight into this interplay came from across the Atlantic. Writing in Paris in 1835, de Tocqueville reviewed his American tour of a few years earlier in a prophetic framework ("in America, I saw more than America"[34]) and examined with

[34] De Tocqueville, I, 15.

particular scrutiny the specific constitutional and legal aspects of the American experiment. Acknowledging his dependence on Story's *Commentaries on the Constitution*, de Tocqueville concluded as President Jackson had discovered, that it was the federal courts with their territorial and personal jurisdiction, and, above all, their jurisdiction to determine jurisdiction, that constituted the critical nexus of the American Union. Yet above and beyond purely governmental relationships, de Tocqueville also put his finger on the creative tension which arose between the constraint of the emerging American law and the exuberance of American nationalism, and he concluded: ". . . without this admixture of lawyer-like sobriety with the democratic principle, I question whether democratic institutions could long be maintained."[35]

[35] *Ibid.*, 286.

CHAPTER XXV

Symbols of an Age

A MATTER OF COPYRIGHT

In addition to writing his commentaries and changing the content and character of legal education, Story used one other weapon to blunt the thrust of the codification movement. This was the judicial opinion, wherein he turned a venerable document of the law into a modernized technique of judicature. For what Story did was to take what had been a terse and often obscure memorandum of a decision in a particular dispute and change it into a comprehensive and systematic exposition of whatever law bore on the point in question. Thus, each such expression of his views, particularly in important cases, was not so much an award of an individual judgment as a codification in miniature.

To be sure, this transformation was not exclusively Story's work, but he played a critical and decisive role in it, and, moreover, he was well aware of the didactic value of his product (". . . do not omit to have your decisions reported," he advised a fledgling judge[1]). He was also aware of its financial value. His involvement in both aspects had run from an ambitious program to

[1] Letter to Joseph Hopkinson, Dec. 16, 1828, in Burton A. Konkle, *Joseph Hopkinson* (Philadelphia, 1931), 260.

market his circuit-court reports to being, *de facto* at least, joint venturer in the twelve volumes published under the name and aegis of Henry Wheaton during the latter's tenure as Supreme Court reporter, from 1816 to 1827. While Story apparently received no material gain from the Wheaton reports, he did increase the award of the reporter, thanks to extrajudicial contributions of learned notes and erudite appendices, plus enthusiastic, if anonymous, book reviews. His efforts, altruistic at the time, enormously complicated the question of who owned what in the product. Wheaton's immediate reward was the $1,000 per annum provided under the Reporter's Act of 1817[2] (a statute which Story helped enact), but there was also a general if diffuse understanding that compensation would also come from the sale of the reports. While some friends and at least one foe, Justice William Johnson, were acquainted with Story's assistance to Wheaton, their association was not particularly well known. "I blush to see," Wheaton once acknowledged, "that Chief Justice Spencer [of New York] has very much praised Mr. Wheaton's note on guarantees in *Lanusse v. Barker* in my 2nd volume. *You* know how much of that praise *I* deserve."[3]

The law explosion, the ever-widening federal jurisdiction, and the quality of the product combined to give the Wheaton reports an extraordinary popularity, with which went, paradoxically enough, something of an increasing embarrassment of riches. Fairly early in his career Wheaton was complaining of the "monstrous bulk"[4] of one of his volumes, and along in the next decade Story was expressing the general opinion that "the business of reporting"[5] should be managed more sparingly. When Richard Peters of Philadelphia succeeded to Wheaton's position in 1827, he moved to winnow and update the work of his predecessors

[2] *United States Statutes at Large*, III, 376 (1817).

[3] Wheaton to Story, June 14, 1819, Wheaton Papers. The case is actually in Wheaton's third volume, at 148, and the note is claimed by Story in a memorandum reprinted in W. W. Story, I, 283.

[4] Letter from Henry Wheaton, July 2, 1820, in Wheaton Papers.

[5] Joseph Story to Jeremiah Mason, Jan. 8, 1827, in Hillard, *Mason*, 254.

through a summarized edition. While it was an excellent editorial product, the foreword to the new work suggested an uneasy legal position:

> It is not considered that his work will interfere with the interests of those gentlemen who have preceded the reporter in the station he has the honour to hold. Deeply as he is impressed with the absolute necessity of this understanding, he would regret exceedingly such an interference. Their volumes will always be standards for reference, and of the highest authority; and every member of the profession, who has the ability to purchase them, will own them. The legal rights of the proprietors of these most able and valuable works, where they exist, will be carefully respected. Nothing will be inserted in the contemplated publication, but matter in the public record, and which from their nature and other circumstances, are not the subject of literary property. The opinions of the court are public property.[6]

Peters turned out to be a prophet of the law, but an inept (or perhaps an extraordinarily astute) judge of sales. Contrary to his assertion, lawyers who were able to afford the original reports showed no inclination to buy them for $180 when the synoptic version was available for $36. From faraway Denmark, where he was serving as American minister, Wheaton irately watched sales plummet, vainly wrote Webster and Story of his concern, and then returned to America on leave of absence to vindicate his rights. Seeking a permanent injunction and an accounting, he filed suit in the federal circuit court in Philadelphia, where his case was considered and dismissed.[7] Wheaton accordingly appealed to the Supreme Court and, accompanying his cause, was reported on arrival as looking "very mad."[8]

[6] *Condensed Reports of Cases in the Supreme Court of the United States,* 3rd edition (6v., Philadelphia, 1844), I, *vi.*
[7] *Wheaton v. Peters,* 29 FED. CASES 862 (1832).
[8] Horace Binney to John Sergeant, Jan. 15, 1834, in Warren, *Supreme Court,* I, 785 n.2.

Apparently his outraged concern continued to the day of final decision, for he looked "strongly excited"[9] when the determinative opinion was read by Mr. Justice McLean in mid-March of 1834. Story had left the term early, doubtless to avoid any embarrassment in being present at a conclusion which Peters won on all counts. McLean's opinion was thoroughly Jacksonian. In a hammer-and-tongs resolution of one of the most complex questions in the law, the rights inhering in intellectual products, it resolved doubts in favor of competition and against monopoly as it declared the opinions of the court in the public domain and held only the marginal notes in the reports capable of being the subject of literary property. It was also Jacksonian enough to denounce the possibility of the national copyright authority being a source of independent judicial power and to combine its thrust with a flourish of states'-rights rhetoric. ("It is clear there can be no common law of the United States. The Federal Government is composed of . . . sovereign . . . states, each [with] its local usages, customs, and common law."[10] Yet the opinion also was Jacksonian when at the crucial climax it held the federal copyright statute not only controlling but preemptive and required that it be read *strictissimi juris*— specifically that the eighty copies of the reports which Wheaton had deposited with the Secretary of State under the Reporter's Act could not suffice to satisfy the requirement of a deposit of one copy required under the copyright statute.[11]

Perhaps the cruelest cut which Wheaton endured was the dedication of the synoptic reports to Chief Justice Marshall, and it may well have been this circumstance which roused him to a vituperative fury against Story exceeding by far anything Thomas Jefferson had to say. In explaining why Marshall's vote went against him on his appeal, Wheaton declared:

[9] Letter from Charles Sumner, March 19, 1834, in Story Papers, Library of Congress.
[10] *Wheaton v. Peters,* 8 PETERS at 673 (1834).
[11] *United States Statutes at Large,* I, 125 (1790).

I answer that he never studied the cause, and I have the high-est authority for this assertion. He pinned his faith on the sleeve of his prevaricating brother, believing that, if the lat-ter had any leaning it was toward me on the friendship the hypocrite once possessed—and which doubtless still continued to pour in that venerable man's ear.[12]

Any doubt as to the identity of the "prevaricating brother" and "the hypocrite" was removed in other references, for Wheaton asserted that Story had conspired with the district judge to deny him justice at the trial level, and ascribed to Webster an asser-tion that Peters had "something in writing under the hand of one of their learned bench, which if made public, would condemn him to infamy."[13]

Wheaton's charges seem almost as preposterous as his legal theory that the opinions of the Supreme Court were *inter vivos* gifts to him from the individual justices and thereby his personal property. He did, however, have some ground for complaint. The statute was read with extraordinary literality, and, more-over, Story appears to have been rash enough to correspond with the district judge while the case was under advisement in Phil-adelphia.[14]

Wheaton was not the only one to remonstrate over the de-cision. Chancellor Kent wrote that "to deny the common law and to construe the statute with such severity is not palatable to us humble authors."[15] Story's reply was illuminating, if for noth-ing more than the contrast it afforded to his response on the posthumous Jefferson correspondence. More noteworthy was the forbearance he manifested in the face of Wheaton's strictures, which unquestionably must have reached his ears. In any event,

[12] Henry Wheaton to Eliza Lyman, his sister, May 14, 1837, in E. B. Baker, *Henry Wheaton* (1937), 127.
[13] *Ibid.*
[14] See John F. Whicher, *The Creative Arts and the Judicial Process* (New York, 1965), 186-201.
[15] Letter from James Kent, April 11, 1834, in *Proceedings of the Mass. His-torical Society,* 2nd series, XIV (1901), 417.

the combined circumstances suggest an apprehension that the ex-reporters had been given something less than perfect justice and explain why Justice Story chose to be absent when the final opinion was read.

> I am sorry for the controversy between Mr. Wheaton and Peters, and did all I could to prevent a public discussion of the delicate subject of copyright, in which we all have so deep an interest . . . (s)trict construction of the statute of Congress we adopted with vast reluctance . . . I wish Congress would make some additional provisions on the subject, to protect authors of whom I think no one is more meritorious than Mr. Wheaton. You, as a judge, have frequently had occasion to know how many bitter cups we are not at liberty to pass by.[16]

A MATTER OF DEPOSITS

Imagine, if you will, the excitement that would have attended a disclosure that Mr. Justice Frankfurter not only had been the president and a member of the board of the Cambridge Trust Company during most of his years on the Supreme Court, but had repeatedly intervened with the holders of the public purse to secure and retain a large government deposit in that institution. The certainty of the excitement is matched only by the impossibility of such dual service in the present day and age. However, today's standards should not be projected backward. Mr. Justice Story for many years had been judge, president of one bank, and vice-president of another.[17] None of his contemporaries thought that there was anything untoward in this state of affairs. Or almost none of them.

On the contrary, while the Jacksonian revolution was changing basic attitudes, there persisted the mercantilistic view of the

---

[16] Letter to James Kent, May 17, 1834, in W. W. Story, I, 182.
[17] See, generally, Dunne, "Mr. Justice Story and the American Law of Banking," *American Journal of Legal History*, V (1961), 205.

corporation as an arm of government carrying out a public purpose, and the resulting assumption of propriety when a man
prominent in public life undertook supplementary public service
as a bank officer. Indeed, such was this long-lived perception of
the communal character of the corporation that one of Story's
eulogists saw nothing improper in recalling that as Speaker of
the Massachusetts House of Representatives the future Justice
had "exerted his influence"[18] to obtain the charter of the Merchants' Bank of Salem, an institution with which he was closely
associated for over twenty years.

Similarly characteristic were the repeated and formal supplica-
tions of Story's board of directors that he use his influence to
obtain a government deposit. In fact, the only remonstrance over
Story's banking connection arose not because the president of the
Merchants' Bank was also a member of the United States Supreme
Court, but, rather (in a complaint to the Treasury filed by a com-
peting Salem bank of Jacksonian persuasion), that government
funds were kept in a bank headed by one of the "bitter, uncompromising opponents of the administration."[19] Unfortunately, the
vigorous and imaginative competition came at a time when the
Treasury portfolio was held by Louis McLane, who apparently
shared Story's views on banking matters, and who saw to it "that
the public money was left undisturbed in the Merchants Bank."[20]

Secretary McLane was less successful in seeing that the government deposit remained undisturbed at the Bank of the United
States. However, he did manage to fight a delaying action in the
campaign against the bank which President Jackson launched to
hasten the demise of that institution, already foreshadowed in his
successful veto of its charter renewal. The *coup de grâce* aimed
at crippling the bank's operational function by terminating the

18 John Treadwell to W. W. Story, Aug. 25, 1847, in W. W. Story, I, 205.
19 *Ibid*. II, 159.
20 *Ibid*. McLane, however, took another view of other aspects of Story's
public philosophy. "You fear Judge Marshall," he once wrote to Martin
Van Buren, "I fear a thousand times more Judge Story and a line of such
miserably frivolous bookworms . . ." (Letter of July 20, 1830, in Warren,
Supreme Court, I, 719-20.)

deposit of the eight to nine millions in Treasury funds which by statutory mandate were committed to the bank's safekeeping. There was one exception to the mandate: the Secretary of the Treasury could "at any time otherwise order and direct."[21] McLane not only had no intention of ordering withdrawal of the funds but actively pressed the bank's case for recharter. These efforts in part caused him to be transferred to the Department of State in June, 1833, with William J. Duane of Philadelphia as his Treasury successor. Duane proved equally intransigent on ending the government's deposit. Prior to the veto, he had successfully persuaded Jackson to withhold public criticism of the bank, but he found himself dismissed within four months of appointment. Finally Roger Brooke Taney, future Chief Justice of the United States, was selected for the post. Three days after taking office, Taney announced that deposits of government funds would henceforward be made in groups of seven state-chartered institutions rather than in the federal bank.

The action was hotly attacked when Congress convened in Washington in late 1833, and it led to Taney's rejection by the Senate when the President submitted his name for formal confirmation. Following long-time procedure, Senator Daniel Webster requested Story's extrajudicial opinion in the deposit controversy. The reply, written on Christmas Day of 1833, must have come as something of a disappointment. Differing from Webster, who thought the funds could be removed only in the threat of insolvency, Story stated his view that no such condition was implied under the statute. However, speaking with all the authority of a jurist, a law writer, and the president of a state-chartered bank, he suggested doubts as to the legal authority of the new depositaries to fulfill certain conditions of their federal contract. Then, not satisfied with a delicate matter of interwoven national and state law which might come before him for judgment, he went on to plant a barb in the man who would one day be his chief. Asserting that Taney's power over the deposit was that of

[21] *United States Statutes at Large*, III, 274 (1816).

a trustee rather than an officer in the executive branch, he insisted that

> [the decision] belongs to the Secretary and to him alone, and any interference by the President to control or influence his judgment, much more to deter him from exercising his judgment, is, on the part of the President, a departure from his duty, and if the Secretary acts upon the opinion of the President, and not upon his own, I think he virtually violates the charter and abandons his trust.[22]

A MATTER OF ARSON

On August 13, 1834, a public meeting was held in Cambridge at which Story spoke in a solemn and impressive manner. That he dominated the proceedings was characteristic not only of the way he had sunk his roots in his new home town, but also of his outgoing and enthusiastic nature generally. "Judge Story," ran one Harvard reminiscence, "with fully two men's stated work, had time for every good cause and worthy enterprise. There was no public meeting for a needed charity, for educational interests, in behalf of art or letters, or for the advancement of a conservatively liberal theology, in which his advocacy was not an essential part of the program."[23] The Cambridge meeting fell under the latter classification, for it had been called to protest the burning of a convent in Charlestown by an anti-Catholic mob on the night of the preceding August 11.

Not that Story felt any affinity for the works of Catholicism. Rather, in his early poetic effort, *Power of Solitude*, he had gently deprecated monkish superstition in the best style of the Enlightenment. Yet as a child, at a time when Guy Fawkes torches blazed the length of New England, he had been taken aside by his father and told that the Catholic religion had many excellent and pious men. It was this inherited attitude which made

[22] Letter to Daniel Webster, Dec. 25, 1833, in W. W. Story, II, 156.
[23] Andrew Peabody, *Harvard Reminiscences* (Boston, 1888), 58.

the Charleston arson as much a sign of advancement as of regression. That Rome should be met with violent resistance was quite consistent with one element in the Yankee tradition. Yet there was another which appealed to order and rationality, and it was this, with Story as spokesman for the establishment, which asserted a countervailing view in deeply regretting "that in this land of religious liberty, proclaiming its duty to give all citizens and inhabitants an equal protection, a scene should have occurred so inconsistent with law, with justice . . . and with religion."[24]

Unquestionably Story's concern was heightened by the fact that the burning of the convent seemed not an isolated phenomenom. Rather, the episode appeared part and parcel of a political and social order in which despotism in the center produced King Mob ascendant throughout the country. Or so it seemed to the anti-Jacksonian opposition, who increasingly adopted the name of Whig and looked upon themselves as the intellectual and political descendants of Britain's anti-Tory opposition. A characteristic screed came from New York's Chancellor Kent some four months before the burning of the convent: "This elective American monarchy frightens me. The experiment, with its foundations laid on universal suffrage & an unfettered & licentious press, is of too violent a nature for our excitable people."[25]

And the "excitable people" were behaving appallingly. Just a month prior to the firing of the convent an anti-Negro riot in New York took both life and property and did so without public comment. Shortly thereafter, the scenes were repeated in Philadelphia. "The worst and most fatal symptom of the times," wrote a foreign observer, "is that the perpetration of these outrages . . . excites no sensation. The destruction of the churches and school houses of the blacks in New York was looked on as a show."[26] There was, to be sure, a leaven of hope and humanity at work,

[24] Letter to Bishop Fenwick, Aug. 13, 1834, in Anon., *The Charlestown Convent: Its Destruction by a Mob* (1870), 22-23.
[25] Letter from James Kent, April 11, 1834, in *Proceedings of the Mass. Historical Society*, 2nd series, XIV (1901), 418.
[26] Chevalier, 390.

but nonetheless the scales seemed distressingly unbalanced in the increasing outburst of "murder, outrage, and destruction which has been exhibited throughout the United States."[27]

Story seemingly had a preview of this national wave of unrest when a relative by marriage was brutally murdered in Salem in the summer of 1831,[28] and the general state of affairs worsened in the ensuing years. With the opening of 1835, still a new crime of violence was recorded—the first attempted assassination of a President of the United States. To be sure, the assailant was deranged, but his act could have been prompted by the increasingly violent aspect of his environment and in any event it seemed an accurate, if ominous, prelude to the long, hot summer which followed. In July a mob enraged by a bank failure held Baltimore for three days and burned the homes of the leading citizens ("destroyed by the mobility," noted the seldom punning John Quincy Adams).[29] Down in Charlestown another mob, led by no less than ex-Governor Hayne, demonstrated the right of nullification by sacking post offices in a quest for abolitionist literature and did so with the connivance of the local postmaster and the approbation of the Postmaster General. In Mississippi, mobs hung suspected slave rebels and suspected card sharks with marked impartiality. And then the geographical cycle seemed to complete itself with another Northern incident when, in October of 1835, a Boston mob of two thousand almost succeeded in lynching William Lloyd Garrison, prominent abolitionist, who for his own safety was lodged in jail.

This time it was an English traveler's turn to be shocked, first at the event, next at the public reaction:

and even Judge Story, when I asked him whether there was not a public prosecutor who might prosecute for the assault on Garrison . . . replied that he had given his advice (which

[27] *Ibid.*, 385.
[28] See Lewis, "The Murder of Captain Joseph White," *American Bar Assn. Journal,* LIV (1968), 460.
[29] J. Q. Adams, *Memoirs,* IX, 252.

had been formally asked) against any notice whatever being taken of the outrage,—the feeling being so strong against the discussion of slavery, and the rioters being so respectable in the city.[30]

Niles' Weekly Register found that the "spirit of riot and a disposition to 'take the law into their own hands' prevails in every quarter"; in a two-week period it had observed "*five hundred* articles relating to the various excitements" and concluded, "*Society seems everywhere unhinged.*"[31] Others observed a regression in individual morality. "The old Yankee character appears nearly extinct," noted one diarist in bemoaning the "spirit of riot and insubordination."[32] And John Quincy Adams wondered whether the unprecedented affluence might not be at the root of the trouble as he seemed to foresee both sectional and class war: "We are in a state of profound peace and over-pampered with prosperity; yet the elements of exterminating war seem to be in vehement fermentation . . ."[33]

At the opening of the next century, the hardbitten William Graham Sumner offered an explanation of violence in the age of Jackson:

On reflection, it will not be found strange that the period 1829 to 1837 should have been marked by a great deal of violence and turbulence. It is not possible that a growing nation should spread over new territory, and feel the thrill of its young energies contending with nature in all her rude force, without social commotions and a certain recklessness and uproar. The contagion of those forms of disorder produces other and less excusable forms.[34]

[30] Martineau, *Autobiography* (1877), II, 24-25.
[31] Aug. 13 and Sept. 5, 1835.
[32] Philip Hone, *Diary*, ed. Bayard Tuckerman (2v., New York, 1889), II, 108, 110.
[33] J. Q. Adams, *Memoirs*, IX, 254.
[34] William G. Sumner, *Andrew Jackson as a Public Man* (New York, 1968; reprint of 1882 edition) 364-65.

CHAPTER XXVI

A Coming Together

THE WHIG MIND

Story's interrogator on the near-lynching of Garrison was Harriet Martineau, English writer and intellectual. She landed in America in mid-September of 1834, and quickly learned of current political attitudes.

> The first gentleman who greeted . . . my arrival in the United States, a few minutes after I had landed, informed me without delay, that I had arrived at an unhappy crisis; that the institutions of the country would be in ruins before my return to England; that the levelling spirit was desolating society; and that the United States were on the verge of a military despotism.[1]

This was but the first of many warnings. She wondered about the imminence of military dictatorship in view of the absence of soldiers, save for a few she saw at West Point; otherwise, the views seemed remarkably similar to those she had heard in response to reform efforts in her own Britain. Doubtless the malaise was the same in both cases—the frustration of men of affairs

[1] Martineau, *Society in America* (1837), I, 10.

stripped of power, removed from a national exuberance which they did not share, much less dominate, and with respect to which a generally increasing affluence, their own included, made exclusion all the more bitter.

Certainly in its American application the mob anarchy throughout the land seemed to them the natural concomitant of despotism in the center as foretold by the pages of Gibbon. For Story and his cultured contemporaries had read their *Decline and Fall* all too well, and the parallel seemed not only obvious but unavoidable—the barracks emperor, absolutism masquerading under republican forms, and blatant self-serving in public life. And, in truth, the popularized Presidency did have its distressing manifestations. "The capital of the Union presented a revolting spectacle," wrote a critical German historian. "Flattery, servility, espionage, tale-bearing, and intrigue thrived as they scarcely had in the most infamous European courts."[2] Foremost perhaps was an aura of surveillance. Within days of the first Jackson inaugural, the Chief Justice himself was writing of the "system of espionage . . . pursued by the hunters after office, [even] if not encouraged by the person to whom the retailers of [illegible] would wish to pay their court."[3] And certainly nothing in the ensuing years tended to quiet the growing sense of apprehension. "If I talk too free, burn my letter," Kent once wrote to Story.[4]

Yet rhetoric became a prison as the Whigs carried public oratory into a stylized private dialogue, and that which began as a flourish of opposition became instead an indispensable part of private conversations, wherein participants sought to outdo each other in predictions of disaster. The depressive underside of Story's complex union of optimism and depression was almost tailor-made for this milieu, and he joined the chorus of despair in both private

[2] Von Holst, *A Constitutional and Political History of the United States,* trans. Laler (hereinafter cited as von Holst), II (1888), 25-26.
[3] Letter to Thomas Marshall, March 20, 1829, in Marshall Papers, Virginia Historical Society, Richmond.
[4] James Kent to Story, April 11, 1834, in *Proceedings of the Mass. Historical Society,* 2nd series, XIV (1901), 418.

correspondence and public utterance. "[T]he picture you give of public affairs," responded his minister to his appraisal in early 1834, "is dark and humiliating in the extreme,"[5] and by summer he passed to open protest in two vigorous remonstrances. One, an anonymous essay, was a eulogy to Webster and summarized its contents in its title, "Statesmen: Their Rareness and Importance." (". . . we have few, very few statesmen; we have party men and party leaders . . . we have politicians of all sorts . . . we have demagogues of every rank and degree . . ."[6]) Chief Justice Marshall's response to a complimentary copy joined in its pessimistic estimate. "To men who think as you and I do," wrote Marshall, "the present is gloomy enough; and the future presents no cheering prospect."[7]

Story's other undertaking that summer was a lecture, "The Science of Government as a Branch of Popular Government," at the American Institute of Instruction. It gave him an opportunity to counterattack publicly on several fronts. One riposte was directed at the Jacksonian ideal of simple government and, needless to say, simple law.

> If there be any truth . . . it is that in proportion as a government is free, it must be complicated. Simplicity belongs to those only where one will governs all . . . where few arrangements are required, because no checks to power are allowed; where law is not a science but a mandate to be followed and not to be discussed; where it is not a rule for permanent action but a capricious and arbitrary dictate of the hour . . .[8]

The other was an eloquent restatement of Whig foreboding:

> Let not Americans forget, that Greece, immortal Greece has been free; and yet, thousands of years have already rolled

[5] Letter from John Brazer, March 4, 1834, in Story Papers, Library of Congress.
[6] New England Magazine, VII (1834), 89.
[7] Letter from John Marshall, Oct. 6, 1834, in W. W. Story, II, 173.
[8] Miscellaneous Writings, 619.

over her servitude; that Italy, beautiful Italy, has been free, but where is now her republican grandeur? . . . the spirit of liberty is not there; and Rome has become, as it were, the vast sepulcher of her own perished glory.[9]

His own words were in somber contrast to the soaring optimism which had attended his public oratory during the administration of John Quincy Adams, and as time went on his moments of depression deepened and lengthened. Dropping in to see Chancellor Kent on his return from the 1835 term of the Supreme Court, he confessed that Aristotle, Cicero, and Burke had become the polestars of his political thought, and that he found in their words proof positive of the folly of the new times. Indeed, he had been thinking of himself more and more as an American Cicero lately. "I seem almost . . . to be in a dream," he had noted a year earlier, "and to be called back to the last days of the Roman republic, when the people shouted for Caesar, and liberty itself expired with the dark but prophetic words of Cicero."[10] Now he summed it all up to Kent in a terse condemnation that Cicero had prefigured it all—"the evils of democracy as they are and always will be."[11]

A JACKSONIAN THERMIDOR

In addition to pronouncing orthodox Whig doctrines on complexity of government and on the danger of despotism, Story's speech before the American Institute of Instruction wove in a third element as fully Jacksonian as Whig. Its intellectual lineage ran through the Northwest Ordinance to the Puritan foundations of Story's New England. This was an almost unshakable optimism in the perfecting power of education, and Story gave it a particularly political application. Conceding that the science of govern-

[9] *Ibid.*, 623; see also Ruth Welter, *Popular Education and Democratic Thought in America* (New York, 1963), 75.
[10] Letter to Samuel P. P. Fay, Feb. 18, 1834, in W. W. Story, II, 154.
[11] Quoted in *American Law Review*, V (1871), 368.

ment could be taught (for such indeed was the very title of his address) he suggested that the proper mode of instruction was the "constant use of suitable elementary works."[12] And in suiting action to words, he took time from his own incredible schedule to put his *Commentaries on the Constitution* into two simplified texts for nonprofessional use. One, *The Familiar Exposition,* was designed for college students. The other, *Constitutional Class Book,* was written for the grade schools. Perhaps the latter was the most important version of all, for, as Story wrote on Independence Day of 1834: "I shall be glad if the Constitutional Class [Book] should take well with the public, . . . it may have some tendency to infuse into young minds the true principles of our gov't. If they are once well established there, it will be difficult under any extravagancies of party spirit wholly to obliterate them."[13]

And indeed he was more right than he intended, for while universal suffrage might have chilled the Whig mind, universal education commanded an increasingly wide approval, and in the very necessities of the case the underlying forces which nurtured and shaped this movement had other tempering and acculturating consequences. Thus, the Jacksonian theoreticians, who increasingly called themselves Democrats, could, in the very act of asserting the credo of the many, "acknowledge, in general, a strong sympathy with minorities, and consider that their rights have a high moral claim on the respect and justice of majorities; a claim not always fairly recognized in practice by the latter."[14] Yet the plain fact of the matter was that to the extent that a concern for minorities—the Indians, the slaves, the handicapped—had a political base, it lay in the Whig Party. To be sure, much of the Whig concern was an effort to fortify political weakness with an appeal to moral sentiment, but it had an authentic core

Miscellaneous Writings, 637.
Letter to Charles Sumner, July 4, 1834, Harvard College Library.
First editorial, "The Democratic Principle," from *The Democratic Review,* January, 1838, in Edwin Rozwenc, *The Meaning of Jacksonian Democracy* (Boston, 1963; hereinafter cited as Rozwenc), 20.

for all that. Moreover, it provided the ultimate nexus whereby the rising spirit of conscientious concern, almost wholly outside the Jacksonian mainstream, found political outlet.

Tending toward the same end of checking and restraining initial exuberance was the inevitable lesson of experience. Like their Jeffersonian forebears, and indeed as Story's Boston address had suggested, there was more to returning to simplicity than simplistic yearnings. Government simply refused to stay simple as the world about it grew more complex. It became particularly complex and expensive at the state and local levels, but even in Washington and despite heroic efforts, federal expenditures not only increased but did so at a faster pace than population.[15] Moreover, life itself took on a new hedonism fatal to both reform and revolution. A charter Jacksonian disapprovingly described the environment into which his associates had taken office and which would enervate much of their revolutionary spirit:

> . . . They have here adopted the ridiculous English custom of having dinner after dark. We were invited at *five* o'clock, went a little before *six*, and sat down about *seven* . . . There was ham, beef cooked in various ways, mutton, turkey *with* bones and *without*, pork, chicken, partridges, canvas-back ducks, jellies, puddings, olives, grapes, raisins, custards, apples, and half a dozen things I know no name for; Madeira wine, sherry, champagne, and two kinds the names of which I do not recollect.[16]

Yet it was social and economic mutation rather than styles of living which caused the years of 1834–35 to open with a still new form of violence.

An older and more intimate friend of General Jackson's was Major John Eaton, distinguished as the husband of Peggy Eaton. He had been a Tennessee planter like Jackson himself and became Secretary of War in Jackson's cabinet. But when Mrs. Eaton's social problems brought about reconstitution of

[15] See L. White, *The Jacksonians* (1954), 9.
[16] Amos Kendall to Mrs. Kendall, Feb. 10, 1829, in Kendall, 282.

the cabinet and her husband's retirement therefrom, he entered the world of private enterprise as president of the company formed to build and operate the Chesapeake and Ohio canal. In the course of labor difficulties that arose soon after, President Jackson had federal troops called out in response to Eaton's appeal. This was the first instance in American Labor history of intervention by the federal military in labor disputes. . . .[17]

For it was no paradox but rather the very logic of history that the first military repression of the new industrial order in America came not as a reaction of the Whig-Federalist conservatives but as an official counterblow of the Jacksonian state. Or so the vision of one contemporary observer implied. "The old war between the King and the Barons is well nigh ended," wrote Orestes Brownson, who insisted that there was stirring a turbulence in America to which the controversies over banking and the tariff were remote and peripheral. "So is that between the Barons and the Merchants and Manufacturers, landed capital and commercial capital. . . . And now commences the new struggle between the operative and his employer, between wealth and labor."[18] Brownson then looked at both Britain and the United States and saw a common reason why change ended in essentially a renovated status quo: "The middle class is always a firm champion of equality when it concerns humbling a class above it, but is its inveterate foe when it concerns elevating a class below it."[19] Brownson would well advance a specifically American application for his vision and cited the essentially pragmatic Jacksonian center as a radicalism which encompassed shaking the title deeds of their predecessors with a conservatism which demanded securing their own. For when all was said and done, the dominant makers of

Post-publication interpolation written by the late Bray Hammond for insertion at p. 345 in his *Banks and Politics in America* (1957) and reproduced here with the kind permission of Mrs. Hammond.
Brownson, "The Laboring Classes," in Blau (ed.), *American Philosophic Addresses* (New York, 1946), 181.
Ibid., 178.

the Jacksonian revolution sought equality of opportunity, not of reward, and were compelled by their own logic ultimately to turn to social order and the maintenance of private rights under a rule of law.[20]

A SENSE OF RENEWAL

That Jacksonian and Whig shared in large measure a common ethos and in fact edged toward a common center did not make the process of change any the less agonizing, much less encourage any sense of rapprochement. Indeed, the bitter campaign of 1836 in which Martin Van Buren continued the Jacksonian legacy only underscored how much both sides were prisoners of their rhetoric. The Whigs, now doubly despondent at the *arriviste* ascendancy, redoubled their talk of despotism, anarchy, and decay, yet denied it by the immense and zestful activities of their daily lives. Similarly the Jacksonians rang the changes of states rights, strict construction, the common man, and equality of opportunity, all the while using the central government when it suited their purposes to lay the foundations of enterprising capitalistic industrialism.

To both points of view the enfolding mantle of an authentically American law—constitutional, private, and public—provided something of a common shelter. The Whigs, typified by Story and Kent, mixed an enormous amount of rhetoric as they extolled its glories to the sky and privately hoped that its constraints might somehow secure a social tranquillity of vested right and private property. And, after their fashion, so did the Jacksonians as the pressed their own quest for a simple, uncomplicated, and understandable legal order which might legitimate both equality of opportunity and security of reward. Indeed, beneath the differences the common core of Whig and Jacksonian was strikingly implied in the messages which the two doctors of law from Harvard delivered within a short time of each other.

[20] See Meyers, *The Jacksonian Persuasion* (1957), 187.

One came at the Harvard bicentennial in October, 1836, in an impromptu speech of Story's which hailed law as "the great instrument by which society is held together" and then passed to an encomium as fully Jacksonian as Whig in its basic motivation:

> Without it, neither liberty, nor property, nor life, nor that which is dearer than life, a good reputation, is for a moment secure. It is, in short, the great elastic power which pervades and embraces every human relation. It links man to man by so many mutual ties, and duties, and dependencies, that though silent and unseen in its operations, it becomes at once the minister to his social necessities, and the guardian of his social virtues.[21]

A cryptically parallel theme emerged a few months later in a message from Andrew Jackson. It was an extraordinary document reflecting all the strength and ambiguity of the outgoing President. The Indian removal policy was seen as a blessing ("The States which had so long been retarded in their improvement . . . are at length released from the evil"[22]). So was the demise of the federal bank ("the paper money system and its natural associations . . . monopoly and exclusive privileges"[23]). But still another passage indicated that the evolving legal and juristic philosophy of the Jacksonian revolution should not be sought in these triumphal asides. Rather, the core lesson dealing with both the nature of law and the character of its dispensing instrument appeared in an elliptic and elusive reference which epitomized the vindication that nullification had given both *Martin v. Hunter's Lessee* and Section 25 of the Judiciary Act:

> Unconstitutional or oppressive laws may no doubt be passed by Congress. . . . (I)f they are within the reach of judicial

[21] W. W. Story, II, 255.
[22] Richardson, III, 294.
[23] *Ibid.*, 306.

authority, the remedy is easy and peaceful; and if, from the character of the law, it is an abuse of power not within the control of the judiciary, then free discussion . . . will not fail to redress the wrong. But until the law shall be declared void by the courts or repealed by Congress no individual or combination of individuals can be justified in forcibly resisting its execution.[24]

The message was in fact one of farewell. It was dated March 4, 1837, a day fair, bright, springlike, and thus very much like the March 4 eight years earlier. There was also an extraordinary symbolic touch as the outgoing President Jackson and the incoming President Van Buren rode to the inaugural ceremonies in a coach made from the wood of the *U.S.S. Constitution*. Reminiscent of both the old and the new, the basic oak which had formed both ship and coach exemplified the capacity of the basic constitutional material to both admit and constrain the Federalism of the early republic and the exuberant democracy of the Jacksonian revolution of its second growth. To be sure, much of the violence and brutality which made up the dark underside of American life was still there, and slavery continued to present its fatal contradiction to the American dream. Yet through it all persisted a sense of uplifted destiny, and certainly it was this spirit rather than exuberance which was the order of Jackson's last day in the Presidency. Indeed, there was very little of King Mob in the response which greeted the old President as he left the steps of the Capitol. It was a cry, noted Senator Benton, "such as power never commanded; nor man in power received. It was the affection, gratitude, and admiration . . . the acclaim of posterity breaking from the bosoms of contemporaries."[25]

[24] *Ibid.*, 297.
[25] Benton, *Thirty Years' View*, I (1854), 735.

PART EIGHT

The Great Terms

CHAPTER XXVII

The New Order

THE DEAD CHIEF JUSTICE

It was near sunset on July 6, 1835, when John Marshall died in Philadelphia, and the great bell which fifty-nine years earlier, almost to the very day, had proclaimed liberty throughout the land, cracked as it tolled a lamentation. It would never ring again, and to many its silenced voice was conjoined in ominous prophecy with the death of the Chief Justice. For to these the end of Marshall's career, though hardly unforeseen, had been none the less dreaded as a calamity. "[H]is knowledge of constitutional law, his weight of character, his purity of life, and his devotion to the Union," Associate Justice Joseph Story had written a few years earlier, "have gained for him a public confidence, which, in the present crisis of our affairs, cannot be supplied by any other man in the country."[1]

Part of Story's concern was personal. A British traveler observing the majestic old Judge on Story's arm thought the two looked more like father and son than like judicial colleagues. But matching and even surpassing their deep affection was a rapport in political and philosophical conservatism, and the rapport was only the stronger by their common response to "the present crisis of

[1] Letter to Charles Sumner, Feb. 6, 1833, in W. W. Story, II, 120.

347

our affairs," the burgeoning forces of Jacksonian democracy. Appropriately, therefore, Story's pessimism on Marshall's declining health was coupled with an equally bleak political foreview:

> . . . I look to the future with diminished hope and subdued confidence. I fear my country cannot be forewarned . . . so as to provide for the safety and permanence of its institutions. When the Government shall be once thoroughly organized upon the system of party and patronage, it will become so corrupt, that it will be vain to hope for reform or glory.[2]

If the pessimism was exaggerated, the timing was acute, for the Jackson system of "party and patronage" had successively overrun the serried constitutional defenses which the founding fathers had thrown up against popular control of the federal government. Capturing in turn the House, the Presidency, and the Senate (more or less), the Jacksonians by the time of Marshall's death had already filled three of the seven seats on the Supreme Court. And now with the passing of the Chief Justice they gained control of not only the high court but the symbolic diadem of its presiding office. The governmental transformation was complete.

The judicial part of the transformation had been foreshadowed. The last eight years of Marshall's tenure had witnessed an ongoing modification—some would say destruction—of the canons of mercantilist nationalism which the Chief Justice had engrossed upon the institutions of contracts, corporations, and currency at the Great Term of 1819 and upon interstate commerce in 1824. By 1827, a date significantly coincident with the first nationwide Jacksonian victories, Marshall was forced into his only constitutional dissent as his court refused to extend to a logical conclusion his views on the irreformability of contracts. Again, by 1830 the number and vigor of dissents against his austere prohibition of local money experiments made him anticipate an ultimate, perhaps an early, reversal of that ruling. Significantly, a Kentucky case to

[2] Letter to Richard Peters, May 20, 1835, in W. W. Story, II, 194-95.

do just that appeared shortly thereafter on the Court's docket and was kept from final judgment only through the combination of a disagreement among the justices and vacancies in their number. Also on the docket and similarly delayed from final decision was an appeal from Massachusetts which could sharply limit the Chief Justice's previous envelopment of state-granted corporate charters within the contracts clause of the Constitution. Likewise working its way to an ultimate resolution was a controversy from New York which could substantially modify Marshall's soaring vision of the national commerce power.

Side by side with this erosion of Marshall's preemptive Federalism, however, a counter-revaluation of institutional conservatism was at work, and Justice Story was its spearhead. Almost single-handedly he had transformed the Harvard Law School from an institution characterized by an inert curriculum, deadening instruction, and dwindling enrollment to a vital and modernized school working a transformation of legal education and producing a new breed of American lawyers. From both the Supreme Court and his New England circuit court he had hammered out an extraordinary sequence of opinions in admiralty, commercial law, equity, and property that made the reports of his decisions both an addition to legal literature and a model for a revived judge-craft. And on top of all he had written an astonishing succession of encyclopedic *Commentaries—Bailments* (1832), *Constitution* (1833), *Conflicts* (1835), and *Equity Jurisprudence* (1836).

Story's overfull schedule involved an extraordinarily ironic consequence, for his very preoccupation with the activities which carried on Marshall's work also kept him from the dying Chief Justice's side. He mournfully regretted the fact, but in a flash of perceptive insight he also saw that his enforced absence was not without a merciful aspect:

> I have a very crowded docket at Rhode Island. . . . As soon as the Court is over here, I must return to Boston, where the Circuit Court is still open, awaiting my arrival, to try some very important causes. . . . The Law School,

as to my department, also stands suspended until my return; and . . . it happens to be the most busy and important part of the term. . . .

I see not, therefore, how between these double duties, I can possibly go to Philadelphia, though it would be grateful beyond expression to me to be with the Chief Justice, and to cheer his loneliness, and soothe, if I could, his sufferings. If I were to go to Philadelphia at all, I should wish to pass a day or two with him, for to go merely to meet with him, and to bid him an external farewell, would be too distressing to both of us to justify the interview. Indeed, I confess, I should scarcely feel the courage, under the most favorable circumstances, to stand in his presence, and to feel that it was the last time.[3]

There was still another bitter aspect to Marshall's death: the almost certain knowledge that the office of Chief Justice would fall to a nominee unsympathetic to Marshall's views. Story's apprehension was confirmed when, some months after Marshall's death, President Jackson selected Roger Brooke Taney for the succession. There was a double aptness to the nomination. On the surface it appeared that the *bête noire* of Jacksonian democracy had been selected in a final triumph of evil, for Taney, master strategist of the bank war and architect of the downfall of the federal bank, had been previously rejected by the Senate as Secretary of the Treasury and as Associate Justice of the Supreme Court. Yet, a deeper significance exemplifying a basic continuity between fundamentalist Federalism and Jacksonian revisionisms, lay in the fact that Taney would in many ways continue Marshall's judicial centralism and, in some aspects, actually extend it.

The latter development was enshrouded in the future. For the present, Story's reaction to the Taney nomination must have included a surge of personal resentment. By every index of prestige, seniority, and scholarship, the Chief Justiceship should have fallen to Story himself, and had the vacancy occurred during his

[3] Letter to Peters, June 19, 1835, in W. W. Story, II, 199-200.

fleeting rapport with Andrew Jackson in the 1832 nullification crisis, it might have done so. Three years, however, changed many things, even though the very vigor of his disclaimers (". . . I have never for a moment imagined that I should be thought of"[4]) suggested a certain hope against hope. But neither the enthusiasm of his Whig supporters nor his plaudits from London, Paris, and Heidelberg could determine the appointment of a Chief Justice of the United States. Rather, succession to that office was determined by the greatest achievement of John Marshall—the transformation of the Supreme Court from tribunal of justice to an organ of government.

This meant that the succession inevitably had more of a political than a juridical character. It made Roger Taney the inevitable successor. It also forced Story from the role of virtually full-time coadjutor of a living Chief Justice to that of the occasional dissenting surrogate of a dead one. He came to Washington with a heavy heart. "Judge Story arrived last evening," wrote Webster, "in good health, but bad spirits. He thinks the Supreme Court is *gone* and I think so, too; and almost everything is gone, or seems rapidly going."[5]

THE NEW COURT

Like the riderless horse in the cortege of a fallen king, an appropriate symbol and tribute to Marshall was presented as the 1836 term of the Supreme Court ran its course without a successor presiding over the tribunal. Taney's nomination became entangled with both a circuit-court reorganization bill and partisan maneuverings through the opening months of the year, and the new Chief Justice did not take oath until March 28. Meanwhile Story, as senior associate, undertook the interim workaday administration at the Supreme Court. While the temporary prece-

[4] Letter to Peters, July 24, 1835, in W. W. Story, II, 202.
[5] Letter to Mrs. Webster, Jan. 10, 1836, in Webster, *Private Correspondence*, 266.

dence was pleasing enough, his heart was not in the job. More-over, the docket was humdrum, and the only memorable passage in the term reports came in Story's eulogy to the dead Chief Justice: "The Constitution of the United States owes as much to him as any single mind . . ."[6] The eulogy was remarkably re-strained, as were Story's other public tributes, particularly the stately and elegaic verse he proposed as an inscription for a cenotaph:

> *To Marshall reared—the great, the good, the wise;*
> *Born for all ages, honored in all skies;*
> *His was the fame to mortals rarely given,*
> *Begun on earth, but fixed in aim on heaven.*[7]

A truer picture of desolation appeared in the candor of private correspondence:

> I miss the Chief Justice at every turn. I have been several times into the room which he was accustomed to occupy. It yet remains without an inhabitant, and wears an aspect of desolation, and has a noiseless gloom. The table at which he sat, the chair which he occupied, the bed on which he slept,— they are all there, and bring back a train of the most melan-choly reflections. Consider for a moment that I am the last of the Judges who were on the bench when I first took my seat there. I seem a monument of the past age, and a mere record of the dead.[8]

With the end of the term and return to New England more misfortunes came. His family life had always been a thing apart, and in a sense the law in its many phases was his real life. This is

---

[6] 10 PETERS at *vii*. See the parallelism in Arnold Toynbee, *A Study of History*, Somervell abridgement, I (New York and London, 1947), 316.
[7] "Inscription for a Cenotaph," in W. W. Story, II, 206. See also oration "Life, Character, and Services of Chief Justice Marshall," in *Miscellaneous Writings*, 639.
[8] Letter to Harriet Martineau, Feb. 8, 1836, in W. W. Story, II, 226.

not to say that Story was not the very paradigm of husband and father, but possibly some of the inadequacies and some of the tragedies of home life reinforced an already strong inclination. Certainly a succession of losses of small children left its mark. Obviously, too, it left a mark on Mrs. Story, in a sickliness which a collective diagnosis appraised in mid-1836 as holding a "menacing aspect," with surgery being among the alternatives considered and apparently discarded.[9] By late fall political distress followed family misfortune as the Democratic forces rolled to a third term in the Presidency with the election of Martin Van Buren. Particularly dismaying here must have been the circumstance that Daniel Webster, one of the two anti-Jacksonians to contest the election, carried only Massachusetts and that by the slimmest of margins.

The stage was thus appropriately set for the 1837 term and for a dramatic judicial vindication of the new order. The Jacksonian years had already left their mark on the *dramatis personae* in the accession of five of the seven incumbents of the Supreme Court. The appointments had come unevenly. The first, early in the administration, had fallen to John McLean of Ohio and Henry Baldwin of Pennsylvania. Three more occurred in 1835—James M. Wayne of Georgia, Roger B. Taney of Maryland, and Philip P. Barbour of Virginia, whose nomination went to the Senate the same day as Taney's. However, of the latter, only Wayne had been seated before the 1837 term. For Story, on a purely personal level, these changes in the Court were not an entire loss. From almost the first he felt an extraordinary friendship for McLean, and he also applauded the appointment of Baldwin.

Events would force a reappraisal of the latter judgment, for Baldwin, occasionally unbalanced but still a legal writer of some skill, was to use this talent to Story's discomfiture. Yet in a sense Baldwin would not add to discomfiture as much as he would continue it, for his barbs merely carried on a tradition which

[9] See John G. Warner to Joseph Story, July 25, 1836, in Story Papers, Library of Congress.

Justice William Johnson had started years before. And while Story obviously grieved with each death of a member of the old Marshall Court, he must have felt no unusual pang when Wayne, a Georgia Unionist, took Johnson's seat. Indeed, an extraordinary omission from Story's writings appears to be the complete absence of any expression of sentiment on the passing of Justice Johnson.

THE OLD QUESTIONS

The 1837 term marked the twenty-fifth year of Story's service on the Court. With the possible exception of 1819 it was also to be the most significant term he ever attended. There were, in fact, a number of parallels between the two terms. Each involved a trilogy of great constitutional cases, linked in two of the three instances by the same constitutional question. Moreover, an additional touch of theater was provided by the fact that each term was held in a newly decorated courtroom, an appropriate symbol for the inauguration of a renewed and invigorated constitutional law. Finally, at each term Justice Story had considerable extrajudicial connection with the subject matter of the constitutional litigation.

Needless to say there were differences. For Story, 1819 was the term of jubilee; 1837 was to be a term of lamentation. But if the Justice looked mournfully to the past, the country, with enormous self-confidence and lustihood, was moving into a new and exciting future characterized at one and the same time by aspiration and vulgarity, self-seeking and altruism, ethical renewal and ingrained amorality. And the problems which resulted from the democratization of politics, and the proliferation of enterprise, and the revolutions in technology, daily underscored the growing inadequacy of the neo-Federalist doctrines which the Supreme Court had propounded in 1819.

For, given the enormous distances and the bursting diversity of the country, the two-dimensional and essentially mercantilist framework outlined in 1819, for all its nationalist sentiment, was increasingly irrelevant to cope with industrialization, urbanization, and immigration. Now capital and credit, the forms and functions of business enterprise, the nature of commercial commitments, and the ever-increasing flow of men and materials all required a new and positive dimension, and already the Marshall Court (over the dissent of the Chief Justice, to be sure) had provided it in the area of contracts and insolvency.

And now three further aspects of the same basic question were presented. One concerned the latitude of function of corporate enterprise, which was indispensable to an industrial age whose needs for entrepreneurial capital outstripped individual or even family resources. Yet the general use and fullest function of corporate organization was constrained by the possibility, which the Marshall Court had previously suggested, of subordination to the grandfather rights of first arrivals.

The monetary issue of capital and credit ran along much the same line but was sharpened by the overriding practical fact of the Jacksonian destruction of the second Bank of the United States notwithstanding a constitutional and indeed a political vindication by the Marshall Court at the 1819 term. The end of the bank as a national institution meant that state monetary authority had to fill the void, and the bank itself had moved from federal to Pennsylvania incorporation. This very circumstance luminously illustrated the linkage between the several issues before the Court, as Charles Jared Ingersoll of the Philadelphia bar was advising his legislature that prospective constitutional developments permitted it to take back the charter it had granted the bank and to do so irrespective of what the Marshall Court had previously said on the point.

And finally there was the problem of dealing with the dynamics of the new order in terms of the sheer physical impact of its human and industrial components. National policy favored an unrestricted immigration from Europe to fill the expanding industries and the opening lands of the West. But there were problems of movement, activity, and concentration; however necessary an earlier veto might have been to striking down the local impediments to commerce, the necessity of legitimating legitimate local police and welfare activity now assumed an imperative character.

Hence, the issue between the answers of 1819 and the questions of 1837 was not whether the answers of the earlier day would be overruled. Rather, hidden beneath the rhetoric of politics and the brocade of legalism was the issue of *how* they would be. The key issue was whether the new questions would produce a constitutional continuity structured in a framework which preserved the vital spirit of 1819 or whether the centrifugal exuberance of the Jacksonian revolution would carry constitutional forms back to the regression and disintegration of preconstitutional confederation.

CHAPTER XXVIII

Bridges, Bank Notes, and Immigrants

THE QUESTIONS

On June 17, 1786, the eleventh anniversary of the Battle of Bunker Hill, the Charles River Bridge connecting Boston and Charlestown was opened, and by invitation of the bridge company a stately procession of the members of the Massachusetts legislature crossed over to commemorate the battle on the spot where it was fought. It was a symbolic opening note; the bridge was fated to have an embattled future. At the time, however, only felicity was apparent, for it was a structural wonder and represented a great advance in safety and convenience over the ferry which, since the middle of the seventeenth century, had afforded the only means of passage.

The legislators crossed for free, but all others paid a toll, the *quid pro quo* which the commonwealth of Massachusetts had authorized as a reward to the company putting up the bridge in the first place. According to ancient English custom, the business of operating a bridge, a ferry, or a wharf was undertaken not on the basis of entrepreneurial choice but on that of a sovereign grant awarded in the public interest. In line with this tradition the commonwealth had in 1650 granted the ferrying rights between Boston and Charlestown to Harvard College. In 1785 the grant was revoked and the right of passage given instead to the Charles River Bridge Company. The company was authorized to collect tolls for forty years, after which the bridge would become the property of the commonwealth. During the forty-year period an annual payment of $1,200 per year from the tolls was to be made to Harvard as compensation for the loss of its privilege. In addition, the company committed itself to settle a reasonable sum upon the school after the bridge reverted to free use.

The bridge company flourished with the ongoing urbanization of Boston, and its stock sold at a substantial premium. In 1792, an inkling of a competitive future appeared with the chartering of another bridge some distance away. In anticipation of a possible loss of revenue, the Charles River Bridge tolls were extended for an additional thirty years. However, as the original toll period approached its close, the extension decision came under increasing public protest on the basis both of the amounts charged and of the services rendered. The upshot was the chartering of the Warren Company to erect a bridge virtually alongside the Charles structure and to do so on terms far more favorable to the traveling public. The Warren Bridge was to become toll free when its costs had been recovered and in no event later than six years after construction.

The new bridge project had two significant Jacksonian characteristics. In the first place, it exemplified Jacksonian laissez-faire by combining private gain and public good, for its promoters were willing to undergo whatever sacrifice the bridge entailed in return for the enhancement in value of their urban real-estate holdings on the other side of the Charles. But even more important was the fact that its competition destroyed the value of the Charles River Bridge as completely as if the legislature repealed the charter out of hand. It thereby undercut by indirection the prohibition which the Marshall Court had laid on the unilateral abrogation of corporate privileges, and which Story had powerfully reinforced in his circuit court when he held that even a reserved power to amend a charter could not be used to abrogate vested rights.[1] It was against this background that the Charles River Bridge Company sought a restraining order against its competitor from the Massachusetts courts. Unsuccessful at this level, it appealed to the United States Supreme Court, where *Charles River Bridge v. Warren Bridge* was argued in 1831, but where, for six years thereafter, vacancies, absences, and judicial disagreements prevented a resolution of the controversy.

Much the same issues, sequence, and economic background characterized the other two great cases of 1837. One concerned commerce, the other credit. The first, *Mayor of New York v. Miln*, was an immigration controversy involving the validity of a New York City requirement that the masters of incoming vessels deliver a passenger manifest to the local police authorities and assume responsibility for the passengers' not becoming public charges. The other, *Briscoe v. Bank of Kentucky*, tested the constitutionality of a note-issuing bank that was both state-chartered and state-owned. Externally dissimilar, the two lawsuits, like the bridge controversy, were apparently covered by prior and ruling decisions of the Marshall Court which had vigorously asserted that currency and interstate and foreign commerce were matters that had been delivered by the Constitution to the national government and correspondingly prohibited to the states.

Hence, all three cases presented the single and basic question of whether the states could respond to new conditions by giving a new name to old things. Something of a common thread was also provided by the extrajudicial associations and declarations of Justice Story. He had been an enthusiastic supporter of the federal bank. Moreover, notwithstanding his onetime presidency of a state-chartered banking institution, he had argued in his *Commentaries on the Constitution* that only practice, not text, afforded the states power to incorporate note-issuing banks, and he had tendered the 1812–15 inflation as an example of a currency under state control.[2] The greatest amount of personal in-

---

[1] *Allen v. McKeen*, 1 FED. CASES 489 (1833).
[2] Story, *Commentaries on the Constitution* (1833), III, 19.

volvement, however, came in the bridge case. Doubtless Story had crossed the bridge many times, starting with his student days at Harvard. But there was more here than sentimental recollection. There was the issue of a fellow of the Harvard Corporation and a professor in its law school sitting as a judge in a case when an item of university income was directly involved in the litigation. Under the standards of the age, wiser perhaps than succeeding ones which made a conflict-of-interest statute as a definitive answer, neither Story nor anyone else saw anything untoward in concurrent service. And there was a certain offset: Professor Greenleaf of the Harvard Law School was retained to argue the defense of the Warren Bridge, and Webster to defend the rights of the Charles structure. The fact that two of Story's closest associates were ranged on opposite sides tended to insure at one swoop judicial impartiality and splendor of argument.

THE ANSWERS

On January 19, 1837, reargument opened in *Charles River Bridge v. Warren Bridge,* and it continued for the following week. Notwithstanding his growing concern for the outcome, Story seemed to appraise the forensic rhetoric with both enthusiasm and detachment: ". . . Greenleaf's argument was excellent—full of ability, point, learning, condensed thought, and strong illustration. . . . Webster's closing reply was in his best manner, but with a little too much *fierté* here and there. . . . On the whole, it was a glorious exhibition for old Massachusetts."[3]

When the Court reached its decision—in favor of the Warren Bridge—his true feelings on the issue became apparent. To Greenleaf he sent an urbane note of congratulation, but a letter to his wife etched his dismay: "Mr. Greenleaf has gained the cause, and I am sorry for it. . . . A case of grosser injustice . . . never existed. I feel humiliated."[4]

[3] Letter to Charles Sumner, Jan. 25, 1837, in W. W. Story, II, 266.
[4] Letter to Mrs. Story, Feb. 14, 1837, in W. W. Story, II, 268.

The depth of his concern became public with the publication of the opinions, and his extended dissent stood in singular contrast, both in style and in tone, to the majority views expressed by the new Chief Justice. For in a tour de force reminiscent of Marshall's terse and lucid nationalistic prose ("throughout this vast republic, from St. Croix to the Gulf of Mexico. . . ."[5]) Taney approvingly viewed the surging American scene, and masterfully flanked the hard doctrines of the Dartmouth case:

> . . . [I]n a country like ours, free, active, and enterprising, continually advancing in numbers and wealth; new channels of communications are daily found necessary, both for travel and trade, and are essential to the comfort, convenience, and prosperity of the people.[6]

Conceding that vested rights must be "sacredly guarded," Taney put the case into its sharpest focus: Should the implications of governmental grants of monopolistic privilege be resolved against "a company of adventurers" and in favor of the public? Noting that a recent English decision had so held, and observing that it would be anomalous indeed for monopoly to be constrained in Britain and indulged in America, he used the unthinkable alternatives to infuse Jacksonian laissez-faire into constitutional construction:

> [Otherwise] we shall be thrown back to the improvements of the last century, and obliged to stand still until the claims of the old turnpike corporations shall be satisfied, and they shall permit these States to avail themselves of the lights of modern science, and to partake of the benefit of those improvements which are now adding to the wealth and prosperity, and the convenience and comfort, of every other part of the civilized world.[7]

[5] *McCulloch v. Maryland*, 4 WHEATON at 408 (1819).
[6] *Charles River Bridge v. Warren Bridge*, 11 PETERS at 547 (1837).
[7] 11 PETERS at 553.

Taney's opinion, breathing new vigor into the doctrine of state power, provided, in effect, the resolution of the other two cases. Formally, however, these were decided in a series of essentially lackluster opinions of other Jacksonian appointees. In the immigrant case, Justice Barbour called the New York statute an exercise of the state's reserved police power and upheld it accordingly.[8] In much the same mode Justice McLean upheld the Kentucky-chartered bank as a legitimate use of state chartering authority, and obscured (with particular appositeness to the right which Massachusetts once held to buy into Story's bank) that if a state might own part of the stock of a bank, no principle prevented it from owning the whole.[9]

Story's principal response was a characteristically learned 35,000-word dissent in *Charles River Bridge*. It was almost a set piece of a Story opinion, and it should have been, for he had first written it back in 1821 and presumably had polished it during the interim. Yet it also contrasted strangely not only with the Chief Justice's majority views but also with some of his own, particularly *De Lovio v. Boit*.[10] Back in 1815, Story had scoffed at the idea that Lord Coke's *Institutes* and the statutes of Richard II could possibly be relevant norms for the judicial power of the United States. Now he venerated Lord Coke and sought relevance in medieval precedents on royal fisheries and manorial advowsons even though he had to clamber over English authorities to do it ("I am aware, that Mr. Justice Blackstone . . . has laid down some rules apparently varying from what has been stated . . . Much relevance has also been placed upon the language of Lord Stowell"[11]). Indeed, one is almost tempted to apply a subsequent verse from the Justice's pen to his bridge case concurrence:

> *Spare me quotations, which, though learn'd, are long,*
> *On points remote at best and rarely strong;*

[8] *Mayor of the City of New York v. Miln,* 11 Peters 102 (1837).
[9] *Briscoe v. Bank of the Commonwealth of Kentucky,* 11 Peters 257 (1837).
[10] See, *supra*, pages 129-32.
[11] 11 Peters at 591 and 596.

How sad to find our time consumed by speech,
Feeble in logic, feebler still in reach,
Yet urged in words of high and bold pretence,
As if the sound made up for lack of sense.[12]

Yet he remained both the scholar and the pragmatist. Implicitly reproving the Chief Justice for emphasizing the monopolistic character of the Charles River Bridge ("when it is suggested, that a grant is . . . a monopoly, the mind almost instantaneously prepares itself to reject every construction which does not pare it dow to the narrowest limits"[13]), he gave his own practical view of the matter:

> I can conceive of no surer plan to arrest all public improvements, founded on private capital . . . than to make the outlay of that capital uncertain . . . both as to security, and as to productiveness . . . The very agitation of a question of this sort, is sufficient to alarm every stockholder . . .[14]

All this was peripheral to his main point, as moving as it was irrelevant:

> I stand upon the old law; upon law established more than three centuries ago, in cases contested with as much ability and learning as any in the annals of our jurisprudence, in resisting . . . encroachments upon the rights and liberties of the citizens, secured by public grants. I will not consent to shake their title deeds by any speculative niceties or novelties.[15]

In selection of the principal issue, Story agreed with Taney: the bridge case was indeed the critical point and all else postscript. Accordingly, Story's dissents in the immigration and bank cases were shorter, but what they lacked in length they made up in

[12] W. W. Story, II, 413.
[13] 11 PETERS at 606-07.
[14] *Ibid.*, 608.
[15] *Ibid.*, 598.

additional citation of authority. In each he called upon the dead Chief Justice, and his *Briscoe* plea was typical of both: "Mr. Chief Justice Marshall is not here to speak for himself, and knowing full well the grounds of his opinion, in which I concurred, that this act is unconstitutional, I have felt an earnest desire to vindicate his memory from the imputation of rashness or want of deep reflection."[16]

It was, of course, curious on the face of things that the shade of John Marshall should be called upon for only two of the three cases, and the two lesser ones at that. In fact, an anonymous reviewer of Volume Eleven of Mr. Peters' reports noted the fact, but simply went on to assume that Marshall's disapproval extended to the bridge case ("in two, out of three constitutional judgments in this volume, if no more, as it appears . . . that of Chief Justice Marshall was different"[17]). There was a more fundamental reason for the asymmetry in the Story dissent, however, and explanation came in 1850 by way of a footnote in Professor Greenleaf's edition of an English work on property. Marshall, it seemed, after the first argument of the cause, had opted for the constitutionality of the Warren Bridge—or so Greenleaf reported he had been "credibly informed."[18]

But the shadow of John Marshall may also have cast itself over another part of the 1837 term, in prompting Story's charitable and restrained reaction to another of its incidents—Justice Baldwin's publication of his concurring opinions as part of a polemic work, *A General View of the Origin and Nature of the Constitution.* Not only was it specifically stated to be a rebuttal to Story's *Commentaries on the Constitution,* but insult was added to injury when the author said he was ignoring all constitutional expositions

[16] *Ibid.,* 350.
[17] *North American Review,* XLVI (1838), 155. The Harvard Library "key" to the *North American Review* identifies the anonymous reviewer as Charles S. Daveis, a prominent Maine lawyer and a friend of Story. My thanks to Prof. Merle Fainsod for assistance at Harvard.
[18] William Cruise, *A Digest of the Law of Real Property,* ed. Greenleaf (3v., Boston, 1850), II, 68 n. I am indebted to Prof. Stanley Kutner for this reference.

"other than those which are found in the opinions of the court, delivered with few exceptions, by the late venerated Chief Justice."[19]

Whatever the nuances of the latter phrase, Story responded in sorrow rather than in anger. In part his reaction was doubtless based on the fact that two years earlier Baldwin had done what he should have done and had gone to the dying Marshall's side. "I had no doubt he would," Story then commented, "for there is no person on earth . . . for whom he felt so much reverence and respect."[20] Now he declined to challenge the *General View*, and merely appealed to Marshall for his position: "I have no reply to make to it, I have no desire to make any . . . Our late friend, Mr. Chief Justice Marshall, approved all the doctrines in the Commentaries on the Constitution. Under such circumstances, I am quite consoled, although another Judge disapproves them."[21]

THE LAMENTATIONS

Not all reaction to the dominant Jacksonian opinions reflected the injured hauteur which Story extended to Baldwin, for Taney's *Charles River Bridge* opinion was a particular focus of Whig wrath. Webster assured Story that his dissent in that case left the Chief Justice "not an inch of ground to stand on,"[22] and young Charles Sumner adopted a British simile to write that reading Taney after Story was "hog wash after champagne."[23] He reported a similar reaction from Chancellor Kent: "The Chancellor abused Taney & yr. associates to my heart's content. He thought Taney's opinion in the Warren Bridge case was miserable and yours gigantic."[24] In fact, Kent had difficulty in reading Taney's

[19] Baldwin, *A General View of the Origin and Nature of the Constitution and Government of the United States* (1837), 7.
[20] Letter to Richard Peters, July 24, 1835, in W. W. Story, II, 201.
[21] Letter to Richard Peters, June 14, 1837, *ibid.*, 273-74.
[22] Letter from Daniel Webster, February, 1837, *ibid.*, 269.
[23] Letter from Charles Sumner, Mar. 25, 1837, in *Proceedings of the Mass. Historical Society*, 2nd series, XV (1902) 211.
[24] Letter from Charles Sumner, Nov. 28, 1837, in Story Papers, Library of Congress.

views through; he dropped the pamphlet in shuddering disgust on the first effort and managed to finish it later by an effort of will but with increased repugnance.

But the Jacksonians were also capable of attack, and a spirited one came in *The United States Magazine and Democratic Review*. Only a year old and "dedicated to "that high and holy DEMOCRATIC PRINCIPLE,"[25] the journal opened the year 1838 with both a slashing assault and a spirited defense in an article entitled "The Supreme Court of the United States, Its Judges and Jurisdiction." Anonymously written by Charles Jared Ingersoll of the Philadelphia bar, the polemic opened up its analysis of the Court with felicitation over the "late *renovation* . . . of this august body" and a castigation of the "blind veneration" hitherto accorded it.[26] He then warmed to his theme: "The immense and unexampled prepotency of putting judicial vetoes on laws . . . after they have long been in force—the vast constructive faculty, unknown in any other age or nation, has become of late, the ordinary, the favorite occupation of the Supreme Court . . ."[27]

In his thirty-page attack on this subject, Ingersoll remained immensely respectful toward Marshall, but singled out Story for particular attention, and traced his judicial career from his last-choice appointment in a mode which combined flattering estimate and needling asides:

> . . . the choice fell at last on a very young man, Joseph Story . . . ; Mr. Speaker Story would have never been Mr. Justice Story but for his well ascertained, as was then thought, root and branch democracy . . . Learned, indefatigable, and enthusiastic, no man living has contributed more to the literature of the law, and no member of the Supreme Court, has, for twenty-five years, left his impression more distinctly on [its] proceedings . . .[28]

[25] *The United States Magazine and Democratic Review* (hereinafter cited as *U.S. Magazine*) I (1837), 1.
[26] *Ibid.*, 143
[27] *Ibid.*, 147.
[28] *Ibid.*, 156.

Ingersoll then passed to his bill of particulars. He took particular issue with Story's course in the Fairfax litigation, castigating him, on the first decision, for "RASHLY . . . (whether right or wrong) reversing a decree of the highest court of Virginia" and on the second for his "peremptory and profuse argument of forty pages."[29] Other Story opinions also came in for reproach, but the fire of Ingersoll's wrath was especially reserved for the *Dartmouth College* decision, "a very Cyclops of jurisprudence—*monstrum horrendum*," and the reference to "the English authorities paraded as precedents" made it clear he had Story's concurrence in view.[30]

Ingersoll brought his polemic to a close with a touch of barbed humor in describing the 1835 term, when the absence of a full bench foreclosed constitutional argument and adjudication and produced an asserted depression in the Justices. This he ascribed to the fact that the ladies ceased to visit the Court to hear argument in great cases and to lionize the Justices at dinner parties as men vested with great power. The consequence, he said, was that members of the Court were bored to distraction and hardly able to await a motion to adjourn—to dinner. He ended, however, seriously enough and on a note of Jacksonian orthodoxy—that the new Supreme Court would join the executive, the Congress, and the states in "the great and glorious cause of reducing government and enlarging freedom as much as possible."[31]

Up in New York, Caleb Sprague Henry, who, like Story, was liberal in religion but conservative in politics, expressed outrage at the journalistic attack—"flippant, flagrantly unjust, vulgar in its spirit, addressed to the bad passions of the vulgar & ignorant."[32] He had a countering string of adjectives for the counter article he desired Story to write for his *New York Review:* "Thoroughgoing, strong, full of dignified scorn, laying down the *true* principles, signalizing the bad, & defending the court where unjustly

[29] *Ibid.*, 161.
[30] *Ibid.*, 162.
[31] *Ibid.*, 172.
[32] Letter from C. S. Henry in Story Papers, Library of Congress. The letter is undated, but the content suggests it was written in mid-January, 1838.

attacked. Take the calm, lofty, searching air—of ability—& superiority tone, London Quarterly like. Let us make a lofty stand for the right, the noble, the true . . ."[33]

Giving repeated assurance of anonymity, Henry urgently requested a manuscript for the April issue, and indeed his magazine for that month did contain an unsigned defense of the Court in the form of a review of Volume Eleven of Mr. Peters' reports. It is not done in Story's style, however, and several items—such as some quotations which do not appear in his bridge dissent and the reference to the Dartmouth College case in terms of "the prosperity of all our literary, charitable, and religious establishments"[34] (rather than including business corporations), suggest it did not fully reflect his point of view. Otherwise, the piece was almost a point-counterpoint response to the Ingersoll polemic as it defended the Marshall Court's decisions *seriatim* and passed to "the decisions of the Supreme Court under the new dynasty."[35] After a detailed review of the 1837 term, it concluded: "[I]n reading these decisions, we perceive at once an altered tone and narrower spirit . . . The change is so great and so ominous, that a great gloom is cast over the future. We seem to have sunk suddenly below the horizon, to have lost the light of the sun, and to hold our way *per incertam lunam, sub luce maligna*."[36]

Indeed, the uncertain moon had already risen, for even before the Court adjourned from the term of 1837, a financial panic broke on the country, and, in a seeming exemplification Story's warnings on the inadequacies of state-sponsored money, banks suspended specie payments. Story felt that he was indeed the prophet vindicated in seeing here the logical consequences of the destruction of the Bank of the United States and "the last infatuated act of folly,"[37] the Jacksonian specie circular. Moreover, as summer unfolded, the Van Buren Administration showed that it

[33] *Ibid.*
[34] *New York Review*, II, 372.
[35] *Ibid.*, 379.
[36] *Ibid.*, 385.
[37] Letter to John McLean, May 10, 1837, in W. W. Story, II, 273.

had absolutely no intention of deviating from the path of Jacksonian orthodoxy. From Ohio, Justice McLean, Jackson's first appointee but sounding more and more like a charter member of
the Marshall Court, sourly read the new President's first message
and noted that "the voice from the Hermitage is to govern."[38]

It was at this distressing juncture that the permanent nature of
Mrs. Story's illness was confirmed. "Mrs. Story has become a
permanent invalid," Story wrote Harriet Martineau. "I entertain
no hope of her [recovery]."[39] Not surprisingly, his distressing
domestic situation, the reverses on constitutional law, the changed
character of the Court, and the turbulent state of public affairs
turned his thoughts to withdrawal and escape, perhaps in full-time
teaching and scholarship or perhaps in commercial enterprise. For
the second time since his appointment he seriously considered resigning, and in fact even before the 1837 term had adjourned he
had been in correspondence with Sumner on the possibilities of
the presidency of a newly formed insurance company, just as two
decades before he had been tempted by the possibility of a lucra-
tive Baltimore law practice.

Story's opinions over those two decades may have shown sharp
differences in their orientation and outlook, but his reaction remained the same. Somewhere in his nature a Calvinist strain
prompted him to kick against the goad, and his final conclusion
to the web of troubles in 1837 was the same as his reaction in
1816. He stayed on the Court.

[38] Letter from John McLean, Sept. 12, 1837, in Story Papers, Library of
Congress.
[39] Letter to Harriet Martineau, Apr. 7, 1837, in W. W. Story, II, 276.

CHAPTER XXIX

The Great Terms

THE LAW

Undoubtedly, one element in Story's decision to stay on the bench was set out in a couplet by Charles Sumner:

> *The Law School is doing well*
> *All goes as merry as a wedding bell.*[1]

And thanks to the Justice, the law school was not only doing well but flourishing. Enrollments were high and its national reputation was growing apace; it was both setting the model for American legal education and raising up a new breed of lawyers. He had now been engaged in his professorship for almost a decade. The enrollment had climbed to sixty, and a substantial addition was in prospect. The luster of his name attracted a national student body. His enthusiasm, which tempered the harsh discipline and abolished the "written" (i.e., read) lecture, galvanized the entire institution. And its success was due in large measure to the fact that its environment and operation both reflected and influenced Story's work, giving it a final dimension and enabling the threefold role of judge, writer, and teacher to merge in the total influence he

[1] Letter from Charles Sumner, Jan. 18, 1837, Story Papers, Library of Congress.

was bringing to bear on the organic development of a distinctively American law.

In fact it was more than coincidence that at the very time the judicial reverses of the 1837 term were about to unfold, his own counterattack against the jurisprudential side of the Jacksonian revolution succeeded. To be sure, the facts of life were overwhelmingly on his side and against the arcadian delusion which saw a simple, short, and legislatively adopted code as the source of all law, the judiciary as finders of fact, and every man as his own lawyer. And this was in effect what he said on a Massachusetts commission in a half-a-loaf recommendation of a limited codification of the criminal law. Declining appointment to serve further, he nonetheless wrote home, almost as soon as he arrived in Washington for the 1837 term, for news of further developments, and what he heard must have pleased him. "Codification is at a standstill," wrote Sumner, and Greenleaf added, "I should not be surprised if the whole subject should sleep for the present."[2] But the subject was not sleeping; in the sense contemplated by its extreme enthusiasts it had died. But there were other causes than over-optimism, and here Story's hand was evident, for his commentaries were, in effect, miniature codes and his latest literary efforts held an especial application for both the codification movement and the Charles River Bridge controversy.

The latest focus of his writings and research had been equity, that supple and elastic jurisprudence which both filled the interstices and softened the rigors of the common law. Elusive even in definition, stressing a remedial and natural justice, it came out of the chancellor's court of medieval England, and claimed a sweep of parties and of remedies—injunctions, specific performance, declaratory judgments, interpleader rather than simple money judgments. It also involved a framework of values at almost complete variance with codification concepts—judges instead of juries, sophistication instead of simplicity, discretion instead of automa-

[2] Letters from Charles Sumner, Feb. 5, 1837, and Simon Greenleaf, Feb. 7, 1837, Story Papers, Library of Congress.

tism, and general principles instead of specific rules. And as Dean Roscoe Pound had noted in calling Story the father of American equity, it was his opinions from the bench, his speeches and articles, and, above all, his luminous commentaries, that not only brought equity into the mainstream of American law but did so at the high tide of the codification movement.

Indeed, the Charles River Bridge case itself could be taken as partial vindication of this work, for it was a suit in equity calling on a jurisdiction which the Massachusetts courts lacked when Story was a practicing member of their bar. And it was a void he had vainly sought to supply during his service as a state legislator and as a member of the state constitutional convention. Perhaps it was a small consolation, but the fact remained that the bridge company could not even have sued as it did, even in a losing cause, under the common law.

To Story, a brighter symbol of the same advance was the great success of his *Commentaries on Equity Jurisprudence*, which in its two-volume compass had succeeded in capturing the basic principles of this field of law. Yet, compendious as it was, the book was only a beginning. Practical supplementation was needed by a counterpart volume on procedure, and Story was hard at work to provide it. And in a significant manifestation of some Calvinist strain, his lamentations on the constitutional decisions of the Great Term did not keep him from the most pressing of schedules.

> . . . I am compelled to give up to public and irresistible duty much of the time that I should be glad to devote to my friends. For the last six weeks I have been under the severest tasks, and discipline, and anxiety, that I could . . . The Circuit Court has been constantly in session, and I have been compelled to be there. There are nearly seventy law students, and every day that I command any leisure I have been obliged to give them lectures. My work "Equity Pleadings" is in press, and one third of it remains to be written before I go to Washington.[3]

3 Letter to Francis Lieber, Nov. 11, 1837, in W. W. Story, II, 283.

What drove him on? There are any number of explanations. Perhaps the best came from a compliment that he had paid Kent, but wherein he really held a mirror to his own face: "the high path of duty, and unconquerable love of the law."[4]

THE HIGH PREROGATIVE

The Jacksonian revolution seemed even more ascendant with the convening of the 1838 term. The Supreme Court now consisted of nine Justices, two additional seats having been created as a response to territorial expansion and filled by the newly appointed John Catron of Tennessee and John McKinley of Alabama. Justice McLean had not been enthusiastic about his new colleagues. "McKinley's temper is not unlike Baldwin's and Catron is full of himself,"[5] he had written Story the previous summer. Story too was less than pleased, but his reaction was based on procedure rather than personalities: "The addition to our numbers has most sensibly affected our facility as well as rapidity of doing business . . . I verily believe, if there were twelve judges we would get no business done at all . . ."[6]

Story found the term "dull, and dry and tedious,"[7] and made all the more melancholy by a Washington duel fought with rifles ("we are now come to that in this goodly city"[8]); the Justices were invited to attend the funeral, but all declined save Justice Baldwin. Undoubtedly the tragedy added to Story's sense of depression, and he was glad when the term was over. "To me an attendance here is but a melancholy renewal of the memory of departed days, and pleasures never to return."[9]

Doubtless his depression combined with his nearness to events to obscure the resounding vindication and renewal which the

[4] Joseph Story to James Kent, Dec. 22, 1836, *ibid.*, 258.
[5] Letter from John McLean, Sept. 12, 1837, Story Papers, Library of Congress.
[6] Letter to Charles Sumner, March 15, 1838, in W. W. Story, II, 296.
[7] *Ibid.*
[8] Letter to Mrs. Story, Feb. 25, 1838, in W. W. Story, II, 286.
[9] Letter to John Brazer, March 5, 1838, *ibid.*, 290.

1838 term of the Court gave "the memory of departed days."
For in 1838 this tribunal made up overwhelmingly of Jacksonian
appointees expounded the national judicial power in a mode surpassing anything John Marshall had ever attempted and asserted
a high and independent prerogative against both the executive and
legislative arms. In one case it affirmed the issuance of the extraordinary writ of mandamus—whose very name bore the royal plural-
ity in a command to a government officer to do his duty—ordering
a Cabinet officer to perform an official act irrespective of the
wishes of the Chief Executive. In the other it announced its constitutional capability of exercising original jurisdiction without the
necessity of a congressional statute providing process and procedures.

The first case arose out of the claim of a postal contractor;[10]
the other involved a boundary dispute between Rhode Island and
Massachusetts.[11] Both cases turned ultimately on a view of the
character and sanction of the judicial power of the United States.
Both cases were remarkable for what the final opinions said, for
what they did not say, and for the way they overrode venerated
doctrines.

The postal case finished what *Marbury v. Madison* had begun,
with the Jacksonian Court issuing the very writ that John Marshall had refused. To be sure, Marshall's refusal was based on the
constitutional ground that Congress could not affect the original
jurisdiction of the Supreme Court, and not on the constitutional
ground urged by President Jefferson—that the separation of powers removed the President and his officers not only from the ambit of judicial writs but even from that of subpoena[12] And this
is precisely what Amos Kendall, holdover Postmaster General,
told the United States Circuit Court for the District of Columbia
in the summer of 1837 when it issued its writ of mandamus order-

[10] *Kendall v. U.S. ex rel. Stokes*, 12 PETERS 524 (1838). See also White, *The Jacksonians* (1954), 278-79.

[11] *Rhode Island v. Massachusetts*, 12 PETERS 657 (1838).

[12] See, e.g., letter to Spencer Roane, Sept. 6, 1819, in Jefferson, *Works*, XII 135.

ing him to pay a postal contractor in accordance with an applicable statute. Kendall, who believed the claim was fraudulent and who had persuaded President Jackson to a like view, declined to appear even to submit a pleading contesting jurisdiction. Instead, he addressed several letters to the chief judge denying that the circuit court "could constitutionally inquire into the official conduct of the president or heads of departments."[13]

The circuit court overruled his position, and Kendall had the benefit of formidable legal representation when his appeal was argued at the 1838 term of the Supreme Court. The Jacksonian Court split on the question of whether the writ might issue under the circumstances. The minority position was illustrative, for it assumed, contrary to Kendall's basic position, that mandamus might be constitutionally authorized by Congress against officers in the executive branch, and concluded that Congress had not done it here. Contrariwise, Justice Thompson's majority opinion held that Congress could and did authorize the Circuit Court for the District of Columbia to issue the writ. But the majority opinion was also significant for what it did not say. Excised therefrom was an irate riposte to an asserted argument of the Attorney General which supposedly reiterated the point that the Postmaster General was subject only to the President and beyond judicial control. In reading his opinion, Thompson had included a paragraph which denounced the point as "vesting in the president a dispensing power which has no countenance . . ."[14] and then excised his denunciation when the Attorney General insisted that he should not be understood as having said any such thing.

The Attorney General's disclaimer of Jeffersonian orthodoxy, which thus made the postal case something of a judicial triumph, was paralleled and perhaps bettered in this regard by the boundary controversy. In the postal dispute it was unclear whether Congress had given the court which had the case the authority to proceed; in the boundary case it was plain that Congress had not.

[13] *U.S. ex rel. Stokes v. Kendall*, 26 FED. CASES at 703 (1837).
[14] Quoted in Warren, *Supreme Court*, II, 46.

Nonetheless Rhode Island proceeded with its suit, insisting that it could be heard by the Supreme Court as a matter of original constitutional jurisdiction even if Congress had not provided the specific ways and means. There was some jurisprudential philosophy to support this position; there was also authority on the other side, for congressional statute clearly controlled where and when the court sat at all, and there was corollary doubt as to whether it could proceed in any area until Congress regulated its processes, furnished a rule of decision, and made provision for execution. On this question, however, the Jacksonian point of view was clear, for Ingersoll's condemnatory article in *The United States Magazine and Democratic Review* had included a prior exercise of nonlegislated jurisdiction in its bill of indictment ("In 1832, the Empire State was compelled, after protest, to appear and answer the complaint of New Jersey, although there is no legislation to regulate this constitutional power"[15]).

Speaking for the Court, however, Justice Baldwin read an extraordinary opinion which built an assertion of national judicial power upon the very states'-rights premises Baldwin had asserted in the *General View*—that the Supreme Court acquired its jurisdiction in the boundary dispute as the representative, not of the nation, but of the several states "by their own consent and delegated authority, as their agent."[16] It apparently was quite characteristic for Baldwin to deduce extraordinary conclusions, and the federal judge who sat with him on the circuit subsequently wrote Story that in view of Baldwin's erratic legal logic and unpredictable behavior, the only charitable view "of any of his conduct, is, that he is partially deranged at all times."[17] Story did not sit in the case, but his self-disqualification did not preclude an opinion on Baldwin's opinion—"full of his elaborate citations and comments in his peculiar way." Yet there were more aspects to the case than Baldwin's making a virtue out of adversity. One was that at Bald-

[15] *U.S. Magazine*, I, 166-67.
[16] 12 PETERS at 720.
[17] Letter from Joseph Hopkinson to Joseph Story, May, 1833, in Konkle, *Joseph Hopkinson* (Philadelphia, 1931), 286.

win's opinion upholding an independent judicial power was written at all. Another was the opinion's lofty aloofness to the argument that Massachusetts had no intention of handing over six thousand of its citizens like czarist serfs in compliance with an unconstitutional mandate of the Supreme Court. Here, perhaps, response was unnecessary, for Rhode Island had already spoken to it—"Does Massachusetts threaten? Is Massachusetts ready to become a nullifying state . . . ?"[18]

The question was a good one, and its answer proved a point. Response to the two great cases of 1838 was not nullification at the state level or statutory chastisement at the federal one. To be sure, criticism, implicit or explicit, came. Congress effectively canceled the judicial penalties laid on Kendall as a consequence of his disregarding the writ, but, more significantly, it ignored a recommendation from President Van Buren that the Circuit Court of the District be stripped of its power to issue the writ against other executive officers.

But even more than the inaction of Congress, the entrenched status of the nationalist Constitution and, necessarily, of the Supreme Court as its prophetic expositor could be seen in the words of two spokesmen of indisputable Jacksonian character. One was in the dissents of Chief Justice Taney in the mandamus and boundary cases. The other was a letter to Story written by Charles Jared Ingersoll, author of the *Democratic Review*'s attack on the Court itself.

Taney's dissents were particularly illustrative. In neither did he suggest the supine views of the national judicial power proposed by the losing litigants. In the mandamus case, he argued that Congress had not authorized the circuit court to do what it did. In the boundary controversy he pleaded for judicial self-denial in essentially political controversies and not the necessity of congressional intermediation to the court's prerogatives.

But most telling, perhaps, was the Ingersoll letter, which Story had received upon the close of the 1837 term. While Story prob-

[18] 12 PETERS at 709.

ably was unaware of Ingersoll's authorship of the condemnatory Supreme Court article, he undoubtedly was familiar with Ingersoll's hostility to corporate privilege and considered him a radical for it. Ingersoll wrote to the point: "I always was a dissentient from the Dartmouth College case, and that I hold all public charters to be public property is true, and in these sentiments I believe I am sustained by the English authorities. If that makes me a radical, sobeit—there is no magic in the word."[19] But Ingersoll did not write to dispute, but, rather, to tell Story of the birthday present he had given his youngest son. The gift was a set of Story's *Commentaries on the Constitution,* and it was given as a token from father to son as "one of the most valuable works he can master."[20]

[19] Letter from Charles Jared Ingersoll, April 9, 1837, in Story Papers, Library of Congress.
[20] *Ibid.*

PART NINE

The Sunset Years

CHAPTER XXX

False Hope, False Dawn

IN BRIEF ASCENDANCY

"The nomination of Harrison runs like wildfire on the prairies,"[1] Justice Story wrote from Washington in early 1840 in an observation which posed an interesting question, for the farthest west the Justice had ever been was Niagara Falls and that in 1825. Nonetheless this comment which he sent a Harvard professor admirably illustrated the growing determination of the Whig Party to beat the Jacksonian Democrats at their own game in an electoral appeal wrapped up in the frontier trappings of log cabins, hard cider, and the common man.

And not only was Justice Story a Whig, but at sixty he was an elder statesman of the party, counselor of its leaders, and high strategist in its councils. He was cautious enough about his political activity, and it would be two more years before he would avow his partisan faith even in private correspondence. "I am a Whig," he wrote Henry Clay in 1842, "and although I do not pretend to mingle in the common politics of the day, there are great measures, upon which I have a decided opinion and, which I would not disguise if I could."[2] Among the "great measures"

[1] Letter to Simon Greenleaf, Feb. 6, 1840, in W. W. Story, II, 327.
[2] Letter to Henry Clay, Aug. 3, 1842, in Swisher, 430; see also Newmeyer, "A Note on the Whig Politics of Justice Joseph Story," *Mississippi Valley Historical Review*, XLVIII (1961), 480.

on which his views were well known—indeed, had been well known for a quarter of a century—were the merits of a national bank, a protective tariff, and a bankruptcy law.

Yet it was not so much the merit of these proposals—by 1840 the canons of the Whig Party—as it was the cumulative misfortunes of twelve years of Democratic Presidential power which turned the unfortunate Martin Van Buren out of the White House in that year's election and brought William Henry Harrison to the Presidency. There was, to be sure, a singularly Machiavellian touch in the victory which showed how well the Whigs had learned their political lessons, for they had nominated an obscure anti-Jackson Democrat for the Vice-Presidency and thereby assured the maximum popular support for the ticket. Their grand strategy was immensely successful, and the assurance of victory was evident in a letter which Story wrote as he prepared to leave for Washington for the 1841 term:

> I hope that the Court will have a harmonious session; and I am sure that the Chief Justice and a majority of my brethren will do all that is proper to accomplish the purpose. The change in the Administration will produce no change in my own conduct. I mean to stand by the Court and do all I can to sustain its dignity and the public confidence in it. . . .
>
> I hope General Harrison will require Congress again to take the purse-strings in their own hands, and to demand back what they have so unconstitutionally surrendered to Jackson and Van Buren. The power of removal may, and ought to be, regulated by Congress . . .[3]

It was the first term in many years that he truly anticipated, and it turned out to be a momentous and memorable one. For the Whigs the term also held a mournful and prophetic overtone, by reason of the sudden death of Justice Barbour on February 24, 1841, and the events which followed. Story felt a strong sense of personal loss in the matter, for he had liked Barbour from the start ("a very conscientious and pains-taking Judge, and I think

[3] Letter to Richard Peters, Dec. 3, 1840, in W. W. Story, II, 341-42.

will improve as he goes on"[4]) and had written a touching eulogy to him (". . . not only equal to all the functions of his high
station, but above them,—*par negotiis, et supra*"[5]) But his sadness
was compounded, his sense of decorum was shocked, and his political instincts were outraged at what followed—that with only a
few days left in power, and before Barbour was so much as
buried, the outgoing Van Buren Administration managed to hus-
tle through the nomination and confirmation of Peter V. Daniel
as Barbour's successor and thereby denied the Whigs the first
fruits of their victory.

Even under the best of circumstances the appointment would
not have sat well, for Story saw Daniel as a man of "prodigously
small calibre."[6] Yet for all its stealthy and shabby character, he
did not permit the episode to upset him unduly, and upon his return to Massachusetts the sense of victory was still obvious.
"Judge Story has returned," wrote Charles Sumner, ". . . with
more health and spirits than I have known him blessed with for a
long time."[7]

Then the optimism ceased. Death again operated to abort the
Whig victory, but this time in a far more serious fashion. On
April 4, 1841, President Harrison died, and John Tyler assumed
the office. Almost immediately, events began to vindicate the
portent of the Barbour succession. The uncontemplated and unwanted President, entrenched in the executive arm, threw his
weight against the Whig legislative program, "and its crowning
dome,"[8] a new federal bank, was buried beneath a succession of
Presidential vetoes. By late summer the breach between Tyler and
his adopted party was permanent, and save for Secretary of State
Daniel Webster (who was engrossed in diplomatic negotiations)
the Cabinet resigned en masse.

[4] Letter to Charles Sumner, Jan. 25, 1837, *ibid.*, 266.
[5] W. W. Story, II, 353.
[6] George Templeton Strong, *Diary*, ed. Nevins and Thomas (4v., New
York, 1952), I, 157.
[7] Charles Sumner to Francis Lieber, March 23, 1841, in Edward Pierre,
Memoir and Letters of Charles Sumner (4v., Boston, 1877–94), II, 175.
[8] Webster, quoted in von Holst, II (1888), 488 n.2.

Story's covert collaboration with Webster in negotiating the northeastern boundary of the United States engendered no sense of loyalty to the Tyler Administration. On the contrary, he felt an ongoing and deepening bitterness over what he regarded as the consequences of a double perversion of the Constitution. One was the manner of selecting the Vice-President. The other was the veto power. The first he saw as completely betraying the intent of the founding fathers, a President and Vice-President "equally worthy and fit" for the chief magistracy; the second, when aggressively used by a minority President, he feared made it impossible "to maintain the original balance."[9] The extent of his concern was strikingly shown at a Salem dinner party in late 1841. Story exhibited nothing of the attitudes with which he began the year. Rather, there was much reaction talked, and young Richard Henry Dana noted that no one talked more than Story, "who began life as a radical."[10] Lord Howard of Morpeth, befitting a foreign visitor, merely listened. He subsequently recorded what he heard:

> The judge our host talked with incessant but pleasant and kindly flow; the conversation approached very near to treason against their own constitution; they pronounce it an utter failure, especially with respect to the election of fit men for the office of President; . . . they talk much as Lord Grey would talk of the present proceedings of the Reform Parliament.[11]

BANKRUPTCY

Yet Story should not have been so hard on President Tyler, who, in an effort to conciliate the Whigs, had sacrificed his own strict-constructionist views to approve the one Whig proposal probably closest to the Justice's heart—a national bankruptcy act. Story had worked for such a statute almost since taking his seat

[9] Letter to John Berrien, July 23, 1842, in W. W. Story, II, 406.
[10] R. H. Dana, *Journal*, ed. Lucid (1968; hereinafter cited as Dana), I, 53.
[11] Quoted in Schlesinger, *The Age of Jackson* (1946), 323 n.4.

on the Court, but far more underlay its passage than his years of persuasion.

The principal factor was the panic of 1837, which not only had turned the Jacksonians out of office, but had also left an estimated 100,000 ruined businessmen in its wake. Technically they were not bankrupts, for the national bankruptcy power had gone unused since 1801. They had not much to look for in local law either, for the Supreme Court had substantially disabled the states from dealing with the problem. In 1819 it had decided *Sturgis v. Crowninshield* and forbidden local laws that operated retrospectively. Again, in 1827 in *Ogden v. Saunders* it had approved *in futuro* laws but only with a strictly local application. In 1840 *Suydam v. Broadnax*[12] reiterated the judicial prohibition against applying such laws to interstate contracts.

Thus, for years what Webster called "want of power in the states and want of will in congress"[13] had left many debtors both figuratively and literally in a state of hopeless bondage, for imprisonment for debt still prevailed. Yet new circumstances forced a new surge of effort. Thus, even before the election, in April of 1840, Webster had introduced a bankruptcy bill drawn in large part by Story and modeled after the Massachusetts Insolvent Act of 1838. While the forthcoming election proved an effective delaying agent, the circumstances of the initial debate suggested some significant changes. In an obvious and doctrinaire reaction, the Jacksonians objected to giving the national government a plenary power to wipe out local debts. Less obvious but fundamentally more predictable and dismaying was the response of many of the onetime Southern nationalists, who, pressed between the millstones of a burden of debt and a concern for slavery, opted for the limitations of ancient British precedent in order to restrict the federal power to the narrowest possible scope. Yet notwithstanding such opposition, Webster proposed a broad act which broke new ground by making bankruptcy applicable to

[12] 14 PETERS 67 (1840).
[13] Webster, *loc. cit. supra* (note 8).

any debtors other than businessmen and by permitting voluntary proceedings.

While the first proposal came to naught, less than three months after the convening of the first and special session of the Twenty-seventh Congress a similar measure finally passed. Passage was due more to horse trading and logrolling in the legislative process than to merit, and indeed a determined effort to repeal the law was made before the year was out. Story sounded more like a prisoner with a reprieve than a judge with a law as he noted with deep relief: "The Bankrupt Act has had a breathing spell. . . . I, at least, will do all I can to give it a fair operation, and a cheap one."[14] His wish was that Congress would let the courts probe the deficiencies of the act and make the necessary adjustments. He did not get it. In early 1842 Congress repeated its experiment, and a future President summed up legislative sentiment:

> . . . such a law!—[it] places the relation of debtor and cred-
> itor, throughout the several States, under the . . . Federal
> courts . . . deprives these states of the power to regulate this
> . . . subject according to their own laws. I have recently
> seen a decision of Judge Story, in a newspaper, by which
> the attachment laws of Massachusetts are declared to be pros-
> trated under our bankrupt system.[15]

Story had done more than impair the attachment laws of Massachusetts. In *Ex Parte Eames*, he had asserted with perhaps unnecessary didacticism that the federal statute *"ipso facto,* suspended all actions upon future cases, arising under the state insolvent laws, where the insolvent persons were within the purview of the Bankrupt Act."[16] It was, however, to *Ex Parte Foster*[17] that Congressman Buchanan doubtless referred, and if pressed Story would have agreed that such was the precise intent of the bankrupt statute, and that, moreover, the act was but one element—along with *Swift v. Tyson* and the corporation de-

[14] Letter to John Pitman, Feb. 10, 1842, in W. W. Story, II, 416.
[15] Speech of James Buchanan, May 9, 1842, in *Congressional Globe*, 27th Cong., 2nd Sess. (1842), Appendix, 385.
[16] 8 FED. CASES at 237 (1843).
[17] 9 FED. CASES 508 (1842).

cisions—to create a relevant and authentically American law of commerce.

Perversely, however, Story's activism in securing and enforcing the Bankrupt Act played a substantial part both in effecting repeal of the law and in securing a judicial reversal of his own decisions under it. The latter point involved the question of whether attachments issuing out of state courts prior to final judgment were "liens" which were preempted from bankruptcy process by the very terms of the act. Involved in it was the larger issue whether state or federal courts held the final power of decision in state–federal collisions, and this in turn involved the superintendence of one tribunal by another. Story had anticipated all these questions in *Martin v. Hunter's Lessee* when he held that in any system of divided jurisprudence a final power of decision had to reside somewhere. And this, in effect, was what he said in *Ex Parte Foster*, where he concluded on the basis of common-law precedent that an intermediate attachment was not a "lien" within the meaning of the bankruptcy statute no matter how many times the Massachusetts courts had called it that.

The New Hampshire precedent was to the same effect, and when the question came before that state's Supreme Court, Chief Justice Joel Parker stood by the state tradition, *Ex Parte Foster* notwithstanding, and acidly noted that Story's decision in the latter case "contributed in no small degree, to the repeal which has followed so hard upon the enactment of the Act of 1841."[18]

When *In Re Bellows* brought the same question to the United States Circuit Court for New Hampshire, Story rejoined with sarcasm and some hauteur that the point had already been "fully discussed and fully decided" and that if he were to change his conclusion, it would be at the behest of "some tribunal whose views I am bound to obey."[19] This was obviously not the Supreme Court of New Hampshire.

Within months, the New Hampshire Supreme Court noted that the question had been decided differently in other federal cir-

[18] *Kitteredge v. Warren,* 14 N.H. at 517 (1844).
[19] *In Re Bellows,* 3 FED. CASES at 138 (1844).

cuits, and that Story's *Commentaries on the Law of Bailments* had denominated attachments as "lien." Noting that it would "make no comment on the general tone of [Story's] opinion,"[20] it went on to reaffirm its earlier holding and asserted that it would afford due protection to all state officers enforcing it. The governor of the state then invited legislative attention to the conflict, and on December 26, 1844, the New Hampshire House overwhelming passed a resolution commending its own high court for opposing "the unwarrantable and dangerous assumptions of the Circuit Court of the United States."[21]

Story probably knew nothing of the state court's assertion when, on the last day of 1844, he wrote an opinion on a bankruptcy matter out of New Orleans and used a technical point of pleading as the base for a towering *obiter dictum* which was virtually a commentary on the law of bankruptcy. No target was disclosed in the opinion, but in a letter to his son Story indicated why he had written as he had: "The opinion covers the whole ground . . . in the New Hampshire cases . . ."[22] Alone of his colleagues Justice Catron protested the advisory nature of the opinion, and, unabashed and unrepentant, so did the Supreme Court of New Hampshire. When the question came before it three years after Story's death, it held that Story's opinion, even from the bench of the Supreme Court of the United States, "settles nothing."[23] Ironically, Story's own Court agreed. Abjuring "arbitrary and fanciful" interpretations of the act and disclaiming any intention of laying "a strong hand" on state tribunals, the Supreme Court held that preliminary attachments were liens all the time and wrote what seemed to be the final and melancholy obituary to the Whig legislative program and to Story's efforts on its behalf.[24]

---

[20] *Kitteredge v. Emerson*, 15 N.H. at 244 (1844).
[21] Quoted in Shirley, 342.
[22] Letter to W. W. Story, Jan. 1, 1845, in W. W. Story, II, 509. The case was *Ex Parte The City Bank of New Orleans*, 3 HOWARD 292 (1845).
[23] *Peck v. Jeness*, 16 N.H. at 529 (1845).
[24] *Peck v. Jeness*, 7 HOWARD at 620 and 626 (1849).

CHAPTER XXXI

Two Orders, One Law

THE MODERN CORPORATION

One aspect of bankruptcy controversy interlocked with another legal development in which Story was also playing a critical role. This was the transmutation of the corporation into an instrument of industrial and finance capitalism. The process was slow and episodic, not only involving a refining and recasting of ancient legal precedents but throwing up delicate questions of American constitutional law. Thus, on the question of bringing state-chartered corporations within the ambit of a federal bankruptcy statute, Story wrote Webster: "Is it quite certain, that State Rights, as to the creation and dissolution of corporations, are not thus virtually infringed? I confess, that I feel no small doubt, whether Congress can regulate State Corporations by any other laws than the State laws."[1]

His doubt probably kept corporations out of the 1841 statute; it also reflected, consciously or otherwise, the older view in which the corporation was but a vehicle of communal service invested with governmental power for public purposes. Formally at least he had disposed of that view in his *Dartmouth College* concurrence, where he had explicitly extended the corporate

[1] Letter to Daniel Webster, May 10, 1840, in W. W. Story, II, 332.

form to business enterprise, shifted its rationale from public service to vested right and private property, and enshrouded it in the protection of the federal Constitution. His constitutional doubt, coming atop his common-law creativity, thus set the stage for an environment in which the new form of enterprise found sanctuary from state interference in an expansive reading of the contracts clause and immunity from the national power in a rigorous application of the federal principle.

The Taney Court completed his germinal work in this area, and the collaboration between the new Chief Justice and his senior associate was here creative, ongoing, and every bit as viable as the association with John Marshall had ever been. Thus, the doctrine of the common seal—the medieval rubric which required a soulless corporation to communicate and otherwise act only under its visible, talismanic *sigillum*—had been banished from American law by Story only over Marshall's dissent. (Indeed, one of Story's singular international triumphs came when the British courts followed his lead on the point. The Court of King's Bench, regretting that his opinions could not be cited as directly controlling precedents, nevertheless noted that they were "intrinsically entitled" to the highest respect and observed that their holding had been almost unanimously followed by all courts in "the United States in America" (*sic*).[2]

Paralleling this liberalization of the internal corporate procedures was Taney's liberalizing efforts in terms of ever-expanding territorial operations. The occasion came in 1839 with the case of *Bank of Augusta v. Earle*,[3] an appeal from the federal court in Alabama concerning the legitimacy of the purchase of a promissory note by a bank outside the state of its incorporation. The defense was that the bank had no extraterritorial power to do any such thing, and consequently that it held no rights in the instrument. On circuit, where the case was first heard, Justice McKin-

---

[2] *Beverly v. Lincoln Gas Light and Coke Co.,* 112 ENGLISH REPORTS at 321 (1837).
[3] 13 PETERS 519 (1839).

ley agreed and thereby, according to Story, "frightened half the lawyers and all the corporations of the country out of their proprieties."[4] On a somewhat graver note he wrote Justice Mc-Lean that the circuit decision would "most seriously affect all banks, insurance companies, and manufacturing companies doing an interstate business."[5]

When the case was argued before the Supreme Court, Webster made a virtue out of adversity and insisted that corporations were to be regarded as citizens of the state of their incorporation for all purposes and were therefore invested with all privileges and immunities with which the Constitution endowed citizens. Justice Baldwin agreed. At the other pole, Justice McKinley held fast to his fundamentalist views. The Chief Justice steered brilliantly between these extremes. As a concession to McKinley he agreed that a state, if it wished, could bar a corporation from its borders. He then reached the result proposed by Webster and adopted by Baldwin, by finding the absence of a positive bar to corporate entry the equivalent of a state's implied invitation to entry extended upon an expectation of like treatment for its own corporations elsewhere. The basis of this concept was Story's *Commentaries on the Conflict of Laws,* which was cited with appropriate references. The author was flattered and grateful. "I hope you will allow me to say," he wrote Taney, "that [your opinion] does great honor to yourself as well as the court."[6]

Further developments proved how solid was the basic Taney–Story rapport, how deceptive had been the opposition suggested by their differing opinions in the Charles River Bridge case, and how the seeming confrontation in that controversy was more a matter of emphasis than category. To be sure, Taney was willing to reward enterprise more liberally than Story; more importantly, however, he agreed with Story that the rights of property were to be "sacredly preserved" and proved it in invalidating an Illinois

[4] Letter to Charles Sumner, June 17, 1838, in Warren, *Supreme Court,* II, 50.
[5] Letter to John McLean, May 25, 1838, McLean Papers, Library of Congress.
[6] Letter to Roger B. Taney, Apr. 19, 1839, in Swisher, 385.

statute which attempted to impair foreclosure rights.[7] Story's congratulatory letter could well have been written to Marshall:

> I read the opinion with the highest satisfaction, and entirely concur in it. I think your opinion is drawn up with great ability, and in my judgment is entirely conclusive. . . . There are times in which the Court is called upon to support every sound constitutional doctrine in support of the rights of property and of creditors.[8]

But the crowning touch in the legal development of the rights and immunities in the legal infrastructure of new industrialism came when the Taney Court not only entered where the Marshall Court refused to tread, but actually reversed the great Chief Justice to do so. This concerned the process—which might literally be called naturalization were a natural person involved—where by Webster's argument for corporate citizenship was granted for the purposes of federal jurisdiction.[9] This new dispensation accordingly overruled the previous views of John Marshall in which the corporation was merely the collective aggregate of its members.[10] Story, however, felt that this was no price at all and insisted that the Court's revised holding merely brought the law into line with Marshall's later views. He was also glad for his own account:

> I . . . rejoice, that the Supreme Court has at last come to the conclusion, that a corporation is a citizen, an artificial citizen, I agree, but still a citizen. It gets rid of a great anomaly in our jurisprudence. This was always Judge Washington's opinion. I have held the same opinion for very many years, and Mr. Chief Justice Marshall had, before his death, arrived at the conclusion, that our early decisions were wrong.[11]

[7] *Bronson v. Kenzie*, 1 HOWARD 311 (1843).
[8] Letter to Roger B. Taney, Mar. 25, 1843, in Warren, *Supreme Court* II, 103-4.
[9] *Louisville . . . R. R. Co. v. Letson*, 2 HOWARD 497 (1844).
[10] *Bank of the United States v. De Vaux*, 5 CRANCH 61 (1809).
[11] Letter to James Kent, Aug. 31, 1844, in W. W. Story, II, 469.

SLAVERY: MEN AND MERCHANDISE

The surge of national economic development which took its Northern form in industrialization and the corporate revolution wore a Southern face in the expanded plantation system. The developments were alike in involving a concentration of men and capital on a hitherto unprecedented scale. Both had their legal and indeed their constitutional consequences—on one side the transmutation of the corporation, and on the other a concerned and growing reexamination of the institution of slavery.

And there the similarity ended. Corporate development followed a lineal and relatively consistent process whereby a private juridical entity was endowed with the characteristics of humanity and citizenship. Conversely, the reappraisal of slavery differed as to both sequence and result. Useless to one order, indispensable to the other, the South's peculiar institution was caught up in a renewed attack and an expanded defense, in a milieu reflecting the rising sensitivity of a national and international conscience on one side and the tensions of constitutional development on the other. Its upshot, following a tortured and ambiguous sequence, was the opposite of that attending the corporation, for instead of personality and citizenship it was repression and dehumanization.

The fundamental dilemma was well illustrated in a phrase out of Story's opinion in *Hagan v. Forson*, where he considered whether an amount in controversy met the requirements of federal jurisdiction. The specific issue concerned the presumptive value of a slave woman and her child, and here Story's equivocal language resolving the legal issue permitted him to have both his Unitarian conscience and his judicial nationalism: "It is not supposed that their value can be equal to $2,000.00."[12]

On a more general note, the same ambiguity ran like a thread throughout his entire public career as an overriding concern for institutional continuity constantly checked the impulse of a keen

---

[12] *Hagan v. Forson,* 10 PETERS at 160.

sense of justice. Jeremiah Mason had glimpsed it years before when he first met Story, then ostensibly a Jeffersonian radical: "I said to myself, 'this young man will go for *the law*,' and I invited him home for dinner."[13] And so it was with slavery. Of his personal detestation there could be no doubt, for he had gone out of his way to denounce it in charges to federal grand juries, had broken his judicial silence for political address on one and only one occasion to condemn the Missouri Compromise, and had written a towering circuit-court opinion proclaiming the international slave trade a violation of international law.

Yet always there was the restraining qualification. The condemnatory references in his grand-jury charges and town-meeting speech were virtually unique among his vast writings, and the judicial condemnation of the slave trade was by his own admission only "abstractly considered,"[14] for in that case his final judgment was what it would have been under the earlier, traditional law. And more than this—he contributed what he called his widow's mite to the African Colonization Society. Doubtless the latter action earned him the epithet "colonizationist,"[15] which was among the milder terms contemporary advocates of radical reform reserved for the protagonists of the delusion that the remedy for slavery and all its fruits might be painless and relatively costless. Yet Story never shared the complete delusion. Rather, his support of the Society was offered in the hope of rousing the slaveholding conscience against a day when the institution of slavery, penned in territorially and circumscribed juridically, might somehow be constitutionally terminated.

Story never threw his ideas on the latter point into any systematic and comprehensive form, but his hopes were not without support in the pattern of both national and world events. Indeed, starting with Lord Mansfield, who in the eighteenth century had abruptly nonsuited a West Indies planter who sought to recover

13 Dana, II, 229.
14 Letter to Ezekiel Bacon, Nov. 19, 1842, in W. W. Story, II, 431.
15 W. P. Garrison, *The Story of His Life—William Lloyd Garrison* (hereinafter cited as Garrison), IV (1889), 414.

a slave on English soil through the ancient writ of *de homine re-plegiando*—that medieval process whereby manor lords once re-captured absent villeins—slavery was increasingly seen as a local and anachronistic relic of barbarism which would sooner or later fall of its own weight before an ever-widening enlightenment. Much of this process had been followed in the United States, in-cluding Story's own state of Massachusetts. In other states slav-ery had been ended by the action of state conventions, and a vigorous attack on the institution had been made in Virginia itself at the constitutional convention of 1830.

Yet while the ancient institutions of servitude came under in-creasingly heavy attack from Brazil to Russia, and the first wide-spread legal emancipation had been effected in the British West Indies, a formidable counteroffensive was building in the United States. The fear of slave revolts tightened the Southern apparatus of repression, and philosophically Southern polemics passed from defending slavery as a sad necessity to proclaiming it a positive good. But even more importantly, a movement to expand slave territory via the annexation of Texas was gathering increasing force. And out of this milieu came a new round of constitutional and statutory controversy which illustrated the pervasive conse-quences that slavery held for everything it touched.

Two such controversies were presented at the 1841 term of the Supreme Court. One concerned a provision of the Mississippi constitution forbidding the importation of slaves, as merchandise, into that state.[16] The other involved the status of freeborn Afri-cans who had resorted to mutiny and homicide to obtain their liberty. Ostensibly dissimilar, the cases were alike in prompting a reexamination of the fundamental nature of slavery in its Amer-ican environment and in forcing Story's implicit conclusion—adopted in a startling exception to his hostility toward the doc-trine of concurrent powers, on the one hand, and his deep inclina-tion to juridical comity, on the other—that American slavery was a legal anomaly which survived only by a perversely fortuitous

[16] *Groves v. Slaughter*, 15 PETERS 449 (1841).

junction of constitutional and municipal law, and which was to be penned in the narrowest permissible limits.

The Mississippi question involved the power of a state to bar the importation of slaves. In this case the motive of the bar was economic rather than humanitarian, for it sought to prevent a drain of money from Mississippi and to stabilize slave prices within it. The provision, however, was drawn into controversy about a suit over notes given on the purchase price of slaves brought into the state in violation of its prohibition, and the litigation concerned not one question but two. Primary was the issue of whether more legislation was needed to make the state's constitutional constraint effective. Beyond this lay the question of whether the bar, if valid without implementation, was void because of a collision with the plenary national control of interstate commerce.

The other case before the Court presented the foreign and international aspects of the same basic issue. Officially styled *The Amistad*,[17] it was more popularly known from one end of the country to the other as "the case of the African captives." The official name was that of a ship, the popular one that of its "cargo" —free Africans enslaved in violation of the laws of Spain, transported to Cuba, and who, after an obviously untrue certification as slaves by official Spanish documents, were in the process of being transshipped. En route, they revolted, killed the captain and three of the crew, and attempted to sail back to Africa, but were taken by an American man-of-war and, together with their ship, were libeled as prize before the federal district court of Connecticut. The prize claim, however, was but one of many suits which followed. The owner demanded the Africans as slaves, the Africans sued for their freedom, and the Van Buren Administration demanded return of the ship and its unwilling passengers to the Spanish authorities on the basis of a treaty with Spain which

---

[17] 15 PETERS 518 (1841). See also Anon., *The Amistad Case* (1968 reprinting); "Africans Taken on the Amistad," H. R. Exec. Doc. 185 (1840); Argument of John Quincy Adams before the Supreme Court (1841); and William A. Owens, *Black Mutiny* (Philadelphia, 1953).

provided for the surrender of pirates and stolen merchandise.

Presentation of the two questions accordingly gave the 1841 term of the Supreme Court critically important historical aspects, not quite in Story's anticipation of a Whig renewal, but, rather, on the internal and external aspects of the American dilemma. Indeed, it was indicative of a certain dramatic character that the two cases provided the closing reports in Mr. Peters' volume for that year.

Penultimate was the Mississippi importation ban, where the report showed Justice Smith Thompson speaking for a majority of the Court in an opinion which avoided (some would say dodged) the basic constitutional issue. He upheld the notes on the ground that the ban was nugatory without further legislation. Justice McLean, concurring, nonetheless added a dictum that the commerce clause did not prevent state action of the type in question, and his comment in turn sparked an array of advisory views from his colleagues on the two points of issue. The range of their hypothesis somewhat obscured the fact that Justice Story joined McKinley in coming to grips with the root issues and dissented on the ground that the notes were utterly void.

Story drove the implications of his dissent home in a letter to Senator Robert J. Walker of Mississippi when he insisted that his position meant that Mississippi's importation prohibition was consistent with the commerce clause of the Constitution, "especially as interpreted in the late decisions of the Supreme Court."[18] He did not go into detail, but the legitimacy of local police arrangements impeding that commerce had already been validated (over his dissent, to be sure) at the Great Term of 1837. But whatever his views otherwise on the preemptive sway of specific national authority, his concept of state superiority in this case drew on the nature of slavery and on the keystone point he had made in the opinion he wrote for the Court in the case of the African captives.

For in the opinion which closed out the 1841 reports Story

[18] Letter to Robert J. Walker, May 22, 1841, in Manuscript Collections, The New York Historical Society, New York, N.Y.

stripped John Quincy Adams' eight-hour argument on behalf of the Africans ("extraordinary . . . for its power, for its bitter sarcasm"[19]) to the bare legal bones. Speaking for the Court, he analyzed the Spanish–American treaty, found that its linguistic ambiguities must be construed on the side of freedom "where human life and human liberty are in issue"[20] and, accordingly, decreed that the Africans were neither murderers nor pirates nor merchandise, but, rather, freemen who gained their inalienable rights by legitimate self-help and who should be liberated forthwith.[21] It was not one of his better efforts, but what his subdued reasoning lacked in rhetoric it made up in securing support within the Court. Nat Turner had made revolts for freedom, irrespective of the status of the rebels, an unpopular subject at home. Moreover, British refusals to return to their owners slaves shipwrecked in the newly emancipated West Indies made extended discussion of international affairs equally unnecessary and undesirable. Thus, within the area permitted for legal and constitutional maneuver, Story had made a noble effort to achieve the double compaction of slavery. It was not enough, and a bitter test lay ahead.

SLAVERY: THE AMERICAN FUGITIVE

Even if the unquestioned juridical status of the African captives had been that of slaves, as long as they were foreign slaves (and in the absence of a specific treaty obligation) they could have made a formidable legal argument for their freedom and for a full-dress trial in obtaining it. This was not the situation in the case of an assertedly American fugitive slave who, when tried in that status, had fewer rights than an accused criminal. For the criminal could be removed from his state of refuge only upon executive demand supported by due judicial proof, but under the

[19] Letter to Mrs. Story, Feb. 28, 1841, in W. W. Story, II, 348.
[20] 15 PETERS at 596.
[21] Some of the captives were taken back to Africa by a New England religious group, and the leader of the rebels ultimately became a participant in the slave trade. See, generally, Owens, *Black Mutiny* (1968).

federal Fugitive Slave Act of 1793 an owner or his agent might retake an alleged fugitive slave by *force majeure* and then effect removal from the state of refuge pursuant to a certificate granted by a state or federal magistrate upon *ex parte* testimony.

When young Joseph Story was a student at Harvard, well into the nineteenth century, the New England papers routinely printed descriptions of runaways, and state officers routinely participated in their recapture and return. The rising tide of anti-slavery sentiment gradually constricted such cooperation, and assistance was replaced with "personal liberty" laws providing that no one might be removed from the state without a certificate of a state magistrate and frequently conditioning the critical finding of fact upon a jury trial.

It was just one year after the cases of the Mississippi importation ban and the African captives that the collision of one of these state statutes and the federal Fugitive Slave Act presented Story the bitterest decision of his entire career. It came in *Prigg v. Pennsylvania*,[22] a controversy which arose when the agent of a Maryland slaveowner seized a fugitive slave woman together with her child and removed them from Pennsylvania without obtaining the state certificate which the statute of the latter state required in such cases. The agent was indicted for kidnapping in Pennsylvania, and was convicted. His subsequent appeal to the Supreme Court drew into issue the constitutionality of all such state laws and secondarily (for the point was not specifically briefed and argued) the legitimacy of the federal law as well.

Indeed, it was on the latter point that the Northern polemicists concentrated their heaviest constitutional fire. One line of attack insisted that both the basic constitutional provision and its statutory implementation were in conflict with other portions of the Constitution, particularly the jury-trial requirements of the Sixth Amendment. Even more radical and arresting was the argument that since neither the word "slave" nor "slavery" was used in the Constitution, fugitive slaves—whatever their ancestors' obligations

[22] *Prigg v. Pennsylvania*, 16 PETERS at 539 (1842).

may have been—were not "persons held to service" within the meaning of the constitutional text.

In resolving the case on behalf of a majority of the Court, Story placed the thrust of his analysis on his construction of concurrent powers. Forsaking the latitudinarianism he had shown in the Mississippi import case, he reverted to his basic view of national preemption and struck down all state legislation, friendly or hostile, which bore on the subject.

He wrote with awareness of the momentous issues involved ("Few questions which have ever come before this Court involve more delicate or more important considerations"[23]) and then passed to his threshold premise—that the fugitive-slave provision of the Constitution was "a fundamental article, without the adoption of which the Union could not have been formed."[24] To this was annexed, as a middle term, a proposition he had earlier announced in a different context, to the effect that not only was the Fugitive Slave Act valid but Congress *had* to enact it lest the constitutional covenant become "a delusive and empty annunciation."[25] And this brought him his final point, that any state legislation on the subject by its very existence added to, and thereby impeded, the plenary federal power.

To be sure, there were a few embellishments. There was a learned citation of Blackstone on recapture. For Northern readers there was a characterization of slavery as a "mere municipal regulation, founded on and limited to the range of territorial laws."[26] For the Southern point of view there was an assurance that the opinion did not prohibit fugitive-slave patrols or the imprisonment of suspected runaways. But the upshot of his judgment was the ouster of all state involvement from the recapture process, save only for the attestation of a state magistrate as provided under the federal act, and this, Story held, might be forbidden by the individual states.

23 *Ibid.*, 610.
24 *Ibid.*, 611.
25 *Ibid.*, 614.
26 *Ibid.*, 611.

While Chief Justice Taney and Justice Daniel protested the decision as virtually disabling the operation of the federal law in view of the small number of available federal officials, other Southern reaction was approbatory, particularly of the recognition of the historical origin of the recapture provision.[27] But this very point, historical exegesis, excited strong Northern criticism.

> Story delivered this opinion . . . disregarding all other rules of interpretation, and resorting to history to make the clause apply to slaves. And yet no judge has ever scouted more contemptuously than Story the idea of going out of the words of law or the constitution, and being governed by what history may say were the intents of the authors.[28]

Far more bitter was condemnation which was based on moral grounds: "The enormity of this decision . . . cannot be exhibited in words. . . . *It is not law*. . . . It is to be spit upon, hooted at, trampled in the dust resolutely and openly."[29]

There was no question but that Story was deeply wounded by criticism of the latter type. In a somewhat self-commiserating mood, he recalled his *La Jeune Eugénie* opinion as he wrote an old friend that he had always been opposed to slavery, but "I take my standard . . . *as a Judge* from the Constitution."[30] On a more spirited note, he thundered from his Harvard classroom at the "madmen" who would pull down the house of Union to exorcise its defects.

Doubtless part of his sensitivity grew out of developments in the famous Latimer recapture, which occurred that very fall in the streets of Boston and which subsequently occasioned a tumultous meeting in Faneuil Hall. Latimer, a fugitive slave, was

---

[27] See, e.g., Cobb, *The Law of Negro Slavery* (Philadelphia and Savannah, 1858) and Alexander H. Stephens, *The Reviewers Reviewed* (New York, 1872), 132.

[28] Lysander Spooner, *The Unconstitutionality of Slavery* (New York, 1967, reprint of 1860 edition), 283.

[29] *The Liberator*, Mar. 11, 1842, quoted in Garrison, III (1889), 59.

[30] Letter to Ezekiel Bacon, Nov. 19, 1842, in W. W. Story, II, 431.

taken by the agents of his ex-master and lodged in the city jail. He remained there when the Chief Justice of the Massachusetts Supreme Court, on the strength of Story's *Prigg* opinion, refused to allow him a writ of habeas corpus. Probably it was only the *de facto* ransom of the prisoner by the abolitionists which forestalled a removal proceeding in Story's circuit court, and indeed the frequency of such occurrence was underscored shortly thereafter when Massachusetts forbade all its officers, from Chief Justice to jailer, to participate in recapture proceedings.[31]

And perhaps it was a similar concern over his own juridical involvement during his days as a United States commissioner which made Story's son take almost twenty pages of *The Life and Letters of Joseph Story*[32] to enter an extended defense of the *Prigg* decision—that it nullified the Fugitive Slave Act, that this consequence made the opinion a "charter of freedom," which gave the free states a voice in a uniform recapture process, and that, moreover, the jury issue was still open.

Yet a complete appraisal as to whether *Prigg* had this effect must be sought not so much in the views of the judge as in those of his judges. A most severe censure came from Wendell Phillips, his former student, who gave an appraisal a year after Story's death and it was not *nil nisi bonum:*

> No oath of office, no obligations to the constitution of the United States can excuse an outrage on justice and humanity. . . . The course of a Judge, no matter how pure his private character, no matter how high his fame as a jurist, who helps a master to regain his slave shall, whether he is alive or dead, be branded as infamous so far as my voice and pen can effect it.[33]

---

[31] See, generally, Leonard Levy, *The Law of the Commonwealth and Chief Justice Shaw* (1957), 78-85.
[32] See W. W. Story, II, 381-98.
[33] *The Liberator,* Sept. 11, 1846, quoted in Sherwin, *Prophet of Liberty* (1958), 749.

CHAPTER XXXII

The 34th Section

THE UNIQUE DISTINCTION

Story achieved two posthumous distinctions in 1938. In that year Congress passed the Chandler Act and thereby finally vindicated his vision of a comprehensive bankruptcy system. In that year also, his own Court accorded him a different type of recognition by adjudging him its only member to write an unconstitutional opinion in a leading constitutional case.[1] The almost incredible distinction was underscored by being given to one whose threefold accomplishment as justice, writer, and teacher made him regarded—from Commager to Cooley, from de Tocqueville to Lord Bryce—as the paramount authority on the Constitution in general and on the constitutional bounds of the national judicial power in particular.

It must also be stressed that Story does not hold his adjudicated distinction merely because he was subsequently overruled on a point of constitutional law. On the contrary, Story himself—by

---

[1] *Erie R. R. v. Tompkins*, 304 U.S. at 64 (1938). The circumstances of the opinion are set out in Mason, *Harlan Fiske Stone* (1956), 478-81. Justice Butler dissented. Justice Reed, concurring, held in effect that Story did not write an unconstitutional opinion but merely misconstrued a statute. Prof. Philip Kurland suggests that this concurrence "may yet prove to be his most important opinion" (Kurland, "Mr. Justice Frankfurter, the Supreme Court, and the Erie Doctrine in Diversity Cases," *Yale Law Journal*, LXVII [1957], 190).

singular irony, in his unconstitutional opinion of *Swift v. Tyson*[2] emphasized that in the very necessity of the case judicial opinions must be "re-examined, reversed, and qualified . . . whenever found to be either defective, or ill-founded, or incorrect."[3]

His salutary rule of correction has an especial pertinence for opinions construing a Constitution which, in Chief Justice Marshall's words, is intended to endure for ages and consequently to be adapted to various crises in human affairs. To repeat, Story's distinction did not arise from being reversed in the ongoing application of the judicial power or the United States; rather, it attached because he was adjudged to have egregiously misconceived the scope and sanction of that power itself.

Story's unconstitutional opinion was based upon his construction of Section 34 of the Judiciary Act of 1789, which provided the rules of decision for the federal courts in trials at common law. However, it was cut from the same cloth as his great opinion in *Martin v. Hunter's Lessee* construing Section 25 of that very act. Indeed, there was a remarkable conplementarity between the two opinions. One came at the beginning of Story's judicial career, one at the end. One announced the judicial superintendence of the Supreme Court, as a *national* tribunal, over matters of fundamental public law; the other provided the same role in the area of private law. Both drew on knowledge of the history and juristic background of the constitutional text, a firsthand examination of available sources, and an acquaintance with the generation that had written both the Constitution and the Judiciary Act. Both also presupposed a transcendental natural law, ascertainable by reason and verifiable by experience. Both were also part and parcel of the larger lifetime effort by which Story had sought to expand the national judicial power to what he saw as its full constitutional dimension—his towering admiralty opinion in *De Lovio v. Boit*, his lifetime quest for a bankruptcy statute, and his tireless if unsuccessful effort to secure a common-law criminal jurisdiction.

[2] 16 PETERS 1 (1842).
[3] *Ibid.*, at 18.

Another component of his lifetime of effort was an ongoing construction of Section 34 which, as originally drawn, provided: "The laws of the several states, except where the constitution, treaties, or statutes of the United States shall otherwise require or provide, shall be regarded as rules of decision in trials at common law in the courts of the United States in cases where they apply."[4] Here was posed a problem of interdependent variables, for the very "laws of the several States" which the federal courts were commanded to follow depended in part upon a definition of, and in part supplied the definition to, "the cases where [such laws] apply." The latter phrase was, of course, the important one, and its exegesis had stretched out across Story's entire judicial career. Paradoxically, the capstone of this effort came in 1842 when Story took up the opening lines and in *Swift v. Tyson* held that the word "laws" did not include state court decisions. These, he insisted, were not laws but merely evidence of what the law was, and, were, moreover, subject to frequent and pervasive revision. For this reason and as a consequence of his separate and more fundamental conclusion that the cases where state decisions—*or* state statutes—did not apply included the instruments and incidents of interstate or foreign commerce, he declared that federal courts must be guided by their own decisional logic in pronouncing an American commercial law.

THE ROOTS

Swift v. Tyson had far more to it than facilitating trade—even though when conjoined to *Letson* its potential for corporate development was formidable—or even bringing the judicial dispensation of the Constitution to a full dimension. Rather, it was part of an Enlightenment view of perfectibility in which the concerns of commerce and the manipulative techniques of the law were seen as the humble building materials for a soaring edifice. Story had sketched its outline almost twenty years earlier: "What a magnificent spectacle will it be, to witness the establishment of

[4] *United States Statutes at Large,* I, 92 (1789).

such a beautiful system of juridical ethics . . . the universal empire of juridical reason, mingling with the . . . concerns of commerce throughout the world."[5]

Unfortunately his vision did not come to pass. While some state courts were inclined to follow the federal lead on points of commercial law, others persisted in their ways to the result that American law was indeed a hydra-headed creature. Moreover, within the Supreme Court itself, a dissenting concern mounted that the failure to heed state decisions in common-law trials was, in effect, a rationalization for a self-aggrandizement of the federal judiciary. And, finally, just as in the area of constitutional jurisprudence, the division between national and local in private law involved dynamics rather than equilibrium, with the consequence that federal domination of the instruments of commerce ran on to an ever-increasing localization. There was another element at work also—an increasing skepticism as to the values and outlook of the Enlightenment.

While this philosophical and ethical demarche was the basic component of the Supreme Court's 1938 reversal of Story, two parallel premises obscured its significance. One premise was pragmatic—that since *Swift v. Tyson* had not ended the anomaly of state and federal courts sitting on opposite sides of the street and pronouncing different views of law on the same common-law controversy, the desired uniformity might be had by forcing the federal tribunal to follow the state rule, good, bad, or indifferent. A second was historical—that a textual analysis by "a competent scholar" of the proposed and enacted versions of Section 34 showed that Story had mistakenly read "laws" as excluding judicial precedents.[6] At the root, however, largely concealed by this overlay but most important of all, the decision was cosmological

---

[5] "The Progress of Jurisprudence," in *Miscellaneous Writings*, 215.
[6] The Court adopted the view of Warren, "New Light on the Federal Judiciary Act of 1789," *Harvard Law Review*, XXXVII (1923), 49, that this was the significance of changing "The Statute law of the several States in force for the time being and their unwritten and common law now in use" to "the laws of the several states . . ."

and even theological, involving a view of man and the universe which ran all the way back to *Antigone* and Plato's *Republic*. And on this line of encounter *Erie Railroad* marks a critical point of inflexion of that movement of the law which Professor Paul Freund describes as away from idealism in metaphysics and the categorical imperative in morals toward pragmatism and utilitarianism.

While one of Story's most formidable defenders, Professor William Crosskey, has insisted that *Swift v. Tyson* did not involve an exercise in "juristic metaphysics," the contrary views of both supporters and opponents is singularly persuasive as to both *Swift* and, by consequence, *Erie*.[7] For, unquestionably, the lawyers who wrote Article III of the Constitution and the Judiciary Act of 1789 no more doubted the objectivity of "the true law" than they did the fact of their own existence, and their attitude is epitomized by a passage from James Wilson, constitutional draftsman and charter member of the Supreme Court: "Order, proportion, and fitness pervade the universe. Around us, we see; within us, we feel; above us, we admire a rule, from which a deviation cannot, or should not, or will not be made."[8]

Indeed, in denouncing the *Prigg* opinion, William Lloyd Garrison had put the point admirably: *"It is not law."*[9] And this is precisely what Story declared in *Swift v. Tyson*. It was his great successors in title to the scholar's seat on the Supreme Court who suggested the basis of this point of view and of its logical contrary. Thus, Justice Cardozo summed up Story's constitutional position as presupposing that "the law declared by courts "had a Platonic or ideal existence before the act of declaration."[10] Justice Holmes vigorously expressed the opposite point of view as he assailed the concept of a "mystic overlaw,"[11] insisted that the

7 Crosskey, II, 858; see also 856-60 and 912-19.
8 "Of the General Principles of Law and Obligation," in James Wilson, *Works*, ed. Andrews (2v., Chicago, 1896), I, 49.
9 See, *supra*, page 401.
10 *Great Northern R. Co. v. Sunburst Oil Co.*, 287 U.S. at 365 (1932).
11 *United States v. Thompson*, 257 U.S. at 432 (1921).

common law was the identifiable voice of a sovereignty and not a "brooding omniscience in the sky,"[12] and asserted in dissent a proposition that was adopted as ruling law in *Erie Railroad:* that there is no such thing as "a transcendental body of law outside any particular State but obligatory within it."[13] And Justice Frankfurter summed it all up: that *Erie Railroad* "did not merely overrule a venerable case, it overruled a particular way of looking at the law."[14]

There are some other circumstances relevant to the *Erie* decision. One, noted by Dean Shulman of the Yale Law School, was that the case did offer some judicial concession to state power at a time when the Supreme Court was otherwise validating unprecedented expansion of federal authority and function. And in this respect it is surely not without significance that a leading apologia for the *Erie* opinion used the idiom of John C. Calhoun and the compact theory of the Constitution to summarize its thrust —"that the federal courts defer to the states on matters outside the states' grant of power to the nation."[15] Yet one need not adopt the idiom or viewpoint of Calhoun to admit that the expansive dynamics of Story's nationalist–natural-law jurisdiction had been badly overextended and was due for some salutary pruning. Indeed, most significant of all was the fact that *Erie* was itself part of a larger process of a cleansing reaction to the excesses of a natural-law jurisprudence which had imposed a paralyzing overlay on legal thought generally and whose constitutional aspect had persistently forestalled the national power itself in efforts toward economic and social reform.

Ironically, however, the very act of stripping the ultranaturalist overlay from constitutional jurisprudence freed *Swift v. Tyson* to rule American private law from its grave by filling the inter-

---

[12] *Southern Pacific v. Jensen,* 244 U.S. at 222 (1917).
[13] *Black and White Taxicab and Transfer Co. v. Brown and Yellow Taxicab and Transfer Co.,* 276 U.S. at 533 (1928).
[14] *Guaranty Trust v. York,* 326 U.S. at 101 (1945).
[15] Friendly, "In Praise of *Erie*—and of the New Federal Common Law," *New York University Law Review,* XXXIX (1964), 384.

stices—or building on the base—of the great organic statutes ranging from securities markets to labor relations. The formal premises of that rule are another matter, and this even though the tripod base of *Erie* has become badly eroded with the passage of time. As with *Swift v. Tyson* before it, there continues the anomaly of state and federal courts on the same street reaching different judgments on the same facts. Indeed, the anomaly is now compounded, for federal litigants are denied the elementary common-law process of reexamination and reform of precedents. Thus, the federal courts struggle to apply early-nineteenth-century decisions to twentieth-century facts while the state tribunals are free, in Story's words, to reexamine, reverse, and qualify anachronistic precedents. Yet the persistence of the discrepancy at least suggests that (1) an unfounded assumption underlay both *Swift* and *Erie*, that conflict between state and national law is critically related to the federal rule of decision, and (2) an equally valid hypothesis might propose this situation as the ineluctable consequence of a federal system.

And so with the two other formal premises from which *Erie* proceeded. On the historical front, it now seems conceded that the textual exegesis of the various drafts of Section 34 "confirm Story's interpretation more than . . . refute it."[16] The view of the nature of the law is undergoing change. In part it is due to a reexamination of the circumstance—whether metaphysical fact or psychological necessity—that law is something more than the coercion of a sovereignty and, whether viewed as pure act or as brooding omniscience, must exert its own claim to miracle, mystery, and authority.

And, finally, to use a phrase all lawyers and many laymen intuitively comprehend, Story was superbly "right on the law." Certainly this was the inescapable conclusion of those draftsmen who wrote his view into the Uniform Commercial Code. And, likewise, it might be argued that it was also the conclusion of Charles Dickens.

[16] *Ibid.*, 389.

MR. MICAWBER'S I.O.U.

How often the dedicated reformer, loving humanity in the abstract, is utterly friendless, neurotic, and insecure in all individual relationships, and, conversely, how frequently the political conservative, or even the political reactionary, nonetheless remains "simple and authentic, gregarious and humane, generous and affectionate."[17] This was Story, whose warmth, humor and compassion made him particularly fond of Dickens; and while his testimonial to the author sits curiously with his basic social and political attitudes, there is no questioning its enthusiastic sincerity:

> . . . what interests me most is the strong sympathy which he everywhere exhibits for the poor, the forlorn, and the wretched; and his stern contrasts between the cold selfishness and indifference of the rich, and of the so-called philosophic guardians of paupers, dressed in brief authority, and the humble virtues of the humblest race of laborers.[18]

Unfortunately he never lived to read much of Dickens' work. One wonders how he would have responded to *Bleak House*. Certainly he would have loved *David Copperfield*, not only for itself but also for the delightful way it put the point which came before him for decision in *Swift v. Tyson*. The facts of the two episodes were profoundly different, as were much of the legal technicalities; nonetheless, the core issue was the same: Did a preexisting debt constitute "value"? Or, to put the point another way: Can promising what one is already bound to do serve as a foundation for a subsequent, separate, and legally enforceable commitment?

Dickens sketched the issue in describing the reluctance of Mr. Micawber to depart from London while still owing money and how that impecunious man brilliantly resolved his problem:

[17] Commager, "Joseph Story," in *Gaspar Bacon Lectures* (1953), 93.
[18] Letter to Mrs. Story, Feb. 13, 1845, in W. W. Story, II, 517.

"To leave this metropolis," said Mr. Micawber, "and my friend, Mr. Thomas Traddles, without acquitting myself of the pecuniary part of this obligation, would weigh upon my mind to an insupportable extent. I have, therefore, prepared for my friend Mr. Thomas Traddles, and I now hold in my hand, a document, which accomplishes the desired object. I beg to hand to my friend Mr. Thomas Traddles my I.O.U. for forty-one, ten, eleven and a half, and I am happy to recover my moral dignity, and to know that I can once more walk erect before my fellow man!"

With this introduction (which greatly affected him), Mr. Micawber placed his I.O.U. in the hands of Traddles, and said he wished him well in every relation of life. I am persuaded, not only that this was quite the same to Mr. Micawber as paying the money, but that Traddles himself hardly knew the difference until he had had time to think about it.[19]

While there was no doubt in Mr. Micawber's mind that "value" had been given—particularly, *mutatis mutandis*, in the case of negotiation of a note or draft—courts had split on the point. Thus, in 1844 the latest decision of New York appeared in the negative,[20] while other tribunals were supportive. However, the difficulty in discerning a transcendentally valid rule cast no doubt on the assumption that one existed, as the very language which Chancellor Kent used on a similarly obscure point plainly indicated—"a little difficult to know what is the true rule of the law merchant in the United States."[21]

But it also must be emphasized that "the true rule" did not suggest itself by inner enlightenment, but was revealed through the experimental processes of commercial practice. And as Story had suggested in *Commentaries on the Conflict of Laws* in a juridical application of Adam Smith's invisible hand, any nation which refused to accommodate the principles underlying general com-

[19] Charles Dickens, *David Copperfield* (Universal Library edition), 537.
[20] *Coddington v. Bay*, 20 JOHNSON 637 (1822).
[21] Kent, *Commentaries on American Law*, III (1828), 64.

mercial practice would be penalized by having its trading business reduced to the state of that of a savage tribe.

It was this very flexibility in applying the lessons of experience which led Story to insist that decisions were but evidence of a more fundamental law and accordingly should be subject to an ongoing plasticity. Hence, on the question of whether a preexisting debt was "value," he omitted legal citations and drew on his own experience as judge and bank president as well as his knowledge of general business practices to suggest why an affirmative answer was in order:

> [W]hy upon principle should not a pre-existing debt be deemed such a valuable consideration? It is for the benefit and convenience of the commercial world, to give as wide an extent as practicable to the credit and circulation of negotiable paper, that it may pass not only as security for new purchases and advances made upon the transfer thereof, but also in payment of and as security for pre-existing debts. The creditor is thereby enabled to realize or to secure his debt, and thus may safely give a prolonged credit, or forbear from taking any legal steps to enforce his rights. The debtor also has the advantage of making his negotiable securities of equivalent value to cash. But to establish the opposite conclusion, that negotiable paper cannot be applied in payment of or as security for pre-existing debts, without letting in . . . equities between the original and antecedent parties, and the value and circulation of such securities must be essentially diminished, and the debtor driven to the embarrassment of making a sale thereof, often at a ruinous discount, to some third person, and then by circuity to apply the proceeds to the payment of his debts.[22]

But this was only half the issue. Even more basic was the point whether the New York decision, right or wrong, was required to be followed by Section 34. And on this point Story had returned

---

[22] 16 PETERS at 20. Unquestionably, these considerations resulted in the "value" rule of *Swift v. Tyson* being codified in Sections 25 of the Negotiable Instruments Act and 3-303 (b) of the Uniform Commercial Code.

an answer thirty years before, during his first term on the Supreme Court and his first swing around circuit. In fact he laid the cornerstone of *Swift v. Tyson* in his first Supreme Court opinion on *United States v. Crosby*[23] wherein he insisted that local law, and local law alone, could determine title to real estate. But there was a corollary to this and he also gave it early. In almost the first opinion he wrote on circuit, he read Section 34 to the effect that "the laws of the states are to be regarded only as rules of decision, and not as exclusive or peremptory injunctions."[24] And, more important, he read it as having no application where "the subject matter of the suit is extraterritorial."[25]

And thus through three decades on the Court, he gradually developed the rule of allocation which he announced in *Swift v. Tyson* as the "true" interpretation of Section 34, limiting its application:

to state laws strictly local, that is to say, to the positive statutes of the state, and the construction thereof . . . adopted by the local tribunals, and to rights and titles to real estate, and other matters immovable and intraterritorial in their nature and character. It never has been supposed (by the Supreme Court) that the section did apply . . . to questions of a more general nature . . . especially to questions of general commercial law. . . . The law respecting negotiable instruments may be truly declared in the language of Cicero, adopted by Lord Mansfield . . . to be in great measure, not the law of a single country only, but of the commercial world. *Non erit alia lex Romae, alia Athenis, alia nunc, alia posthac, set et apud omnes gentes, et omni tempore, una cademque lex obtenibit.*[26]

23 7 CRANCH 115 (1812).
24 *Van Reimsdyck v. Kane*, 28 FED. CASES at 1062 (1812).
25 *Ibid.*, at 1065.
26 16 PETERS at 18-19. See also, e.g., *United States v. Hoar*, 26 FED. CASES 329 (1821); *Halsey v. Fairbanks*, 11 FED. CASES 295 (1826); *Cook v. Hammond*, 6 FED. CASES 399 (1827); *Wallace v. Agry*, 29 FED. CASES 67 (1827); *Donnell v. Columbian Insurance Co.*, 7 FED. CASES 889 (1836); *Robinson v. The Commonwealth Ins. Co.*, 20 FED. CASES 1002 (1838); *Williams v. The Suffolk Ins. Co.*, 29 FED. CASES 1402 (1838).

And equally important is the fact that *Swift v. Tyson* was the constitutional judgment of a unanimous Court. To be sure, Justice Catron grumbled at never having heard the point on transfer by way of pledge before the preceding evening, but his concurrence only underscored the basic agreement which Story's Jacksonian colleagues gave his views. For in the endorsement of federal jurisdiction over general commercial law, the members of the Taney Court were really confirming their obligation to what the idiom of their age still occasionally called *"jus gentium,"* or "private international law," a field of law they were constitutionally bound to declare and enforce.[27]

Significantly, a Jacksonian suggestion to clip the wings of the federal courts was phrased in terms of limiting jurisdiction "to matters arising out of the Constitution and the law merchant."[28] Again it was Justice Thompson, always a strong states'-rights man, who sent *Swift v. Tyson* up from his circuit court by disagreeing with the district judge who had held the state decision controlling. But the most significant vindication of Story's views and vision came ten years after his death when the most fundamentalist of Story's states'-rights colleagues, Justice Daniel, refused in *Watson v. Tarpley*[29] to enforce a Mississippi statute which forbade action on bills of exchange until after maturity and thereby precluded suit upon dishonor by nonacceptance. Story had greeted Daniel's appointment to the Court with a demeaning comment— truly rare for him—on his new associate's capacity, but he could well have reconsidered his comment had he witnessed Daniel's rigorous application of *Swift v. Tyson* in striking down "a violation of the general commercial law, which a state [had] no power to impose, and which the courts of the United States [were] bound to disregard."[30]

---

[27] See Crosskey, I, 563-77, and II, 859-62.
[28] Letter from Worden Pope to Andrew Jackson, Dec. 25, 1829, in Warren, *Supreme Court*, II, 177-78.
[29] 18 HOWARD 517 (1855).
[30] *Ibid.*, 521. Mr. John P. Frank said Justice Daniel would have anticipated *Erie Railroad* "if he had thought of it." (Frank, *Justice Daniel Dissenting* [1964], 169.)

A PHILADELPHIA LEGACY

Section 34 is currently Section 1652 of Title 28 of the United States Code. It now makes the laws of the several states the rules of decision in "civil actions" instead of the former phrasing, "in trials at common law," and thereby includes trials in equity. As such it both honors and affronts Story's memory. It is a measure of Story's accomplishment as the father of American equity that the nationwide adoption of equity has permitted the union with law in the text of the statute. It is a measure of how much his influence has faded that the standard of reference for equity is now whatever precedent, good, bad, or indifferent, may seem territorially available, rather than the ongoing, self-correcting systematic and comprehensive body of transcendent law which he—and the Congress which first wrote the Judiciary Act—contemplated. For Section 34 contained no directions on what the federal courts should regard as their rules of decision in equity proceedings. On the contrary, the Judiciary Act merely reflected the self-evident fact that "there is, or at least seems to be, under the Constitution of the United States, an inherent difficulty in separating the supreme jurisdiction at law from that in equity."[31] This meant that the "local exception" which Story had permitted in *Swift v. Tyson* had no allowance in the latter field: ". . . the equity jurisdiction of this court is wholly independent of the local laws of any state, and is the same . . . in all the states . . . it is the same in its nature and extent, as the equity jurisdiction of England, from which ours is derived, and is governed by the same principles."[32]

This circumstance also featured in the argument in *Swift v. Tyson,* as the counsel who sought to have the New York opinion rule the decision realized the implications the law–equity distinction held for his case and reached out, lawyerlike, to meet it. His name was Richard Henry Dana, and he was already winning a distinction in the law to match what his authorship of *Two Years*

[31] Story, "Chancery Jurisdiction," in *Miscellaneous Writings,* 170-71.
[32] *Gordon v. Hobart,* 10 FED. CASES at 797 (1836).

Before the Mast had already won for him. A product of the Harvard Law School, he had gone into the law with reluctance, feeling it "hard, dry, uninteresting, uncertain, and slavish."[33] Story's lectures changed all that. "He combined, in a remarkable manner," Dana later recalled, ". . . the two great faculties of creating enthusiasm in study, and establishing relations of confidence and affection with his pupils. We felt that he was our father in the law, an elder brother, the patriarch of a common family. We felt as if we were . . . privileged to pursue the study of a great science. . . ."[34]

And Story must have been particularly pleased with the way his old student neither dodged nor blurred the issue but met it with spirited forthrightness. To be sure, it was making the best out of a bad cause, for there were some states which did not have a formal system of equity, and to one, Louisiana, it was utterly unknown in any historical sense. But the young attorney did say what could be said—that state courts without the formal system did frequently and indeed habitually apply equitable principles under the forms of the common law.

What he did not and could not say had been asserted by Story many years earlier, as a young legislator unsuccessfully trying to bring equity to Massachusetts:

> Courts of Equity, as contradistinguished from Courts of Law, have jurisdiction in cases, where the latter from their manner of proceeding, either cannot decide at all upon the subject, or cannot decide conformable with the principles of substantial justice. Whenever a *complete, certain,* and *adequate* remedy exists at law, Courts of Equity have generally no jurisdiction. Their peculiar province is to supply the defects of law in cases of *frauds, accidents, mistakes,* or *trusts.*[35]

[33] Dana, I, 37.
[34] Letter to W. W. Story, May 3, 1851, in W. W. Story, II, 319.
[35] Report to the General Court, Jan. 16, 1808, reprinted in *American Journal of Legal History*, XIV (1970), 78-79. I am indebted to Prof. Surrency for the discovery of this report.

And Story went on to list the specific instances where equity might intervene and compel a different result than that obtaining or obtainable under the common law—partners' and merchants' accounts, legacies, trusts, mortgages, dower, and partition. And, more to the point, litigants in later years proved his point by voting with their feet when, as inhabitants of states without equity, they took out-of-state residence so as to secure equitable relief under the diversity jurisdiction of the federal courts. Indeed, the most striking example grew out of liquidation of the Hollowell and Augusta Bank of Augusta, Maine: litigants who sought a common-law recovery in equityless Massachusetts were non-suited,[36] but those fortunate enough to sue in equity—on the same facts—in Story's circuit court had a complete recovery.[37]

Yet as Story also noted in his legislative report, "equity follows the law" and presupposed the existence of substantive legal rights which its ancient procedures would then enforce. This mixture of substance and procedure was strikingly illustrated by the great case of *Vidal v. Philadelphia*,[38] decided by the Supreme Court in 1844. The substantive issue, at the root, was whether Christianity formed part of the common law. The procedural one was whether equity might give effect to a trust with an imprecise bounty. The two seemingly diverse conditions were united in an attack by the passed-over French relatives of a Philadelphia philanthropist in seeking to recover a fortune left in trust for the establishment of a school. The residents of the school were designated as being poor, white orphans. One regulation of the school was that no minister of religion should so much as set foot therein. If the relatives could prove the trust void for vagueness or hostility to religion the money was theirs.

On the basis of the old law—and Justice Story as its expositor—they had encouraging reasons on both counts. On the first point the Supreme Court itself had spoken, and Story's had constituted

---

[36] *Spear v. Grant*, 16 MASS. 9 (1819).
[37] *Wood v. Dummer*, 30 FED. CASES 435 (1824); see Crosskey, II, 895-96.
[38] 2 HOWARD 127 (1844).

a concurring opinion, in the case of *Baptist Association v. Hart's Executors*[39] back in 1819 to the effect that without a statute—and none was involved in the will case—a trust could not be enforced where the beneficiaries were so imprecisely designated. On the second, Story had gone out of his way in his inaugural lecture at Harvard to insist that Christianity was part of the common law and to castigate Thomas Jefferson for suggesting the contrary.

Since 1819, however, researches into legal history had shown that, contrary to prior assumptions, English courts had not needed a statute to enforce trusts with imprecisely named beneficiaries. This aspect of the litigation together with the obvious emotional appeal of a thrust based on religion led counsel for the relatives to concentrate their fire on the "clergyman exclusion" provision of the trust. Story noted how argument assumed a semitheological aspect, and another observer said the entire proceeding sounded like a camp meeting without hymns, with Webster rivaling any preacher in America. And the conclusion certainly appeared to be justified on reports of Webster's homiletics: "[He said:] 'Suffer the little children to come unto me,' accenting the word children. He repeated it, accenting the word little. Then rolling his eyes heavenward and extending his arms, he repeated it thus: 'Suffer the little children to come unto *Me*, unto *Me*, unto *Me*, suffer the little children to come.' So he went on for three days."[40]

The sermon was in vain. Story wrote for a unanimous court and sustained the will. On the issue of preciseness of designation he went one better and included some early English citations upholding jurisdiction which he had discovered in his own research. The religious question was somewhat more difficult. Nonetheless,

[39] 4 WHEATON at 1 (1819). Story wrote a concurring opinion which was reprinted as a note on pp. 1-23 of the report. "I regret that your opinion was not delivered as that of the Court," wrote reporter Wheaton, "for I think the Chief Justice does not excel in those causes which require a minute investigation of the authorities." (Letter to Story, April 30, 1819, Wheaton Papers.) Story subsequently incorporated much of it into *Equity Jurisprudence* and claimed his authorship lest he "otherwise seem to have appropriated so large a portion of the labors of another." (Story, *Equity Jurisprudence*, 9th edition [1866], 360.)

[40] John Wentworth, quoted in Warren, *Supreme Court*, II, 130-31.

he nimbly wove round his earlier rhetoric, insisting that Christianity was indeed part of the common law but that this was a proposition "to be received with its appropriate qualifications."[41] He thus ultimately came to grips with the specific issue and held that the exclusion of clerics did not necessarily mean that the proposed school was antireligious. On the contrary he insisted that religious instruction could well be given by laymen as part of the provision which required the orphans to be taught the general principles of ethics and morality.

His legal logic was underlain by his Unitarian outlook whereby his growing political conservatism was accompanied by religious outlooks which ran quite the other way, in a decided liberal bent. Unquestionably it was given something of a fortification a year before when an English decision overturned a bequest on the grounds that Unitarians were not "pious and godly persons."[42] Moreover, at home he saw the current round of Know-Nothing church burning as another melancholy confirmation that predatory religious prejudice was the natural product of demogoguery and mob rule. These circumstances were, however, but the cumulation of a lifetime of experience and it left Story particularly insusceptible to Webster's preaching, as a friend's bantering note of many years before had foreshadowed:

> You are of the sect of Independents, who do not submit with a good grace to be catechized in any matters affecting the conscience. . . . I have discovered already that Unitarians are no better than Mohamatans and that in the attempt to reconcile some of the dogmas of the Christian scheme, they are exposing the scheme itself of the most mortal perils.[43]

And when Story wrote in the will contest opinion that religious instruction in the school might be given by laymen, he was

[41] 2 HOWARD at 198.
[42] See W. W. Story, II, 450-51.
[43] Letter from Samuel P. P. Fay, Feb. 17, 1828, Story Papers, Library of Congress.

but suggesting a particular application to his own example that the works of religion might be carried on without a special priesthood, or perhaps—as the dedication and application of his own life were proving—by a priesthood of all believers. In either event, his incredibly crowded schedule as judge, teacher, and writer always had a place for the works of the church, and this included both his local congregation and its national convocation. And thus it was particularly appropriate that within two months of the Philadelphia will contest he gave concrete proof that the work of the Lord belongs to all as he became the new president of the American Unitarian Association and its annual meeting on May 28, 1844, opened with "Hon. Joseph Story in the chair."[44]

[44] 19th Annual Report, American Unitarian Society (1844), 3.

CHAPTER XXXIII

The Westering

THE SEA OF TROUBLES

For all the disappointments that the Jacksonian and post-Jacksonian periods afforded, Story managed to live a full and satisfying life through them—or at least until the end of the 1842 term. From this point on, almost in the fashion of a Greek tragedy, a host of troubles began to converge upon him. The *Prigg* decision brought an unprecedented flood of Northern abuse upon his head and doubtless was one of the factors which led to the breaking of his health in the latter part of the year. As a consequence he missed a term of the Supreme Court for the first time in his third of a century of service, and in further consequence he underwent a shocking and painful affront from his colleagues. And this was only the beginning of still more painful circumstances—the burgeoning slave power, the rising democracy, the second winnowing of the hand of death on his Court, and an electoral triumph of the Democratic Party.

He fell ill in November of 1842. In addition to the *Prigg* turmoil, a lifetime of overwork was also a significant cause, and his persistent dedication was evident in a premature assumption of recovery and an abortive attempt to leave for the 1843 term. The resulting relapse struck him down until spring, and he used the enforced leisure to complete the third edition of his work on equity jurisprudence and to launch his eighth commentary, a work on bills of exchange. He dedicated it to his associate in the law school, Simon Greenleaf, but the act itself carried a haunting and prophetic note; Story stated that his original intent had been to dedicate the whole of his professional works to Greenleaf, but "advancing years admonish me, that the term of my life may not be so far prolonged, as to enable me to reach the full consummation of my purposes."[1] The reception was enthusiastic, although one review suggested a changing temperament in his reading public: "It has one fault, . . . common to his other works, which may however be excusable in a judge before whom the same questions may . . . arise. We mean the indeterminate mode in which most points are frequently discussed, throwing together the arguments and authorities, *pro* and *con,* and leaving the student's mind in a sad state of perplexity and unhappiness."[2]

His recovery stretched almost to summer, and at one point included the possibility of the therapy of a long sea voyage. Indeed, an erroneous report that he was to visit London caused a stir from the Inns of Court to Westminister Hall, and Edward Everett, the American minister to Britain, found himself "persecuted as a deluder"[3] when the *Britannia* arrived without the distinguished American jurist. The sea voyage turned out to be unnecessary, but Story's illness was none the less real, and indeed had been prolonged by a distressing incident involving the discharge of Richard Peters, his confidant, as reporter for the Supreme Court.

The incident had been building up for some time. Justices Catron and Baldwin regarded the reporter with hostility, and there was discontent among other members of the Court over the delay in publication of the reports. The upshort was dismissal at the beginning of the 1843 term, an action undertaken in the absence of Story and McKinley, and moreover carried by the mar-

---

[1] Story, *Commentaries on the Law of Bills of Exchange* (1843), *vii.*
[2] *American Law Magazine,* I (1843), 448.
[3] Letter from Edward Everett, May 18, 1843, in W. W. Story, II, 443.

gin of four justices to three. Time was when Story cast the critical vote in appointing the reporter. Now the office was filled without so much as a consultation. Story was crushed by the news, and Sumner wrote Justice McLean of his reaction: "I think that nothing has occurred at Washington which has affected his spirits so deeply. His sleep was destroyed the night after he received your letter."[4] Yet far more ominous was the uncharacteristic note of resigned passivity which followed: "But let it pass, I no longer ever expect to see revived the kind and frank courtesy of the old Court, and I am content to take things as they are."[5]

ALARMS AND EXCURSIONS

Story's sense of alienation was heightened upon his arrival in Washington for the 1844 term, for a vacant chair on the dais mutely testified to the passing of Justice Smith Thompson the preceding December. Shortly thereafter, early in 1845, came news of the death of former Justice Duvall, who had taken his seat the same day as Story and who had retired because of the infirmities of age in 1834. And then in April Justice Baldwin died, and Story commented on the news with characteristic benevolence: "Poor Baldwin is gone."[6]

His brief comment compressed personal sentiment with institutional concern, for he wrote Kent of a hope that Baldwin's succession would be "nobly . . . filled."[7] He also expressed the expectation that the hope would not be realized, and his growing despair over party and faction was borne out when the succession to Thompson became a bone of contention between the Democratic and Whig parties. Yet, however unseemly, the squabble manifested a concern which had been increasingly on his own

4 Charles Sumner to John McLean, Feb. 2, 1843, in Warren, *Supreme Court*, II, 107 n.1.
5 Letter to John McLean, Feb. 9, 1843, *ibid.*, 107.
6 Letter to James Kent, Apr. 25, 1844, *ibid.*, 116.
7 *Ibid.*

mind, and this was timing his own departure from the Court so that his successor might be chosen by a President who shared his outlook.

In fact he had been weighing this course of action four years before, only to have the unanticipated death of Harrison foreclose the possibility. Now what he foresaw as the "sure and certain election"[8] of Henry Clay appeared to reopen it. Quite apart from the question of his health—and he had developed a "constant dread"[9] of another breakdown—he saw nothing on the horizon to warrant his staying on the Court, and even the foreseen Whig victory did not afford reassurance of reversing powerful forces which were threatening to carry constitutional forms before them. The forces of slavery were poised to bring about what Story called the "grossly unconstitutional"[10] annexation of Texas. Mob rule showed its face in the growing Know-Nothing movement, and here Story commented that the only difference between riots in a despotism and in a republic was that the latter government lacked the apparatus of efficient repression.

And then in November came the cruelest cut of all—the defeat of Clay for the Presidency by James K. Polk. Story was "thunderstruck"[11] when he heard the news of Polk's nomination. He had turned to verse upon Mrs. Polk's previous departure from Washington and had disconsolately suggested that the separation of the Polks from the capital was permanent:

> *Lady, I heard with saddened heart*
> *The melancholy strain;*
> *So soon from these fair scenes to part*
> *Ne'er to return again.*[12]

[8] Letter to John McLean, Oct. 9, 1843 in Francis Weisenburger, *The Life of John McLean* (Columbus, O., 1937), 104.
[9] Letter to James Kent, Aug. 31, 1844, in W. W. Story, II, 469.
[10] Letter to Ezekiel Bacon, April 1, 1844, in W. W. Story, II, 481.
[11] Letter to John McLean, Aug. 16, 1844, in Eugene McCormac, *James K. Polk* (Berkeley, 1922), 246.
[12] Quoted in Charles G. Sellers, *James K. Polk, Jacksonian* (Princeton, 1957), 340.

While Story the poet may have been pleased, Story the politician was dismayed, by the turn of events which undid the cadenced prophecy. Undoubtedly the news contributed substantially to Story's sense of being "fatigued and exhausted" and was the critical factor in steeling his decision to leave the Court as he noted, "I have done my share of the work, and have earned my title to a little indulgence."[13]

And such was the load of writing, judging, and teaching that he actually looked forward to the grinding trip to Washington as an opportunity for thought and recollection. In part his sense of relaxation must have come from the thought that the trip would be the last of the long journeys south which had begun almost forty years before. The city and the country had changed so much in the four ensuing decades, and he had done his part in effecting the transformation. One factor appeared on the very calendar of the Court, for the ever-mounting volume and importance of its work had caused the opening day of the term to be advanced to the second Monday of December.

Certainly nothing he saw or heard in Washington suggested that the country was changing for the better. The election had made the annexation of Texas a foregone conclusion, and the expulsion of a Massachusetts representative looking into the patently unconstitutional Negro Seamen's Act deepened his gloom over the expansionist character of Southern slavery. He was also depressed by the obvious national sympathy for the Dorr rebels, whose efforts to overturn Rhode Island's seemingly irreformable colonial charter caused him (in view of the "late alarming crisis of public affairs in Rhode Island"[14]) to instruct Newport's federal grand jury on treason vis-à-vis state and nation, and who in his view, as he wrote the local federal judge, were attempting "to involve your state in a civil war [and] to break down your form of republican government."[15]

[13] Letter to Richard Peters, Nov. 27, 1844, in W. W. Story, II, 484.
[14] 3 STORY'S REPORTS at 615 (1842).
[15] Letter to John Pitman, Jan. 14, 1845, in W. W. Story, II, 516.

And the business of the Court seemingly bore out the way things were going. In the case of *Fox v. Ohio*,[16] argued but not decided, a majority of his colleagues leaned to the proposition that notwithstanding the double-jeopardy provision of the Constitution and the long prohibition of the common and natural law, the nation and the state might still inflict successive punishments for the same single act. And in *Cary v. Curtis*, he broke into outright dissent over what he saw as a holding that Congress might "take from a citizen all right of action in any court to recover back money claimed illegally . . . by its officers."[17] A letter summed it all up:

> In every way which I look to the future, I can see little or no ground of hope for our country. We are rapidly on the decline. Corruption and profligacy, demagogism and recklessness characterize the times, and I for one am unable to see where the thing is to end. You, as a young man, should cling to hope, I, as an old man, know that it is all in vain.[18]

Yet things were not quite as bleak as he suggested, and he was undertaking not a surrender but, rather, a redeployment. The blade he had forged, the national judicial power, was in being. To be sure, it often went unused or, what was worse, misused. Nonetheless, it hung on the wall awaiting a future champion at some future day, and the Fabian nature of Story's judicial resignation could be inferred from a subsequent observation coming from another source: "If anything can *retard* (*stop it* you can not) the jacobinical torrent which is sweeping past and undermining the foundations of . . . our institutions, the barrier of sound law and conservative influences which the Harvard Law School is building up, will do it."[19]

---

[16] 5 HOWARD 410 (1847).
[17] 3 HOWARD at 253 (1845).
[18] Letter to Charles Sumner, Jan. 4, 1845, in W. W. Story, II, 519.
[19] Benjamin D. Silliman to Charles Sumner, June 29, 1846, in Handlin, 199-200.

THE UNFINISHED SCHEDULE

Story was a little more explicit in writing to his old friend Ezekiel Bacon. It was a singularly moving letter, because the two had corresponded excitedly almost a half century earlier in planning to achieve Story's accession to the Court. Now the subject was in precisely the opposite direction, and Story disclosed the dilemma which pulled him between respect for an institution and a concern for his own integrity:

New men and new opinions have succeeded. The doctrines of the Constitution . . . which in former times received the support of the whole Court, no longer maintain their ascendancy. I am the last member, now living, of the old Court, and I cannot consent to remain where I can no longer hope to see those doctrines recognized and enforced. For the future I must be in a dead minority of the Court, with the painful alternative of either expressing an open dissent . . . or, by my silence, seeming to acquiesce. . . . The former course would lead the public, as well as my breathren, to believe that I was determined . . . to diminish the just influence of the Court and might subject me to the imputation of being, from motives of mortified ambition, or political hostility, earnest to excite popular prejudices against the Court. The latter course would subject me to the opposite imputation of having either abandoned my old principles, or of having, in sluggish indolence, ceased to care what doctrines prevailed. Either alternative is equally disagreeable to me, and utterly repugnant to my past habits of life and to my present feelings.[20]

He resolved the dilemma in favor of leaving. He kept his plans to himself, save for a few confidants, for his friends had talked him out of resigning on previous occasions and he correctly anticipated a public outcry when the news was announced. Henry Clay, to whom he made an advance disclosure, was more understanding.

[20] Letter to Ezekiel Bacon, April 12, 1845, in W. W. Story, II, 528.

I am not surprized that the weighty, some of them painful motives, enumerated in your friendly letter of the 22nd ultimo, should prompt you to desire to retire from the bench of the S. Court, deeply as I, in common with many others, will lament that event. We shall regard the last remaining light of the truly august old Court as extinguished. Your friends would rejoice if you could reconcile it to your feelings to continue; but most certainly, after what you have said to me, the question should be left to your exclusive judgment.

I lament that there is nothing in the political prospects before us to encourage you to abide in your station. If indeed this Nation be resolved to cast away the blessings which encompass it, and to add another sad example to those which History records of the corruption & downfall of Republics, no organization of the Supreme Court, however enlightened, virtuous & patriotic its members might be, can avert the calamity.[21]

His initial schedule called for resignation at the end of the term, in early March, but a concern for a backlog of cases which had already been argued before his circuit court forced him to put off his severance until the end of summer. Accordingly, he worked away at opinion writing with the anticipation of a schoolboy about to be released on a holiday. Yet it was not idleness that he anticipated, but rather his full-time connection with the law school, which had replaced the Supreme Court as the citadel of his ideas.

Indeed, the despair saturating his letters to Sumner and Bacon was genuine enough at the moment, but it was also an index of his ability to throw himself completely into the concept or idea before him. Certainly little of it showed through on July 3 when the sixteenth anniversary of the reconstitution of the school under his aegis was celebrated, and Rufus Choate most appropriately spoke on "The Position and Functions of the American Bar, as an

[21] Letter from Henry Clay, Feb. 9, 1845, in Manuscript Collections, The Historical Society of Pennsylvania, Philadelphia.

Element of Conservatism in the State."[22] Story could have well written the key passage himself, for it epitomized why he had left the bench and come full time to Harvard: "it contributes, or ought to . . . contribute, more than all things else, or as much as anything else, to preserve our organic forms, our civil and social order, our public and private justice, our constitutions of government—even the Union itself."[23]

And along the latter line, preservation of the Union unquestionably played a part in Story's decision to elect full-time scholastic duty. Primary, of course, was his concern to lay the groundwork for institutional resistance to what he saw as corruption and demogoguery, but he also envisioned the law as a unifying national force. Indeed, concern for a diverse student body had prompted Greenleaf to write years before of "advertising our Law School in the *Southern* papers earlier in the season."[24] (To be sure, the reception was not all favorable; a Louisiana reviewer asked "[W]hat will the South become, if her young men are taught her laws in colleges, filled with professors averse to her institutions, and are taught to read her constitution by light thrown through the false prism of uncongenial minds?"[25])

And there was still much writing to do. He had already set the goal of turning out a legal *summa* on maritime and commercial law, and here he worked in the late spring of 1845 putting the finishing touches on his work on promissory notes. Still ahead was the tenth commentary—a masterwork on admiralty—and beyond that the one which Professor Commager says above all others we miss—his memoirs.

In an ironic climax to a life overflowing with achievement,

[22] *Addresses and Orations of Rufus Choate*, 8th edition (Boston, 1905), 133.
[23] *Ibid.*, 137-38.
[24] Simon Greenleaf to Joseph Story, Feb. 16, 1838, Story Papers, Library of Congress.
[25] "Story's Commentaries," *Southern Quarterly Review*, II (1842), 420. The anonymous reviewer also commented, "We do not know what connection, if any, exists between Dr. Story and his publisher, but the haste with which second editions of his writings have followed the first, indicates a disregard of the rights of *first purchasers* . . ."

Story failed his last assignments. He never wrote the tenth commentary or his memoirs. He never associated himself with the law school as a full-time teacher. He did not finish his circuit-court opinions. He did not even submit his resignation. Once before his overcrowded schedule had foreclosed more important business, when it kept him from the dying Marshall's side. Now the amount and complexity of his unfinished circuit-court work achieved the same result.

To be sure, he came close, and he had all his opinions written save one when he came down with what appeared to be a summer cold in early September. But the enormous energy had spent itself, and the powers of recuperation were gone. A violent stricture followed, probably a heart attack, which "baffled the highest medical skill,"[26] his condition worsened, and he died at 9 P.M. on September 10, 1845. It was eight days before his sixty-seventh birthday.

From one end of the country to the other appropriate proceedings mourned his loss and hailed his contributions. From around the world came tributes to his extraordinary genius. Chief Justice Taney, who in public proceedings hailed Story for both public and private virtue, reiterated his sentiments in private correspondence. ("What a loss the court has sustained in the death of Judge Story! It is irreparable, utterly irreparable in this generation; for there is nobody equal to him."[27]) There were a hundred other epitaphs, inadequate for all their floridity, and particularly inadequate were his own dying words: "If I were not thus ill, my letter of resignation would have been now on its way to Washington. I should have completed my judicial life."[28]

A JUDICIAL LIFE

Yet Story's judicial life did not end on September 10, 1845. His

[26] Greenleaf, "Memoir of Judge Joseph Story," *American Law Magazine*, VI (1846), 263.
[27] Roger B. Taney to Richard Peters, November, 1845, in Swisher, 442.
[28] W. W. Story, II, 547.

name and ideas continued in the reports in *Fox v. Ohio* when Justice McLean vainly dissented from the Court's constitutional validation of double punishment for a single act and found his only satisfaction in knowing "that the lamented Justice Story, when this case was discussed by the judges the last term that he attended the Supreme Court . . . coincided with the views here presented."[29] Story's judicial life and legacy, however, are far more than a posthumous appearance in sentimental dissent. Rather, his is truly the case of *Si monumentum requeris, circumspice*.

The world of the law hears his pervasive imprint, ranging from his *Commentaries on Equity Jurisprudence*, first published in Boston in 1836 and after many editions last published in London in 1920, to the *Commentaries on the Conflict of Laws*, whose passages were made the code of a foreign country and even a treaty, to the current English textbook whose opening lines matter-of-factly state: "A letter of credit, according to Story . . ."[30] His imprint is on the modern corporation; it is on the comprehensive and plenary bankruptcy law finally given effect by the Chandler Act of 1938. It is on his decision on "value" in *Swift v. Tyson* written into the Uniform Commercial Code which itself seeks to achieve the goal of *Swift v Tyson* in a national law of business.

Above all, however, there is his work in laying the juridical basis of the American nation-state which was first asserted in *Martin v. Hunter's Lessee* and whose minor premise Justice Holmes, at once his successor in title and great intellectual antagonist, summed up in doubting that the United States would come to an end if the Supreme Court could not invalidate congressional legislation but in being convinced that such a result would follow if a national superintendence were lost over state law.

But *Martin v. Hunter's Lessee* has a major premise—that the Union is older than the States. Elaborately restated in his *Commentaries on the Constitution*, his nationalist doctrine has been

29 5 HOWARD at 440 (1847).
30 Arthur G. Davis, *Letters of Credit* (London, 1954), 1.

repeated down through the years in both scholarly dissertation and state paper, but never more decisively than in Lincoln's war message of July 4, 1861, and now stands appraised as "a legal classic of timeless importance."[31] And within the nationalist framework he helped to build, his legal legacy, even when cast into seemingly obstructionist forms, effects a vital purpose in subserving the very democracy which he feared so much. For, as de Tocqueville observed, ". . . without this admixture of lawyerlike sobriety with the democratic principle, I question whether democratic institutions could long be maintained. . . ."[32]

Yet each man also leaves a personal as well as an intellectual legacy, and here all of Story's shortcomings—vanity, faith touched with doubt, hope darkened with despair, an ongoing apprehension of humanity en masse—never impaired his charity. He was as much distinguished, said the judge who trained him, "by his never-failing kindness as by his legal attainments,"[33] and in a personal democracy which persistently belied his political theorizing, this kindness was extended to family and stranger, to high and low. It appeared in his exemplary behavior as husband and father. ("[O]ur dear little boy is now almost nine months old . . . [I] picture him in your arms, dancing to my old favorite tune, or hallooing 'dad, dad, dad.' "[34]) It appeared in his kindness to a penniless immigrant seeking encyclopedia articles. ("The only condition this kind-hearted man made was that I should not publish the fact that he had contributed the articles until some period subsequent to their appearance."[35]) It appeared in his affability with coachmen, innkeepers, and his fellow passengers on the Boston–Cambridge omnibus. Most of all it appeared in the generous tolerance he granted those who challenged his own deeply felt

---

[31] "Representative Books Reflecting American Life and Thought," Library of Congress release (1960). See also Masters, *Lincoln the Man* (1931), and Wilson, *Patriotic Gore* (1962).

[32] De Tocqueville, I, 286.

[33] Samuel Putnam to W. W. Story, May 28, 1846, in W. W. Story, I, 85.

[34] Letter to Mrs. Story, March 12. 1812, in W. W. Story, I, 218.

[35] Lewis Harley, *Francis Lieber* (New York, 1889), 57.

views—to Harriet Martineau's praise of Jacksonian democracy, to Richard Henry Dana's criticism of his judicial administration of seamen's protective legislation, and to Charles Sumner's youthful pacifism.

And it was doubtless this recognition of a warm and generous heart which correspondingly caused those who deplored his failure to give his personal ethic a social application to nonetheless temper their condemnation. For as James Russell Lowell put it in *The Biglow Papers:*

> *He never said a word too much—*
> *Except of Story, or some such,*
> *Whom though condemned by others strict,*
> *The heart refuses to convict.*[36]

Hence, perhaps Story's epitaph should not be sought in the caption of a major statute or in the title of a learned commentary, nor in the resolution of an arcane point of law in a leading case. Rather, a line as good as any lies in the close of an obscure letter of early 1809. It was written when Congressman Story was preparing to break with President Jefferson and to return home with his political fortunes at crisis and his future enshrouded with doubt. But it was not these concerns but quite another that Story mentioned to his wife: "The post boy waits. It is a cold rainy night. I ought not to keep him shivering at a late hour."[37]

[36] Quoted in Garrison, III (1889), 181. And such was Story's charm that his old student Richard Henry Dana passed over the *Prigg* decision to invoke Story's name in protesting slave recapture proceedings: ". . . this room, where once Story sat in judgment—now a slave pen" ("The Rendition of Anthony Burns," in *Speeches in Stirring Times* [Boston, 1910]), 321.
[37] Letter to Mrs. Story, Jan. 15, 1809, Story Papers, Essex Institute, Salem.

Bibliography

The problem of selectivity, which haunts the effort to describe Story's crowded and varied life, returns with a vengeance in the framing of his bibliography. Throughout the text I have attempted to cite those authors upon whose works I have relied (although, with all good intentions, I am sure that I have failed to give all credit where credit was due). The listing below sets out works which I found in one way or another particularly helpful or which bear any especial relationship to a Story biography.

My selectivity has been highly eclectic. Here, as in the text, I have tried to keep the legal material to a minimum. For example, as a proxy of almost all the enormous amount of material on the *Erie Railroad* decision, I have listed Judge Henry Friendly's 1964 Cardozo lecture and a note from the *Yale Law Journal*, each of which contains a comprehensive array of citations in the matter. Again, on the questions of editions, I have sometimes listed the one which I used, sometimes the latest, and sometimes (e.g., in Story's works) the earliest. Finally, and after some hesitation, I have listed some of my own periodical articles which contain material not included in the text.

On qualitative appraisals I must acknowledge a debt to three authors whose insights have seemed to me extraordinarily luminous and penetrating. Considering the ephemerality of views and styles in history, Henry Adams' work on the Jefferson–Madison era seems actually to improve with age. While closer at hand in terms of origins, and still to undergo the test of time, Bray Hammond's *Banks and Politics in America* appears to me to have high promise of being a timeless classic of American historiography, and I would pass a like appraisal on Richard Ward's slim volume *Andrew Jackson: Symbol for an Age.*

435

One last word: In preparing the following listing I could not resist the opportunity to strike a blow against a pedantic constraint on common sense and have accordingly listed de Tocqueville under *d* and von Holst under *v*.

Abbott, Charles, *The Law Relative to Merchant Ships and Seamen,* ed. Joseph Story. Boston, 1810.

An Account of the Funeral Honours Bestowed upon the Remains of Capt. Lawrence and Lieut. Ludlow. Boston, 1813. Pamphlet Collection, Boston Athenaeum.

Adams, Henry, *The Life of Albert Gallatin.* Philadelphia, 1879.

————, *John Randolph.* Boston and New York, 1898.

————, *History of the United States under the Administration of Thomas Jefferson,* 2v. New York, 1930.

————, *History of the United States under the Administration of James Madison,* 2v. New York, 1930.

Adams, John Quincy, *Memoirs,* ed. Charles Francis Adams, 12v. Philadelphia, 1874–77.

————, *Writings,* ed. Worthington C. Ford, 7v. New York, 1913–17.

Allen, Carleton K., *Law in the Making.* Oxford, 1939.

American Jurist.

American Law Reporter.

American State Papers, ed. Gales and Seaton, 38v. Washington, D.C., 1832–61.

Amory, Thomas, *Life of James Sullivan,* 2v. Boston, 1859.

Annals of Congress, ed. Gales and Seaton, 42v. Washington, D.C., 1834–56.

Anonymous, *The Amistad Case.* New York, 1938; first published in 1841.

Anonymous, *The Charlestown Convent: Its Destruction by a Mob.* Boston, 1870.

Baldwin, Henry, *A General View of the Origin and Nature of the Constitution and Government of the United States.* Philadelphia, 1837.

Bauer, Elizabeth, *Commentaries on the Constitution.* New York, 1952.

Baxter, Maurice, "Should the Dartmouth College Case Have Been Reargued?," *New England Quarterly,* Vol. XXXIII (1960).

Bentley, William, *Diary,* 4v. Salem, 1905–14.

Benton, Thomas Hart, *Thirty Years' View,* 2v. New York and London, 1854–58.

Beveridge, Albert J., *The Life of John Marshall,* 4v. Boston, 1916–19.

Blackstone, William, *Commentaries on the Laws of England,* 4v. London, 1966; reprint of 1765-1769 edition.

Blake, Francis, *An Examination of the Constitutionality of the Embargo Laws.* Worcester, Mass., 1808. Pamphlet Collection, Essex Institute, Salem, Mass.

Blau, Joseph (ed.), *Social Theories of Jacksonian Democracy.* New York, 1947.

Brant, Irving, *James Madison,* 6v. Indianapolis and New York, 1941–56.

Brown, Everett (ed.), *The Missouri Compromise and Presidential Politics.* St. Louis, 1926.

Chambers, William N., *Old Bullion Benton.* Boston, 1956.

Chevalier, Michel, *Society, Manners, and Politics in the United States.* New York, 1839 (Reprinted 1966).

Clay, Henry, *Papers,* ed. Hopkins, 3v. Lexington, Ky., 1959–63.

Cobb, Thomas R. R., *The Law of Negro Slavery.* Philadelphia and Savannah, 1858.

Coke, Edward, *Institutes of the Laws of England,* 4v. London, 1797. Philadelphia, 1836.

Columbian Centinel (Boston).

Commager, Henry S., "Joseph Story," in *Gaspar Bacon Lectures on the Constitution of the United States, 1940–1950.* Boston, 1953.

———, *Documents of American History.* New York, 1948.

Congressional Globe, ed. Blair and Rives, 109v. Washington, D.C., 1834–73.

Cranch's Supreme Court Reports, Vols. 1–9.

Crosskey, William W., *Politics and the Constitution,* 2v. Chicago, 1953.

Crowninshield Papers, Peabody Museum, Salem, Mass.

Dallas' Supreme Court Reports, Vols. 1–4.

Dana, Richard Henry, Jr., *Journal,* ed. Lucid, 3v. Cambridge, 1968.

Dangerfield, George, *The Era of Good Feelings.* New York, 1952.

Derby, Perley, and Gardner, Frank, "Elisha Story of Boston and Some of His Descendants," *Essex Institute Historical Collections,* Vol. L (1914).

de Tocqueville, Alexis, *Democracy in America,* 2v. New York, 1960.

Deutsch, Eberhard, "Development of the Theory of Admiralty Jurisdiction in the United States," *Tulane Law Review,* Vol. XXXV (1960).

Dodd, Edwin M., *American Business Corporations until 1860.* Cambridge, 1954.

Dowd, Morgan D., "Justice Joseph Story: A Study of the Legal Philosophy of a Jeffersonian Judge," *Vanderbilt Law Review*, Vol. XVIII (1965).

———, "Justice Joseph Story and the Politics of Appointment," *American Journal of Legal History*, Vol. IX (1965).

DuBois, W. E. B., *The Suppression of the African Slave-Trade to the United States.* New York, 1965.

Dunne, Gerald T., "Mr. Justice Story and the American Law of Banking," *American Journal of Legal History*, Vol. V (1961).

———, "The American Blackstone," *Washington University Law Quarterly*, Vol. 1963.

———, "Joseph Story: The Salem Years," *Essex Institute Historical Collections*, Vol. CI (1965).

———, "The Story–Livingston Correspondence, 1812–1822," *American Journal of Legal History*, Vol. X (1966).

Du Ponceau, Peter, *Jurisdiction of the Courts of the United States.* Philadelphia, 1824.

Emerson, Ralph Waldo, *Letters,* ed. Ralph L. Rusk, 6v. New York, 1939.

Federal Cases, 31v. This series includes, with a key (Vol. XXX), Story's circuit opinions from the Gallison, Mason, Sumner and (W.W.) Story reports.

Felt, Joseph B., *Annals of Salem.* Salem, 2v. 1845.

Fessenden, Thomas, *An Essay on the Law of Patents for New Inventions.* Boston, 1822.

Forbes, Esther, *The Runnings of the Tide.* Boston, 1948.

Frank, John P., *Justice Daniel Dissenting.* Cambridge, 1964.

Friedman, Leon, and Israll, Fred (eds.), *The Justices of the United States Supreme Court,* 4v. New York, 1969.

Friendly, Henry, "In Praise of *Erie*—and of the New Federal Common Law," *New York University Law Review*, Vol. XXXIX (1964).

"From Judicial Grant to Legislative Power: The Admiralty Clause in the Nineteenth Century," *Harvard Law Review*, Vol. LXVII (1954).

Gabriel, Ralph G., *The Course of American Democratic Thought.* New York, 1940.

Gallison, John, Manuscript Diary, Massachusetts Historical Society, Boston.

Gallison's Circuit Court Reports, Vols. 1 and 2.

Garraty, John A. (ed.), *Quarrels That Shaped the Constitution.* New York, 1952.

Garrison, Wendell P., *The Story of His Life—William Lloyd Garrison*, 4v. New York, 1885–89.

Gilmore, Grant, *Security Interests in Personal Property Security*, 2v. Boston, 1965.

Gunther, Gerald, *John Marshall's Defense of McCulloch v. Maryland*. Stanford, 1969.

Haines, Charles G., *The Role of the Supreme Court in American Government and Politics, 1789–1835*. New York, 1960.

—————— and Sherwood, Foster, *The Role of the Supreme Court . . . , 1835–1864*. Berkeley and Los Angeles, 1957.

Hammond, Bray, *Banks and Politics in America*. Princeton, 1956.

Handlin, Oscar and Mary, *Commonwealth*. Cambridge, 1969.

Harris, Robert J., *The Judicial Power of the United States*. Baton Rouge, 1940.

Heaney, Howell, "The Letters of Joseph Story," *American Journal of Legal History*, Vol. II (1959).

Henderson, Gerard C., *Position of Foreign Corporations in American Constitutional Law*. Cambridge, 1918.

Hillard, George S., *Memoir and Correspondence of Jeremiah Mason*. Cambridge, 1873.

——————, *Life, Letters, and Journals of George Ticknor*, 2v. Boston, 1909.

Howard's Supreme Court Reports, Vols. 1–24.

Jackson, Andrew, *Correspondence*, ed. John S. Bassett, 7v. Washington, D.C., 1926–35.

Jefferson, Thomas, *Memoirs, Correspondence, and Miscellanies*. Charlottesville, 1829.

——————, *Works*, ed. Paul Leicester Ford, 12v. New York and London, 1904–5.

Jennings, Walter W., *The American Embargo*. Iowa City, 1921.

Johnson, Andrew, "Nathan Dane and American Legal Literature," *American Journal of Legal History*, Vol. VII (1963).

Journal of Debates and Proceedings in the Convention of Delegates, Chosen to Revise the Constitution of Massachusetts. Boston, 1853.

Keeffe, Arthur John, "In Praise of Joseph Story, *Swift v. Tyson*, and 'the' True National Common Law," *The American University Law Review*, Vol. XVIII (1969).

Kendall, Amos, *Autobiography*, ed. William Stickney. Boston, 1872.

Kent, James, *Commentaries on American Law*, 3v. New York, 1826–30.

Leslie, William R., "The Influence of Joseph Story's Theory of Conflict of Laws on Constitutional Nationalism," *Mississippi Valley*

Historical Review, Vol. XXXV (1948).

————, "Similarities in Lord Mansfield's and Joseph Story's View of Fundamental Law," *American Journal of Legal History,* Vol. I (1957).

Laurer, T. E., "The Common Law Background of Riparian Doctrine," *Missouri Law Review,* Vol. XXVIII (1963).

Lewis, Walker, *Without Fear of Favor: A Biography of Roger B. Taney.* Boston, 1965.

————, *Speak for Yourself, Daniel.* Boston, 1969.

Lewis, William D. (ed.), *Great American Lawyers,* 8v. Philadelphia, 1907–9.

Levy, Leonard, *Chief Justice Shaw and the Law of the Commonwealth,* Cambridge, 1957.

Livermore, Shaw, *The Twilight of Federalism.* Princeton, 1962.

Lodge, Henry Cabot, *Life and Letters of George Cabot.* Boston, 1877.

Lord, John K., *A History of Dartmouth College.* Concord, N.H., 1913.

Lorenzen, Ernest, "Story's *Commentaries on the Conflict of Laws*—100 Years After," *Harvard Law Review,* Vol. XLVIII (1934).

McClellan, James, *Joseph Story and the American Constitution.* Ph.D. diss., University of Virginia, 1964.

McLean, John, Papers. Library of Congress, Washington.

Madison, James, *Writings,* ed. Gaillard Hunt, 9v. New York, 1900–1910.

Magrath, C. Peter, *Yazoo: Law and Politics in the Young Republic.* Providence, 1966.

Mannix, Daniel P., *Black Cargoes.* New York, 1962.

Marshall, John, *Life of George Washington,* 5v. Philadelphia, 1804–7.

————, Papers. Library of Congress, Washington.

————, Papers. Virginia Historical Society, Richmond.

Martineau, Harriet, *Society in America,* 3v. London, 1837.

————, *Autobiography,* 3v. London, 1877.

Mason, Alpheus, *Harlan Fiske Stone.* New York, 1956.

Mason's Circuit Court Reports, Vols. 1–5.

Masters, Edgar Lee, *Lincoln the Man.* New York, 1931.

Merchants-Warren National Bank, Salem, Mass., Corporate Records.

Meyers, Marvin, *The Jacksonian Persuasion.* Stanford, Calif., 1957.

Miller, Perry, (ed.), *The Legal Mind in America.* Garden City, N.Y., 1962.

————, *The Life of the Mind in America.* New York, 1965.

Moore, Glover, *The Missouri Controversy, 1819–1821*. Lexington, Ky., 1953.

Morgan, Donald, *Justice William Johnson*. Columbia, S.C., 1954.

———, *Congress and the Constitution*. Cambridge, 1966.

Morison, Samuel E., *Life and Letters of Harrison Gray Otis*, 2v. Boston and New York, 1913.

———, *Three Centuries of Harvard*. Cambridge, 1936.

Myers, Gustavus, *History of the Supreme Court*. Chicago, 1912.

Nadelmann, Kurt H., "Joseph Story's Contribution to American Conflicts Law: A Comment," *American Journal of Legal History*, Vol. V (1961).

National Archives, Judicial Records, Washington.

National Intelligencer (Washington).

Newmeyer, R. Kent, *Joseph Story: A Political and Constitutional Study*. Ph.D. diss., University of Nebraska, 1959.

———, "A Note on the Whig Politics of Justice Joseph Story," *Mississippi Valley Historical Review*, Vol. XLVIII (1961).

———, "Joseph Story and the War of 1812: A Judicial Nationalist," *The Historian*, Vol. XXVI (1964).

———, "Daniel Webster as de Tocqueville's Lawyer: The Dartmouth College Case Again," *American Journal of Legal History*, Vol. XI (1967).

Niles' Weekly Register (Washington).

North American Review (Boston).

One Hundred Years of the Salem Savings Bank. Salem, 1918.

Parker, Theodore, *Additional Speeches, Addresses, and Occasional Sermons*, 2v. Boston, 1855-1867.

Parrington, Vernon, *Main Currents in American Thought*, 3v. New York, 1927–30.

Peters' Supreme Court Reports, Vols. 1–16.

Peterson, Merrill, *The Jefferson Image in the American Mind*. New York, 1960.

Phillips, James D., *Salem and the Indies*. Boston and New York, 1947.

Plumer, William, Jr., *Life of William Plumer*. Boston, 1857.

Porter, Kenneth, *The Jacksons and the Lees*, 2v. Cambridge, 1937.

Pound, Roscoe, "The Place of Judge Story in the Making of American Law," *American Law Review*, Vol. XLVIII (1914).

Prager, Frank D., "The Influence of Mr. Justice Story on American Patent Law," *American Journal of Legal History*, Vol. V (1961).

———, "The Changing Views of Justice Story on the Construction of Patents," *American Journal of Legal History*, Vol. IV (1960).

Quincy, Josiah, *Figures of the Past.* Boston, 1926.

Register of Debates, ed. Gales and Seaton, 29v. Washington, D.C., 1825–37.

Richardson, James (ed.), *Messages and Addresses of the Presidents,* 10v. Washington, D.C., 1896.

Robinson, William A., *Jeffersonian Democracy in New England,* New Haven, 1916.

Roper, Donald M., "Judicial Unanimity and the Marshall Court—A Road to Reappraisal," *American Journal of Legal History,* Vol. IX (1965).

Salem Gazette.

Salem *Register.*

Schlesinger, Arthur M., Jr., *The Age of Jackson.* Boston, 1945.

Schwartz, Mortimer, and Hogan, John (eds.), *Joseph Story.* New York, 1959.

Sears, Louis M., *Jefferson and the Embargo.* Durham, N.C., 1927.

Sherwin, Oscar, *Prophet of Liberty: The Life and Times of Wendell Phillips.* New York, 1958.

Shirley, John M., *The Dartmouth College Causes and the Supreme Court of the United States.* St. Louis, 1879.

States Documents on Federal Relations, ed. H. V. Ames. Philadelphia, 1906.

Storrow, Ann Gillam, *Letters to Jared Sparks,* ed. F. B. Blanshard, Northampton, Mass. 1921.

Story, Joseph, *American Precedents of Declarations* (anon.), Boston, 1802.

————, *The Power of Solitude.* Salem, 1802.

————, *A Selection of Pleadings in Civil Actions.* Salem, 1805.

————, *Commentaries on the Law of Bailments.* Boston, 1832.

————, *Commentaries on the Constitution,* 3v. Boston, 1833.

————, *Commentaries on the Conflict of Laws.* Boston, 1834.

————, *Commentaries on Equity Jurisprudence,* 2v. Boston, 1836.

————, *Commentaries on Equity Pleadings.* Boston, 1838.

————, *Commentaries on the Law of Agency.* Boston, 1839.

————, *Commentaries on the Law of Partnership.* Boston, 1844.

————, *Commentaries on the Law of Bills of Exchange.* Boston, 1843.

————, *Commentaries on the Law of Promissory Notes.* Boston, 1845.

————, *Digest of the Law* (MS.). Story Papers Treasure Room, Harvard Law School, Cambridge.

————, Letters, in *Proceedings of the Massachusetts Historical Society,* 2nd series, Vol. XIV (1901).

———, *Miscellaneous Writings*, ed. William W. Story. Boston, 1852.
———, Papers. Essex Institute, Salem.
———, Papers. Library of Congress, Washington, D.C.
———, Papers. University of Texas, Austin.
Story, William W., *Life and Letters of Joseph Story*, 2v. Boston, 1851.
Story's Circuit Court Reports, Vols. 1–3.
Sumner's Circuit Court Reports, Vols. 1–3.
Sutherland, Arthur, *The Law at Harvard*. Cambridge, 1967.
Swisher, Carl B., *Roger B. Taney*. New York, 1935.
Town Records, Marblehead, Mass.
Town Records, Salem, Mass.
Tyack, David, *George Ticknor and the Boston Brahmins*. Cambridge, 1967.
United States Magazine and Democratic Review.
United States Statutes at Large, Vols. I–XVII. Boston, 1848–71.
Upshur, Abel, *Our Federal Government*. Petersburg, 1840.
Valladão, Haroldo, "The Influence of Joseph Story on Latin American Rules of Conflict of Laws," *American Journal of Comparative Law*, Vol. III (1954).
von Holst, Hermann, *A Constitutional and Political History of the United States,* trans. Laler, 8v. Chicago, 1881–92.
Ward, John W., *Andrew Jackson: Symbol for an Age*. New York, 1962.
Warren, Charles, *History of the Harvard Law School*, 3v. Boston, 1908.
———, *History of the American Bar*. Boston, 1911.
———, "New Light on the Judiciary Act of 1789," *Harvard Law Review*, XXXVI (1923).
———, *The Supreme Court in United States History*, 2v. Boston, 1937.
———, *Bankruptcy in United States History*. Cambridge, 1935.
———, *The Story–Marshall Correspondence*. New York, 1942.
Webster, Daniel, *Private Correspondence*, ed. Fletcher Webster, 2v. Boston, 1857.
———, *Writings and Speeches*, ed. J. W. McIntyre, 18v. Boston, 1903.
Wheaton, Henry, Papers, Pierpont Morgan Library, New York.
Wheaton's Supreme Court Reports, Vols. 1–12.
White, Leonard, *The Jeffersonians*. New York, 1951.
———, *The Jacksonians*. New York, 1954.
Whitney, William, "The Crowninshields of Salem," *Essex Institute Historical Collections*, Vol. XCIV (1958).

Wilbur, Earl, *History of Unitarianism.* Cambridge, 1952.

Wilson, Edmund, *Patriotic Gore.* New York, 1962.

Wiltse, Charles M., *John C. Calhoun,* 3v. Indianapolis, 1944–51.

Woodward, Grace, *The Cherokees.* Norman, Okla., 1963.

Wroth, L. Kinvin, "The Massachusetts Vice Admiralty Court and the Federal Admiralty Jurisdiction," *American Journal of Legal History,* Vol. VI (1966).

Index

About the Author

A native of St. Louis, Mr. Dunne is a graduate of Georgetown University and St. Louis University Law School. During World War II, he served on a destroyer in the Pacific. He joined the Federal Reserve Bank's legal staff in 1949 and became General Counsel in 1963; in 1967 he was appointed to his present position of Vice President. He is also Visiting Professor of Law at the University of Missouri.

Mr. Dunne is married to the former Nancy O'Neill, and they have six children.